# SUSTAINABLE URBAN DEVELOPMENT

## About the Editor

**Dr. R. B. Singh** is presently Reader in the Department of Geography, Delhi School of Economics, University of Delhi and Steering Committee Member of the IGU Commission on Land-Use/Cover Change; Secretary General, National Association of Geographers, India (NAGI); Secretary, Hydrology Section, Asia-Oceania Geoscience Society, Singapore; Member, Board of Studies, TERI Institute of Advanced Studies. Ex South Asian Representative in Commonwealth Geographical Bureau (1992-2000). He has to his credit 26 books/research volumes and more than 145 research papers. The UNESCO/ISSC (Paris) awarded him 1998 Research and Study Grants Award in Social and Human Sciences. Dr. Singh was trained in Remote Sensing and GIS technology in the field of environment under GRID-UNEP/UNITAR programme in Switzerland. He is also associated with three prestigious collaborative research programmes such as ICSSR-IDPAD as Project Director, CIDA-SICI partnership programme as Chief Co-investigator and DFID as Project Director.

# SUSTAINABLE URBAN DEVELOPMENT

*Edited by*
R. B. Singh

CONCEPT PUBLISHING COMPANY, NEW DELHI-110 059

**Cataloging in Publication Data—DK**
*Courtesy:* D.K. Agencies (P) Ltd. <docinfo@dkagencies.com>

**Sustainable urban development** / edited by R.B. Singh.
p. cm.
Contributed articles.
Conceptual and empirical case studies from India and other Asian countries.
Includes bibliographical references.
Includes index.
ISBN 8180692957

1. Urbanization—India—Case studies. 2. Urbanization—Asia—Case studies. 3. Sustainable development—India —Case studies. 4. Sustainable development—Asia—Case studies. I. Singh, R. B. (Ram Babu), 1955-

DDC 307.141 609 54 22



ISBN 81-8069-295-7

First Published 2006



*Published and Printed by*
Ashok Kumar Mittal
**Concept Publishing Company**
A/15-16, Commercial Block, Mohan Garden
New Delhi-110059 (India)

*Phone*: 25351460, 25351794
*Fax*: 091-11-25357103
*Email* : publishing@conceptpub.com

# Preface

Indian urbanization is taking place in a rapid pace and in a different context. Rapid urbanization and industrialization accompanied by major changes in social, economic, environmental and technological arena is impacting adversely on traditional land-use, water resources, environmental quality and management practices in cities of developing countries in general and the Indian cities in particular. India's modern urbanization has its root in the colonial period when the British selected Calcutta, Bombay and Madras as regional trading centres and fortified ports. The unprecedented growth of towns and cities in India has been a result of modernization process and the main cause of their incredibly rapid growth has been the agricultural and industrial, development. About 28 per cent of India's population was urbanized in 2001 with 285 million people nearly as many as the entire population of the USA. Rapid population growth pressurizing the limited natural resources has triggered off stream of migrants from the rural areas to large cities. India achieved more than 700 per cent increase in urban population in the last century. The mainstream debate on urbanization and urban population addresses issues of economic growth and the debate on sustainable cities and especially their environmental problems. The rapid growth of population and industrialization and consequent urbanization have emerged as a major factor responsible for environmental degradation in different ways and on different scales. The most significant and worrying trend is of increasing levels of pollution and increase in slum areas. It has also put pressure in the available basic amenities. Safe drinking water supply, sanitation and even fresh air become scarce. Living space in our cities are shrinking and making it more and more crowded.

Urbanization and urban growth on unprecedented scale pose fundamental questions as to whether this magnitude of urban development can be sustained. The present trend of urbanization in developing countries in general, and in India in particular, is heading towards a situation, which may be termed as 'Urban Disaster'. Cities and towns in Asian countries face a difficult future. Urban infrastructure and housing are inadequate and cannot absorb the massive migration from the countryside. Urban economic and social conditions are deteriorating, resulting in high levels of unemployment and social unrest. In these adverse circumstances, Indian urban areas must become the focus for a new policy initiative emphasizing population control, rural development, sustainable agricultural development and rural hazard mitigation. The idea of introducing regional economies through decentralized multi-level planning, local autonomy and people's participation combining the top-down and bottom-up approaches is emerging. At this hour of distress the concept of sustainable cities and also the concept of healthy cities can be the policy framework for the future of the cities. The concept of sustainable cities is closely connected with environment and economy to safeguard natural resources, which in turn lead to minimum acceptable quality of life. There is a constant struggle with issues of air pollution congestion of human population and availability of green space. Healthy city is a model for local governance way in which local government can work to address the determinants of health. In a sustainable city, there is a sense of great opportunity and hope that a new world can be built in which, economic development, social development, and environmental protections are independent. They are also reinforcing components of sustainable urban development. This may be realised through effective partnership among public, private and civic sectors at all levels.

Our Hon'ble President Dr. A.P.J. Abdul Kalam has also emphasized on these concepts. Provisions of Urban facilities in Rural Areas (PURA) may also be the solution of migration and consequently it would help in managing urban environment. The interdisciplinary and multi-dimensional nature and potentiality of Geography provide enough opportunity in this direction. By virtue of their earth bound vision and human welfare oriented approach, the geographers should come forward and make an attempt to understand the future of our cities and suggest corrective measures.

The present book comprises 26 chapters relating to conceptual and empirical case studies from India and other Asian countries. The book also combines an academic understanding with an empirical approach to the sustainable urban development together with policy perspectives. The volume is useful for students, researchers, and teachers coming from geography, urban studies, town planning, atmospheric sciences, environmental studies and policy science.

Department of Geography
Delhi School of Economics
University of Delhi, Delhi-110007

**R.B. Singh**

# List of Contributors

1. **A.K. Gupta**
Geological Survey of India, NH-5P, N.I.T., Faridabad -121001, India

2. **A.K. Jain**
Addl. Commissioner (Plg.), Delhi Development Authority, Delhi, India

3. **Anoop Kumar**
Department of Geography, Government P.G. College, Pratapgarh, Rajasthan-312 605, India

4. **Bhojraj Singh**
Rana Pratap Post Graduate College, Sultanpur, India

5. **D.K. Mishra**
Department of Geography, Delhi School of Economics, University of Delhi, Delhi-110007, India

6. **des. Martin Raithelhuber**
South Asia Institute, Dept. of Geography, INF 330, D-69120 Heidelberg, Germany

7. **Govind Prasad**
Department of Geography, Rana Pratap Post-Graduate College, Sultanpur, India

8. **H.M. Kothari**
Department of Sociology, Government P.G. College, Pratapgarh, Rajasthan-312 605, India

9. **H.S. Saini**
Geological Survey of India, NH-5P, N.I.T., Faridabad-121001, India

10. **Hiromichi Nagashima**
Department of Geography, Kokushikan University, Tokyo, Japan

11. **H.P. Susiripala**
Urban Development Authority, Sri Lanka

12. **H.R. Suri**
Former President, Institute of Town Planners, India 4-A, Ring Road, I.P. Estate, New Delhi-110 002, India

13. **J.M. Giovannoni**
Institute of Environmental Engineering, Ecole Polytechnique Fédérale de Lausanne CH-1015, Lausanne, Switzerland

14. **Jag Mohan**
Department of Geography, Delhi School of Economics, University of Delhi, Delhi-110007, India

15. **Jemes S. Gardner**
Natural Resources Institute, University of Manitoba, Winnipeg, Mb., Canada

16. **Jiro Yonekura**
Faculty of Business and Commerce, Hiroshima Shudo University. Numata-cho, Asa-minami-ku, Hiroshima 731-31, Japan

17. **N.D. Mani**
Department of Rural Development, Gandhigram Rural Institute, Deemed University, Gandhigram, Tamil Nadu, India

18. **P.S. Datta**
Nuclear Research Laboratory, Indian Agricultural Research Institute, New Delhi-110012, India

19. **R.B. Singh**
Department of Geography, Delhi School of Economics, University of Delhi, Delhi-110007, India

20. **R.B. Bhagat**
Department of Geography, Maharshi Dayanand University, Rohtak-124001, India

21. **R.C. Gupta**
Emeritus Fellow AICTE and formerly Professor and Head, Department of Regional Planning, School of Planning and Architecture, New Delhi, India

22. **Randhir Singh Sangwan**
Department of Geography, University College, Rohtak-124001, India

23. **Ravi S. Singh**
Department of Geography, Kisan P.G. College, Bahraich-271801, U.P., India

24. **S.A.I. Mujtaba**
Geological Survey of India, NH-5P, N.I.T., Faridabad-121001, India

**25. S. Hasan Ansari**
Department of Geography,
M.D. University, Rohtak,
India

**26. S. Mohan**
National Institute for
Science, Technology and
Development Studies, Dr.
K.S. Krishnan Marg,
New Delhi-110012, India

**27. Shahab Fazal**
Lecturer, Department of
Geography,
Aligarh Muslim University,
Aligarh, India

**28. Sneh Sangwan**
Department of Geography,
B.P.S.M. Girls College,
Khanpur Kalan (Sonipat),
India

**29. Sukehiro Gotoh**
National Institute for
Environmental Studies,
Japan Environment Agency
Tsukuba Ibaraki 305,
Japan

**30. Takashi Hattori**
Cabinet Councillors'
Office on Internal Affairs,
Cabinet Secretariat,
Government of Japan,
Tokyo, 100-8914, Japan

**31. Udit Ratna**
Associate Town and
Country Planner, TCPO,
Ministry of Urban
Development,
Government of India,
Delhi, India

# CONTENTS

## SECTION–III : ASIAN CASE STUDIES

# SECTION-I

# Concepts

1

# Environmental and Infrastructural Sustainability

## Major Challenges Facing Indian Metropolitan Cities

R. C. GUPTA

### URBAN GROWTH AND SUSTAINABILITY

Post-Independence India has been witnessing a massive increase in urban population which by year 2001 is expected to be 365 million with a heavy concentration of 73 million accounted by 8 large metros which would be more than the combined 1985 population of France, UK, Italy and Germany. According to experts our urbanisation levels would stabilise at around 50 per cent between 2011 and 2020 by which time we will have at least three mega cities of over 20 million population. Looking at the present grim status of infrastructure in our cities generally and metropolitan ones particularly, such a massive increase would create catastrophic conditions calling for massive public investments in physical and social infrastructure including shelter, just to maintain basic minimum standards of living. Mobilisation of such huge resources seem to be impossible, apart from encountering the unmanageable implications of such massive concentrations. This would call for a radical departure from present day monocentric urban development related policies to a firmly rooted regional development approach, enabling a poly-nodal urban pattern for the balanced development at large. This can be made possible through a multi-pronged policy containing metropolitan and large cities and accelerated development of small and medium sized secondary cities. These measures would help in bringing about sustainability in development programmes.

In the context of developing countries particularly, 'Sustainability' appears to have negative correlation with size, scale and intensity of urban development programmes. This is amply born out in respect of our large cities and metropolises, by the increasing environmental and ecological disorders, housing and infrastructure shortages, traffic and transportation problems, socio-economic dichotomies and their implications on socio-cultural environments, proliferations of slums and squatter settlements and informal sector, and overall pressure of the urban metropolitan functions. The net result is the deterioration in the overall quality of life and loss of bio-physical, socio-economic and spatio physical aspects of sustainability.

It is now universally recognised that as the cities explode into metropolitan giants, the traditional economic argument that they concentrate labour and resources resulting in increased productivity sustaining the increasing population, is no longer true. Environmental degradation, resource depletion, shrinking availability of land, and acute infrastructure shortages particularly water and power and an eroding quality of life seem to have stretched them to breaking point, rendering such form of urban development environmentally and infrastructurally unsustainable both in the short and long run.

With an expanding economy, the future generation would undoubtedly be better off, however the quality of environment that they would inherit would have deteriorated affecting the health of the community in several ways. A glaring example is Thailand where 10 per cent economic growth resulted in corresponding increase of 10 per cent in pollution levels. In India even the 6-7 per cent economic growth projected consequent to economic liberalisation by the government is likely to lead to similar situation and even worse. According to a World Bank estimate India is losing at least $9.7 billion annually due to health problems and loss of workdays caused by polluted water, air and environmental degradation representing 4-5 per cent of the GDP at 1992 levels. This according to a report is 'enough to offset much annual growth reflected in traditional accounts'. In fact, the deteriorating city environments are nullifying much natural growth and this has serious implications in metropolitan cities which are estimated 50 per cent of the country's GDP.

## METROPOLITAN EXPLOSION AND IMPLICATION

The projected population growth of our large cities and metropolises, particularly the bigger ones, in the next 20 years, is going to make the situation more complex and environmentally grim, areas like Housing, Power, Water and Waste Disposal, Transport and Health will be hit the hardest. Mumbai expected to grow into a staggering 23 million megacity by 2011, while continuing to retain its primacy as the nerve centre of the economy with renewed vigour. On the other hand Mumbai might also be saddled with equally formidable physical, social and environmental problems affecting lives of citizens. It would require to develop an additional 11,000 hectares of land for additional housing for low and middle income families, which will be roughly one-half of the present area developed of Greater Mumbai. From where would this land come and what would the imminent future urban sprawl lead to in regard to the rural countryside and the urban ecosystem? The water supply will need to be doubled from the 1992 supply of 3922 mld to 7957 mld which would entail importing water from greater distances like in Tokyo. Private vehicles on the road would double to 61.1 per 1000 adding to its already high vehicle density of 455 per sq. km. Mumbai already has the highest vehicle density in the world. Most of our metropolitan cities would face similar situations, in the wake of unabated growth being experienced in recent decades. The call of the hour is for a strong, concerted and comprehensive regional settlement policies directed at metropolitan containment and accelerated growth of small and medium cities to avert the crisis.

What is true of Mumbai regarding infrastructural stresses and strains and rapid deterioration in the quality of life in the wake of urban explosion holds good for other metropolitan and megacities as well. Deterioration in the physical environment finds a parallel in the deterioration of the social environment measured as the index of well-being. According to a 1992 WHO study in Delhi based on a sample of 520 city dwellers, it was revealed that 'Urban Neurosis' affects both the affluent and the poorer sections in varying measures. While pollution, overcrowding, traffic congestion and lack of basic facilities are all sources of stress in cities of developing countries, the report has singled out 'Overcrowding' as the root cause for deteriorating environment. This is amply borne out by the exceedingly high density prevailing in our megacities *viz.*: Calcutta 23,669 persons per sq. km. followed by Chennai (21,811); Mumbai (16,434 excluding New Mumbai); Bangalore (14,387) and Delhi (14,313) compared to national average of 267 persons per. sq. km. in 1991. Deterioration in the city's physical environment is further abetted by the fact that 35-40 per cent lowest income families continue to live in slums and squatter settlements due to non-availability and non-affordability of organised shelter.

## WATER SUPPLY CRISIS

The poor state of basic infrastructure provision water, sanitation and power is a glaring pointer to the high degree of unsustainability which plagues our cities. Regarding water supply, while the Government norm for urban water supply is 140 litres per capita per day, no Indian city comes near the target, the supply ranges from a low of 20 to a high of 80 LPCD. According to a ADB study on water availability, Mumbai received 5 hour supply a day of which 24 per cent was lost through pilferage and leaking. Calcutta while having a 10 hours supply was saddled with a 36 per cent loss, whereas Delhi had a 7 hours supply with 30 per cent loss. Chennai, the most water starved mega city had only 3 hours supply. Singapore, on the other hand, has been able to provide 24 hours supply with 90 per cent accountability indicating a vast difference in the quality of life. According to a UN estimate water supply position in most developing countries would get more acute whereas per capita demand of water would continue to rise creating highly unsustainable situations.

## WATER POLLUTION AND ENVIRONMENTAL HAZARD

Almost all the surface water in India is so heavily polluted that it is unfit for drinking. The Ganges receives untreated sewage from 29 urban centres with population in excess of one lakh contaminating its water supply. Contaminated water is considered to be the single biggest cause of sickness and deaths in India, and affects the urban water supply situation, coupled with contaminated borewells and depleting ground water reserves due to over exploitation. In India water borne diseases are estimated to cause a loss of 73 million work days annually, and national loss of productivity ranging from $ 3.1 billion to $ 8.3 billion annually. The contamination is further abetted by discharge of untreated industrial effluents in our river systems particularly where they traverse the urban areas. According to a CPCB study in 1992 in Delhi, it was estimated that 300 million litres of industrial (chemical) waste water was added to the Yamuna river daily, in addition to the 1700 million litres of mostly untreated sewage. The state of the river reached such levels of pollution that the Board declared the river water unfit even for bathing purposes. The above would give a general idea of water pollution levels in our large cities and metropolises, and the problems posed by heavy urban-industrial concentrations in achieving sustainable form of city development.

Environmental problems related to water pollution as a result of untreated sewage and sullage finding their way into the natural water system is not confined to our large cities and metropolises alone but are rampant in all water front urban developments. A case in point is the lake studded medieval city of Udaipur in Rajasthan, sustained for nearly six centuries by an inter-connected lake system of Pichola and six sister lakes, until two decades ago when the process of devastation started, consequent to large scale urban developments taking place on lake fringes and immediate catchment areas, with the growth and expansion of the city. About 60 lakh litres of sewage and 40 tonnes of solid waste are dumped in and around the lakes everyday. Siltation due to rampant deforestation has reduced the depth of the Pichola in places by a third, and the entire lake-ecosystem has been disturbed, creating a major ecological and environmental hazard for the historic but expanding city. Even though the government, though belatedly, had imposed a blanket ban on construction around the lakes in 1997, construction of major buildings and complexes has continued unabated adding to the unsustainability of the city. A holistic approach is called for to channelise the city's expansion away from the lake-regime area, establish a proper sewage disposal system, prohibit further construction along the lakes, and most importantly undertake massive afforestation programmes to check siltation in order to save the lakes which constitute a critical environment asset of the city.

## SANITATION AND SOLID WASTE MANAGEMENT

Of all civic amenities, sanitation barely exists in most Indian cities. Out of 4000 urban centres, only 300 have an underground sewage system and that too partial wherein only 28 per cent of urban households are connected to public sewers. Only 18 million households in India have water sealed closets. According to Sulabh International in most cities in India, one-third defecate in the open, and another one-third have manually cleaned latrines. Besides 70 per cent of what gets flushed goes untreated into our river systems, which speaks eloquently of the poor sanitary conditions in our cities. Statistically the picture is much more alarming at the national level. The picture of garbage disposal is equally dismal. On a national city average, hardly 60 per cent of the garbage generated in our cities gets collected, but not necessarily scientifically disposed of. Among our mega cities the collection rate in Mumbai (5800 tonnes daily) and Calcutta (3200 tonnes daily) is pleasantly upto 90 per cent, compared to only 62 per cent in Delhi.

Delhi presently generates 6000 tonnes of garbage daily, and it is reported that three operational landfill sites, Ghazipur (70Ac), Bhalswa (40Ac) and Okhla (18Ac) will be filled up in the next couple of years, and the Civic authorities are already scouting for new sites stretching over 450 acres to meet the demands which shall be increasing as the population increases. Even then the environmental problems particularly groundwater pollution, which are already attributed to the present sites would multiply manifolds. According to TERI while the total municipal solid waste in our cities today is 48.7 million tonnes, we should be prepared to deal with over 280 million tonnes by year 2047. Very few cities practice scientific methods of sanitary landfills or convert the waste into compost or energy leading to highly unhygienic conditions in and around the dumping sites, even though these may be located on the city outskirts.

## ELUSIVE POWER SUPPLY

Urban power supply is another sector of essential infrastructure which presents a very depressing picture of both growing shortfall between demand and supply as well as erratic supply owing to sub-standard distribution network and inefficient management. The picture is equally worse in our metropolitan and mega cities whose demand for energy has continued to increase rapidly. As mega cities move towards higher energy consumption influenced by rising incomes and population growth, according to an estimate India will need an additional 124 GW of power by the year 2007 requiring a capital outlay of $ 124 billion. Delhi alone would need to spend Rs. 1400 crore over a three year period to restore a balance between demand and supply positions.

## UNSUSTAINABILITY OF THE TRANSPORT SYSTEM

Today India's largest cities are among the world's worst hit by traffic problems. Growing congestion, accidents, emissions, overcrowding of public transport and poor management of pedestrian and cycle network are acute enough with 23 million vehicles today and would deteriorate beyond repair in the next ten years when the vehicle population in expected to double. The travel demand is expected to rise in all our major metropolitan cities and between 5 to 7 per cent in Delhi and Bangalore. Calcutta would require a system and network to sustain 38 billion passengers km a year compared to present 29 billion, Bangalore 41 billion passenger km compared to present 32, and Delhi a staggering 108 billion passenger km compared to present 80. This calls for a radical change not only in the transport system planning for these mega cities, but also in urban development strategies at national and regional levels directed at metropolitan containment, in a bid to impart them and their functional components, a measure of sustainability without inhibiting growth.

The transport system including transport infrastructure particularly, road capacities and network in our large cities is grossly inadequate, inefficient and non-functional as further revealed by some glaring statistics. At 2.5 million vehicles, Delhi has more vehicles than the combined vehiclular population of the three other mega cities of Calcutta, Chennai and Mumbai. Despite this higher level of vehicle ownership, higher number of trips and increased use of energy per capita, Delhi's Mass Rapid Transport System (MRTS) is yet at the planning stage, although its first phase covering 55.3 km stretch is now targetted to be completed by the year 2005 at a cost of Rs 8000 crore. The situation is going to worsen during the long intervening period, unless interim strategies are formulated and operationalised. While commuting time in our four mega cities has gone up by one-third on an average during last 10 years, apart from larger travel time and loss of productivity, discomfort, higher emission levels and degradation of environment, it has also resulted in expensive drain on energy. Road space is highly inadequate at 6 per cent for Calcutta and 10 per cent in Mumbai creating more and more congestion and crawling traffic movement.

## ATMOSPHERIC POLLUTION HAZARDS

Air pollution in our mega cities is a lethal fallout of the burgeoning traffic. Six of India's 10 largest cities—Ahmedabad, Kanpur, Nagpur, Mumbai, Calcutta and Delhi—have severe air pollution, at least three times higher than WHO standards. Delhi's situation in consequential health hazards is considered to be worst. According to a WHO study, cars in Delhi release 23 tonnes of SPM daily compared to 15 tonnes in Mumbai and 11 tonnes in Calcutta and 9 tonnes in Bangalore and a further 33 per cent increase is anticipated by the year 2001, besides the lethal lead emissions, one of the most dangerous pollutants in our environment. According to CPCB the lead levels were brought down form 0.56 per litre to 0.15 per litre with the introduction of unleaded fuel and it is now being made compulsory in all the State capitals as a significant measure towards controlling air pollution caused by vehicles. Benzene emissions, however, continue to defy attempts towards neutralisation and shall pose major problems particularly in the wake of increase in aviation fumes consequent to air passenger traffic projected to increase from currently 50 million to 120 million in 2005.

Apart from traffic emission, industrial pollution of the atmosphere is another growing menace in our metropolitan and mega cities. Unless right policies for location and technological upgradation of manufacturing processes and related environmental safeguards are inbuilt and strictly adhered to, industrial pollution of the atmosphere is likely to increase rapidly in the coming years with liberalisation policies directed at increased economic growth. Acid rain is expected to hit Delhi in the next century, thanks to the high sulphur content in our emissions and the massive burning of coal in distant China, which could destroy the diminishing green belts of the metropolis, and being highly toxic would greatly affect animal and bird life.

Noise pollution is another fallout of burgeoning traffic in our mega cities. Even in silent zones day and night time noise levels are reported to be higher at 79-65 dB for Calcutta, 66-52 dB for Mumbai and 63-49 dB for Chennai, compared to CPCB standard of 50-40 dB. (Ministry of Environment and Forest, GoI).

## CONCLUDING REMARKS

### Need for Innovating Planning and Management

It is recognised that despite their failings and shortcomings, cities, particularly the metropolitan ones do play an important role as vehicles of national and regional growth. Urban India contributes more than 50 per cent of the country's GDP although containing less than one-third of population. Urban development policy should aim at optimising the productive advantages of urban centres, while at the same time minimising and mitigating the negative impacts of urbanisation. Despite India having to cope with world's biggest urban population by 2001, our cities have neither the management systems nor the financial resources projected at Rs. 43,500 crore to provide basic civic facilities. What we need is a complete revamping of the urban management structure and practices and massive programmes of resource mobilisation through involvement of the private sector and innovative the financial planning to cope with this huge task. The above cited statistics and factual picture in respect of the current status of essential infrastructure provisions in our cities reveal the high degree of infrastructural and environmental unsustainability particularly in metropolitan and mega cities which in the wake of unprecedented growth may well lead to extremely chaotic conditions by the turn of the century. Already bursting through natural increase and unabated migration, their capacity to absorb the additional demands of the people in every sphere—physical, infrastructural, social, financial—is being called into question.

The fact that our metros and mega cities have reached their environmental limits of sustainability is more than established, which has had severe repercussions not only on the urban quality of life and efficient functioning of the urban system, but also has had huge negative impact on the rural hinterland in as much as they are being starved of resources to serve the cities. It is quite a paradoxical situation that while in the form of metros and mega cities "We have created white elephants which have sucked in all material and human resources, government planning and intervention, and despite this the quality of life in terms of facilities and amenities has declined in our cities." According to the report prepared for Habitat II World Resources 1996-97 "by 2010 the world will have 33 mega cities with population of more than 8 million poor and many of the world's poor will be living in urban conditions worse than rural poor".

In the face of this depressing scenario a multi pronged approach is called for taming the metropolises to bring them within the environmental thresholds of life support systems and devise appropriate urban and regional development strategies directed at metropolitan decentralisation, and development of alternative centres of growth, to establish a balanced regional settlement pattern comprising a hierarchical system of functionally related cities as an imperative to sustainability. Equally important is to devise new paradigms for city structuring and development to make them environmentally compatible and infrastructurally manageable, which are essential attributes of sustainable urban development.

***Note*** : The author has drawn upon various official and unofficial reports and documents for data and information on various aspects discussed herein, which are too numerous to individually list down. Statistics are also quoted from Prabha Chandran's feature article 'India in 2011, Cities of Future', *India Today* Plus, June 1997.

2

# Urban Issues and an Agenda for the Next Century

**A. K. JAIN**

We are at the threshold of the twenty-first century. The twentieth century has been an era of transition, progress, urbanisation and development. The first half of the century was underlined by the World Wars, destruction and new polarisations. The highlights of second half of the century have been reconstruction, development and rapid urbanisation. It has been marked by scientific technological revolution and rapid growth of the economy. While on one hand, there had been collapse of colonial regimes and independence of several major countries, at the same time the world witnessed widening gulf between the rich and poor nations. The political and socio-economic conditions are manifested and reflected by the human settlement.

During the last 50 years of India's Independence our cities manifest both triumph and tragedy. We have achieved the technological and organisational capacity: yet we seek to be moving further from the realisation of this potential. The majority of population suffer a growing sense of loss and frustration as their lives, families and their hopes for the future disintegrate. Millions of people lack secure and adequate shelter and basic sustenance. Their problems continue growing because of population growth, urbanisation, displacement and growing pressures of economy.

## CROSS-CUTTING ISSUES

One of the central focus of urban development is the alleviation of urban poverty. The cities manifest vast gulf of income and living standards. The living conditions in pavements, poorly served slums and squatter settlements are bordering inhuman levels. One out of every three persons lives below the poverty line. It is also a fact that about 90 per cent of our urban poor live in unplanned settlements and self-built housing, lacking even rudimentary services. The planning framework has not been able to serve these vast populations. It is necessary to evolve a new framework to channelise the energies and resources of the poor in an affordable, a better serviced and self-generating settlements.

Improved services, environment and housing enable the poor to integrate themselves with the network of transactions in the urban system as a whole. This propensity, which is highly desirable from the point of view of socio-economic development, underscores the need for launching programmes of *in-situ* upgradation and old city improvement as starting points of the urban process. The strategy may comprise of formulating around the sub-standard areas several programmes of physical, social and economic upgradation, which could promote backward and forward linkages between housing and other programmes, such as nutrition, health, environmental improvement, education and employment. However, the strategy of development should contain a strong commitment to the widest possible public participation.

An integrated package of socio-education and urban basic services should be developed which may cover nutrition, water supply, health care, pre-school learning, immunisation, functional literacy, community based rehabilitation, hygiene and sanitation, recreational and cultural development. The focus of such package should be mother and child.

From an affordability and cost recovery perspective, the urban service and projects assume altogether a new complexion. It helps to evolve realistic policy approach and alternative financial measures, such as taxation *versus* user charges, inter-governmental fiscal, transfers, general and cross-sectional subsidies. The sustainability of urban development which is ensured by the market-oriented approach, has a distinct advantage over the normative approach. However, the market- oriented approach may leave the poor to their own devices. Usually it does not conform to the poverty orientation of development programmes.

## EMERGING PRIORITIES

Emerging priorities of urban development are the environment, urban poverty, infrastructure, basic services, equity and capacity building which are linked to the question of resources. This calls for adopting a new urban management and action oriented planning. The watchwords are environment, equity, efficiency, energy and excellence, so that urban planning acts as a powerful tool of economic growth, social justice and political control. There is a need of urban and legal reforms facilitating strategic initiatives and action planning approach.

## INFRASTRUCTURE

**For growth of economy, it is necessary to focus on infrastructure including transportation, railways, roads, power, water and sanitation. At present there is a wide gap between infrastructure demand and supply. Against an estimated need of Rs. 4000-4500 billion over next 5 years (Rakesh Mohan), the availability in the government sector is hardly one-tenth. This calls for radical changes in governance, management and planning. It is necessary to evolve new partnerships, mobilise national and international resources and revitalise the overall economy. The priorities should be well worked out and no chance be taken to underutilise human capacity or investments.**

## SUSTAINABLE DEVELOPMENT

The issues of sustainable development, viability of long-term partnerships, welfare facilities, social services and equity should not be played down. On the contrary, innovative sectors of infrastructure development and environment can be opened up to partnerships and private sector which have been the domain and burden of the government.

## NEW MODELS OF GOVERNANCE AND DEVELOPMENT

There is a debate on new models of planning and urban management. With the 73rd and 74th Constitutional Amendment Acts and emphasis on maket economy, there is a need to reorient planning strategy towards a new coalition between the local government, urban authority and the private sector.

## FUTURE TRENDS

Based on objective laws of development of human society and scientific-technological advancement, the following trends can be outlined for city planning during the next century :

- Future demand of infrastructure will overtake the level of building and housing constructions.
- "Environment, Employment and Equity" will be the major concerns of city development.
- The structure of a city will be determined not by its geometry but by the human activities within it.

- Possibly many cities will be replaced by conurbations.
- In place of the Master Plan approach which is authoritarian, there will be the emergence of 'Systems Approach,' which will be evolutionary, flexible and participatory. This would provide basic tissue, structure and skeleton as the support for infrastructure, housing, transport and other activities.
- Support elements and systems will be adaptable according to demand and development of energy, environment and activities.
- Solar energy will hold the key of power supply during the next century. Renewable and non-polluting (green) energy sources will overtake present power sources.
- Much higher use of sub-terranean space and Earth Tunnels for climatic control, utilities, transport and other infrastructure will be witnessed during the coming century.
- Recycling of water and elimination of wastes.
- Bio-technology will play a major role in waste treatment and for conservation of natural bio-diversity.
- Evolution of 'Intelligent Infrastructure' and new automation systems, including Telecommunications, Transmission super highways, etc. Buildings will cease to be inert masses, but would imbibe computer controlled smart systems.

## NEED FOR A NEW PLANNING APPROACH

The planning approach and the efforts of development have not been able to make a dent in the basic problems like water, power, sanitation, transport, land and housing. Our cities continue to face the problems of poverty, pollution and productivity. Environment and employment continue to confront our settlements. This has led to unrest among the professionals and the planners have been introspecting and groping for innovations. It is becoming rather obvious that the approach towards planning and development has to change from functional to organisational, from development to sustainable and from technological to managerial. The human settlements should embody diversity in place of uniformity. From centralised planning, there is a need to adopt a decentralised and participatory approach. It is being increasingly realised that in place of hierarchical cellular structure the emphasis has to shift to horizontalisation, from universal to contextual, and from mechanical efficiency to human emotions.

The twenty first century city will have to not only meet highly advanced requirements of energy, ecology and technology, but also radically re-define and re-formulate the philosophy of living, work and recreation. The cities will have to offer a new spatial, visual and symbolic interpretation of physical environment.

## AN AGENDA FOR THE NEW CENTURY

It is essential to identify the problems, document the transformations and project the trends with respect to various relevant issues, like land-use and housing, income-generation, employment, water, sanitation, food, energy, transportation, communications, education, health and public safety. This would underline the need to devise a mechanism to launch search for prototypes, designs and new ideas, with focus on the relevant issues. Some of the priority areas could be the following :

- Higher priority for urban poverty, environment, municipal services, communications and mass transport.
- Ongoing urban interchanges *vis-a-vis*, sustainable development.
- Recognition of the positive role of the city.
- Support for local urban initiatives.
- New action partnership between the public, private and voluntary sectors.
- Vision-based planning and restructuring of land-use and zoning concepts.
- Innovations based upon experience.
- Supports and resources to strengthen and multiply local initiatives.
- Integrated and regenerative community development process.
- New channels for participation and investments.
- Opportunities for productivity and income generation.
- Improved quality of life, including safety and pollution control.
- Assignment of cosmopolitan character of the mega city through innovations in management and administration, cultural and technical inventiveness and political and economic leadership.
- Exploring creative potential and reducing gap between ideas and implementation of innovation by adopting a system where concepts and ideas are more important than procedures, by creating new partnerships and communication networks.
- Capacity building and empowerment of voluntary, community groups, women and informal sectors.

In this context, new attitudes and approaches should replace the present ones with the following key themes:

- Holistic in place of reductionist.
- Diversity in place of uniformity.
- Decentralised in place of centralised.
- Small scale in place of large scale.
- Collaboration in place of independence.
- Partnership in place of autocratic.
- Facilitator in place of manager.
- Participatory in place of pre-planned.
- Organisational in place of functional.
- Urbanistic in place of architectonic.
- Sustainability in place of development.

These call for a new paradigm of Urban Planning, Management and Research with the following considerations:

- The introduction of short and medium-term integrated Action Planning which complement comprehensive long-term development objectives.
- Simplification of procedures and integration of the management of urban development.
- Better utilisation and the increase of the revenue base for local bodies.
- A new urban land policy to match with the National Housing Policy, whereby the local authorities act as facilitators to harness the resources of private sector.
- Upgrading technology in Infrastructure services and transportation.
- Exploring new options for financing of infrastructure, land development, housing, conservation, environmental improvement and slum/jhuggi-jhopri rehabilitation.
- Adoption of Multi-Year Investment Planning to match priorities of stage budgets/5 year plans with urban projects.
- A new approach towards Development Controls, mobilising private sector in land assembly, provision of services and

community facilities and concepts like Accommodation, Reservation, Transfer of Development Rights (TDR), Excess Condemnation, etc.

– Networking with international, national and local agencies and programmes.

## CONCLUSION

The organisations, educational institutes and professionals in the field of habitat have the responsibility to set a new direction and re-direct the resources and power at their command to take the step to a new era. It must involve transformation and innovation in the relationships among people, governments, financial institutions, etc. The success of this collective enterprise depends upon the preparatory process and involvement of grass-root level initiatives of people. Civic engagement, sustainability and equity should be the guiding principles of preparing an agenda for the next millennium.

It should provide a holistic perspective and engage action on cross-cutting issues. It should support the efforts of people working to address their needs within the context of local communities and eco-systems. It is time not simply to mark an ending to this millennium but to move beyond it, to envision and embrace the possibilities of a new era.

# 3
# From Downstream to Upstream Technology

**SUKEHIRO GOTOH**

The ultimate aim of IHDP Industrial Transformation is to understand the human drives and mechanisms that could enable a transformation of the whole industrial system towards sustainability, and in physical terms to decouple industrial activities from their environmental impacts.

## MATERIAL FLOWS OF CURRENT INDUSTRIAL SOCIETY

The present industrial society or system, which has been highly developed and runs on the market economy, consists of basically three components, *i.e.*, production, consumption and residue management. Figure 3.1 shows schematically major material flows connecting these three sub-sytems, and the whole industrial structure. Also shown in Figure 3.1 is that, productive activities take place relatively in the upstream area, while consumption and residue management in the midstream and downstream area, respectively.

The present industrial society may be characterized by its linear material flows. Energy and material uses from upstream through midstream to downstream in this industrial system are directly related to environmental impacts whose total magnitude is so significant that the present global industrial society could be termed as simply non-sustainable.

In order to decouple industrial activities from environmental impacts that are associated with various activities of production, consumption and residue management, two approaches are considered essential towards sustainability. One is to reduce the total amount of energy and material uses, another is to close the material cycle or recycle to the maximum extent possible which is allowed by the second law of thermodynamics. A reduction of Factor Four proposed by Ernst von Weizsacker *et al.* in 1994, and the even more dramatic Factor Ten Clubs are examples of the first approach, and the Recycle Society proposed way back in 1974 by Glenn Seaborg, an American Nobel laureate in chemistry, is one of the classical examples of the second approach.

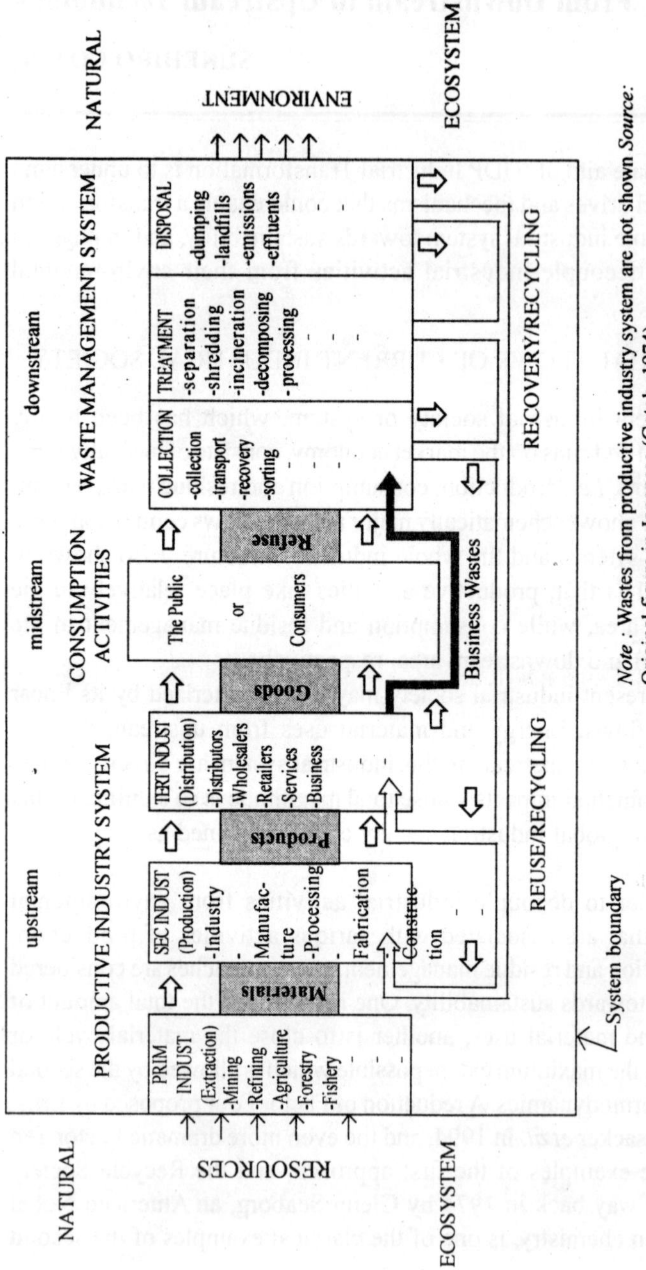


*Note* : Wastes from productive industry system are not shown *Source:* Original figure in Japanese (Gotoh, 1974)

**Fig. 3.1 : Material Flows in the Industrial Ecosystem or Society—A Rheocritical View**

## The Role of Technology in Industrial Transformation towards Sustainability

Technology may be defined as a means by which a certain specific objective based on our human needs and wants is to be achieved. In this regard, technology is destined to be replaced constantly by a more efficient one. Also in the course of development of the present industrial system, technology has been playing one of the central roles.

From a standpoint of industrial transformation, however, the role of technology for the purpose of reducing environmental impacts has to be reconsidered.

Most of the conventional so-called environmental technology have been reactive, curative and corrective in its nature. For example, technology used to control and treat flue gases and wastewaters is the one to react, cure and correct the upstream production process from causing environmental pollutions. Because this type of technology is usually applied at the end of the upstream production process, it is called the "end-of-pipe" technology. The important point here is that although a considerable amount of environmental impacts could be reduced by applying this technology still their major portion will remain because the upstream production process *per se* will not be changed. Often it will be the case from our Japanese experience that the more downstream end-of-pipe disposal technology is applied the more production will be made upstream thus the total amount of environmental impacts to be incurred will be increased. This may be illustrated by the observation that the more municipal waste incinerators or landfills are constructed in the downstream area the more waste will be generated over the midstream and upstream areas.

Technology for sustainable activities of production, consumption and residue management at the firm and/or household level must be, in principle, proactive, preventive and adaptive. Furthermore, it should be innovative from the very beginning of decision process for its research and development.

## Technological Change Envisioned for Industrial Transformation

Technology currently applied and used in the present industrial system must be completely reviewed and changed for sustainable activities

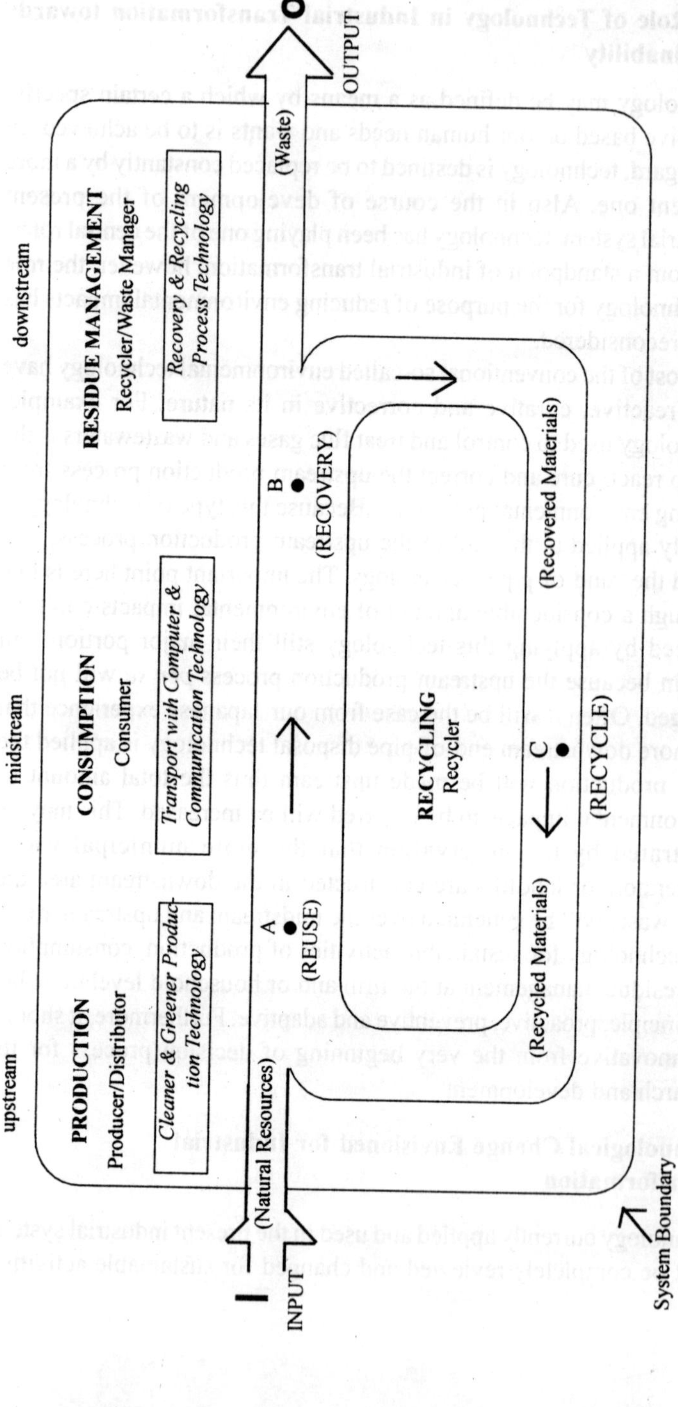


**Fig. 3.2 :** Technological Change and the Recycle Society for Sustainability

of production, consumption and residue management. The following is the so-called "cleaner and greener" technology that should substitute for the conventional industrial technology.

Firstly, in the downstream area where the end-of-pipe disposal technology is used, recovery and recycling technology is to be applied to facilitate closing the material cycle.

Secondly, in the midstream area where activities associated with the distribution of commercial goods and services, consumption, and collection of residues, are the major sources of environmental burden, the present automotive transport technology, which can be identifed as critical from a standpoint of sustainability, has to be reviewed. In this connection, transportation systems that are well planned and controlled, but to be flexibly operated by means of highly efficient computer and communication techniques must be developed.

Thirdly, in the upstream area where most production activities are conducted and most decisions leading to the usage of energy and materials are made, the conventional mass-production system pursuing the extreme of economy of scale for cost reduction but as a result wasting natural resources, should be replaced by a well planned and streamlined production system which is incorporating the lifecycle thinking into the total quality management. Technology used in this context has been called for years the cleaner production or waste (residue) minimization technology.

And finally, Figure 3.2 indicates the direction of technological change for industrial transformation, and also shows the subsequent structure of recycle society.

# 4

# Integrating Policies for Combating Climate Change

## A Case Study of Japanese Inter-Ministerial Coordination for the Kyoto Protocol

**TAKASHI HATTORI**

## INTRODUCTION

In December 1997, Japan hosted the third session of the Conference of the Parties (COP3) to the United Nations Framework Convention on Climate Change (UNFCCC) in Kyoto. For Japan, the Kyoto Protocol was a challenge in dealing with the international treaty-making process and, at the same time, in resolving domestic differences. Considering the inter-ministerial conflicts that arose when facing this multi-faceted inter-sectional issue, the Japanese Government set up a joint conference consisting of relevant advisory councils from the ministries and agencies concerned to facilitate the decision-making process in formulating a policy to combat climate change.

The 'Joint Conference on Relevant Advisory Councils on Domestic Measures Addressing the Global Warming Issue' (hereafter called the Joint Conference) was established in August 1997. Following the Prime Minister's decision, 18 private representatives from 9 advisory councils were appointed to bring this inter-ministerial issue together in a single forum. The Joint Conference met 5 times and, in November 1997, before the COP3, adopted a report outlining the basic direction of policies and measures to be undertaken by the Japanese Government.

In preparing for the Joint Conference, the various ministries and agencies were forced to combine each of their separate measures into one integrated policy of the Japanese Government. In accordance with the open process set by the Joint Conference, this inter-ministerial coordination worked to create the momentum necessary to formulate such an integrated policy. The Joint Conference played a significant role as the mechanism responsible for bringing about the shifts in positions that were necessary for the various ministries and agencies to deal with the requested concerns.

This chapter attempts to shed some light on this recent attempt by the Japanese Government to integrate policies by creating a new high level mechanism in which advisory councils of relevant ministries and agencies are involved. It examines how the mechanism influenced Japanese decision-making on climate change and, in particular, how it changed the relationship between the public and private sectors in the decision-making process. Through examining the case of policy formulation in the lead up to the Kyoto Protocol negotiations, this chapter considers the role of this new mechanism in integrating policies in order to solve such multi-faceted, inter-sectional issues as climate change.

The case study focuses on investigating the relationships between the actors in the decision-making process.[1] The classical models of Allison (1971) suggest that the level of analysis must be carefully considered in case studies. His 'rational actor model' (Model I) would explain the outcome as a final choice but put the decision-making process into a black box. His 'organizational process model' (Model II) would come closer to analyzing the inter-ministerial conflicts on the issue utilizing standard organizational operating procedures, while his 'governmental politics model' (Model III) would take care of governmental actions resulting from bargaining by players in positions with vested interests.

The level of analysis for this case study requires coming down from Model I to Model II or Model III, but with some modifications. With this issue, analysis of the governmental decision-making process should not rely solely on the various public sector agencies but must also consider the private sectors. This chapter includes actors from both the public and private sectors, and examines how the process was affected by the different interests and positions of the actors. In such an analysis, the decision-making process resembles a negotiation process.

Summarizing Faure and Rubin (1993), analysis of a negotiation process must include the following 5 elements: actors, structure, strategies, process, and outcomes. Actors can be individuals, groups, organizations, or nation-states. Faure and Rubin first determine who the actors are and then consider the structural constraints of the negotiation, the strategies taken by the actors to achieve their objectives, the particular course of the negotiation, and the final outcomes of the negotiation. This chapter adopts Faure and Rubin's basic ideas for analyzing negotiations and applies them to each step of the Japanese decision-making process on climate change.

I divide this chapter into 4 sections. The first provides background information on the establishment of the Joint Conference, focussing on inter-ministerial coordination. The second section discusses how the Joint Conference influenced the formulation of Japan's proposed numerical target for the Kyoto Protocol negotiations. The third then demonstrates how the Joint Conference helped deepen Japanese policies and measures to combat climate change. Finally, based on the case study of the Joint Conference, the fourth section draws some general conclusions on mechanisms for integrating multifaceted, inter-sectional policies and measures.

## BACKGROUND

The Joint Conference was established on August 22, 1997, by the 'Prime Minister's Decision'. The stated purpose of the Joint Conference opaquely asserted that "Since the measures [to combat climate change] cover a broad range of policy areas, to effectively implement the various measures, it [is] necessary for the whole government to promote coordinated and systematic linkages among the various measures" (Article 1).

The Joint Conference was able to obtain a combination of characteristics unique and unprecedented in the history of policy formulation by the Japanese Government.

First, the Joint Conference was created as an advisory group directly linked to the Chief of State. It is usual for government ministries and agencies to establish advisory councils for their own purposes. Each of these advisory councils is based on a certain law that sets its objectives and mandates to help research and discuss important matters related to the objectives of its ministry or agency. In some cases, Ministers or Director-Generals of government ministries or agencies create temporary advisory groups to meet urgent objectives such as the "unrestrained absorption of specific knowledge, and maneuvering of public opinion and bureaucracy" (Abe *et al.*, 1990, p. 60). The Joint Conference was a case where the Prime Minister created and took the leadership of an advisory group to absorb knowledge and formulate policy direction.

Second, the Joint Conference assembled private representatives already serving on various advisory councils. Usually, members of advisory groups are chosen directly from various areas of the private sector to represent a wide cross-section of the parties concerned. The Joint Conference also met this requirement—it consisted of representatives from industry, labour and consumer groups, as well as experts on the environment and energy. At the same time, the members of the Joint Conference represented the advisory councils to which they belonged. These members mostly served as the Chairs of advisory councils or their subcommittees, and were recommended by each ministry or agency to represent their advisory councils.

Third, because of the above characteristics, the Joint Conference was operated in conjunction with the relevant ministries and agencies. The general affairs of the Joint Conference—what was to be discussed when—were carried out by the Cabinet Secretariat in consultation with the Environmental Agency and the Ministry of International Trade and Industry (MITI)[2]. Furthermore, each topic for discussion in the Joint Conference was prepared by the relevant ministries and agencies. The establishment and management of the Joint Conference was a coordinated effort of the Japanese Government as a whole.

As we have seen, various actors from both public and private sectors were involved in the decision-making process of the Joint Conference. In any decision-making process, each actor shows different interests and holds different stakes or standpoints. The actors regulate the process from their own aspirations and restraints.

Japanese Prime Minister Ryutaro Hashimoto decided on and ordered the creation of the Joint Conference. On returning from his trip to Denver and New York in June 1997, after attending the Economic Summit and the Special Session of the United Nations General Assembly (UNGASS), Prime Minister Hashimoto instructed the Cabinet Secretariat to begin preparing to bring the COP3 to a successful conclusion. On July 15, 1997, he directly asked the Ministers and Vice-Ministers of the 3 main government agencies involved—the Environment Agency, MITI, and the Ministry of Foreign Affairs—for their best efforts.

Specifically, the Prime Minister's instruction, issued to the 3 agency heads on July 15, was the following :

> Looking toward the third session of the Conference of the Parties of the United Nations Framework Convention on Climate Change to be held in Kyoto this December, Japan, as

host country, must take a leading role to bring the matter to a conclusion.

Regarding this matter, there are conflicts among developed countries, between developed countries and developing countries, and among developing countries. I know it is a very difficult issue, since there are many different views on, for example, how to decide a quantitative target regarding greenhouse gases, when the target year should be set, how policy measures to achieve the target should be met, whether developing countries should strengthen their obligations, and whether they should accept the evolution. As you three ministers know well, there are also many points of view within Japan.

In this situation, by placing the Cabinet Secretariat in the central position, together with the three ministries and agencies involved, Japan must construct a comprehensive strategy to adequately deal with the matter at the seventh session of the Ad Hoc Group on the Berlin Mandate (AGBM7), to be held from the 31st of this month and during the further developments in the fall.

First, I ask your cooperation to make a concrete plan for Japan to cope with future negotiations, while leaving some room for flexibility, by the time of the AGBM meeting at the end of this month.

Next, I strongly ask your every effort to lead the Kyoto Conference to a success, by actively proceeding with your attempts against the global-warming problem.

Furthermore, in future treatment of the matter, please coordinate the relevant advisory councils, such as the Central Environment Council, the Advisory Committee for Energy, and the Industrial Structure Council, by, for instance, creating a joint conference, to nurture systematic linkages among such advisory councils (The Prime Minister's instruction on July 15, 1997).

The Prime Minister's instruction specifically directed the Cabinet Secretariat and the main ministries and agencies to form the new forum of the Joint Conference.

Before the Prime Minister's instruction, the Environment Agency and MITI, along with other ministries and agencies, had continued their turf battles over the issue. Each ministry and agency divided the issue into pieces, which were pursued by each in different ways. The Environment Agency had asked its advisory council, the Central Environment Council, to advise it on a solution to the issue. MITI asked its advisory councils, the Advisory Committee for Energy and the Industrial Structure Council, to advise it on policies and measures to counter the problem. Other ministries and agencies had also been challenged to find solutions to this difficult problem; Table 4.1 shows those attempts by the relevant ministries and agencies.

The turf battles among the ministries and agencies had caused delays in producing a numerical target to be proposed at the Kyoto Protocol negotiations. The Japanese Government failed to produce a numerical target because of the different positions taken by relevant ministries and agencies. In December 1996, at AGBM5, Japan presented a formula for a numerical target: this differentiation formula allowed each industrial country to choose a numerical target for carbon dioxide emissions by either maintaining its emissions at not more than *p* tons of carbon per capita or by reducing its emissions by not less than *q* per cent below the 1990 level. But Japan did not specify a number for "*p*" or "*q*" even after the next AGBM or the Denver Summit—the proposal for a specific numerical target had to transcend the inter-ministerial conflicts.

The difficulty of producing a proposed numerical target was rooted in the difficulty of collecting and evaluating the various policies and measures scattered across various ministries and agencies. The final report by the Joint Conference stated: "The issue of global warming is an environmental issue as well as an economic and energy issue, because greenhouse gases are largely a result of industrial activities and the consumption of energy by people in their daily lives. Their release is also closely linked to transport/traffic policy and housing/construction policy. Therefore, any countermeasures must cover a broad range of policy area in the industrial, transport, and commercial/residential sectors, and coordinated and systematic linkages among the various measures must be maintained" [3. (1)].

The Prime Minister declared the successful completion of the COP3 to be the Cabinet's most important issue and, when the relevant ministries and agencies failed to coordinate the inter-ministerial issues, the Cabinet Secretariat supported the Prime Minister by taking on a

**Table 4.1:** Relevant Advisory Councils

| Advisory Council | Law/Cabinet Order | Mandate | Remarks |
|---|---|---|---|
| Central Environment Council [Environment Agency] | Basic Environment Law, Article 41 | Environmental conservation | Started to discuss policies on global warming—August 1997. (Planning and Policy Committee) |
| Advisory Committee for Energy [Ministry of International Trade and Industry (MITI)] | Law Establishing Advisory Committee for Energy | Securing stable and rational energy supply | Discussed prospects of energy supply and demand. (Supply and Demand Committee) |
| Industrial Structure Council [MITI] | Organizational Order of MITI, Article 101 | Industrial structure | Presented the "Global Environmental Vision" report—March 1997. (Global Environment Committee) |
| Economic Council [Economic Planning Agency (EPA)] | Organizational Order of EPA, Article 41 | Economic policy and Planning | Started to discuss implications of global environmental policies on economic society—July 1997. (Committee on Prospects of Economic Society) |
| Social Policy Council [EPA] | Law Establishing EPA, Article 8 | Improving environment and standard of living, and consumer protection | Proposed transformation to an environment-friendly society—November 1996. (General Policy Committee) |
| Building Council [Ministry of Construction (MOC)] | Organizational Order of MOC, Article 74 | Building | Proposed strengthening countermeasures in the housing field—March 1997. (Building Administration Committee) |

*Contd.*

**Table 4.1 :** *(Contd.)*

| Advisory Council | Law/Cabinet Order | Mandate | Remarks |
|---|---|---|---|
| Road Council [MOC] | Road Law, Ariticle 79 | Road construction planning | Started to build a new 5–year road construction plan. |
| Transport Policy Council [Ministry of Transport (MOT)] | Organizational Order of MOT, Article 108 | Transport policy and planning | Developed a report on measures in the transport sector to deal with the global warming problem — April 1997. (General Committee) |
| Telecommunications Council [Ministry of Post and Telecommunications (MPT)] | Organizational Order of MPT, Article 87 | Telecommunications | Showed effects of telecommunications to reduce the load in "21st Century Telecommunications Vision" — June 1997. |

coordination role and becoming involved in the issue. The Cabinet Secretariat had to fulfil the Prime Minister's initiative and started preparing for the establishment of the Joint Conference by consulting with the relevant ministries and agencies.

The Environment Agency showed some initial hesitation toward the establishment of the Joint Conference. It was cautious about whether the Joint Conference would restrict the discussions of the Central Environment Council that had determined the directions of the Environment Agency's policies on climate change. However, the Joint Conference placed no official restriction on discussions by any advisory council. The Environment Agency could—and did—hold meetings of the Central Environment Council parallel to those of the Joint Conference.

MITI expected the establishment of the Joint Conference to play two roles. First, in the formulation of policy to combat climate change, it intended the Joint Conference to reflect the discussions of all relevant ministries, not just those of the Central Environment Council. It felt that the Joint Conference would be the most suitable forum to advance relevant ministry policies with the help of advisory councils. MITI utilized the Joint Conference to effectively infuse its own policies and measures into the development of climate change policies.

At the same time, MITI aimed at inducing other ministries, such as the Ministry of Construction and the Ministry of Transport, to implement measures sufficient to further cut the expected future emissions of greenhouse gases. MITI is in charge of policies in most of the industrial sector, but does not have major authority over construction or transportation policies that are covered by other ministries and agencies. 'The establishment of the Joint Conference helped MITI rationalize its requests when asking other ministries and agencies to cooperate with policy integration.

Other ministries and agencies accepted the establishment of the Joint Conference[3]. Being involved with the matter from within the jurisdiction of the ministries and agencies is almost standard operating procedure for a bureaucracy (Wilson, 1989). Furthermore, these ministries and agencies were more likely to prefer cooperating with the Cabinet Secretariat than to being given orders by MITI. All government ministries and agencies approved the establishment of the Joint Conference before the official Prime Minister's Decision on August 22, 1997.

Members of the Joint Conference were chosen on the recommendations of the relevant ministries and agencies. Each government agency recommended two representatives from members of each advisory council, having in mind the chairperson of the council or its subcommittee. Avoiding redundancy and keeping balance among the private sectors, the Prime Minister and the Cabinet Secretariat selected 18 members of the Joint Conference.

Consequently, members covered the various aspects of policies on climate change. They may be divided into the following five categories:

*Environment Experts* (3 persons): university professors (current or past) from the fields of environmental technology, law, and economics.

*Other Experts* (5 persons): scholars and members of think-tanks in the fields of energy, transportation, construction, economics, and telecommunications.

*Industrial Leaders* (6 persons): one representative each from the Keidanren and the electricity, steel, automobile, electronic appliance, and computer industries.

*Labour and Consumer* (2 persons): one representative each from a labour union and a consumer group.

*Mass Communication* (2 persons): a representative from the newspaper industry and a member of a think-tank.

In addition to representing the advisory councils of relevant ministries and agencies, the members covered most layers of Japanese society with regard to climate change policies.[4]

In sum, the Joint Conference was established as the Prime Minister's advisory group that assembled a variety of private representatives from the advisory councils of relevant government agencies. Although the public actors had different interests and motivations for participating in the Joint Conference, they succeeded in cooperating to bring about its establishment. The establishment of the Joint Conference fell within the acceptable range for all the public actors. Consequently, the Joint Conference started to function as a part of the decision-making process for integrating Japanese policy on climate change.

## FORMULATING THE JAPANESE NUMERICAL TARGET PROPOSAL

On October 6, 1997, Chief Cabinet Secretary Kanezo Muraoka announced the Japanese numerical target proposal.[5] As a base reduction rate for all industrial countries, Japan proposed a reduction of carbon dioxide, methane, and nitrous oxide to 5 per cent below 1990 levels to be in place by the period from 2008 to 2012. The 5 per cent reduction was a symbolic figure to create impetus in the international negotiations and bring other countries to the negotiating table before the COP3. It proposed a new differentiation formula to vary the actual level of reduction based on each country's circumstances, which reduced the burden on Japan to a 2.5 per cent reduction, but asked all participating industrial countries to reduce greenhouse gas emissions to at least the 1990 level.

To arrive at this proposal, the Cabinet Secretariat held informal meetings with the Environment Agency, the Ministry of Foreign Affairs, and MITI.[6] The Cabinet Secretariat, with strong interests in the outcome, mediated the inter-ministerial coordination among the three agencies. The establishment of the Joint Conference represented the Cabinet Secretariat's strong commitment to inter-ministerial coordination in the formation of climate change policy.

At the informal meetings, based on their own estimates, the three agencies—the Environment Agency, the Ministry of Foreign Affairs, and MITI—proposed to reduce greenhouse gas emissions by 7 per cent, 5 per cent and 0 per cent, respectively, from the 1990 level by the year 2010. These numbers were not presented at the meeting of the Joint Conference; only the result of the inter-ministerial coordination was presented at the third meeting of the Joint Conference on October 13, 1997.

However, the Joint Conference certainly demonstrated its function in the process of deciding the Japanese numerical target proposal.

MITI is in charge of energy policies. After the Denver Summit, the Agency of Natural Resources and Energy in MITI accelerated its trial calculations of energy prospects in 2010, both in a business-as-usual scenario and with policy-based lower adjustments. It assembled a number of measures that were technically and economically feasible in the industrial, transport, and commercial/residential sectors, and applied the measures to each sector until carbon dioxide emissions from total energy consumption in 2010 stabilized at the 1990 level.[7] This exercise done by MITI had to be accepted by other relevant ministries and agencies in charge of such measures.

The establishment of the Joint Conference helped MITI convince other ministries and agencies to accept a sector-by-sector reduction rate by the year 2010: A 7 per cent decrease in the industrial sector instead of a 5 per cent increase; a 17 per cent increase in the transport sector instead of a 40 per cent increase; a zero per cent increase in the commercial/residential sector instead of a 16 per cent increase. MITI took it for granted that the Japanese numerical target proposal had to be complied with by Japan itself. Using the contribution to the Joint Conference as one of its reasons, MITI persuaded the other ministries and agencies to approve the measures that would need to be introduced to gain the MITI's zero per cent cut as the Japanese proposal. MITI and other relevant ministries and agencies presented the chosen measures at the meetings of the Joint Conference.

The Environment Agency proposed the 7 per cent cut based on the "scientific" results of its analysis by the Asian-Pacific Integrated Model (AIM)[8]. It claimed that a substantial reduction would be necessary to maintain the world's climate as it was, and that this would be feasible according to the policies suggested in the AIM analysis. The representative of the Environment Agency's Central Environment Council reported the result of the AIM analysis at the first meeting of the Joint Conference.

The Ministry of Foreign Affairs insisted on a 5 per cent cut by 2010 to meet the "internationally acceptable" rate of reduction. Surrounded by the European Union, which insisted on 15 per cent reduction, and the United States, whose figure was still unknown, it asserted that it was necessary to propose a rate that would save face in the international arena. At the meetings of the Joint Conference, the Ministry of Foreign Affairs presented progress reports on international negotiations.[9]

The members of the Joint Conference expressed their thoughts on numerical targets:[10] "It is important to change our way of thinking from merely accumulating measures that are technically and economically feasible at present to decide which measures need to be met and what should be achieved. Since there is a calculation by one NGO indicating that a greater than 14.8 per cent reduction of carbon dioxide is possible, we must examine numerical targets carefully" (expressed at the second meeting). "The idea that a 7.6 per cent reduction is technically feasible was presented at the Central Environment Council" (at the first meeting). "The industrial sector will make its best efforts based on the Keidanren's voluntary plan. Suppressing carbon dioxide emissions to the 1990 level is the bottom line" (at the second meeting). These remarks—14.8 per cent, 7.6 per cent and zero per cent reductions—offset one another, and did not shift the outcome of the Japanese numerical target proposal.

At the informal inter-ministerial meetings of the 3 government agencies held parallel to the Joint Conference, the Cabinet Secretariat created a method for Japan to reach consensus on its own proposal.[11] By the differentiation formula designed into the proposal, Japan could reduce its own requirement to 2.5 per cent from the 5 per cent benchmark. By including in the proposal a 2 per cent buffer to be sanctioned for non-compliance, Japan could further reduce its requirement to 0.5 per cent, which would be achieved on the 3-gas basis, instead of being limited to carbon dioxide.

At the third meeting of the Joint Conference, where the Japanese proposal was introduced to the members, the members expressed their opinions regarding the numerical target:[12] "There was an opinion at the Central Environment Council that 5 per cent is an attainable figure if efforts are made." "I have strong concerns on the feasibility of realising this figure. Even zero per cent in 2010 means a 15 per cent cut from the current status." "The Japanese Government's proposal is realistic and well considered." "The target of the Japanese Government's proposal is too low."

The Chairperson of the Joint Conference concluded the discussion by saying that the Joint Conference should not be the place to discuss numerical targets that must be determined by international negotiations. He stressed that the Prime Minister had requested the Joint Conference to indicate the basic directions for measures needed to prevent global warming, focusing on comprehensive measures to restrain energy demand.[13]

In sum, how did the Joint Conference influence the inter-ministerial decision-making process in formulating the Japanese numerical target? The Cabinet Secretariat organized informal inter-ministerial meetings and produced the Japanese Government's proposal to the AGBM negotiations. During the course of making the decision of the numerical proposal, each government agency considered the proceedings of the Joint Conference to various extents, and tried to muster support for its positions there. Furthermore, behind the scenes, MITI used the Joint Conference to persuade other ministries and agencies to support its proposal. The remarks by the members of the Joint Conference covered a wide range of views that offsets one another, and let the inter-ministerial agreement proceed as it was. The Joint Conference helped nurture the momentum needed for the coordinated inter-ministerial process to formulate the Japanese proposal on time.

## INTEGRATING POLICIES FOR COMBATING CLIMATE CHANGE

In what way did the Joint Conference influence the government's policies and measures to combat climate change?

The Prime Minister's Decision on August 22, 1997 stated that "the Joint Conference should examine major policies and measures in the industrial, transport, and commercial/residential sectors to deal with the global warming problem" (Article 2). The Joint Conference held 5 meetings before the COP3 and produced a report to the Prime Minister.

At the first meeting, on August 27, after the Prime Minister's opening speech and the selection of the Chairperson and the Deputy Chairperson, relevant ministries and agencies explained information necessary to discuss the issue. The Ministry of Foreign Affairs offered a basic outline of the climate change negotiations that had taken place from UNFCCC to AGBM7. The Environment Agency explained the current situation and projected carbon dioxide emissions; MITI's Agency of Natural Resources and Energy explained the current situation and projected energy consumption. Finally, based on the factors causing an increase in energy consumption, MITI presented a menu of policies and measures to be discussed at the Joint Conference.

At the second meeting, on September 26, relevant ministries presented their versions of policies and measures in the industrial and transport sectors.[14] The policies and measures were those technically and economically feasible ones that each ministry and agency had prepared through inter-ministerial coordination. At the meeting, the Cabinet Secretariat reported the results of public opinion research on the global warming problem, and the Chairperson proposed public hearings by the Joint Conference.

At the third meeting, on October 13, after the Ministry of Foreign Affairs explained the Japanese numerical target proposal, relevant ministries presented their policies and measures in the commercial/

residential sector.[15] The Economic Planning Agency explained options for a re-evaluation of lifestyles as material for discussion, and the Environment Agency and MITI presented economic modalities such as carbon taxes and emissions trading. The members of the Joint Conference then discussed the direction of policies and measures based on the information the ministries and agencies had presented.

After these 3 meetings, the Joint Conference held 2 public hearings to gain wider involvement from the general public who held opinions on policies and measures to combat climate change. The Joint Conference held one hearing in Tokyo on October 27 and the other in Osaka on October 30. A total of 28 persons from various backgrounds, including representatives of environmental NGOs, presented their opinions in front of the members of the Joint Conference and exchanged their ideas. Furthermore, many opinions via facsimile and Internet were sent to the Joint Conference and were presented at the fourth meeting.

The Joint Conference started to compile its report to the Prime Minister at the fourth meeting, on November 7, and finished it at the fifth meeting, on November 13. The Chairperson of the Joint Conference handed the report to the Prime Minister on November 14.

Consulting with the Chairperson and Deputy Chairperson, the Cabinet Secretariat prepared a draft outline of the report based on reports by the relevant ministries and agencies, remarks by the members at the meetings, and general opinions expressed at the public hearings. The draft outline was presented to the members for their comments at the fourth meeting.

Based on the members' comments, the Cabinet Secretariat drafted the report under the supervision of the Chairperson and the Deputy Chairperson. Before the fifth meeting, the draft report was sent to members and relevant government agencies for their comments. The Chairperson and the Deputy Chairperson scrutinized the comments and revised the report that was presented at the fifth meeting. The members gave comments on the revised report, carried out further revisions, and produced the final report.

In this report-generating process, the members of the Joint Conference gave comments on the draft outline and the draft report reflecting a desire to modify the policies and measures set by relevant ministries and agencies. The members gave comments, exchanged views between each other, and requested further developments from the government. The report needed to be unanimously approved; it gave each member the chance to advance policies and measures. Comparison between the draft outline and the final report helps clarify the roles of the Joint Conference members and their effects on the policy formulation. The report-generating process showed competition over the public-private axis and a trade-off between environmental conservation and economic growth (see Fig. 4.1).

Each vector in the two-dimensional diagram represents the effect of the members of the Joint Conference in the report generating process. The origin of the vector stands for the starting point set by the draft outline at the fourth meeting. The head of the vector symbolizes the outcome shown in the final report. Thus, the vector shows the change produced by exchange of views and discussions among the members of the Joint Conference and between them and the government.

The X-axis represents the degree of involvement or commitment by either public sector or private sector. The more left-hand side, the point of the vector represents the involvement or commitment of public sectors. And, the more right-hand side, the spot stands for private sectors' involvement. Here, private sectors include both industry and general people. The X-axis represents whether governments or private sectors take actions in major elements of the report.

The Y-axis depicts the trade-off between environmental conservation and economic growth in the report generating process. The point at the upper side represents the more environmental-friendly actions would be taken. And, the point at the lower side represents the stance of the report that is more conscious about economic growth, or industrial competitiveness. The Y-axis represents where each discussion point of the report was set in the environment and economic dichotomy.

As a whole, this conceptual diagram stands for the effects of the Joint Conference due to the exchange of views and discussions by the members from private sectors. The existence of the vector itself stands for the existence of the effects or roles of the Joint Conference in one way or another. The following of this section exemplifies major discussion points shown in the meetings of the Joint Conference.

Regarding the basic direction of the measures, the outline stated that "technically and economically feasible measures were thoroughly researched." The final report clarifies the different standpoints of the

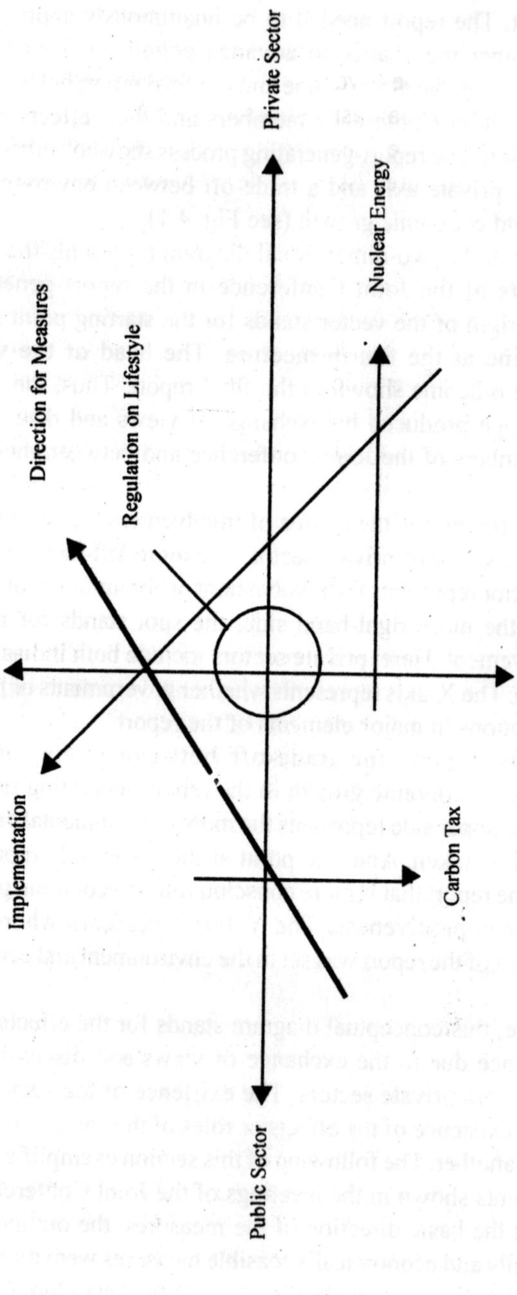


**Fig. 4.1: Conceptual Diagram of the Effect of the Joint Conference**

government and the Joint Conference: The report states that "the Joint Conference examined reports on the technically and economically feasible measures that the government has proposed for the industrial, transport, and commercial/residential sectors" [2. (2)].

The Joint Conference specified the conditions under which the projected carbon dioxide emissions were calculated; these were simply written in the draft outline as "in the case of about 2 per cent economic growth after the year 2000." The final report states that "These figures and other projections presented below were calculated using the socio-economic framework—such as economic growth rates, population trends, and progress in introducing non-fossil energy sources and promoting energy conservation presented in Japan's second report [to UNFCCC]" [3. (2)]. The Joint Conference emphasized that the calculation was based on conditions set by the government. The Joint Conference tried not to discount the possibility of additional cuts in greenhouse gas emissions by the implementation of further policies or measures.

The Joint Conference rejected the draft outline that simply approved the government's policies and measures and reserved its approval by stating in the final report that "While the discussion was subject to time constraints, the conference considered that the direction of the measures as a whole was basically appropriate" [3. (3)]. The Joint Conference further stated in the final report that "... in order to halt global warming, greenhouse gases need to be cut significantly in the long run. Given this situation, we can hardly be content with the... measures, but must instead engage in even greater efforts on a continual basis toward further greenhouse gas reductions—for the realization of greenhouse gas reduction measures, aside from supply-side $CO_2$ cuts, and the enhancement of energy conservation efforts at all levels of society" [3. (3)].

Furthermore, the members of the Joint Conference added to the report the statement that "To ensure that these measures produce steady results, rigorous follow-up studies will be required on what they have managed to accomplish on the energy supply side and in each of the energy demand sectors (industry, transport, and commercial/residential)" (7).

Some members, who were categorized above as the Industrial Leaders, tried to defend the phrase in the draft outline stating that "To cut the carbon dioxide emissions further [than stabilization at the 1990 level], it would be necessary to consider introducing measures to directly restrict energy consumption. We decided not to take such measures, taking into account the impact on economic growth and people's daily lives, and the balance with continued long-term policies to prevent global warming." However, other members, who were mainly categorized as the Environment Experts, rejected the phrase. It was omitted from the final report and replaced with "To achieve this, energy demand has to be kept to around current levels, which will be no easy matter" [3. (3)]. The Joint Conference shifted the report further in the direction of environmental protection than the government had initially considered in the draft outline.

Regarding the supply-side measures, policies on nuclear energy were an issue where the members of the Joint Conference expressed various views. The draft outline stated the necessity to "promote the introduction of nuclear energy (an additional 70.5 million kilowatts of generating capacity in 2010)." The final report affirms that "The basic supply-side measures are the introduction of new forms of energy to the equivalent of 19.1 million kilolitres of oil annually... and 70.5 million kilowatts of extra nuclear power (the equivalent of around 20 new nuclear power plants), based on the current 'Oil-Alternative Energy Supply Targets' [September 1994 Cabinet Decision." (3. (3)].

To reach this agreement, however, the members of the Joint Conference debated the pros and cons of the government's nuclear energy policies. However, the members, both in favour of and against nuclear energy use, mentioned the necessity of obtaining the acceptance of the public:[16] "We need to build consensus among local governments, residents, and mass media in order to promote nuclear energy." "It is necessary to let people understand that we must rely upon nuclear energy." "People cannot effortlessly consent to nuclear plants. There are arguments showing we can lower our standard of living in order to reduce nuclear energy." "We must show alternatives to the general public."

As a result, the Joint Conference added to the final report the statement that "To implement these measures, it will be vital not only to ensure nuclear energy's safety but also to gain the support of the public" [3. (3)], and "Because of limited time at the conference, discussions focused only on the energy-demand dimension of greenhouse gas emissions. But policies related to supply are equally important and are expected to be discussed in future deliberations in related councils" [2. (1)]. The Joint Conference shifted the report in the direction of securing more transparent involvement of the private sector in nuclear energy policies.

Regarding views on economic modalities, most members of the Joint Conference were reluctant to introduce a carbon tax in the present situation. The draft outline stated, "we will continue to examine whether or not to introduce a carbon tax, since there are various pros and cons in the institutional design of the objective, range, stage, rate, and so on".

At the second meeting, the members started the discussion on economic modalities.[17] One of the members spoke out strongly against a carbon tax: "I oppose the introduction of carbon tax in Japan unless it is introduced all over the world at the same time. It would distort the structure of Japanese trade and industry, and the detrimental side-effects would exceed its merits".

Another member refuted the argument: "Carbon tax is income transfer from people to government; the government can use the revenue for policies and measures on climate change. The effects can be positive in the long run, and do not necessarily damage the economy. The major industries in Japan will produce highly energy-efficient products, and would probably turn out to be winners, not losers. Regarding international competitiveness, measures at the border (such as tax exemption to exports) may work to reduce the side-effects."

At the third meeting, after the government's neutral presentation, some members expressed their opinions against the carbon tax:[18] "Introducing a carbon tax would lead to shrinkage, transference, and hollowing of the production bases in Japan. Tax must be discussed not only in terms of environmental protection but in terms of the configuration of the entire tax system, taking economic revitalization into account." "According to past data, in spite of the 57 per cent increase in the price of electricity following the first oil shock, the demand continued to increase at an average of 5.8 per cent over a 5-year period, and in spite of the 52 per cent increase following the second oil shock, the demand increased 3.6 per cent. The price increase did not affect the demand." "We are not presently in such a situation that it is necessary to introduce a high rate tax. Even if spread thinly and widely, serious examination is necessary."

At the fourth meeting, where the draft outline was presented, the members drifted toward the view not to levy a carbon tax in the present situation. "At the public hearings we organized, industry groups and labour unions expressed opposition to a carbon tax. Among the members of the Joint Conference, I am the only one in favour of introducing a carbon tax. Why don't we write in the report that we won't levy a carbon tax? If we only write 'various pros and cons', we are at the same level as the TV commentators." "Carbon tax is a potential tool in cases such as when introduced concurrently throughout the world. Many opposed the introduction of a carbon tax only under the current circumstances. We should not ignore the carbon tax, which would imply we killed the carbon tax."

Those who opposed the carbon tax also expressed their opinions: "If we take a vote, we should write that we won't levy a carbon tax." "Only Japan is considering introducing a carbon tax. We should clearly write that we denied the carbon tax."

One of the members of the Joint Conference carried a neutral opinion: "Not only a carbon tax, but also other incentives in the form of tax breaks and subsidies, are economic modalities for inducing certain human behaviours. We should not hate the very sight of a carbon tax, rather, we should write that we should use economic modalities as a tool."

Thus, the final report states: "Economic modalities entail offering economic incentives using the market mechanism in order to encourage the various economic entities to take actions appropriate to environmental conservation. Economic modalities contributing to $CO_2$ emission reductions would include supplementary economic measures, such as subsidies, loans, and tax breaks, as well as measures relating to economic burdens, such as a carbon tax and emission rights trading" [3. (4)].

It concludes, "With regard to a carbon tax, the conference debated such aspects as its expected efficiency and the impact it would have on the economy. While it would perhaps be inadvisable to introduce a carbon tax at this point of time, continued consideration will be needed on the pros and cons of this concept in line with the changing situation" [3. (4)]. The Joint Conference as a whole shifted the discussion to the direction of not levying a carbon tax at present.

Furthermore, in the final report, the members of the Joint Conference concluded the regulation on lifestyle as "In terms of lifestyle, emphasis will be placed first on voluntary efforts by citizens to conserve energy. Follow-up studies of the results will be conducted and, where the situation does not improve, new measures including regulations will have to be considered to achieve the desired results" [3. (4)]. The issue was written in the draft outline as: "to re-evaluate lifestyle, some feel that strict regulations must be introduced rather than wait for voluntary actions by people, while others feel that measures must be limited to incentives offered to the people." The Joint Conference put regulation on lifestyle as an option in the event that the other policies and measures should become ineffective.

Regarding implementation of policies and measures on climate change, the Joint Conference pushed the government to integrate their actions in the future. "The Government should implement concrete measures in response to the basic direction for measures for the prevention of global warming indicated by this Joint Conference." In the final report the phrase was changed to "... the relevant ministries and agencies should work together to probe deeply into the needs and to comprehensively and systematically formulate measures that can produce good results" (7). This led to formation of a new institution called the Global Warming Prevention Headquarters, headed by the Prime Minister, after the COP3.

Furthermore, the final report states that "We intend to proceed in our respective councils on work toward the realization of policies for 2010 and thereafter" (7). At the fifth meeting, the members of the Joint Conference pointed out the significance of the Joint Conference. The Joint Conference continued to evaluate the government's policies and measures set by the Global Warming Prevention Headquarters.

In sum, after presentations by the government, the Joint Conference managed the report-generating process. The members of the Joint Conference had different views on policies and measures. The Joint Conference managed to shift the direction of measures toward environmental conservation, but did not include a carbon tax. It also shifted the position on nuclear energy policies toward the seeking of public support. Although it postponed any regulations on lifestyle, it asked the government to integrate policies and measures in the implementation stage. Through the report-generating process, the Joint Conference used its role to deepen the government's policies and measures.

## Discussion

Focusing on actor relationships in the decision-making process, the case study presents the structure of the process, the strategies taken by each actor, the process of policy formulation, and the outcomes of the Joint Conference. The establishment of the Joint Conference shifted the Japanese decision-making process from the work of separate government departments to the Prime Minister's initiative. Previously, ministries and agencies each asked their advisory councils separately to discuss the relevant issues. However, the up-coming COP3 forced Japan to integrate the outcome of the advisory councils in a single forum. The Joint Conference helped formulate Japan's proposed numerical target on time and facilitated the deepening of policies and measures during the report-generating process.

This mechanism of integrating policies may be needed for other multi-faceted, inter-sectional issues. The features of the Joint Conference may offer some lessons useful for other occasions.

First, leadership from the top helped the mechanism work. The Prime Minister and the Cabinet Secretariat chose to be directly involved in the decision-making process of climate change policies through the establishment of the Joint Conference. Controlling the agenda and time schedule, this leadership helped centralize the policy formulation and avoided separate and disorganized policies and measures being generated by individual ministries and agencies.

Second, setting a clear objective helped the mechanism work. Bringing the COP3 to a successful conclusion was the highest priority of the Japanese Government. The establishment and proceedings of the Joint Conference served this objective by producing both a proposed numerical target and a report showing the basic direction for measures. The inter-ministerial coordination and cooperation of the private sector helped the parties to pursue objectives beyond their initial positions.

Third, taking implementation into account was a necessary condition for the mechanism to work. Integrating policies in a single forum must be followed up by implementing each policy and measure in each section. The Joint Conference gathered private representatives from various layers of Japanese society and let them serve as representatives of the relevant advisory councils. The relevant government agencies must comply with the report since they themselves participated in the process and are being watched by the advisory councils that participated in the process.

NOTES

1. I draw the case materials mostly from government documents, personal memos, and informal communications with public-sector and private-sector personnel. Since I have been deeply involved in the establishment and management of the Joint Conference, I, as a practitioner, am taking the role of the researcher that participates more or less in the object of research, not just the observer of the object. See the "action research" of Checkland (1981).
2. Article 4. The Prime Minister's Decision. August 22, 1997.
3. In addition to the Environment Agency, MITI, and the Ministry of Foreign Affairs, major relevant government agencies for the Joint Conference were: the Ministry of Construction, the Ministry of Transport, the Ministry of Post and Telecommunications, the Economic Planning Agency, and the National Police Agency. These ministries and agencies prepared the materials and made presentations at the meetings of the Joint Conference.
4. It should be noted that the list of members did not include representatives of environmental non-governmental organizations (NGOs). The voices of environmental NGOs were represented mainly by a member from the Central Environment Council and the consumer group representative.
5. Press Conference by Chief Cabinet Secretary Kanezo Muraoka on October 6,1997.
6. See Hattori (1999) for details.
7. Japan's carbon dioxide emissions in 2010 from a business-as-usual scenario are projected to be 21 per cent higher than the 1990 level.
8. The Environment Agency's National Institute for Environmental Studies, with Nagoya University, prepared the AIM for analyzing carbon dioxide emissions in the region.
9. The progress reports presented by the Ministry of Foreign Affairs at the Joint Conference were: from UNFCCC to AGBM7 (at the first meeting), the Japanese proposal (at the third meeting), AGBM8 (at the fourth meeting); and the informal ministerial meetings in Tokyo (at the fifth meeting).
10. "The Minutes of the Proceedings: The First Meeting of the Joint Conference of Relevant Advisory Councils on Domestic Measures Addressing the Global Warming Issue." August 27, 1997; "The Minutes of the Proceedings: The Second Meeting of the Joint Conference of Relevant Advisory Councils on Domestic Measures Addressing the Global Warming Issue." September 26, 1997.
11. See Hattori (1999) for the role of the Cabinet Secretariat in reaching the agreement.

12. "The Minutes of the Proceedings: The Third Meeting of the Joint Conference of Relevant Advisory Councils on Domestic Measures Addressing the Global Warming Issue." October 13, 1997.
13. "The Minutes of the Proceedings: The Third Meeting of the Joint Conference of Relevant Advisory Councils on Domestic Measures Addressing the Global Warming Issue." October 13, 1997.
14. MITI's Agency of Natural Resources and Energy explained the policies and measures in the industrial sector, and MITI, the Ministry of Transport, the Ministry of Construction, the National Police Agency, and the Ministry of Posts and Telecommunications explained those in the transport sector.
15. MITI and the Ministry of Construction explained the commercial/housing sector, and the Environment Agency reported the progress of the Government's Lead Action Plan (July, 1995 Cabinet Decision).
16. "The Minutes of the Proceedings: The Fourth Meeting of the Joint Conference of Relevant Advisory Councils on Domestic Measures Addressing the Global Warming Issue." November 7, 1997.
17. "The Minutes of the Proceedings: The Second Meeting of the Joint Conference of Relevant Advisory Councils on Domestic Measures Addressing the Global Warming Issue." September 26, 1997.
18. "The Minutes of the Proceedings: The Third Meeting of the Joint Conference of Relevant Advisory Councils on Domestic Measures Addressing the Global Warming Issue." October 13, 1997.

## REFERENCES

Abe, Hitoshi, Muneyuki Shindo, and Sadafumi Kawato (1990). *An Outline of Politics in Contemporary Japan*. Tokyo, Japan: University of Tokyo Press (in Japanese).

Allison, Graham T. (1971). *Essence of Decision: Explaining the Cuban Missile Crisis.* New York, NY: Harper Collins.

Checkland, Peter B. (1981). *Systems Thinking, Systems Practice*. London: John Wiley & Sons.

Faure, Guy-Olivier, and Jeffrey Z. Rubin (1993). "Organizing Concepts and Questions," in Gunnar Sjostedt, editor, *International Environmental Negotiation*. Newbury Park, CA: Sage.

Hattori, Takashi (1999). "The Road to the Kyoto Conference: An Assessment of the Japanese Two-Dimensional Negotiation." *International Negotiation* 4 (2) in press.

Wilson, James Q. (1989). Bureaucracy: *What Government Agencies Do and Why They Do It.* New York, NY: Basic Books.

# 5

# Atmospheric Environment in Urban Ecosystems

J. M. GIOVANNONI

## INTRODUCTION

For scientists and engineers environmental problems must generally be solved using appropriate techniques and management methods, but they should also try to remember the social aspect. There is a close interaction between human behaviour and the quality of the natural environment. This interaction is probably stronger in urban surroundings because of the high concentration of human activities and the rapid rhythm of life. In this context, the human habitat is valued highly as a place of safety, well-being and repose. The quality of this habitat depends on numerous factors, one of which is the quality of the urban atmospheric environment.

The theme of this article includes three main topics. The first concerns the fact that a town is a heterotrophic ecosystem : it depends completely on other ecosystems and ejects pollutants and waste matter. Air pollution is closely linked to the meteorological conditions and so the second topic is the local climate which can develop in urban agglomerations. Certain typical situations are discussed (smog, pollution domes). Finally, for Switzerland the level of urban atmospheric pollution is compared to that of rural zones and to the current norms.

## THE TOWN AS A HETEROTROPHIC ECOSYSTEM

### The Biosphere

Odum (1976) points out that, viewed from Sirius, the planet Earth appears to be a vast anti-hill, or a spacecraft travelling through the universe. Man is an integral part of the biosphere and his survival depends on how well Earth's natural resources are managed. The biosphere system can be described as a collection of large reservoirs (Fig. 5.1) crossed by flows of energy which are responsible for the circulation of the elements in cycles (carbon, nitrogen, water, sulphur, etc.).

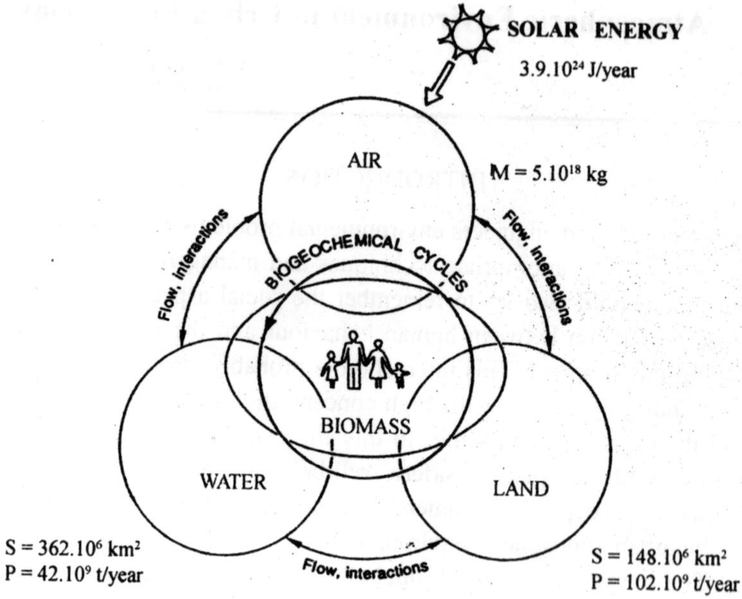


**Fig. 5.1** : The Biosphere System.

The biosphere can be considered as a group of reservoirs crossed by energy flows and matter. Non-linear and retroactive processes can either amortize or amplify the perturbations. Man is a part of the biosphere system : *M*=mass, *S*=surface area, *P*=production of organic matter. The figures are taken from Duvigneaud 1974.

Air pollution is classically described using the "emission-immission" diagram. For this diagram to remain pertinent, it must be remembered that the question of the impact on the environment must be considered within the context of the overall biosphere system. A pollutant should not be studied independently of the biogeochemical cycle to which it belongs. When matter is ejected from one of the biosphere reservoirs (air, water, soil) we must be able to estimate in which of the others it may be distributed and over what period of time (residence time). It is only through knowledge of the cycles that we can learn about this. Non-linear interaction processes also take place in the biosphere, such as the enriching phenomenon in certain radioactive and chemical elements (heavy metals) which occurs along the food chain.

**Urban Ecosystem**

An ecosystem (also called a biogeocenosis) is made up of a biotic community and an inanimate environment which function together. Ecosystems are basic functional units interacting within the biosphere. A lake, a forest, a sea are examples of this. These ecosystems have an autotrophic[1] biotic component, which can fix energy from light and develop the first link in the food chain, and they can function independently using solar energy and the natural element cycles. In contrast, a heterotrophic[2] ecosystem depends on a supply of energy and matter from its surroundings. An urban zone is thus a heterotrophic ecosystem (Fig. 5.2). A town requires inputs of food, combustibles and raw materials. Commerce and industry, traffic, heating and consumer activities produce harmful effects such as noise and odours, and also ejections of pollutants, heat waste matter. These ejections have an impact on the water, air, soil and vegetation reservoirs (urban and peri-urban forests for example), and on buildings and other constructions (deterioration, corrosion). However, it is mainly the effects of Man which draw the most attention. They concern the two interdependent elements of :

- health, shown by a physiological state, and
- well-being, which results from a psychological state.

A town is a heterotrophic ecosystem fed by input flows; its output flows produce impacts on Man and on the other ecosystems.

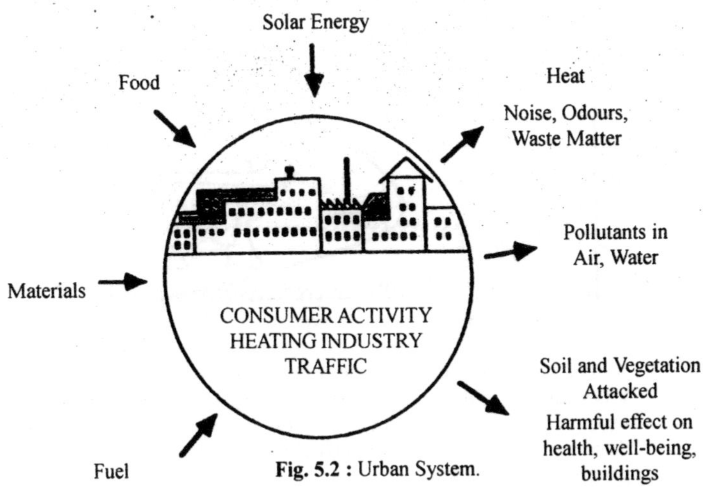


**Fig. 5.2 :** Urban System.

Children and elderly people are in general more sensitive to the effects of atmospheric pollution and for a long time doctors have noted how they influence the increase in respiratory diseases. In certain circles it is also believed that air pollution can effect cardio-vascular diseases.

## URBAN CLIMATE

The level of atmospheric pollution depends on two main factors: emissions (ejection of pollutants) and meteorological conditions.

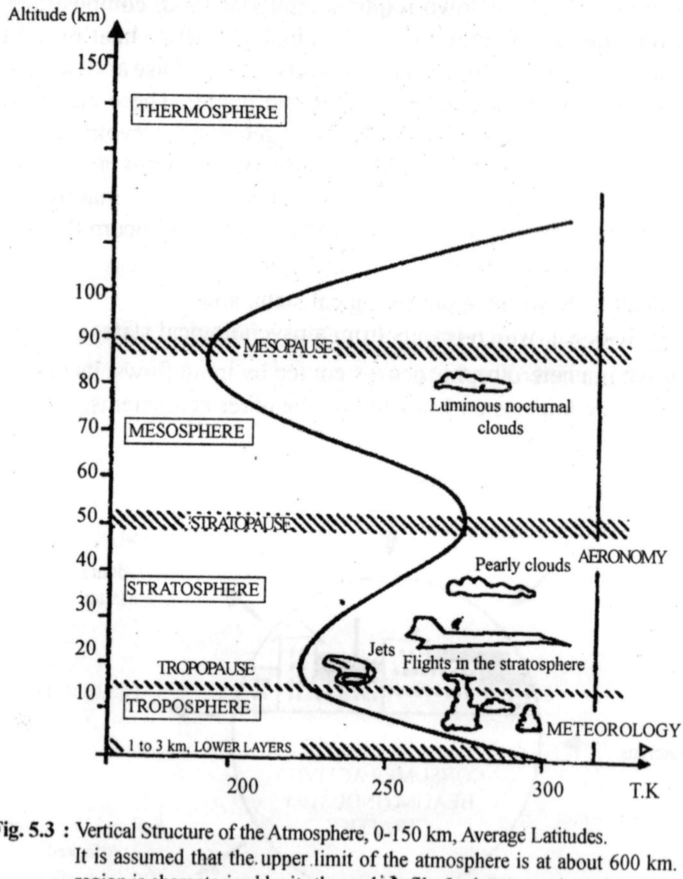


**Fig. 5.3 :** Vertical Structure of the Atmosphere, 0-150 km, Average Latitudes. It is assumed that the upper limit of the atmosphere is at about 600 km. Each region is characterized by its thermal profile. In the troposphere the temperature decreases with altitude, except near the ground where anomalies frequently occur (inversions, instabilities).

These include heat and energy exchanges between the air and the ground and its canopy layer (radiative-energy balance). In an urban context these exchanges can cause what has been called the heat island effect. This effect was discovered in 1833 when Howard analysed the air temperatures in and around London.

**Time and Space Scales**

In terms of climate and air pollution, it is necessary to make a clear distinction between the different time and space scales. From the air reservoir point of view, for example, the urban and rural atmospheric pollution dealt with here mainly concerns the lower layers of the atmosphere, from about 0-3,000 metres (Fig. 5.3). Three types of scale are usually referred to :

(a) *Microscale :* Air pollution over a district or a town is an example of this : the space scale is about 1-100 km$^2$, and the processes are studied during periods varying from one hour to one year;

(b) *Mesoscale :* Air pollution related to dying forests is a problem which arises on a countrywide scale, or over a group of countries. The processes involved are active over several years;

(c) *Macroscale :* The greenhouse effect caused by ejection of $CO_2$ affects the whole world; the ramifications of this phenomenon affect many other sectors such as the carbon cycle, the climate (temperature, rainfall, ice), agriculture, oceans, energy planning and social and economic behaviour. This process can span several centuries.

There is no really clear delimitation between the scales. Sometimes a scale particular to a certain phenomenon is introduced. An urban scale has been proposed by Munn (1981) comprising a range of 5-50 km. This classification is relative, but it is mainly useful for establishing priorities, choosing methods, modelling and for assessing results (degree of problem solution). The pollution of a district is not studied in the same way as a case of pollution in a valley, for example.

## The Heat Island Effect

The heat island effect is due to a difference in air temperature between an agglomeration and its rural surroundings. Typically, the difference is of the order of $\Delta T = 2\text{–}4°C$ and it varies in relation to the size of the agglomeration, the season, place, time, etc. (Landsberg, 1981). The effect does not always appear, for example when the general meteorological conditions mask the effect of phenomena on a local scale. Several factors in the radiative-energy balance contribute to the temperature difference (Fig. 5.4). The main phenomena are :

— diurnal heat retained by buildings,

— reduced infra-red ray emissions due to the "canyon" effect of the urban system,

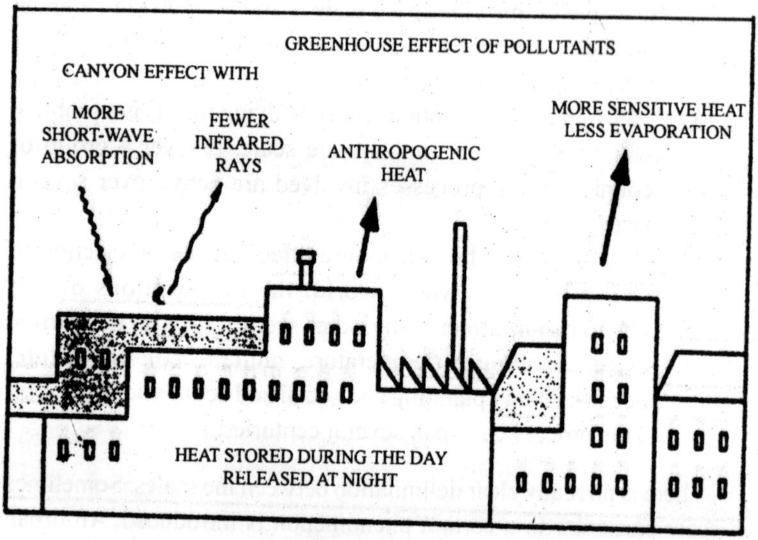


**Fig. 5.4 :** Factors contributing to the Heat Island Effect.

The town-country temperature variation is due to the difference between the radiative-energy balance of an urban zone and a rural zone. Anthropogenic heat ejection plays a greater role in winter (up to 25 or 55 per cent of the incident solar flow), but in general it is the flows caused by the thermal properties of buildings and the relief contours of the town which are most important. These phenomena occur in the urban canopy layer, whose upper limit is at the average height of the buildings (Oke, 1977).

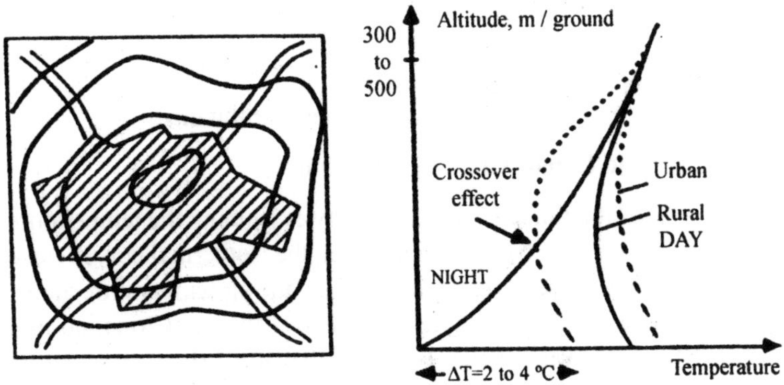


(a) Isothermal Curves at Ground Level

(b) Typical Temperature Profiles (According to Bornstein, 1968)

**Fig. 5.5 :** Urban Heat Island Effect and Field of Air Temperatures.

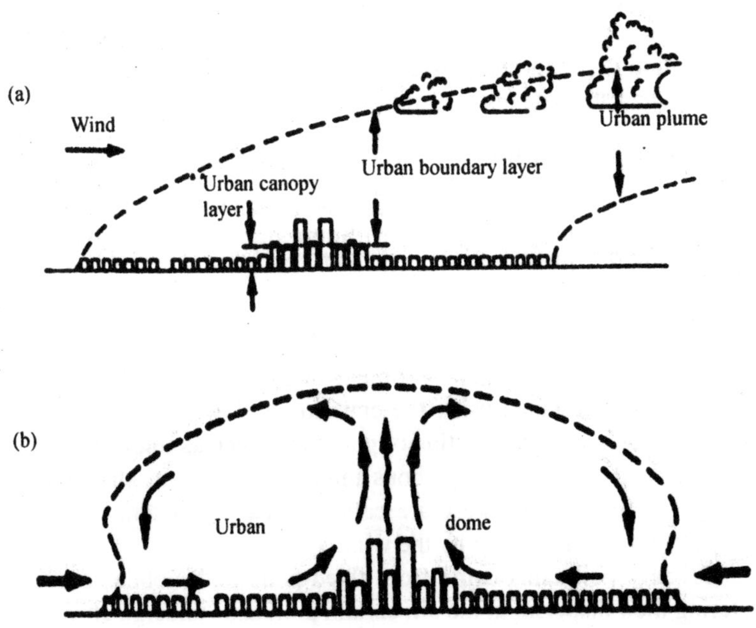


**Fig. 5.6 :** Urban Canopy Layers and Diagram of the Convective Flow Associated with the Heat Island; (a) with moderate wind, (b) in calm weather (taken from Oke, 1977)

— decrease in the evaporation rate, which improves the sensitive heat flow,
— anthropogenic heat ejection, and
— the greenhouse effect of atmospheric pollutants.

### Characteristic Urban Climate Situations

A heat island situation can be detected by examining the temperature measurements (Fig. 5.5). At ground level, the isothermal curves close round the town. Depending on the altitude, the air temperature above the agglomeration can be higher than that of the rural zone, up to a certain height (buoyancy height). Beyond that, the "urban" temperature can be lower than that of the "rural" temperature. In this case we speak of the crossover effect.

This thermal structure produces two types of convection current configurations (Fig. 5.6). With a moderate wind, an urban plume develops and defines the urban boundary layer. Heat and pollutants are dispersed within this boundary layer and transported away from the agglomeration. In calm weather a slow cellular convective circulation is produced. This bell effect encourages pollutant domes to form and stagnate above towns.

## ATMOSPHERIC POLLUTION IN URBAN ZONES

In this section, air pollution is presented in general terms before the formation of smog is discussed. Some data are then given for comparing the quality of urban air with that in rural zones and with the current norms.

### Immissions and Atmospheric Deposition

As already mentioned, the problem of atmospheric pollution is classically represented using the emission-immission diagram (Fig. 5.7). Emissions are the ejection of pollutants, such as sulphur oxides, nitrogen and carbon, hydrocarbons and particles into the atmosphere (in g/s for example). These are called primary pollutants and are dispersed and transported by the wind.

Primary pollutants come from fixed-point and mobile sources. During their dispersal in the air, certain pollutants undergo chemical transformations which give rise to secondary pollutants. Immissions of gases and aerosols are expressed in $\mu g/m^3$, and settling particles in $mg/m^2$ per day. These immissions characterize a pollution situation.

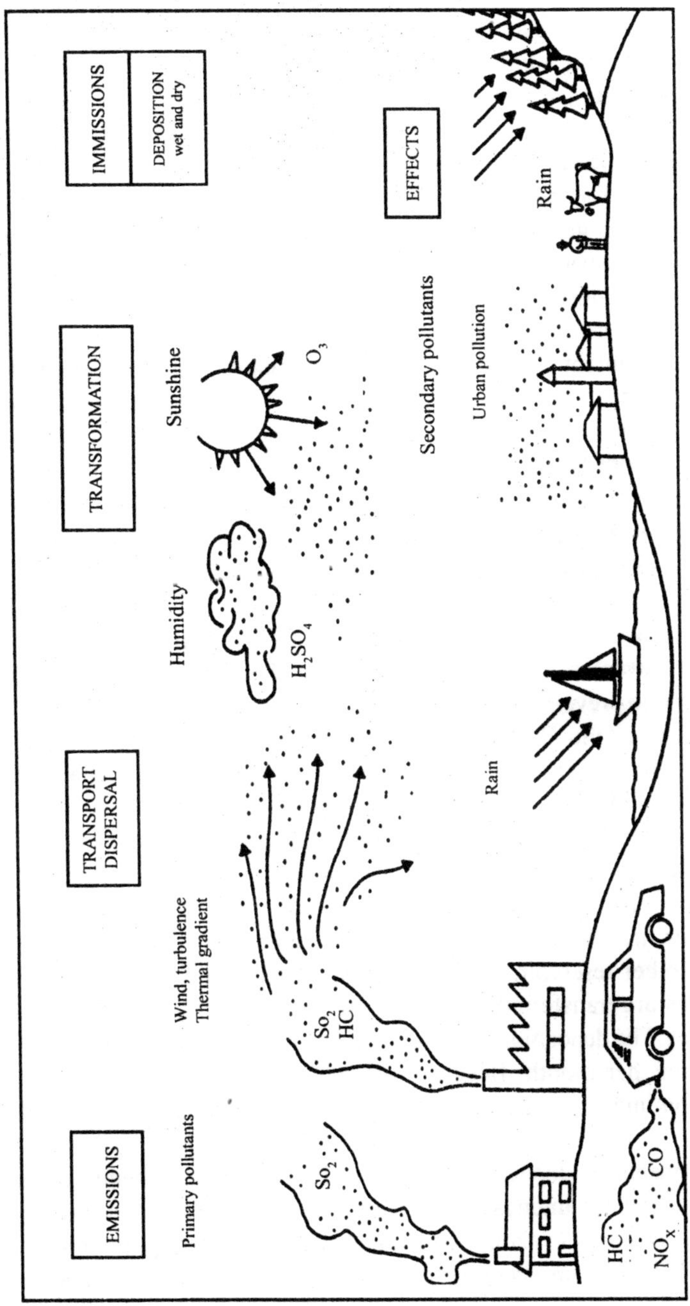


**Fig. 5.7 :** Emission/Immission Sequence.

Atmospheric deposition corresponds to a flow ($mg/m^2$ per month) which produces a transfer of substances into the other reservoirs of the biosphere.

Humidity and solar energy can cause the primary pollutants to undergo chemical changes which produce secondary pollutants. This is the case for the components of smog, for example. Immissions represent the general presence of pollutants in the ambient air. For gases and suspended particles (aerosols) they are expressed in $\mu g/m^3$. For settling dust and particles (upper diameter at 50-100 microns) immissions are measured in $mg/m^2$ per day. Immissions depend mainly on the pollutant considered and the dispersion and transformation condition of the air. Immissions do not depend (or very little) on the receptor and the ground canopy. They can be measured immediately using appropriate technical equipment. Immission values characterize quantitatively a state of atmospheric pollution over a given territory during a fixed period of time. Limit values for immissions have been introduced in order to maintain atmospheric pollution at an acceptable level as regards its effect on Man and his environment. In Switzerland these values are given in the "Ordonnance sur la protection de l'air" (OPair), which came into force in March 1986. Long-term values are intended to prevent chronic harmful effects. These values correspond to annual or monthly average values, for example. The short-term values give information about particular pollution points. The time interval can be half an hour, one hour, or a whole day.

As distinct from immissions, atmospheric deposition includes all the processes which contribute to decreasing the content of a substance present in the air. Atmospheric deposition can be dry or humid. Dry deposits include the transfer of an aerosol or a gas between the air and another reservoir, such as the soil, vegetation or water. Humid deposits are transferred by rainfall etc., and in certain cases by fog and dew. The deposition, therefore, has the nature of a flow, expressed in $mg/m^2$ per month. Because of atmospheric deposits the linear emission-immission diagram can be linked with all the biogeochemical cycles.

Atmospheric deposition is, above all, an interface phenomenon which depends, amongst other things, on the nature of the ground canopy. Deposition should be studied when considering the impact of air pollution on ecosystems. In the urban context, atmospheric deposition is responsible for the damage suffered by monuments and buildings. In addition to acid rain, the importance of the dry acid deposits from the very fine particles produced during the combustion of fossil fuels has been shown (Shaw, 1987).

## Smog

The word "smog" is a combination of "smoke" and "fog". There are basically two types of smog : the classic acid smog (found in London) and the oxidizing photochemical smog (found in Los Angeles). Classic

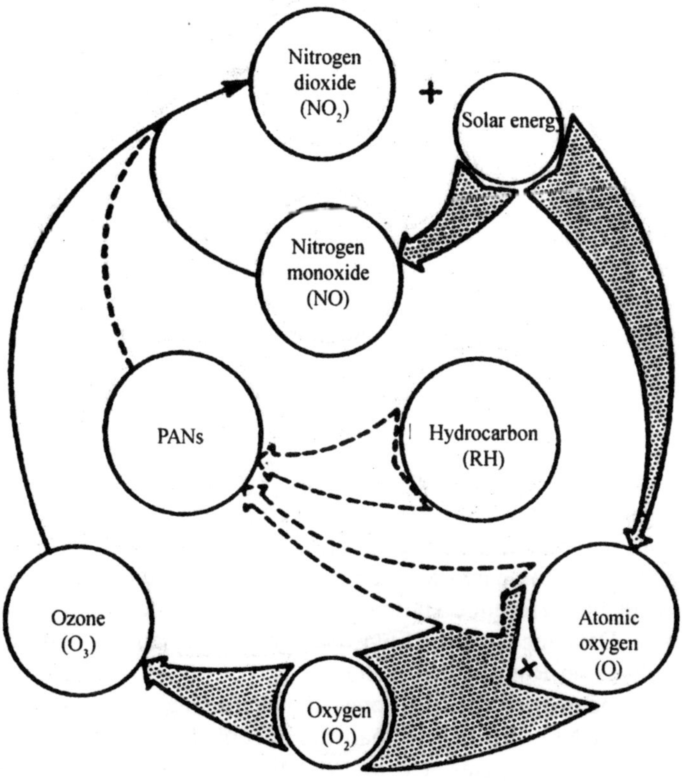


**Fig. 5.8 :** Diagram showing the Formation of Ozone and PANs in Photochemical Smog. Taken from Ross 1974, Section 3 (*Source* : US Dept. of Health, 1970). The paths of the $NO_2$-Ozone and HC–PANs can be traced.

smog forms in winter when the air is damp and there is little sunshine. The $SO_2$ emitted by heating installations is transformed into a sulphuric acid aerosol, which is mainly responsible for the classic smog effects. In contrast to classic smog, the photochemical variety forms in summer in very sunny regions : it is caused by primary pollutants, $NO_x$ and hydrocarbons (HC). These elements, called precursors, produce secondary pollutants, called photochemical oxidants. Among these are ozone (the most abundant), nitric acids, peroxyacetyl nitrates (PAN), etc. Fig. 5.8 shows schematically the formation of photochemical smog, which is a series of complex chemical reactions (see DFI, 1984 Section 3 and Chovin, Roussel, 1973 Section 6).

There were critical cases of atmospheric pollution in Europe in January 1985 and 1987. In Strasbourg, Belgium and the Ruhr Basin a thick winter smog caused the Authorities to declare a pollution alert. Restrictions were imposed on traffic. In Zurich the population was asked to dress more warmly and lower the heating. In Basle there were $SO_2$ alerts. These situations were caused by exceptional meteorological conditions. A mass of cold air caused a blockage in the vicinity of the ground : the heat island effect already mentioned produced pollutant domes above the agglomerations and their prologned presence caused a rapid increase in the air pollution.

## LEVEL OF URBAN ATMOSPHERIC POLLUTION IN SWITZERLAND

*Long-term values:* Fig. 5.9 shows the development of the annual averages of sulphure dioxide ($SO_2$) and nitrogen dioxide ($NO_2$) in different places. The urban stations of Zurich, Dübendorf, Basle and Lugano can be compared with the rural regions of Sion and Payerne, and with the reference station on the Jungfruajoch, situated at 3780 m. Data for Geneva (Ste-Clotilde) and Lausanne (Pierre-de-Plan and César-Roux) are also shown.

In the majority of the urban zones studied the long-term immissions of $SO_2$ and $NO_2$ are higher than the accepted limits, which are 30 $\mu g/m^3$ in both cases. Up to 1984 the $SO_2$ content showed a downward trend. The increase in 1985 was caused by the incidents in January mentioned above. In the last few years, immissions of $NO_2$ have tended to increase. As regards dust suspended in the air, this appears to be increasing, but without exceeding the limit of 70 $\mu g/m^3$ (Fig. 5.10).

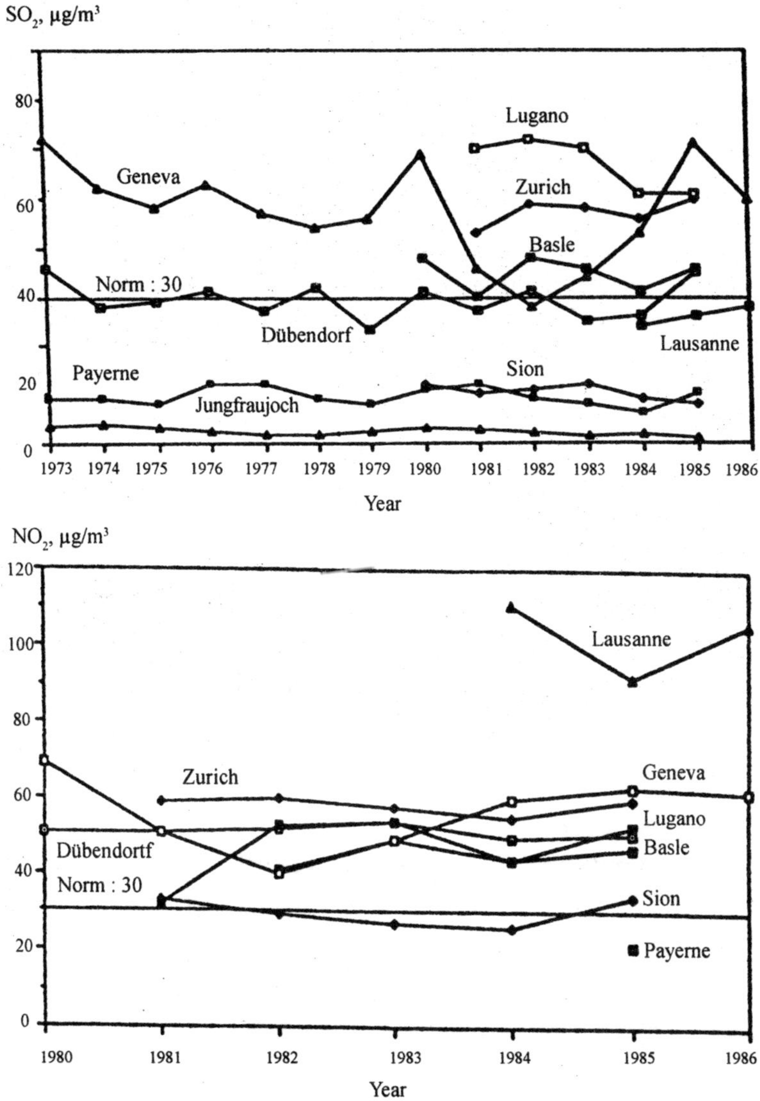


**Fig. 5.9 :** Annual Averages of $SO_2$ and $NO_2$ in Switzerland.

*Sources* : OFPE 1986, SCEG 1987, SHVL 1987. The urban measuring stations in Zurich, Dübendorf, Basle, Lugano, Geneva and Lausanne can be compared with the rural stations in Payerne, Sion and on the Jungfraujoch at 3780 m above sea-level.

The values for long-term immissions given here are for a zone of a few km² around the measuring station. They do not correspond to a spatial average for the town as a whole. This explains in part the large $SO_2$ variances in Geneva. In the same way, the very high $NO_2$ values in Lausanne are for a part of the town known for its high pollution level (rue César-Roux).

The variation in the long-term pollution level is shown in Fig. 5.11, for 4 classes of region. The concentrations of $SO_2$ and $NO_2$ are 2–4 times higher in the agglomerations than in the rural zones. This proportion varies between a factor of 10 and 20 for the hydrocarbons.

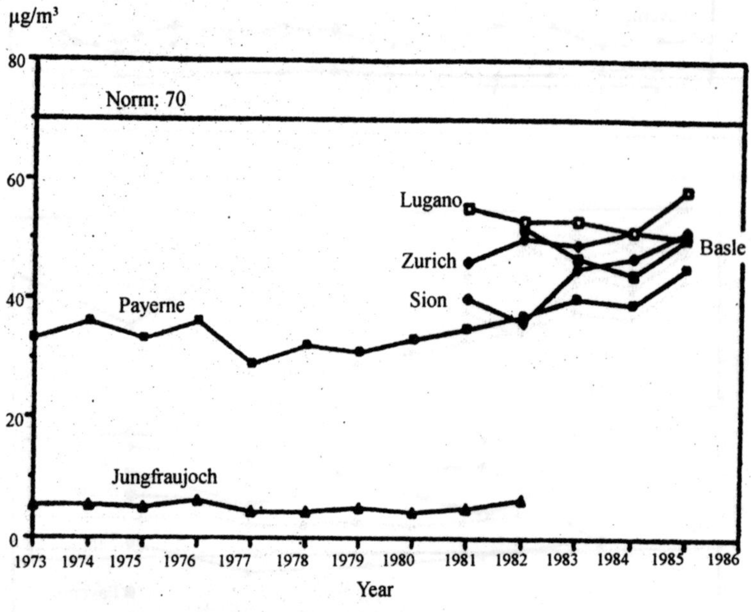


**Fig. 5.10 :** Annual Averages for Dust Suspended in the Air in Switzerland.

*Source*: OFPE 1986. Urban measuring stations: Zurich, Basle, Lugano.

The ozone situation is inverse; in agglomerations ozone dissipates during the night due to nitrogen oxide emitted by traffic.

It should also be noted that the immissions show large monthly variations (Fig. 5.12). Because of heating systems the $SO_2$ content is 4-5 times higher in winter than in summer. The photochemical

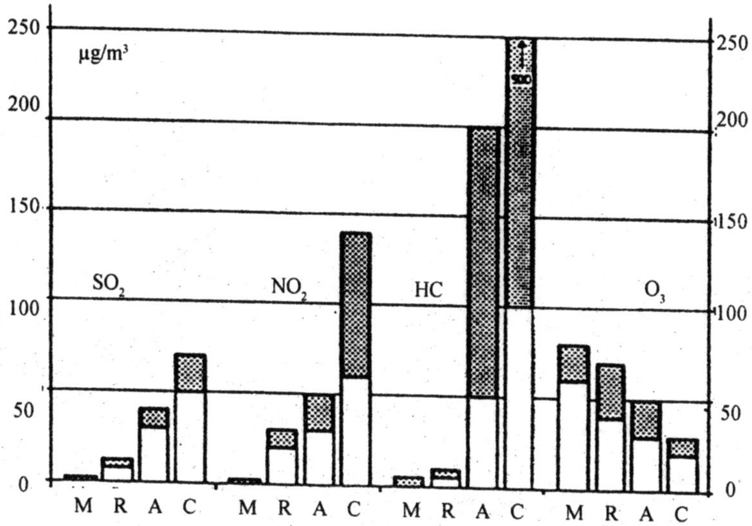


**Fig. 5.11 :** Typical Picture of the Present Quality of the Air in Switzerland (according to OFPE 1986 and DFI 1984). Variations of annual average immissions: M = mountains, Alps over 2,000 m, R = rural regions, A = agglomerations, C = town centres. Unlike other pollutants, the ozone content is higher in rural zones than in urban zones. In the latter the ozone dissipates during the night due to the NO produced by traffic. In rural regions winds can cause ozone to accumulate, or transport it over long distances.

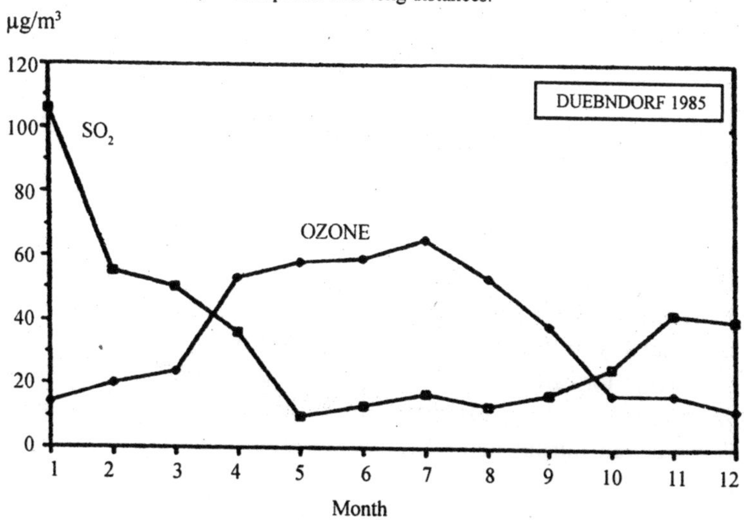


**Fig. 5.12 :** Monthly Averages of $SO_2$ and Ozone Concentrations Measured in Dübendorf, 1985.

*Source* : OFPE 1986.

formation of ozone cycle is inverse because of more intense solar energy in summer.

*Short-term values:* Fig. 5.13 gives an example of short-term $SO_2$ immission values. The three measuring stations are in the centres of Zurich, Geneva and Lausanne. The values shown are called 95 per

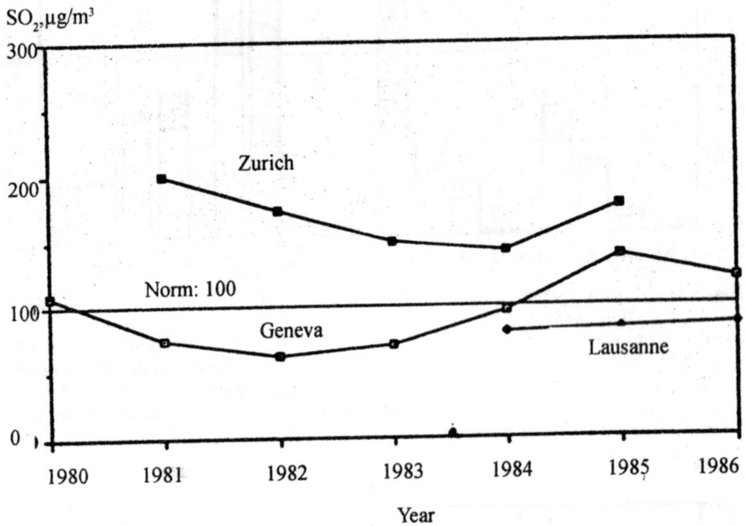


**Fig. 5.13 :** Half-hourly Concentrations of $SO_2$, 95 per cent Values for Zurich, Geneva and Lausanne Measuring Stations, Town Centre.

*Source* : OFPE 1986, SCEG 1987, SHVL 1987.

cent values. The short-term norm of 100 µg/m³ is not exceeded for Lausanne, but for Geneva and Zurich the 95 per cent values are considerably higher than the permissible level.

Except for carbon monoxide, the other pollutants also show high short-term values, *e.g.* ozone, for which the maximum hourly average is exceeded during between 250 and 400 hours per year in the agglomerations (OFPE 1986).

These situations were both the long-term and short-term norms are exceeded are definitely a cause for concern, especially as this state of affairs has existed for several years. In Switzerland the norms did not come into force until March 1986 and it is only since then that the idea that the norm is exceeded is recognized. The present situation corresponds to a transition period. Preventive measures are being taken (control of heating systems, catalysers, etc.) and they will certainly lead to an improvement in the quality of the air in the next few years.

## CONCLUSIONS

An improvement in the quality of life and the urban habitat goes hand-in-hand with improved air hygiene, but this cannot be achieved without pressure stemming from social and political awareness. This seems in fact to exist, and according to a survey made in 1987, 51 per cent of the people questioned put the emphasis on protection of the environment, with air pollution control as a priority. In Switzerland, the Authorities aim to reduce by 1990 emissions of $SO_2$ to their 1950 level, and for nitrogen oxides the 1960 level should be reached by 1995. Legislation has, therefore, been passed forbidding, for example, the sulphur content of extra-light heating oil to exceed 0.2 per cent (since July 1987); from 1st October 1987 the US 83 norms came into force concerning the exhaust gases of private cars.

While it is true that a well-studied problem should result in a well-studied solution, the technical measures must be accompanied by other efforts from the point of view of knowledge and research. An analysis of the situation has thus shown that it will probably not be possible to reduce the nitrogen oxide emissions as planned; in 1995 they will probably still be the same as, or double, those of 1960. To manage the quality of the air effectively it is important to set up a monitoring system so that progress can be checked. Also, efforts should be made to develop data processing and modelling tools. These methods, which are very useful in normal circumstances, can prove even more valuable in cases of accidental pollution. History has already shown how serious the social and economic consequences of these accidents can be.

## ACKNOWLEDGEMENTS

The author wishes to thank Miss Carole Hetzel for translating this article from the original French, and Mrs. Micheline Mattmann for typing the text.

## NOTES

1. Self-nourishing.
2. Deriving nourishment from outside sources.

## REFERENCES

Bornstein, R.D., 1968 : 'Observations of the urban heat island effect in New York' *J. Appl. Meteor.,* 7, 575-582.

CFS, Conseil Fédéral Suisse, 1986 : 'Stratégie de lutte contre la pollution de l'air' *Rapport 86.047.*

CFS, Conseil Fédéral Suisse, 1985 : 'Ordonnance sur la protection de l'air' *OPair* du 16 *novemebre 1985.*

Chovin P., A. Roussel, 1973 : 'Physicochimie et physiopathologie des polluants atmosphériques' *Masson.*

DFI, Département fédéral de l'intérieur, 1984 : 'Dépérissement des forêts et pollution de l'air' *Rapport 301.50/f.*

Duvigneaud P., 1974 : 'La synthèse écologique' *Doin,* Paris.

Giovannoni J.-M., 1987 : 'A laboratory analysis of free convection enhanced by a heat island in a calm and stratified environment' *Boundary Layer,* 41, 9-26.

Giovannoni J.-M., 1987 : 'Estimation de la dépoistion atmosphérique, méthodologie et programme de mesures' *Rapport de l'Institute du génie de l'environnement,* 210.130.

Howard, L., 1833 : 'The climate of London deduced from meteorological observations' *3rd Ed. in 3 Vols.* London, Harvey and Darton.

Landsberg, H.E., 1981 : 'The urban climate' *Academic Press.*

Munn, R.E., 1981 : 'The design of air quality monitoring networks' *Macmillan.*

Odum, E.P., 1976 : 'Ecologie' *Doin,* Paris, traduit de l'anglais par R. Bergeron.

OFPE, Office fédéral de la protection de l'envîronnement, 1986 : 'La pollution de l'air en 1985, réseau NABEL' *Les cahiers de l'enviornnement, 64.*

Oke, T.R., 1977 : 'The urban atmosphere as an environment for air pollution dispersion. Proceedings of the meeting on education and training in meteorological aspects of atmospheric pollution and related environmental problems' *World Meteorological Organization,* 493.

Ross, R.D., 1974 : 'La pollution atmosphérique et l'industrie' *Enterprise Moderne d'Edition.*

Shaw, W., 1987 : 'Air pollution by particles' *Scientific American,* 457, 84-91.

SCEG, Service cantonal d'écotoxicologie, Genève, 1987 : 'Mesure de la qualité de l'air 1986' *Rapport du Département de la prévoyance sociale et de la santé publique.*

SHVL, Service d'hygiène de la ville de Lausanne, 1987 : 'Valeurs d'immissions' *Communication Personnelle.*

# 6

# Urban Development and Environmental Impacts in a Mountain Context

JAMES S. GARDNER AND R. B. SINGH

## PROJECT BACKGROUND

Himachal Pradesh, which came into being as a state in 1971, has experienced remarkable social and economic development in the thirty years of its existence, having relatively high per capita income, literacy and education levels among men and women, and well-developed health and social infrastructure in the Indian national context. Being a hill and mountain state in the north-west Himalaya, it is relatively well-endowed with a variety of natural resources and, by Indian standards, has a small population. Nonetheless, there are parts of the state which are geographically isolated and in which social and economic development in all their forms are lagging. Geographical isolation has had some benefits historically in the sense that some areas have escaped the negative effects of pre-colonial, colonial and post-independence administration and commercial exploitation. Limited and contained deforestation in Kullu and some other districts is an example. However, the final decades of the twentieth century saw an erosion of the isolation factor and ever increasing ascendancy and impact of global economic and political forces in the everyday life in Himachal Pradesh and especially in the Kullu District.

Over the past decade, various researchers and their students attached to this project have studied aspects of environment and resource management in the Kullu District. Why was this area chosen? Firstly, the south to north transect from the plains of the Punjab to the plateau and high mountains of Ladakh which passes through the heart of Himachal is the most complete geo-ecological cross-section of the Himalayan environment. Second, initial field surveys in Kullu and surrounding areas indicated that the widespread deforested landscape, so typical of some of Himalayan regions, was not in evidence to the same degree which suggested a different environmental and land-use history worthy of examination. Thirdly, in the early 1990s it became apparent that the Kullu District was on the threshold of a remarkable and very sudden transformation driven by global economic forces, regional geopolitical forces, new technologies, and national economic liberalization and its effects. Thus, the Kullu District could be seen as a laboratory for the study of rapid social, economic and environmental change. More importantly, research and monitoring of the various changes were seen as important ingredients for policy formulation and evaluation especially as they pertain to social and economic impacts.

One of the most tangible effects of change in Kullu in the 1990s has been the growth of population, growth of settlements, and growth of complex urban functions larger in those settlements. This became especially apparent through the growth of tourist trade and commercial horticulture and the various infrastructures associated with both. In 1997, the central purpose of this project, namely an examination of the environmental and related impacts of these changes and growth in the Kullu District, was articulated. Growth of settlements and urban functions in mountain areas is not confined to the Himalaya, though it is more recent there. This has been and remains an important issue in the Alps of Europe and the Cordillera of western North America. The nature of the mountain environment with its limited space in rugged terrain, competing land-uses, microclimatic and hydrological characteristics, and sometimes sensitive and fragile ecological and human systems presents special challenges for the establishment and maintenance of sustainable environmental and land-use management. Therefore, the focus of this project has been on the environmental impacts of urban growth in the Kullu District with the specific objectives as follows.

## RESEARCH OBJECTIVES

- Document and describe the process of urbanization in the Manali/Kullu area.
- Investigate the impacts of urban development on the local environment and, more broadly on sustainable development in the following areas: water management, solid waste management, sewage management, aggregate extraction, construction in hazards zones, etc.
- Describe local perceptions and knowledge of environmental and livelihood sustainability in the above focus areas.

— Develop sustainability indicators applicable to urban development in mountain ecosystems.
— Develop environmental impact analysis approaches, techniques, and policies suitable for pre-development activities in mountain regions and proper monitoring approaches for those developments in place.
— Strengthen existing linkages and forge new ones between researchers and agencies in Canada and India active in sustainable development and environmental impact analysis in mountain areas.
— Interacts with communities, policy-makers, NGOs and ENGOs, and government and municipal officers and offices pertaining to environmental planning and sustainable development for the purpose of communicating the results of the research.

## RESEARCH RESULTS

### Objective 1

The growth of settlements in the Kullu District and the Manali area in particular, has been complex and driven by a number of factors, both local and external to the area. The resident population of Manali is about 5000, having doubled in the past decade. The upcoming census in 2001 will provide greater assurance of the population estimate which is always difficult in the circumstances of seasonal and highly transient influxes and egresses of people in the area. Census data attached to Manali *per se* also do not reflect the true picture of growth which has occurred outside the municipal limits and is concentrated along and adjacent to the main transportation routes in the area. There are two large components to the transient population of the area: the tourist population, and the migratory labour population connected to the tourist service sector, transportation sector, and commercial horticulture sectors of the local economies.

Tourist visitation, now approaching or over 1 million per year, is concentrated in two seasons: late-spring and early summer, and late-summer and early autumn. Over 90 per cent of the tourists are of domestic origin, mostly from the major urban centres in north India, and their average stay in the area is 3 to 4 days. The economic and infrastructural impacts of tourism in the area are profound and may be exemplified by the expansion of accommodation facilities. Whereas in 1989, there were about 40 small hotels and guest houses in the Manali area, in 1998 there were 693, including several five-star resorts operated by multinational corporations such as Holiday Inns International. The opportunities for service employment in the tourist sector have been taken up by both local residents and by a large cadre of seasonal workers from other parts of the region and beyond. The spinoffs, in addition to accommodations, are exemplified by: restaurants; food stalls; communications services such as telephone, fax and internet: transport services such as taxis, three-wheelers, buses and ponies; retail outlets for all manner of goods; medical services; laundry services; guide and travel services; and so on. In other words, the growth of the tourist sector, in addition to producing population growth and expansion of infrastructure, has resulted in an increase in the number and complexity of functions commonly associated with diversified urban areas.

Other changes are at play in the area as well. Most notably are the development of a diversified horticultural industry in the Kullu Valley and the development and upgrading of surface transport routes of which National Highway 21 is the most important. NH 21 is essential to both the growing tourist industry and the horticultural industry and it serves critical strategic needs for an overland link to northern Kashmir, a fact that became abundantly clear during the "Kargil Crisis" of 1999. Management and maintenance of NH 21 requires year-around attention, a very large financial investment, and the presence of an army of migratory maintenance workers.

NH 21 facilitates the economic growth in the area in both the tourist sector and the horticultural sector. It is an all-weather highway which places Kullu within relatively easy driving distance of the Punjab, Haryana, Delhi and parts of U.P. Other factors have driven that growth. Firstly, the geopolitics of South Asia and, specifically the on-going conflict in Kashmir, has redirected tourist demand away from the traditional mountain destinations in Kashmir and has forced tourist services to relocate in Kullu. Secondly, marketing and publicity of the tourist attractions of Kullu nationally and internationally, largely by the Himachal Pradesh Tourist Development Corporation and the movie industry has been important. Thirdly, the growth of the consumer class (middle class) in India over the past decade has expanded the domestic tourist market substantially. Fourthly, commercial horticulture which focuses on "off season vegetables" and hard fruits such as apples has been supported though the use of specialized varieties, chemical fertilizers, pesticides and herbicides as well as through the transportation to market provided by NH 21. Kullu has always served as a trade route, a meeting place, a source of exotic and medicinal plant products, a spiritual destination, and a home for the gods but the 1990s saw it become networked to global and regional forces in a spectacular fashion which perhaps has been unprecedented elsewhere in mountain areas at least in terms of rapidity of change.

**Objective 2**

Identification and description of the effects of impacts of this growth and development has been the primary focus of the project. We have used the Manali area as the case study area but also have considered the more generalized conditions throughout the Kullu District and Kullu Valley. The material impacts in the landscape have occurred through the infilling of land in and around the main settlements and along the primary transportation routes. The land most affected has been that previously occupied by various agricultural land-uses and that previously unoccupied and variously classified as "wasteland" or unused agricultural or situated adjacent to stream courses and gullies (*nallahas*). Most of the land conversion has occurred at or near the valley floor or on the lower slopes. Small scale agricultural and residential land-uses have developed on land adjacent to the traditional settlements through the land redistribution or *nautor* land scheme of the 1950s. Forest areas surrounding and upslope from the traditional settlements and classified as Protected Forest under the Forest Settlement in the 1890s, and treated as "village use areas" or commons remain in traditional use by the villagers. The total forest coverage in the Kullu District remains largely unchanged over the past 150 years although species composition has been altered. The timber resources of the Protected and other forest areas are, on paper, subject to state authority but in practice are managed through various co-management arrangements between the Forest Department and the villages. Some of our research indicates that traditional forest uses at the village level are relatively unaffected by the hyperactive growth and development in the main centres. More and more of the day-to-day work and management of the forest resources is in the hands of women and women's groups such as the Mahila Mandals as village men become more occupied with cash economy of tourism, horticulture, and related service industries. Rapid growth of Manali and other larger centres in the area has placed greater pressure on the timber resources of the forest areas through illegal cutting. This however, has not as yet led to widespread deforestation.

Primary growth has been focused in and around Manali and Kullu town, as well as in several settlements such as Bhuntar and Katrain on NH 21. Our research has indicated that Manali, a settlement which did not exist as an independent unit a century ago, has grown to the point where it is unsustainable in its present form without significant imports of material and energy resources from external sources. Our "Ecological Footprint Analysis" of Manali demonstrates that the EF area has increased from 2,102 hectares in 1971 to 9,665 hectares in 1998, an increase of over 450 per cent. Manali's Ecological Footprint is now 25 times the actual physical size of the town.

The growth of Manali and the surrounding areas has occurred without commensurate development of proper infrastructure for water supply, sewage collection and disposal, solid waste management, with the exception of recycling of metai, glass and some paper products, and roads and traffic. Because of restricted availability of space for construction, land areas prone to hazards such as flooding, erosion, landslides and debris torrents, have been occupied, thereby increasing vulnerability of people and property of risk from these hazards. Much of the recent construction in the area has minimal built-in protection against earthquake damage, the most significant risk for widespread disaster in the area. Construction of roads and buildings have placed a high demand for aggregate construction materials, which are limited in the area. Most of the aggregate material has been and continues to be mined from stream beds, principally that of the Beas River, which in turn alters the hydraulics during times of high flows, further exacerbating the erosion hazard in and adjacent to the streams. With the growth of settlements and economic development, demand for electrical power has increased. This is general to India as a whole and mountain rivers and streams are perceived as a ready and largely untapped resource for the generation of electricity. Both state and central governments, as well as private companies, are aggressively pursuing development of generating facilities throughout the Kullu District and elsewhere. A number of small, run-off-the-river hydro power sites have been developed, all with no prior environmental impact assessment which includes public consultation. Larger developments, which include those at Malana, Parbati and Larji, likewise have been subject to minimal environmental impact assessment. These projects have substantial environmental and social impacts in the project areas, especially during the construction phase.

The impacts of growth of settlements and urban functions in the region are comprehensive and substantial. Some are of a physical nature and constitute a transformation of the landscape. Others are social, economic and cultural. These are more difficult to identify, describe and explain and their effects may not be seen for some time. It is important to note that change in the Kullu District is being driven largely by external forces at the regional, national and global levels. Like many mountain areas, which have traditionally served as resource hinterlands for centres of population far removed, the Kullu District and many other Himalayan areas continue to serve the same function and are increasingly taking on some of the physical, social and economic characteristics of those distant population centres.

### Objective 3

Our research reveals a significant level of awareness and understanding among local people of the adverse environmental and social consequences of growth of settlements, urban functions, and economies. There is also keen awareness of the economic and material benefits, including health, education, and social benefits, of this as well. Therein lie the incentives for participation. At the level of the local communities and particularly in the traditional villages, the need for balance is well-recognized. However, as noted above, much of the impetus for growth and many of the main actors and forces supporting it, come from outside the region. Tourists are predominantly domestic tourists from other parts of India. Investors are usually from urban areas to the south. The economic conditions which provide these people the means for involvement in the Kullu District are determined by the Indian economy at large, as well as global economic forces. National, state and municipal legislative documents, policies, procedures, and regulations which are designed to guide and regulate growth and minimize negative impacts are relatively well-developed. In practice, however, the regulatory framework is often ignored or avoided at the level of individual projects at the local level. While more policies and regulations might help, the real issue today in a place like the Kullu District is the application and enforcement of those that exist, and continued monitoring of what actually takes place on the ground. The January 12, 2001 Himachal Pradesh Cabinet declaration of a moratorium and restriction on further construction in parts of the Manali area and in some other municipalities in the state, is a promising step which may address the concerns that many local people have voiced. However, the effect will rest as much on enforcement as on the regulation.

**Objective 4**

In studying the application of the Ministry of Environment and Forests environmental impact assessment procedures, we found that, despite the rapid pace of development in the Kullu District, any form of assessment has been carried out for only three projects, all hydropower dam projects. Study of documents and interviews with participants revealed that the assessment process is still in its nascent stages in the mountain regions. Many constraints exist, including the inaccessibility of information, lack of familiarity with EIA, lack of institutional capacity, and the remoteness of some of affected areas and their constituents. Detailed work continues on the application of the process to developments such as micro-hydro and on the public involvement aspects of the process.

**Objective 5**

Development of linkages between Canadian and Indian scholars and others has occurred as planned, except for that part of the project which planned to bring Indian municipal and environmental management officials to Canada to observe rapid urban growth in Canadian mountain areas and meet with their counterparts there. This activity had to be removed from the project as a result of budget restrictions placed on our award.

Dissemination activities of the project have been extensive and numerous and are summarized in several other documents associated with the project. In the course of the project, three principal dissemination workshops with government officials, residents, members of NGOs, academics and students, and others have occurred. Two of these have been held in Manali and one has been held in Delhi. The summaries of these workshops are available in individual reports and as part of the project final report.

**Objective 6**

As above under objective 5. Dissemination activities and interactions with policy-makers at all levels from the local municipalities and villages to the Government of India Planning Commission have occurred. Indeed, this type of activity was integral to the methodology of the project research in that these people were primary sources of information through the interview process. In addition, the media in India have been very active in covering and reporting aspects of this project. Press clippings are available in other reports. As part of the process, it has been our practice to provide individuals who have assisted us and participated in this way, with reports on the results of our work. We hope to continue to do this through the coming year as the results become more refined and consolidated. This is critical at the community level.

## POLICY ISSUES

Policies are created to guide practice and achieve certain objectives within a framework of beliefs, values and political considerations. As such, policies for one group of people and within particular cultural, historical, and political contexts are not likely transferable to other situations. Policies which are guided by such values as equity and equality of opportunity, freedom of expression, and a notion of the common good are probably most acceptable to us. They may not be acceptable to others. It follows that it is presumptuous to impose policy outside the immediate context. Indeed, that is the fundamental flaw in colonialism and other froms of paternalism, including that exercised by central governments. This is a cautionary note to any discussion of policy implications that arise forms a project such as this. In addition, the history of so-called "development work" presents numerous examples of prescriptive results and applications that have been inappropriate and failures because of a lack of attention to, and understanding of, context. To understand context, research is necessary and our work has been guided by this fact. Geography and scale are important in understanding context. Policies which seem fine at an international, national or even regional level may not be appropriate or may have negative consequences at the local level. This is, after all, the basis of current objections to overarching international trade policy agreements for example. One of the core struggles in development work today, especially in the area of management of natural resources and environment, has to do with participation and involvement of local or community level people and their knowledge and aspirations. We knew this before commencing this project and everything which we have found out in the project has simply been a reinforcement.

Therefore, this has been primarily a research project. We have set out to understand and describe the processes and outcomes of rapid growth of settlements, economies, and urban functions in the high mountains of the Kullu District of the Himachal Pradesh Himalaya. In the course of our research, we have found that an elaborate system of land-use and land management has existed in the area for centuries. The first significant external imposition of policies on these systems occurred during the British colonial period and relatively late in it at that. One might say that, as a result of this lateness, the biases of the individual colonial officials, and the relative geographical isolation of the area, the imposition of the external policies regarding land tenure and resource use rights was relatively benign and sensitive to local conditions and established or *de facto* rights. This was particularly evident in the assigned rights to forest use, especially in regard to non-timber forest resources. Post-independence imposition of policy, especially with respect to timber forest resources may not have been equally as benign and sensitive to local conditions in Kullu. Nonetheless, the more recent adoption of a policy of Joint Forest Management by the state government, especially with regard to timber and fuelwood resources is to be applauded and encouraged though it will take time to implement to the point of true co-management of resources.

Our research, demonstrates as well that the processes and events unfolding today in the Kullu District more than ever before are connected to national and global forces of economic growth. Some of the effects have been positive locally while others, especially those related to environmental impacts and increasing exposure to risk from disaster, have been negative. Obviously, policies must be designed in a way to protect against the negative consequences of the social and economic forces at play while encouraging the positive consequences. For the most part, existing policies at the national and state levels are meant to do just that. Problems which arise do so because the procedures and practices associated with the policies are not well-developed. This is seen most forcefully in the lack of enforcement of building and zoning regulations and in the relative lack of public participation in project environmental impact assessment, all of which is mandated by policy. Thus, "development" in the Kullu District is more a matter of enforcement and refinement of policy and involvement of local input and decisions in resource and environmental issues. The implications of our research are less for policy than they are for practice in the local context. While the forces driving change arc external to the area, the policies which regulate the effects and impacts, have to be implemented in a way that is consistent with local historical and established practices and institutions.

## POLICY IMPLICATIONS

On the basis of our research, the following are at present the key areas for attention in terms of policy refinement and implementation in the Kullu District.

- *Management of forest resources:* must be comprehensive to all forest areas including reserved and protected forests, must recognize established village-based rights to use of all forest resources, Joint Forest Management between the Forest Department and villages must be encouraged and continue to be developed especially with respect to the timber and fuelwood resources, forest management at the watershed level for water management and erosion control purposes must continue and be strengthened.
- *Environmental impact assessment:* regulations relating to environmental impact assessment and especially the public participation component of it must be enforced and

encouraged through public education. This is especially critical in regard to major construction projects such as hydro developments and road construction.

— *Land-use zoning and building regulation:* must be refined and enforced to prevent building in hazard areas and construction that is sub-standard and thus subject to greater risk of damage in earthquakes for example, must be refined and enforced to prevent encroachment of residential, agricultural/horticultural, and transportation land-uses into designated forest areas.

— *Regulation of mining activity:* the most pervasive mining activity presently taking place in the Kullu District is the extraction of sands and gravels from stream beds of the area for construction purposes, the hydraulic effects of this activity should be subject to some research and, if as a result it is demonstrated that there are adverse consequences such as accelerated streambed and bank erosion, the activity should be subject to appropriate regulation.

— *Waste management:* neither solid wastes, other than those currently subject to recycling, nor liquid wastes are adequately managed in the Kullu District, there is a need for both investment in infrastructure such as sewage lines and treatment facilities and development of regulations and practices for waste minimization and containment through continuance of the poly bag ban, greater provision of waste bins, public education, composting in commercial and private establishments.

— *Traffic management:* the roads in settlements in the Kullu District are congested with vehicles including three-wheelers, motorcycles, taxis, private cars, buses, trucks, etc. in part because of the numbers of people and vehicles and partly because the roads were not designed for the purpose of motorized traffic, the consequences are found in noise and air pollution, contamination of surface water through runoff, travel delays, and general annoyance, primarily a municipal issue it must be addressed more fully through regulation and restriction on use of certain roads at certain times by certain vehicles, prohibition of vehicle use in some areas, provision of more adequate parking facilities, provision of local public mass transit, and public education and information which encourages other more environmentally friendly forms of locomotion at the local level, there are valuable lessons to be learned here from European mountain communities.

— *Environmental education:* the key to sustainable environmental and resource management, and therefore livelihood sustainability, occurs through the application of knowledge and experience, the traditional resource management regimes in the Kullu District were and remain conservative, essentially sustainable and dependent on informal transmission of knowledge and experience (*i.e.* informal education), mandatory formal education was one of the policy and development priorities for Himachal Pradesh when it came into being in 1971 with the result that residents of the area are relatively well-prepared to work in the globalized village economy and society, environmental education does take place in the schools of the area, our research suggests that this could be enhanced by further incorporation of informal or traditional local knowledge into the formal curricula.

It is difficult to assess the impact of our research and information dissemination activity in the Kullu District and the Manali area in particular. The presence of members of our team, both Canadians and Indians, in the area has certainly been noticed and the fact that many people have been interviewed and interacted with has probably heightened awareness of environmental issues in general. The most significant long-term impacts no doubt will arise as the result of education and training opportunities provided to Canadian and Indian students as a result of their involvement with the project and their interactions in the study area. Other impacts have occurred by way of information dissemination and discussion at our workshops in the local area and in Delhi and through the media. Whether this impact how officials and policy makers see and approach the problems encountered in Kullu and other mountain areas remains to be seen. Some specific products of our work assist or will assist in addressing resource management and environmental sustainability issues. Included are: our logo for the poly bag ban which is distributed in the form of stickers that appear on windows and vehicles throughout Manali and in the form of a crest on T-shirt which are produced and sold by a local retailer; a walking map of Manali which is designed to encourage people to walk for shopping and visiting of sites of interest so as to reduce traffic and is distributed through local hotels and taxi stands; and hazard risk maps for the whole Kullu Valley which can be used by local planning officials.

Finally, through the research we have been able to address some issues of general interest in the study of environmental impact of urban growth, degradation or not of mountain environments and the Himalaya specifically, and the use and management of common property resources.

## CONCLUSIONS

The development issues of the Kullu District are not issues of meeting basic human needs. These were addressed, by and large successfully, through the social development priorities of Himachal Pradesh when it came into being as a state. The development issues are more complex and relate more to addressing the impacts of economic development, some of which are detrimental to the goal of environmental and resource sustainability. Certainly the remoteness factor still operates in this high mountain area such that provision of basic human needs is not everywhere equal and equitable. Areas adjacent to the Kullu District, for example parts of Lahaul and Spiti and the remote reaches of the Sainj and Parbati Valleys do not share the same level of social, educational, and health services and have not participated so directly in the remarkable economic growth and development with its benefits and costs as in Kullu. Migrant workers and their families and other landless people in Kullu do not share the same benefits as others in the area and are more vulnerable to social, economic and natural hazards.

## RESEARCH ACTIVITIES

1. A field visit to the field area, *i.e.* Kullu Valley, was made during November-December, 1998 by the Indian Interns for Urban change detection study.
2. Field Work and Data Collection relating to "Footprint Analysis" of the Manali Urban Area (October-December 1998) by the Canadian Partners.

3. On the basis of completed field research, literature review, consultations with practitioners and policy makers following issues were completed:

   (a) Solid waste management in municipal corporation of Kullu (Singh and Mishra).
   (b) Water supply in Kullu (Singh).
   (c) Tourism development and marketing in Manali and Kullu (Singh).
   (d) Urban growth and exposure to natural hazards (Saczuk & Gardner).
   (e) Environmental Assessment Processes in Manali (Sinclair and Diduck).
   (f) Perceptions of urban sustainability (Sinclair).
   (g) Waste management (Cole and Sinclair).
   (h) Sustainability of Manali urban area through Ecological Footprint analysis (Cole).

4. Extensive fieldwork was conducted by the Indian Interns on "Environmental Impact Statement and Issues in Tourism and Infrastructure" in July 1999 in Kullu and Manali. Both primary and secondary data were collected on land-use,. land-use change and planning issues in the town of Kullu.
5. The Canadian team of Prof. Gardner and Interns conducted fieldwork also in June-November 1999. Their work focused on risk from natural hazard in the built up areas and along the roads from the town of Kullu to Rohtang Pass. The research also highlighted the impact of the growth of Manali.
6. The Indian and Canadian Partners, along with their research teams, conducted joint field research and a workshop in Manali in October 1999. The following aspects were discussed:

   (a) People's Perception of Environmental Impact and Land-use Change (Singh & Pandey).
   (b) Perception of Environment by the Decision Makers and Community Leaders (Singh and Sen Roy).
   (c) Consolidation of Long-Term Climatic Data (Singh & Sen Roy).
   (d) Hazard Risk Assessment and Land Resource Management (Singh & Pandey).

(e) Gender, Handicraft Industry, Mountain Urban Economy (Singh & Rana).
(f) Climatic Variability and Apple Yield in Kullu Valley (Singh & Sen Roy).
(g) Climatic Variability and Crop Yield in Kullu Valley (Singh & Sen Roy).

7. Dissemination workshop held in Manali, May 24-25, 2000 by Indian team partner for CIDA and SICI officials. Scientific field visit on land-use change and Urban Development.
8. Canadian team partners (Dr. Gardner, Dr. Sinclair, and 4 Interns) conducted further research in Manali/Kullu area during June-October, 2000 on hazard mapping and risk assessment; capacity building for environmental education; waste management; environmental impact assessment of hydro development; and use and management of protected areas.

DISSEMINATION ACTIVITIES

- Discussion meeting during visit by Mr. Tom Schatzky of CIDA: Mr. Tom Schatzky from CIDA and Ms. Seema Sharma from SICI visited the Indian Partner at the Department of Geography, University of Delhi on 23rd November, 1998. Apart from presentation of two Research Assistants working in the project, a few other researchers having interest relating to the project, spoke about on-going work undertaken by them.
- A discussion meeting on "Urban Development and its Impact on the Environment", was jointly organized by the CIDA-SICI research team and Himachal Pradesh Mahila Kalyan Mandal on 29th November, 1998 at Mahila Bhawan, Kullu. The main objective of the discussion was to recognize the rapid urban growth, understand its causes and the environmental and social consequences, and to identify policies and practices, which provide direction for minimizing negative impacts and ensuring sustainability. The team decided to develop locally acceptable EIA procedures for development projects proposed in the study area.
- CIDA-SICI dissemination workshop was organized and conducted in Manali in October 1999 to discuss project results with local people and officials. In addition, a group of 35 master's students

from University of Delhi attended a daylong field seminar led by Prof. Gardner and Dr. Singh.

- Joint CIDA-SICI Partnership Programme project workshop held at University of Madras, December 1999 by Dr. Gardner and Dr. Vasant Kumaran to review the results of the Manitoba/Delhi and Waterloo/Madras projects.
- CIDA-SICI dissemination workshop was organized and conducted in the field site at Manali during 24-25th May, 2000 to discuss project results before CIDA representative, Ms. Evelyn Lee; Administrative Director of SICI, Mr. M.K. Lakhtakia; and Programme Officer, Ms. Rachna Thapliyal. A group of 12 researchers from University of Delhi attended a daylong seminar at the Wildlife Awareness and Education Centre and a one-day scientific field visit to the Project Site between Manali to Rohtang Pass, led by Dr. Singh.
- CIDA-SICI Project dissemination workshop was organized at Delhi University during November 3-4, 2000 to discuss project results with researchers, policy makers and community leaders. Over 150 participants attended the workshop. The inaugural address was delivered by Hon'ble Dr. D.N. Tiwari, Member (Science, Technology & Environmental Forests), Planning Commission, Government of India. The valedictory session was attended by the Hon'ble M.P. Bezbaruah, Secretary, Ministry of Tourism, Government of India. SICI was represented by Prof. Vikram Bhatt, Vice President and Ms. Rachna Thapliyal, Programme Officer.
- The Principal Investigator Prof. J.S. Gardner and chief Co-Investigator Dr. R.B. Singh and 3 Indian Interns participated and presented research results and findings before CIDA-SICI workshop organized by the Shastri Indo-Canadian Institute at India International Centre, New Delhi during April 24-26, 2001.

## COMMUNICATING RESEARCH RESULTS TO OFFICIALS/ POLICY MAKERS

1. The field survey conducted by Indian Interns in November-December 1998 had interaction with Government officials and Policy makers.
2. Dissemination of information about the project to the practitioners and Policy makers in and around the field study area was accomplished through interviews (March 1999).

3. Project results at the dissemination workshop in October 1999 and May 2000, were communicated at the workshop to the local officials and policy makers.
   — Member of Legislative Assembly representing the Project region, Mr. Chandersen Thakur
   — Sub-Divisional Magistrate, Manali
   — District Agricultural Officer, Kullu
   — Scientist, G.B. Pant Institute of Environment and Development, Government of India
   — Advocate, Manali
   — District Planning Officer, Kullu
   — Forest Department, Manali

INTERACTION WITH FOLLOWING POLICY MAKERS

- Planning Commission, Government of India
- Municipal Corporation of Kullu
- G. B. Pant Institute of Environment and Development, Kullu, Government of India
- Tourism Development Department of Kullu
- Ministry of Tourism, Government of India
- Central Water Commission, Government of India
- National Institute of Educational Planning and Administration, New Delhi.
- District Pollution Control Board
- Western Himalayan Mountaineering Institute, Manali
- Forest Officers and State Forest Conservator, Shimla, Manali
- District Planning Officer, Kullu
- District Agricultural Officer, Kullu
- District Horticulture Officer, Kullu
- District Town Planning Officer, Kullu
- Sub-Divisional Magistrate, Manali
- District Education Officer, Kullu
- Executive Magistrate, Manali
- Environmental Engineer/Director, H.P. State Pollution Control Board, Shimla
- Member Legislative Assembly (MLA), Shimla, Kullu
- Deputy Commissioner, Kullu

- Director Environmental Assessment Branch, Delhi
- Additional Inspector General of Forests, Delhi
- High Court Advocate, Shimla
- Irrigation and Public Health Department of Kullu
- Tourism Development Departments of Kullu and Manali
- Department of Science and Technology, H.P., Shimla
- Indian Institute of Public Administration, New Delhi
- Institute of Manpower Research, New Delhi
- Indian Law Institute, New Delhi
- R.G. Office (Map), Government of India

## REFERENCES

**Dissemination of Findings Through Publication of Papers**

Berkes, F., Gardner, J. and Sinclair, J., "Comparative Aspects of Mountain Land Resource Management and Sustainability ; Case Studies from India and Canada," *International Journal of Sustainable Development and World Ecology.*

Duffield, C., Gardner, J. S. Berkes, F. and Singh, R.B. "Local Knowledge in the Assessment of Resource Sustainability: Case Studies in Himachal Pradesh, India and British Columbia. Canada", *Mountain Research and Development,* Vol. 18, No. 1, 1998, pp. 35-49.

Haigh, M. J., Singh, R. B. and Krecek, J "Headwater Control : Matters Arising", in *Headwaters-Resources and Soil Conservation,* Eds. M. J. High *et al.*, New Delhi: Oxford & IBH Pub., 1998, pp. 3-24.

Rana, Monica, "Gendered Landscapes: Women and Sustainable Mountain Development in Indian Himalayas," in *Awareness,* a Journal from Singapore, Vol. 7, March 2000.

Sinclair and Diduck, "Public Involvement in EIA—A case study of hydro development in Kullu District, H. P., India," in *Impact Assessment and Project Appraisal.*

Singh R. B., "Land use/cover changes, extreme events and Eco-hydrological responses in the Himalayan Region," *Hydrological Processes,* 1998.

Singh, R. B. "Understanding High Mountain Land Use Towards Sustainable Environmental in Jammu and Kashmir", in *Headwaters-Water Resources and Soil Conservation,* Eds. M.J. Haigh *et al.*, New Delhi: Oxford & IBH Pub. 1998, pp. 409-422.

Singh, "Geographical Information System for Environmental Monitoring and Management," in National Seminar on Environmental Management in Hydro Electric Projects, 1999.

Singh R. B. "Environmental Impact Assessment and Management in Highlands and Headwater Regions," in R.S. Goel (ed.) *Environmental Impact Assessment of Water Resources Projects,* Oxford and IBH Pub., New Delhi, 2000. pp. 343-356.

Singh R. B., and Tingal, "Man-made and Natural Geo-Hazards in Kullu Valley, in R. B. Singh (ed.) *Disaster Management,* Rawat Pub., New Delhi, 2000. pp. 259-286.

Singh R. B. and Baber Ali, "Dynamics of Village Common Land and its Sustainable Management in the Himalayan Upper Beas Basin" S.K. Dash and J. Bahadur (ed.)

*The Himalayan Environment*, New Age International Pub., New Delhi, 1999. pp. 246-257.

Sinclair and Ham, "Household Adaptive Strategies : Shaping Livelihood Security in the Western Himalaya", *Canadian Journal of Development Studies*, Vol. XXI, No. 1, pp. 89-112.

Singh, R.B. and Ghai, S. "Human Induced Hazards and Development in a part of upper Yamuna watershed, Garhwal Himalaya, in eds. A. M. Pathan and S.S. Thingale– *Contributions to Environmental Geoscience*, Aravali Books Int., New Delhi, 2000 pp. 151-160.

**Related Research Volumes Published by Partners**

R.B. Singh (Ed.) : *Urban Sustainability in the Context of Global Change,* Ed., Science Pub., Inc., Enfield (NH), USA and Oxford & IBH Pub. New Delhi, 2001, pp. 282.

F. Berkes and J. S. Gardner (Eds.) : *Sustainability of Mountain Environments in India and Canada,* Natural Resource Inst., Univ. of Manitoba, Winnipeg, 1997, pp. 407, 1997.

R. B. Singh (Ed.) *Sustainable Development of Mountain Environment of India and Canada,* ed., New Delhi Oxford & IBH Pub., 1998, pp. 345.

R. B. Singh and M. J. Haigh (Eds.) : *Sustainable Reconstruction of Highland and Headwater Regions,* ed. Jointly with M.J. Haigh, New Delhi, Oxford & IBH Pub., 1995, pp. 681.

R. B. Singh (Ed.) : *Ecological Techniques and Approaches to Vulnerable Environment,* Science Pub., Inc., Enfield (NH), USA and New Delhi, Oxford & IBH Pub., 1998. pp.255.

Predicting Global Change Impacts on Mountain Hydrology and Ecology : Integrated Catchment Hydrology/Altitudinal Gradient Studies, Editor includes R.B. Singh and others, IGBP Report 43, Royal Swedish Academy of Sciences, Stockholm, 1997. pp. 61.

7

# Urban Housing

## A Study of Privatisation Policy

**H. R. SURI**

The basic purpose for the formulation of a "Policy on Privatisation" is to boost housing stock as well as promote, monitor and programme planned development of Housing by private agencies without much involvement of the Government or Government Funds." For evolving an effective system, we have to examine the ground realities, hurdles, procedural brakes and long standing in built problems. The fundamental premise is that we are short of funds, prices of land are very high and the country cannot afford to waste land. We have to make the best use of our scarce resources. We can also make use of the in-built inertia of the people to develop their own schemes/projects themselves. We have got to help the population in the city/country who cannot help themselves.

### 1. Reality

1. Major portion of the city of Delhi is in existence that we have almost five to six lakh plot holders in the city. It seems that every plot holder in the city is feeling suffocated in the clutches of the rules and regulations prevalent in the city.
2. Percentage of house owners in the city/country is very low. There is higher percentage of tenants. It is noted here that Ninth Five Year Plan is up holding the need for rental housing which is in fact undermining the basic need for increasing the percentage of the house owners. All benefits for the increase in values of the properties in individuals hands goes to the house owners. Increase in house ownership will increase savings and satisfaction. Therefore every decision we make must increase the percentage of the house owners in the city/ country.
3. Delhi/India has tremendous population in lower income group. This high percentage of population living in city cannot afford more than 500-600 sq. ft. of built up space. If we examine in detail the floor areas of the individual plots as well as in the

case of group housing schemes we find that there is no provision for this lower income group of population of the city. A detailed examination will reveal that the planned accommodation in case of plotted development or ground housing is not less than 1100 sq. ft. of built up space/floor area. 60-70 per cent of the population of the city has therefore no affordable place to live in the city and that no space has been planned are being planned for this group of population. Therefore, we find that this population is forced to live in unauthorised areas, in urban villages, in slums or in squatter settlements. This 60 to 70 per cent of the population may be covering only one-tenth of the area of the city.

It may be noted here that in India we have smallest income of a family, it has smallest size of dwelling unit for largest size of the family. On the other hand smallest size of family of the high income groups have largest size of dwelling units. In a developed country a bricklayer has a 3 bedroom house a secretary/engineer has 3 bedroom house and that their prime minister has 3 bedroom house. There is a need for the rationalization of the residential built space.

4. Poor people consisting of more than 50 per cent of the population in the city cannot help itself. Government agencies have to initiate action to provide housing for this lower income group. It is very much doubtful if any private agency will venture in this sector. Builders if forced to provide EWS housing along with high income groups may not accept this. Even if builders offer to build EWS housing as part of their projects, it may not be healthy for the growth of individuals. Such a situation is bound to create an inferiority complex in children and poorer sections of the population.

   It will be interesting to note and examine the activity of each and every builder in the city as to type of accommodation being provided by them. It is very certain that none of the builders has done any amount of work for this lower income group of our population. A detailed examination of all the projects carried out by the Delhi Development Authority will reveal the same situation/facts. DDA is carring out only self financing scheme.

5. Slum department is ineffective therefore it needs to be close down. It has been shunting from MCD to DDA and *vice versa.* The lands in Delhi are generally in the control of DDA, and that the maintenance is basically is the responsibility of the MCD. Therefore the slum department is ineffective. Most of the slum settlements are occupying lands designated for other basic needs of the city. Whatever slum areas are existing are deteriorating everyday.

   The squatter colonies are also occupying land designated for other important uses such as facilities, amenities etc. Shifting of squatters and other such colonies need to be formed as part of the city. Whatever may be it is our duty to see that the basic bone structure of the city alongwith its essential infrastructure remains intact. This action will make them part of the city plan and that the bloodlines and the arteries of the city will keep on working. All facilities and amenities for the residential uses shall remain in position. Whenever at a later date, we have money, or the people of the area can afford, we can redevelop the area as per our then future requirements.
6. The area of city planned for 49.00 lakh in 1962 is today catering to more than double the population. The reasons for this growth are well known. These factors literally reduce the proportionate areas for facility and services to 50 per cent when compared to the original plan proposals. This fact is very serious and Ministry of Urban Affairs and Employment ought to initiate action for re-examining all the planning standards in this context.
7. DDA could not prepare Zonal Plans what to talk of Detailed Development Plans for the First Master Plan of 1962. It is doubtful if DDA has made much progress in making such plan as per MPD 2001. In the absence of detailed development plans there is a need to have atleast a framework of the various parts of the city alongwith facilities and amenities, before any licence can be granted to the private developers in the city.
8. Mobility/transferability is the most important factors for adjustment and adaptability to the right type of accommodation as and when necessary. The situation is ever changing in the life span of every family. In Delhi, mobility/transferability does not exist at all. People have tremendous problems in buying

and selling property. The Apartment Act is in operation in Delhi but it has not been advertised properly, therefore, it is defunct and ineffective. Because of many types of hurdles are being faced by the people, action is required to ease out ULCA and other outdated lease conditions to smoothen the process of transferability, for adjustment and redevelopment. It is interesting to note that Delhi has all the restrictions of lease where as other metro cities have none, similarly East of Kailash, Vasant Vihar etc., are tied down in such problems whereas Greater Kailas I or II have no problems.

9. The banking system is outdated. The entire financing system needs overhauling. In this outdated environment of financing system, an individual in India can normally hope to buy a house/dwelling unit when he is about to retire, whereas in a developed country a young family can easily afford to buy a house.
10. *Discourage ownership of more than two Dwelling Units:* In most of the developed countries, young families are in a position to acquire a home and are quick in adjusting to changing needs. The authorities spend their own funds or raise resources from banks when they are unable to meet the requirement of funds. This increases the cost of the dwelling unit very much. The housing in Ghaziabad is an example of this misadventure. We need to look into this phenomena in detail.
11. Government agencies who resort to departmental construction system as operated by CPWD sometimes take 10-12 years to complete and dispose of such properties. In 10 years time, total cost should be recoverable if we want to ensure viability in the costing of dwelling units. There is a need for strict monitoring, phasing, programming and project management for the execution of the housing projects by the housing boards as well as the private enterprises.

## II. Privatisation and Individual Plotholders in the City

1. Delhi has more than 6 lakh plot holders. Major reconstruction is taking place in all parts of the city. The Notification of 23rd July 1998 has increased the floor areas/FAR to some extent but it is doubtful if plotted development will be able to generate more dwelling units, unless we adopt corrective actions. A

detailed examination will reveal this aspect. It is advisable to delete the column governing dwelling units/per floor in the Notification. It is very much doubtful if DDA has been able to control density in the city. It is, therefore, advisable if people can themselves determine the number of dwelling units on their properties with in the given building bulk/floor area/ground coverage and height etc.

2. One thing is certain; nobody will plan a Mahabir Nagar type of accommodation in Maharani Bagh or *vice-versa.* It is noted here that in this age a person with high income may require a small accommodation.
3. As far as services are concerned we have to plan for population needs in any area in terms of projected growth. With regard to group housing it has been proved the cost of services generally is low for high density and high for low density.
4. Recommendations in my article 'Management of housing stock' within given constraints of funding and resources are very relevant in this regard. The points in brief are given below. We have to maximise the use of scarce resources in the best possible manner and conserve good quality agricultural land:
   (i) No funding for dwelling units having the built-up space more than 150 sq. cm should be permitted in the city/country.
   (ii) Discourage with disincentives, ownership of more than one dwelling unit.
   (iii) Percentage of house owners must be increased in the country.
   (iv) To facilitate housing and to conserve scarce land resources a dwelling unit must be declared as a basic entity against a plot at present. This is in conformity with the Apartment Act already in operation in Delhi.
   (v) Transferability/Mobility must be increased. All hurdles must be eased out.
   (vi) A Hire Purchase system and a System of Tripartite agreement between (a) a developer, (b) a purchaser, and (c) the financial institution bank needs to be introduced in the country. Hire purchase system will help the financing mathematics in the country. A young couple in this system can easily pay back the loan in very small instalments on long term basis.

(vii) Registration of developers/builders and property brokers and estate agents is essential.

(viii) Instalment system based on hire purchase system will make residential accommodation within the aforadable limits of young couples.

## III. Privatisation and 50-60 per cent of the Population in Lower Income Group

It is doubtful if builders and developers will be interested in construction housing for the low income groups. The real problem in the city is this low income groups. Ansal and such other organisations have made fun of this situation and detailed examination reveals that few EWS dwelling units were actually built by them to distract attention and convince the authorities that they are also interested in this group. The biggest evidence of this fact is the track record of most of the builders.

Asking big builders to earmark EWS and LIG housing has been a fiasco in Mumbai. Moreover placing LIG and EWS next to high income group is not a very happy situation. Theory of constructing tenable and non-tenable units by then Janta Government during seventies failed miserably. It is very much certain that construction of housing for the lower income groups will have to the responsibility of Government agencies for the next couple of decades. On the other hand it is also true that the DDA and the other authorities were unable to carry out this assignment.

In 1968, DDA took a decision to build dwelling units which do not cost more than the amount of salary a government officer earned. But somehow DDA got lost on the way. They got busy with HIG housing *i.e.* flats which had an area of 1200 sq. ft. and above. 80 sq. m flats booked by DDA in 1979 have not yet been completed and handed over to the people. It will be worthwhile to cross examine all the issues regarding these projects to find out the root cause of the problem. Considering these facts we may have to consider the following:

1. Housing for the lower income groups has to be the responsibility of the authority for the next couple of decades.

2. District/Zone-wise Housing Boards be formed and entrusted with the task of housing for the poor.
3. The authorities should construct flats/DU's with built up area upto 80 sq. m only.
4. If Government likes to consider housing in the infrastructure category, then group housing projects having flats with built up area upto a maximum of 50 sq. m be taken up in the infrastructure priority sector because in this category maximum help is needed.
5. Authorities should use private consultants for the design and implementation of projects instead of involving themselves. However they should focus on monitoring, phasing and managing the implementation and execution of the projects.
6. Disposal of DUs in the lower income group be through allotment/lottery etc., on the basis of higher purchase system.
7. Funding of all housing projects can be through banks/financial institutions and based on tripartite agreement system as prevalent in Britain and other countries.
8. Major portions of Central and State Housing subsidy should go to the small income groups. Fiscal differential method should be income based for the dispersal of housing units in all income groups.
9. It is high time that the slum department is closed and all funds be diverted to such housing boards.
10. Shifting of squatters etc. should be planned as part of the total city residential development so that all facilities and amenities are available and the city structure remains undisturbed.
11. Slum colonies being planned by the departments of slums at Jonapur are highly questionable.
12. Major portion of the area acquired for the residential land-use be utilised for the lower income group.
13. It is highly illogical that the government acquires land by displacing the poor agriculturists and the hands over such properties to a developer at reduced/fixed rates so that they make money.
14. Selected acquisition of land by the housing boards may be permitted. This will make land available for the lower income groups at cheaper rates.

15. Gradually all settlements/slum areas planned or unplanned be brought into the framework of the city.
16. The process of urban renewal needs initiation into the country. The process will take care of those well located squatter colonies/slums at an appropriate time when we are ready with finances of redevelop. We have to understand that the city has much longer life, buildings come and go.
17. What the city cannot afford is the congestion, choked blood lines and arteries. We must see that we do not distort the basic structure of the city. All its roads, parking, drains, sewerage system, water supply, educational, health and recreational facilities and other social needs have to be protected and enhanced.
18. The basis for the broad re-distribution of land uses in a city needs to be reconsidered. The percentage of saleable areas should be 45 per cent as against 55 per cent being universally adopted at present. It is very difficult to enhance land for such functions at a later date.

## IV. Privatisation and Private Developers/Builders

1. Developers have got to be on their own. All authorities need to do is to streamline the system and remove the brakes and hurdles, if any.
2. Loan for housing projects based on standard and clear cut guidelines should be given priority by banks and other financial institutions.
3. Entire work of development/redevelopment slum/squatter colonies and other anciliary functions has to be business like as far as the authorities are concerned.
4. Land acquired by the authorities from the original owners at very low rates should not be given to a developer on any basis.
5. Builder must use their own resources and methods to collect parcels of land as required under rules being framed.
6. In case of vacant lands/properties which do not form part of any approved scheme, a 55 per cent cut should be made for infrastructure.
7. All the proposals by the developers must form part of the basic structure of the city.

8. Releasing freedom to private developers without the availability of zonal/other details plans is suicidal. It is important that DDA quickly prepares all necessary detailed zonal plans and detailed development plans for speeding up the process of privatisation for the development of housing in the city so that all schemes by the developers properly fits into the overall framework of the city/bone structure of the city.
9. The land/properties for private development in the hands of the builders should form part of the planned areas. In the planned areas already existing, even 1 hactare is also sufficient for the process of privatisation/renewal. This seems to be the only answer to bring in existing haphazard growth, unauthorised colonies and legalised colonies within the framework. This system will also prevent areas from decaying.
10. A system for using foreign funds through banks/financial institutions as well as non-resident Indians needs to be developed and streamlined. Lots of foreign funds are available because of differential bank interest situation in foreign countries as compared to India.
11. Mobility/transferability must be maintained at the maximum level and buying and selling of properties should be made easy.
12. Incentives be given to private builders and developers if they want to develop land for 50 per cent of the population in the lower income group having a maximum dwelling unit size of 50 sq. m.
13. A development charge/cut for socialising funds for the construction of houses for the EWS and other lower income groups be introduced.
14. The development charge for infrastructure is required to be levied and collected.
15. A charge for development of peripheral services is also required alongwith physical and social infrastructure.
16. A development charge has to be levied for development of city parking zones. This is necessary where it is not possible to provide parking spaces in projects.

17. There are some excellent recommendations prepared by the special group constituted by the Ministry of Urban Affairs and Employment a year ago in respect of revision of MPD-2001 such as amalgamation of plots, provision of stilts/ combined basement/common staircases, lifts etc. are very relevant, these need to be adopted.

## CONCLUSION

No one will disagree with the fact that the situation is bad not only in Delhi but in the entire country. To make matters worse, everyone in the country is copying what is being done in Delhi. One-tenth of the population has already consumed 70 per cent of the area of the city. 90 per cent of the population is managing with 30 per cent of the area. Therefore, there is a strong case of rationalisation of urban built space with business like approach after considering the ground realities. Time has come for the city of Delhi to adopt the process of urban renewal thereby giving a lead for the improvement of the environment of human habitation in our country.

While on the subject I would like to list the following articles which need examinations by the Ministry if we mean business:

1. 'Management of the Housing Stock' (within given work of resources) Innovative Strategies.
2. Regional Planning Mechanism in India: An Agenda for Action.
3. Delhi a Healthy City? A Wishful Distant Dream.
4. Spatial Planning: Safer Cities.
5. Urban Land (Ceiling and Regulations) Act on Wrong Foundations.
6. Implementation of 74th Amendment Act in Doldrums.
7. A New Production Line for Spatial Planners.
8. Spatial Planning and Safer Cities.
9. The Recommendations of the expert group on development code constituted by the steering committee of the MOUDE for the review of MP-2001.

# SECTION-II

# Indian Case Studies

# 8

# Urbanisation in India
## A Demographic Reappraisal

R. B. BHAGAT

## INTRODUCTION

The United Nations estimates indicate that at mid 1990s, about 43 per cent of the world population lived in urban areas. With the urban population growing two and half times faster than its rural counterpart, the level of urbanisation is projected to cross the 50 per cent mark in 2005. United Nations projections further show that by 2025, more than three-fifth of the world population will live in urban areas (U. N. 1993; 2000).

The growth rate of urban population of developing regions has been declining recently. It was estimated to be 3.9 per cent per annum during 1980-85, which declined to 3.79 per cent per annum during 1980-85, 3.62, and 3.43 during 1990-95 and 1995-2000 respectively. The decline in the rate of urbanisation is also continuing in developed regions of the world. As a result, some of the European countries have experienced negative urbanisation in the recent past (U. N. 1993; 2000). However, the continued absence, namely, adequate data on rural to urban migration in most developing countries as well as on natural increase in rural and urban areas separately precludes attribution of the slowing down of urban growth in most of the countries to any single demographic process. It reflects the effects the host of factors like the relatively week expansion of urban industries and price shifts unfavourable to manufactured goods, population ageing, policies to alter migration and spatial distribution patterns in some countries, and no doubt other forces (Brockerhoff, 1998; 1999). The arguments of Kelly and William (1984a; 1984b) that the slow growth of agricultural land stock and high growth of population of labour force in developing countries are factors that presumably push rural population toward urban areas are not correct for the recent past. The sluggish performance of manufacturing (as compared to agriculture) remains largely responsible for the observed slower pace of urban growth in developing countries, and may have decelerated urban growth from what otherwise would have been higher rates in the 1980s and 1990s by curbing net rural to urban migration. Even though manufacturing is performing well but cannot generate adequate employment being capital intensive is unlikely to accelerate rural to urban migration. The likely deceleration of rural to urban migration could be the important reason for the slowing down of urbanisation in the developing countries in recent times. The fertility decline could also be the another important factor for lower urban growth in several parts of the developing world particularly in Latin America where total fertility rate declined from 6 in the early 1960s to 3 in the early 1990s (United Nations, 1993).

The push factors like population growth and unemployment etc., and pull factors like opportunities in the urban areas are debated in the studies of India's urbanization. The National Commission on Urbanisation (1988) has termed them as factors of demographic and economic momentum respectively. In this article, specific attempt has been made to examine the contribution of both the types of urban process mentioned above. The main objectives of the study are as follows:

(i) To evaluate the definition of urban from urban development perspective.
(ii) To study the level, trend and regional pattern of urbanisation.
(iii) To examine the relative contribution of natural increase as well as rural to urban migration in urban growth in the recent past.
(iv) To examine India's future urbanisation in the light of new economic policy.

## Sources of Data and Method

Census is the main source of data on urban population for not only India but also most of the countries of the world. Census defines urban areas based on certain criteria. In India since 1961, two important criteria namely: (i) statutory administration, and (ii) economic and demographic aspects have been adopted to declare certain settlements as towns. The former includes civic status of towns such as municipal corporations, municipality, cantonment board, notified area committee, etc., and the latter includes criteria like population size, density of population and percentage of work force in non-agricultural sector.

The former is also known as statutory town and the latter as census town. These two types of town based on two different criteria have added complexity to the urbanisation process in India. For example, the predominance of non-agricultural activities is expected to be found in urban areas, but surprisingly we have significant number of towns in the country, which are predominantly agriculture oriented. Such paradoxical development creates doubts about the quality of urbanisation in India (Bhagat, 1992). Further, the definition of urban area had changed from time to time. Although, the definition of urban areas of 1961 census continued in later censuses, but it has been slightly modified in constituents of non-agricultural activities since 1981 census. According to 1981 census, 75 per cent of male workers in non-agricultural activities is required for a settlement to be declared as urban. In addition to it, at a town level the change in boundary has been frequent, and in several cases adjustment for it is impossible due to lack of relevant information.

The sources of urban growth comprise natural increase in urban areas, migration, re-classification of rural areas into urban areas and the change in the boundaries of existing towns. The migration data and the information on re-classification of rural areas into urban areas are available from the census. But the information on emigration is not available in the country, although its effect is likely to be negligible. The data on natural increase are available from Sample Registration System (SRS) published by Registrar General of India annually. The contribution of migration in the urban growth could be estimated directly from the data available in Migration Tables. However, it underestimates the contribution of migration due to several inadequacies, which are mentioned in the latter section. Alternatively, therefore, the residual method could be preferred in case of India.

### India's Place in World Urbanisation

The urban population of the world was estimated to be 2.96 billion in 2000 (see Table 8.1). It was estimated that nearly 50 million people are added to the world's urban population and about 35 million to the rural population every year. The share of world's population living in urban centres has increased from 39 per cent in 1980 to 48 per cent in 2000. The developed countries have higher urbanisation level (76 per cent in 2000) compared with the developing countries (40 per cent). The urbanisation level has almost stabilised in the developed countries. There was about 3 per cent increase in the level of urbanisation in the developed countries during 1990-2000. On the other hand the increase in the level of urbanisation was faster in developing countries (6 per cent during 1990-2000). The higher level of urbanisation in Africa compared to Asia gives the impression of higher life chances in Africa, which is misleading. Table 8.2 shows that the level of urbanisation in India was 25.7 per cent in 1991, which was lower than the average level of urbanisation in the developing countries (34 per cent in 1990). In south Asia, India has an edge over some of the neighbours in urbanisation. The countries like Bangladesh (18 per cent), Sri Lanka (21 per cent), Bhutan (16 per cent) and Nepal (10 per cent) have lower level of urbanisation than India. But Pakistan has higher level of urbanisation (32 per cent) than India. It is however important to note that the comparison of the level of urbanisation at the world level is affected by definition of urban areas in each countries. For example, in Bangladesh places having a municipality (*Pourashava*), a town committee (*Shahar Committee*) or cantonment board are defined as urban; in Nepal, all localities of 9000 or more inhabitants are declared urban: in Pakistan places with municipal corporation, town committee or cantonment are declared urban; in Sri Lanka also municipalities, urban councils and town are treated as urban. If urbanisation is at all to be considered as process of social and economic change affecting the life chances of people, then there is an urgent need to consider a standard definition across the world. The United Nations Population Division must pay attention to this aspect of urbanisation.

**Table 8.1 :** Percentage of Population Residing in Urban Areas by Region, 1980-2010

| World/Region | 1980 | | 1985 | | 1990 | | 2000 | | 2010 | |
|---|---|---|---|---|---|---|---|---|---|---|
| | % | '000 | % | '000 | % | '000 | % | '000 | % | '000 |
| World | 39 | 1752 | 41 | 1997 | 43 | 2282 | 48 | 2962 | 53 | 3779 |
| More Developed Region | 70 | 797 | 72 | 838 | 73 | 880 | 76 | 968 | 79 | 1060 |
| Less Developed Region | 29 | 954 | 32 | 1159 | 34 | 1401 | 40 | 1993 | 47 | 2717 |
| Africa | 27 | 130 | 30 | 164 | 32 | 205 | 38 | 322 | 44 | 493 |
| Asia | 26 | 678 | 29 | 813 | 31 | 974 | 37 | 1369 | 44 | 1845 |
| Latin America | 65 | 233 | 68 | 273 | 72 | 315 | 77 | 400 | 80 | 482 |

*Source* : World Urbanisation Prospects—The 1992 Revision, United Nations, New York, 1993.

**Table 8.2 :** India : Indicators of Urbanisation

| Census Year | Urban No. of UA/ Towns | Population in Million | Number of Towns/UA per 10 Lakh % Urban Population | Decennial Growth Rate of Rural Population | Population (%) |
|---|---|---|---|---|---|
| 1901 | 1827 | 25.85 | 10.84 | 8.6 | — |
| 1911 | 1815 | 25.94 | 10.29 | 8.0 | 0.35 |
| 1921 | 1949 | 28.08 | 11.18 | 8.7 | 8.27 |
| 1931 | 2072 | 33.45 | 11.99 | 8.4 | 19.12 |
| 1941 | 2250 | 44.15 | 13.86 | 8.2 | 31.97 |
| 1951 | 2843 | 62.44 | 17.29 | 9.5 | 41.42 |
| 1961 | 2365 | 78.93 | 17.97 | 6.6 | 26.41 |
| 1971 | 2590 | 109.11 | 19.91 | 5.9 | 38.23 |
| 1981 | 3387 | 159.46 | 23.34 | 6.4 | 46.14 |
| 1991 | 3768 | 217.17 | 25.72 | 6.0 | 36.10 |
| 2001 | — | 285.35 | 27.78 | — | 31.30 |

***Notes:***

1. As the 1981 Census was not conducted in Assam, the 1981 population figures for India include interpolated figures for Assam.
2. The 1991 Census has not been held in Jammu & Kashmir. The 1991 population figures for India include projected figures for Jammu and Kashmir as projected by the standing committee of experts on population projection (October, 1989).

*Source*: Census of India, 1991.

http. \\www.censusindia.net (2001 Census).

In India on the other hand both civic status as well as demographic aspect are taken as criteria for declaring a settlement as urban. The recent census of India defined the urban places on the basis of the following criteria :

(i) All places with a municipality, corporation, cantonment board or notified town area committee etc.

(ii) All other places which satisfy the following criteria:

(a) Minimum population of 5000

(b) At least 75 per cent of male working population engaged in non-agricultural pursuits; and

(c) A density of population of at least 400 persons per square km.

Besides, the directors of census operation in states/union territories were allowed to include in consultation with the concerned state governments, union territory administration and the Census Commissioner of India, some places having distinct urban characteristics as urban even if such places did not strictly satisfy all the criteria mentioned under the category (b) above (Census of India, 1991). The definition adopted in India assumes that urbanization is the consequences of industrialization, and therefore, urban areas must have preponderance of non-agricultural activities. It also considers only male work force in the non-agricultural sectors ignoring the fact that large number of women are increasingly inundating the labour force in the rural as well as urban areas. The definition also loses its potency when it is examined from the perspectives of areas benefited by green revolution particularly in the states of North-West India, namely Punjab and Haryana. In the wake of green revolution, several village settlements in these two states have good infrastructural facility in terms of electricity supply, transport and communication and other so called urban amenities. But these settlements cannot be classified as urban due to lack of fulfilment of 3/4th male work force being employed in non-agricultural activities. It is worth to mention that a urban status has higher potential of revenue collection in terms of property taxes, sale tax, vehicle tax, entertainment tax, octroi, and service charges. The present definition does not allow the settlement to be classified as urban even if it has higher level of development barring non-agricultural preponderance. It is, therefore, argued that the definition adopted by Census of India is caging the settlements of green revolution areas. This also must be looked from the powerful rural lobbies in these areas which take several benefits like electricity and irrigation subsidy, exemption of income tax etc., but are unwilling to pay on several counts if the settlement is declared urban. On the other hand in the backward states such as M.P. and Chhatisgarh and also in U.P. and Bihar several settlements are declared as urban due to political expediency by granting them urban status like municipality and notified area committee. This amounts to burden of taxes and charges on the poor people who hardly could afford them. This paradox of urban definition is hampering the process of urban development in the country. There is a need to search for alternative definition conducive for the development with social justice. One can think of incorporating social amenities and life chances variables for defining urban areas which could reflect better organisation of human settlements bereft of industrial and gender biases.

## Trend in India's Urbanisation

In order to understand the demographic trend in India's urbanisation, the following indicators of urbanisation have been considered in this study:

(i) Percentage or urban population to total population—This shows the level of urbanisation in an area.
(ii) Decadal growth rate—This provides the change in urban population in percentage related to base year.
(iii) Number of towns per ten-lakh rural population—This indicator shows the extent to which rural areas are served by urban centres.
(iv) Percentage of population in Class I cities/towns—This indicates about the dominance of large towns in the process of urbanisation compared to medium and small towns.

The urban population in India at the beginning of twentieth century was only 25.85 million constituting 10.84 per cent of India's population in 1901 which increased to 285.35 million comprising 27.78 per cent of total population in 2001. The growth rate was highest observed during 1971-81 (46.14) and subsequent slowing down of India's urbanisation. It is also surprising to note that the total number of towns/ Urban Agglomeration (U.A.) per ten lakhs rural population has declined from 8.6 in 1901 to 6.0 in 2001. This shows that more rural population is marginalised from the benefits of urban centres.

Correlation co-efficient between the indicators of urbanisation and socio-economic variables like per capita Net Domestic Product (NDP), literacy, work force in non-agricultural activites and infant mortality rate shows that the decennial growth rate is positively associated with literacy and non-agricultural work force and negatively associated with infant mortality, although the correlation co-efficient are low and insignificant. The percentage of urban population is significantly positively related with non-agricultural work force, per capita income, and literacy and negatively related with infant mortality. The positive association between percentage urban population and percentage of urban population living in class I cities shows that urban population is highiy concentrated in class I cities. The correlation matrix also shows that the higher is the per capita net domestic product the higher is the number of towns per 10 lakh rural population. Literarcy, infant mortality rate and percentage of work force in non-agricultural sector are significantly related with each of the indicators of urbanisation. While literacy and infant mortality have relatively weak relationship with indicators of urbanisation, non-agricultural work force is significantly positively related with percentage of urban population and concentration of population in class I cities. The urban growth over time shows very diverse pattern across states of India and, therefore not significantly related with per capita income either in 1980s or 90s, but the relationship with level of urbanisation was significantly related with per capita income in both the decades of 1980s ($r$=0.51; $N$=16) and 90s ($r$=0.69; $N$=16). This shows that economically better off states have higher level of urbanisation compared to backward states. Some of the states like Punjab, Haryana and Tamil Nadu have picked up urban growth in 1990s after a slowing down in 1980s. Alongside few better off states like Maharashtra and Gujarat have maintained the tempo of urban growth more or less over the last three decades. On the other hand, the backward states like U.P., Bihar, Rajasthan, Madhya Pradesh and Orissa show a consistent decline in urban growth after experiencing a very high urban growth during 1970s. It reflected the predominance of push factor in India's urbanisation. During the 1980s, most of the states irrespective of economic status showed decline in urban growth, which continued in several states during 1990s also except Punjab, Haryana and Tamil Nadu. The urban growth figures over the last few decades show that the level of urbanisation increases marginally in the eastern sector comprising the states of Bihar, West Bengal and Assam. The situation of West Bengal is very depressing as urban growth is consistently declining and the level of urbanisation increases very marginally. The urban growth figures of 1990s clearly show that although urbanisation has continued to slow down in 90s also, but some of the states have reversed its pattern, and some of them maintained their tempo. This indicates that the differential impact of growth impulse at the regional level. The urban growth processes in the country indicate the marginalisation of eastern India in the wake of new economic policy.

**Table 8.3 :** Level of Urbanisation and Urban Growth in Selected States of India, 1971-2001

| State | Level % 1981 | Growth 1971-81 | Level % 1991 | Growth 1981-91 | Level % 2001 | Growth 1991-2001 |
|---|---|---|---|---|---|---|
| Andhra Pradesh | 23.3 | 48.6 | 26.8 | 42.6 | 27.1 | 15.1 |
| Assam | — | — | — | — | 12.7 | 37.2 |
| Bihar+1 | 12.5 | 54.8 | 13.1 | 30.4 | 13.4 | 29.0 |
| Gujarat | 31.1 | 41.4 | 34.4 | 33.6 | 37.4 | 33.4 |
| Haryana | 21.9 | 59.5 | 24.8 | 43.1 | 29.0 | 51.1 |
| Himachal Pradesh | — | — | — | — | 9.8 | 33.7 |
| Kerala | 18.7 | 37.6 | 26.4 | 60.9 | 25.9 | 7.7 |
| Karnataka | 28.9 | 50.7 | 30.9 | 29.1 | 33.9 | 29.4 |
| Madhya Pradesh+2 | 20.3 | 56.0 | 23.2 | 44.9 | 24.9 | 32.1 |
| Maharashtra | 35.0 | 40.0 | 38.73 | 38.7 | 42.4 | 34.5 |
| Orissa | 11.8 | 68.5 | 13.4 | 36.1 | 14.9 | 29.9 |
| Punjab | 27.7 | 44.5 | 29.7 | 29.1 | 33.9 | 37.4 |
| Rajasthan | 21.0 | 58.7 | 22.9 | 39.2 | 23.4 | 31.5 |
| Uttar Pradesh+3 | 17.9 | 60.6 | 19.9 | 38.9 | 21.0 | 32.7 |
| West Bengal | 26.5 | 31.7 | 27.4 | 28.9 | 28.0 | 20.8 |

1 = Jharkhand; 2 = Chhatisgarh; 3 = Uttaranchal (Three newly created states in 2000.)

**Table 8.4 :** Correlation Matrix of Different Indicatiors of Urbanisation and Socio-economic Variables, India, *(N = 16)*

| S. No. | % Urban (1) | Urban Growth (%) (2) | No. of towns per 10 Lakh Rural (3) | % Urban in class I cities (4) | Per Capita Income (5) | % Literacy (6) | IMR (7) | % work force in non-agricultural sector (8) |
|---|---|---|---|---|---|---|---|---|
| 1. | 1.0 | | | | | | | |
| 2. | –0.13 | 1.0 | | | | | | |
| 3. | 0.53 | –0.01 | 1.0 | | | | | |
| 4. | 0.78** | –0.07 | –0.02 | 1.0 | | | | |
| 5. | 0.51 | –0.24 | 0.47 | 0.24 | 1.0 | | | |
| 6. | 0.48 | 0.32 | 0.096 | 0.46 | 0.25 | 1.0 | | |
| 7. | –0.49 | –0.29 | 0.06 | –0.56 | –0.35 | –0.78** | 1.0 | |
| 8. | 0.63* | 0.11 | 0.23 | 0.54 | 0.68* | 0.84** | –0.88** | 1.0 |

* Significant at 0.01 level; ** significant at 0.001 level.

**Table 8.5 :** Trend in Natural Increase in Rural and Urban Areas, India, 1971-1999

| Year | Natural Increase | |
|---|---|---|
| | Rural | Urban |
| 1971-80 | 19.99 | 19.27 |
| 1981-90 | 21.64 | 19.49 |
| 1991-99 | 19.57 | 15.75 |

*Source* : Sample Registration Bulletins for respective years : Office of the Registrar General, India, New Delhi.

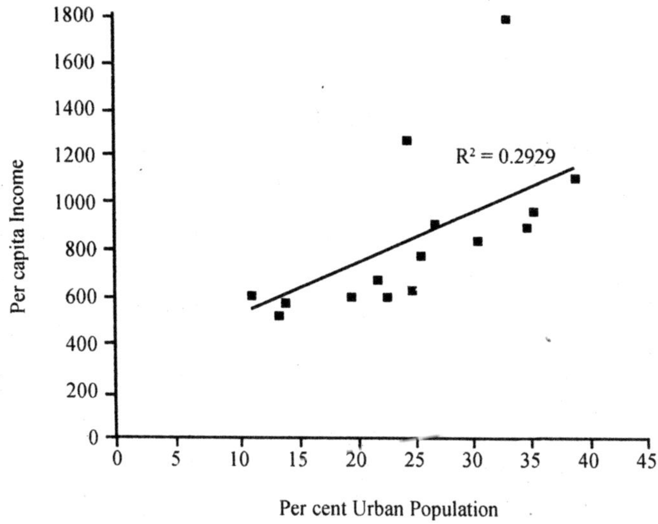


**Fig. 8.1 :** Income and Urbanisation, 1991 (Major States).

## Trend in Natural Increase and Migration

There are three components of urban growth *viz.*, the natural increase, net migration and the areal classification *i.e.*, addition of new towns minus declassification of existing towns. Besides the extension of

**Table 8.6 :** India : Components of Urban Growth, 1971-1991

| Per cent Share | 1971-81 | 1981-91 |
|---|---|---|
| Natural Increase | 41.7 (45.1) | 59.9 (58.7) |
| Net Migration + Changes in Municipal Boundaries | 39.4 (36.1) | 22.6 (23. 7) |
| Reclassification | 18.8 (18.8) | 17.4 (17.5) |

*Source* : Census of India 1991 : Figures in parenthesis are from Pathak and Mehta (1995). Pathak and Mehta have also estimated the component of urban growth like Census but after adjusting for the declassified towns.

**Table 8.7 :** Urban Growth and Share of Natural Increase in Selected States of India

| States | Urban Growth (%) | | | | Share of Natural Increase |
|---|---|---|---|---|---|
| | 1961-1971 | 1971-1981 | 1981-1991 | 1991-2001 | 1981-91 |
| **Relatively Rich States** | | | | | |
| *Industrial* | | | | | |
| Maharashtra | 40.8 | 40.0 | 38.7 | 34.5 | 57.0 |
| Gujarat | 41.0 | 41.4 | 33.6 | 33.4 | 69.9 |
| *Agricultural* | | | | | |
| Punjab | 25.3 | 44.5 | 29.1 | 37.4 | 81.5 |
| Haryana | 35.6 | 59.5 | 43.1 | 51.1 | 62.1 |
| **Relatively Poor States** | | | | | |
| Bihar | 43.9 | 54.8 | 30.4 | 29.0 | 85.5 |
| Rajasthan | 38.5 | 58.7 | 39.2 | 31.5 | 65.3 |
| Orissa | 66.3 | 68.5 | 36.1 | 29.9 | 60.7 |
| Uttar Pradesh+ Uttaranchal | 30.1 | 60.6 | 38.9 | 32.7 | 62.8 |

*Source* : Census of 1991 and www.censusindia.net

boundaries of towns also tend to influence the urban growth. However, sometimes it could be of small magnitude. As it is mentioned, the natural increase reflects the role of demographic momentum, on the other hand migration is sensitive to economic growth. Table 8.4 presents natural increase per thousand population at all India level for the years 1971 to 1999. Although the rural and urban difference in birth rate has remained significantly large in the early years of 1970s which narrowed down in the later 80s, the difference in natural increase between rural and urban areas was not significantly large and remains

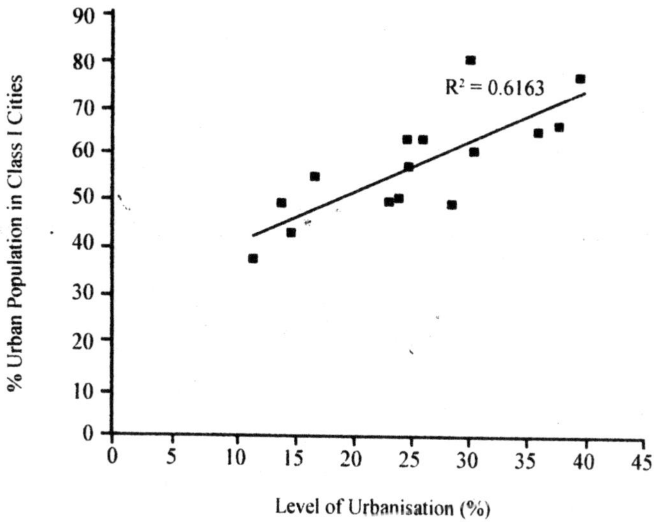


**Fig. 8.2 :** Level of Urbanisation and Concentration of Population in Class I Cities, 1991

almost constant both in 1970s and 1980s. This is due to the fact that level of decline in death rate in both rural and urban areas were not uniform. The urban areas have advantages than the rural areas. The average natural increase was 19.99 per thousand during 1971-1980 for rural areas compared to 19.27 in the urban areas. The natural increase has increased during 1981-90 in the rural areas and remained constant in the urban areas during the same period. This shows that natural increase is not responsible for the slowing down of India's urbanization during 1980s. As a result, the share of natural increase in the decadal growth has increased and the share of migration has declined substantially (see Table 8.5 and 8.6). In the decade of 1990s, the natural increase in urban areas has declined substantially from the level of 19.49 during 1980s to 15.75. This has led to further slowing down of India's urbanization during the 1990s.

As it has been noted that urban growth at all India level has declined during the last decade, this trend is also visible for most of the states of India for the period 1981-1991. Further, it has declined both in better off as well as poorer states. The poorer states like Bihar, Orissa,

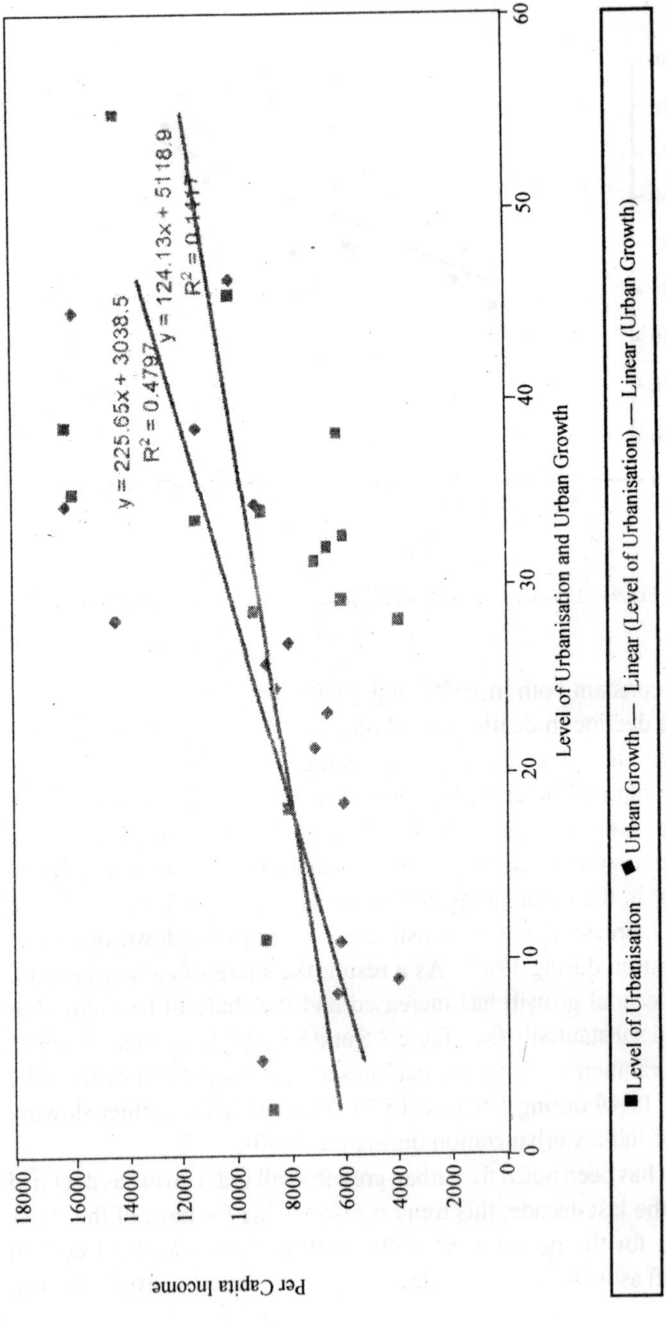


**Fig. 8.3 :** Level and Growth of Urbanisation, 2001

Uttar Pradesh and Rajasthan have shown very high growth rate during 1971-81 (55 per cent and above) which declined to below 40 per cent in these states. It has also declined in better off states like Maharashtra and Gujarat which are industrially advanced and agriculturally developed states like Punjab and Haryana also have registered decline in urban growth during 1981-91. The natural share of increase is very high in the urban growth in relatively poor as well as relatively rich states of India. This clearly shows that the urbanisation in India in recent times is predominantly led by demographic momentum. On the other hand, the role of economic momentum in terms of pull factors are largely restricted to the large cities only wherein the new entrants are finding increasingly difficult to find a foothold due to over increasing size of informal sector and growth nativism.

## EVIDENCES OF DECLINING TREND OF MIGRATION

There are several ways to examine the contribution of migration to the urban areas depending upon the availability of data. One of the ways could be to examine the share of net decadal migration to urban areas to urban growth, but the census data have some limitations in estimating the net decadal migration to urban areas directly from *Migration Tables* as separate information in the wake of change in the area and population due to extension of municipal boundaries during the inter-censal period is not available either for the total or for the migrant population. Secondly, the migration data for new and declassified towns are not available separately and this could introduce error in estimating the contribution of migration in the share of urban growth over a period of time. It is found that shares of migration estimated directly from Migration Tables underestimates the contribution of migration grossly. For example, Premi (1991) estimated 33.6 per cent contribution of net rural to urban migration along with increase due to changes in municipal boundaries compared to 39.4 per cent estimated by Jain (Census of India, 1991) and 36.1 per cent by Pathak and Mehta (1995) for the year 1971-81 using the residual method. Table 8.5 presents share of migration in urban growth along with natural increase and reclassification of towns for the census year 1971 to 1991 based on residual method.

It may be seen that the share of migration along with changes in municipal boundaries was around one-third of the urban growth during 1971-81 which had declined to about one-fifth during 1981-91. The share of new towns adjusted for declassified towns was estimated to be around 19 per cent during 1971-81 compared to nearly 18 per cent during 1981-91. The estimates clearly show that migration to urban areas had drastically declined during the 1980s. This is also reflected in the share of migrants in the total urban population as well as the share of decadal migrants to total migrants at the all India level as well as for the different states of India.

Table 8.8 shows that the percentage of migrants to total urban population as well as decadal (0-9 years) to total urban migrants for the census year 1981 and 1991. It may be seen that share of migrants to total urban population was nearly 39 per cent in 1981 which declined to 32 per cent in 1991. Similarly, the share of decadal migrants to total urban migrants declined from 49 per cent in 1981 to 42 per cent in 1991. The decline was observed for males as well as females separately. This shows the increasing nativity in the urban areas confirming the increasing role of natural increase in India's urbanization. The increasing nativity was observed for most of the states of India except Gujarat, Kerala and Himachal Pradesh where the percentage of migrants to total urban population remained static between the 1981 and 1991 censuses. The increasing nativity was more pronounced in the states of Maharashtra, Orissa, Tamil Nadu, Uttar Pradesh and West Bengal. The decline in the share of migrant population to total urban population was highest in Maharashtra where the share had declined to 34 per cent in 1991 compared to 48 per cent in 1981 followed by West Bengal and Orissa where decline was nearly 10 percentage points between the censuses 1981 and 1991. The share of decadal migrants (0-9 years) had also declined sharply in most of the states of India indicating that the pace of migration has slowed down in the 1980s compared to 1970s (Table 8.9). The share of inter-censal rural to urban migrants (0-9 Years) in the total rural to urban migration was around 50 per cent for males and 44 per cent for females in 1981 which declined to 44 and 40 per cent respectively in 1991. The decline in the recent rural to urban migration was very sharp for males and females in Maharashtra where decline was more than 15 per cent for both the sexes between the censuses 1981 and 1991. In

**Table 8.8 :** India : Trend in Migration into the Urban Areas, 1981-1991

| State/Country | Percentage of Migrants to Total Urban Population* | | Percentage of Inter-censal Urban Migrants to Total Urban Migrants 1981 | | | Percentage of Inter-censal Urban Migrants to Toal Urban Migrants 1991 | | |
|---|---|---|---|---|---|---|---|---|
| | 1981 | 1991 | M | F | Total | M | F | Total |
| India | 38.8 | 32.2 | 48.7 | 45.2 | 46.9 | 43.1 | 40.2 | 41.6 |
| Andhra Pradesh | 38.6 | 34.5 | 57.3 | 54.1 | 54.9 | 49.3 | 46.0 | 47.5 |
| Assam | — | 38.6 | — | — | — | 44.1 | 42.2 | 43.2 |
| Bihar | 38.5 | 31.8 | 53.1 | 42.3 | 47.1 | 42.1 | 32.3 | 35.9 |
| Gujarat | 39.6 | 38.1 | 42.1 | 44.7 | 43.5 | 42.6 | 41.8 | 42.2 |
| J & K | — | — | — | — | — | — | — | — |
| Haryana | 46.8 | 43.6 | 51.5 | 46.7 | 48.9 | 46.3 | 42.0 | 43.9 |
| Himachal Pradesh | 58.8 | 58.9 | 63.6 | 57.4 | 60.8 | 58.1 | 50.9 | 54.6 |
| Karnataka | 37.9 | 32.8 | 52.6 | 47.1 | 49.7 | 48.6 | 44.7 | 46.6 |
| Kerala | 25.0 | 25.5 | 53.9 | 48.0 | 50.4 | 48.3 | 43.7 | 45.5 |
| Madhya Pradesh | 41.8 | 39.1 | 53.6 | 46.8 | 49.9 | 45.5 | 41.5 | 43.2 |
| Maharashtra | 48.3 | 33.8 | 44.3 | 44.4 | 44.3 | 40.3 | 41.0 | 40.7 |
| Orissa | 47.7 | 37.0 | 59.9 | 52.6 | 56.4 | 49.4 | 43.4 | 46.3 |
| Punjab | 42.6 | 40.1 | 42.4 | 53.3 | 41.7 | 41.0 | 38.9 | 39.8 |
| Rajasthan | 32.9 | 30.0 | 55.9 | 43.2 | 48.5 | 49.3 | 39.0 | 43.1 |
| Tamil Nadu | 35.8 | 28.2 | 51.9 | 49.9 | 50.8 | 40.9 | 40.8 | 40.8 |
| Uttar Pradesh | 28.8 | 22.3 | 49.9 | 36.4 | 41.6 | 44.1 | 35.5 | 38.6 |
| West Bengal | 39.4 | 28.5 | 31.3 | 33.4 | 32.3 | 28.3 | 32.1 | 30.3 |

*Source* : Census of India 1991 Floppy Diskette, D-2 Tables. * It includes international migration also.

Punjab, the female migration was much more affected in the 1980s compared with male migration. As such the share of inter-censal (0-9) female migrants to total rural to urban female migration has sharply declined from 51 per cent in 1981 to 41 per cent in 1991 whereas the figures for male was 50 per cent in 1981 compared to 46 per cent in 1991.

The unemployment data available from National Sample Survey show that unemployment was more in urban areas than rural areas

**Table 8.9 :** India : Trend in Inter-censal Rural to Urban Migration (0-9 Years) to Total Rural to Urban Migration, 1981-1991

| State/Country | 1981 | | 1991 | |
|---|---|---|---|---|
| | Male | Female | Male | Female |
| India | 49.7 | 44.3 | 44.2 | 40.1 |
| Andhra Pradesh | 56.4 | 50.9 | 49.0 | 44.8 |
| Bihar | 52.7 | 40.7 | 41.6 | 31.4 |
| Gujarat | 47.1 | 43.3 | 43.4 | 41.8 |
| Haryana | 61.5 | 51.0 | 50.7 | 43.5 |
| Himachal Pradesh | 64.4 | 55.0 | 59.6 | 45.5 |
| Kerala | 51.4 | 45.7 | 46.8 | 42.3 |
| Karnataka | 50.9 | 44.1 | 49.2 | 49.8 |
| Madhya Pradesh | 55.3 | 45.9 | 46.4 | 41.0 |
| Maharashtra | 59.0 | 58.8 | 40.0 | 40.6 |
| Orissa | 58.5 | 50.0 | 48.1 | 41.5 |
| Punjab | 49.8 | 50.7 | 46.4 | 40.6 |
| Rajasthan | 58.3 | 41.2 | 51.6 | 38.5 |
| Tamil Nadu | 48.7 | 46.2 | 40.1 | 39.3 |
| Uttar Pradesh | 51.0 | 37.8 | 45.1 | 34.9 |
| West Bengal | 34.4 | 38.7 | 32.2 | 34.9 |

*Source:* Census of India 1991 Floppy Diskette, D-2 Tables.

and also the unemployment had increased in urban areas during the period 1983 to 1987. There was not much variation in unemployment rates by size class of towns either by weekly or current daily status, but class I (one lakh and above) had shown lower unemployment rate based on usual status approach than other categories of town. On the other hand, some of the metro cities like Mumbai, Madras, Calcutta and Ahmedabad had shown higher unemployment rates compared to other metropolises (NSSO, 1993). The higher unemployment rate during the 1980s possibly have dampening impact on the rural to urban migration and consequently on the urban growth during the decade 1981-91 The more recent data on employment rates during the 1990s did not improve substantially, on the contrary casualisation and feminisation of work has also increased along with decline in regular jobs (Deshpande, 1998; Unni, 2001; Streetkerk, 2001). This shows that underemployment does have increased in the last decade. Further, the growth in employment (0-81 per cent per annum) remains to be far below than the growth of the labour force (1.75 per cent per annum) in the country (Sundaram, 2001). The official data on the growth of employment in organized sector shows that the average growth in employment was only 0.87 per cent per annum during 1991 to 1999 in spite of impressive growth in national income during the said period (over 6 per cent per annum). This has happened as economic growth being capital intensive is likely to generate lesser employment (Ministry of Finance, 2001).

The changes in the economic structure of India are also visible in the trend and regional pattern of urbanisation in the country. The urban growth has further slowed down albeit with decreasing pace during the 1990s at the all India levels. But several states like Punjab, Haryana and Tamil Nadu have picked up urban growth, whereas the eastern sectors of India continues to be sluggish show that the impact of new economic policy has selectively benefited the states. This would reinforce the spatial disorganization of urbanisation process and the dualistic structure of increasingly urbanised and increasingly ruralised space of India. The operation of push factors as evidenced during the 70s no longer seems to be effective because of lack of jobs in the formal sectors and the saturation in the informal sectors of urban areas.

Moreover, the cost of living in urban areas is rising phenomenally. The cost of living as measured in terms of retail price index has increased three times during the 1990s compared to 1980 (Ministry of Finance, 2001). The large metro cities which have a very dominating position in India's urbanisation stand as economic island where new entrants have to face greater difficulties in finding a foothold, let alone jobs. The natives of the big cities have advantages in preparing themselves in terms of opportunities for skill formation. In spite of that it is difficult for the cities even to accommodate is labour force on account of natural increase, let alone the migrants. The likely impact in future will be reduced migration to metropolitan cities.

The slowing down of migration to urban areas was due to rising parochialism in cornering jobs for the natives. In recent years, due to shrinkage of jobs and increasing unemployment among youth the concept of *sons of the soil* is very much appealing to the natives of even in states where such campaign were little invoked by the political parties in the past. In a recent study in Ahmedabad by Desai (1999) found that local people feel that 80 per cent of jobs should be reserved for *sons of the soil,* a feeling or attitude repulsing the migration to urban areas in the wake of growing urban crisis. Further political sentiments are whipped up against migrants in several states of India ruled by regional parties. Thus, India's future urbanization will continue to slow down as large population are likely to live in relatively poorer states of India. This has great social consequences also. The increasing spatial barrier in terms of lack of opportunities in the urban areas as well as political hostility will likely to block the social mobility of the poorer sections of society leading to a situation of fixed rural-urban boundary or a situation of neo-apartheid.

## The Future Urbanisation

India has launched the programmes of economic liberalisation since 1991. Some of the proponents of this strategy thought that of linking the country with the global economy would accelerate rural to urban migration and boost urban growth in 1990s and the following decade. The expectation was evidently based on the assumption that there will be a massive inflow of capital both from within and outside the country resulting in rapid development of infrastructure and industrial growth. This would likely to give impetus to the process of urbanisation in the country since much of the industrial growth and consequent growth in employment would be within or around the existing urban centres (Kundu, 1997). This enthusiasm was not correct as Census 2001 reveals that the declining trend in urban growth was not reversed. It seems that the benefits of liberalisation will accrue to only those who could acquire new skills commensurate with the demands of liberalisation. In view of sluggish growth in employment, it was difficult for the common man and the poor to benefit from the liberalisation. Further, unlikely to the expectation the domestic and foreign investments are coming only in selected sectors concentrated only few pockets of the country in and around metro cities. And the magnitude of foreign investment is very low in India compared to China. For example, in spite of several allurements only approximately $ 3.5 billion (1.8 per cent of total across countries) of the foreign direct investment (FDI) reached to India in 1998 compared to 43.8 billion $ (7 per cent) in China (World Bank, 2001). Moreover, such investments are not likely to benefit the urban centres of non-metropolitan nature, as return, will bc low compared with metro cities having high agglomeration economy. Therefore, the deceleration of urban growth will continue to be in future. On the other hand, critics of new development strategy who have pointed out that the opening of the economy will destabilise the agrarian economy, resulting in high unemployment and massive exodus from rural areas. This would lead to rapid growth of population in urban centres. This view was also proved to be incorrect as it was uphill task for the poor people to survive in a situation of rising cost of living and increasing difficulty to accommodate themselves in the bloated informal sector in view of the increasing casualisation and feminisation of work in the post-liberalisation period. This process has further strained the informal sector—a refuge for poor migrants from rural areas. Thus in view of sluggish growth in employment and increasing casualisation of work in the 1990s, and the persistence of the under currents of *sons of the soil* factor backed by regional-linguistic political parties in different states of India and also the hostility of urban elite, who perceive migrants as a threat to their job security and a burden on the existing social amenities, the pace of urbanization will continue to decelerate in future. On the contrary, the liberalisation as such by benefiting the people and urban centres selectively is likely to widen intra-urban and inter-regional inequality in the level of urbanisation in the country.

REFERENCES


Bhagat, R.B. (1992) "Components of Urban Growth in India with Reference to Haryana : Findings from Recent Censuses" *Nagarlok*, Vol. 25, No. 3 pp. 10-14.

Brockerhoff, M. (1999) "Urban Growth in Developing Countries : A Review of Projections and Predictions", *Population and Development Review*, Vol 25, No. 4, pp. 757-778.

Brockerhoff, M. and Brennam, E. (1998) "The Poverty of Cities in Developing Regions ", *Population and Development Review*, Vol. 24, No. 1, pp. 75-114.

Census of India (1991) "Emerging Trends of Urbanisation in India", Occasional Paper No.1 of 1993, Registrar General, New Delhi.

Desai, A. (1999) "Cultural Integration in Ahmedabad City", *Geographical Review of India*, No. 4, pp. 352-360.

Deshpande, S. and Deshpande, L. (1998) "Impact of Liberalisation of Labour Market in India : What Do Facts from NSSO's 50th Round Show " *Economic and Political Weekly*, Vol. 33, No. 22, pp. L21-L31.

Dube, S. C. (1990) *Indian Society*, National Book Trust, New Delhi.

Jeffers, M. (1939) "The Law of the Primate", *Geographical Review*, 29, pp. 226-232.

Kelley, A.C. and William, J.G. (1984a) "Population Growth, Industrial Revolution, and the Urban Transition", *Population and Development Review*, Vol. 10, No. 3, pp. 419-441.

Kelley, A.C. and William, J.G. (1984b) *What Drives Third World City Growth ? A Dynamic General Equilibrium Approach*, Princeton University Press, Princetion.

Kidwai, A. H. (1991) "Urban Atrophy in Colonial India : Some Demographic Indicators" in I. Banga (ed.) *The City in Indian History : Urban Demography, Society and Politics*, Manohar Publication, New Delhi.

Kundu, A. (1980) *Measurement of Urban Processes in Regionalisation*, Popular Prakashan, Bombay.

Kundu, A. (1993) *In the Name of the Urban Poor : Access to Basic Amenities*, Sage, Delhi.

Kundu, A. (1997) "Trends and Structure of Employment in the 1990s : Implication for Urban Growth", *Economic and Political Weekly*, 32 (4) : 1399-1405.

Kundu, A. (2000) "Globalising Gujarat : Urbanisation, Employment and Poverty" *Economic and Political Weekly*, August 26–Sept. 2, pp. 3172-3182.

Krishan, G. (1993) "The Slowing Down of Indian Urbanisation", *Geography* 78(1) : 80-84.

Malhotra, R. (1997) "Incidence of Poverty in India : Towards a Consensus on Estimating the Poor" *Indian Journal of Labour Economics*, Vol. 40, pp. 67-102.

Mathur, D.P. (1994) "The State of India's Urban Poverty", *Asian Development Review*, Vol. 12, pp. 32-76.

Ministry of Finance, Government of India (2001) *Economic Survey*, 2000-2001, Government of India, New Delhi.

Mohanty, B. (1997) "Impact of Economic Reforms on Weaker Sections of India", *Political Economy of India*, 1997, pp. 142-144.

Mohan, R. (1996) "Urbanisation in India : Patterns and Emerging Policy Issues", in Josef Gugler (ed.) *The Urban Transformation of the Developing World*, Oxford University Press, Oxford, pp. 93-131.

National Commission on Urbanisation (1988) *Report of the National Commission on Urbanisation,* Vol. II, August, Ministry of Urban Affairs, Government of India.

NSSO (1993) *Sarvekshna,* 57th Issue, Vol. 17, No. 2, Ministry of Planning, Government of Inida.

Pathak. P. and Mehta, D. (1995) "Recent Trends in Urbanisation and Rural-Urban Migration in India: Some Explanations and Projections", *Urban India,* Vol. 15, No. 1, pp. 1-17.

Premi, M.K. (1991) "India's Urban Scene and its Future Implication" *Demography* India, Vol. 20, No.1. pp. 41-52.

Preston, S.H. (1979) "Urban Growth in Developing Countries : A Demographic Reappraisal", *Population and Development Review,* Vol. 5, No. 2, pp. 195-215.

Streetkerk, H. (2001) "Thirty Years of Industrial Labour in South Gujarat : Trends and Significance" *Economic and Political Weekly,* Vol. 36, No. 26, pp. 2394-2398.

Sundaram, K. (2001) "Employment-Unemployment Situation in the Nineties" *Economic and Political Weekly,* March 17, 2001, pp. 931-940.

United Nations (1993) *World Urbanisation Prospects :* The 1992 Revision, UN, New York.

United Nations (2000) *World Urbanisation Prospects :* The 1999 Revision, UN, New York.

Unni, J. (2001) "Gender and Informality in Labour Market in South Asia" *Economic and Political Weekly,* Vol. 36, No. 26, pp. 2360-2377.

World Bank (2001) *World Development Report 2000/2001 : Attacking Poverty* (Published for the World Bank), Oxford University Press, Oxford.

# 9

# Integral Vision of Metro Systems in Indian Mega Cities

**UDIT RATNA**

## INTRODUCTION

The transport system is considered as important input in the process of development of a nation. In the wake of urban population explosion especially in Indian metropolitan cities, the need of Mass Rapid Transit System (MRTS) as an efficient transport system to meet the demand of the commuters is increasingly being felt. At present, thirty-five metropolitan cities existing in India, have crossed 107.88 million population, where more than half of the total population spread in all the metropolitan cities is concentrated just in six million plus cities, namely Mumbai, Kolkata, Delhi, Chennai, Bangalore and Hyderabad.

The level of transport demand in million plus cities has exceeded the capacity of bus transport system and is on rising trend due to speedy urbanization and economic growth. The situation in Delhi is rather more deplorable owing to unmanageable traffic volume, inadequate supply of bus transport services and massive increase in number of personalized vehicles every passing year. The supporting infrastructures did not increase proportionately with the vehicular population to cope up the existing demands. Delhi's infrastructure is thus, under tremendous pressure, transport being one of the worst hit. The existing supply of bus transport services is not able to meet the requirements of the commuters as far as safety, reliability and quality of services are concerned. The circular rails play very insignificant role in catering to need of the commuters. In the given scenario, the commuters are forced to shift to personalized mode of transport mainly two-wheelers, cars and para-transit modes, which are highly uneconomic, unsafe and wasteful from limited road space points of view. Keeping in view the traffic and transport bottlenecks, the MRTS is the ultimate panacea in the present millennium.

This chapter addresses the accessibility aspect of commuters by metro rail. The existing scenario of urbanization and motorization in Indian mega cities in general has been discussed. The measures to improve the accessiblity in broad framework of Delhi MRTS have been suggested.

## URBANISATION AND MOTORISATION SCENARIO

### Growth of Population

The country has envisaged enormous population growth during the second half of twentieth century, having registered nearly three-fold increase of population from 361 million in 1951 to 1.03 billion in 2001[1]. The urban population of the country has gone up by four and half times from 62 million to 285 million (Table 9.1), and the population of six cities registered five times increase from 11.74 million to 59.99 million during the corresponding period.

**Table 9.1 :** Urbanisation Scenario in India

*(Population in million)*

| Year | Total Population | Urban Population | % of Urban Population |
|---|---|---|---|
| 1951 | 361.09 | 62.44 | 17.29 |
| 1961 | 439.23 | 78.94 | 17.57 |
| 1971 | 548.16 | 109.99 | 19.91 |
| 1981 | 685.18 | 159.00 | 23.31 |
| 1991 | 844.32 | 217.18 | 25.72 |
| 2001 | 1030.00 | 285.00 | 28.00 |

*Source* : Census of India, 1951-2001.

In contrast to this, Delhi has witnessed most dramatic rate of growth registering a nine-fold increase during the corresponding period mainly due to constant influx of population in search of employment and business from the surrounding area (Table 9.2). The number of million plus cities has grown from 5 in 1951 to 23 in 1991 and 35 in 2001 (Table 9.3). The statistics of growth of metropolitan cities indicates that nearly 60 per cent of urban population of all the metropolitan cities is concentrated in six metro cities.

**Table 9.2 :** Growth of Mega Cities and their Population

*(Population in Million)*

| S.No. | Name of Metro Cities | 2001 | 1991 | 1981 | 1971 | 1961 | 1951 |
|---|---|---|---|---|---|---|---|
| 1. | Mumbai | 16.36 | 12.56 | 8.23 | 5.97 | 4.15 | 2.97 |
| 2. | Kolkata | 13.21 | 10.86 | 9.19 | 7.72 | 5.98 | 4.67 |
| 3. | Delhi | 12.79 | 8.37 | 5.71 | 3.65 | 2.36 | 1.43 |
| 4. | Chennai | 6.42 | 5.36 | 4.28 | 3.17 | 1.95 | 1.54 |
| 5. | Bangalore | 5.68 | 4.11 | 2.91 | 1.65 | 1.20 | NMS |
| 6. | Hyderabad | 5.53 | 4.27 | 2.53 | 1.80 | 1.25 | 1.13 |
| Total | (6 Metro) | 59.99 | 45.53 | 32.85 | 23.96 | 16.89 | 11.74 |

*Source* : Compiled from different Census.

**Table 9.3 :** Growth of Number of Mega Cities and their Population

*(Population in Million)*

| | Year | 2001 | 1991 | 1981 | 1971 | 1961 | 1951 |
|---|---|---|---|---|---|---|---|
| Total | No. of Metros | 35 | 23 | 12 | 9 | 7 | 5 |
| | Population | 107.88 | 70.99 | 42.12 | 27.82 | 18 | 11.74 |

*Source* : Compiled from different Census.

## Growth of Vehicles

The six-mega cities accommodate 9.57 million vehicles (17.4%) of India. Delhi has the highest number of vehicles in the country with almost 10.0 per cent of the nation's vehicle with only 1.34 per cent of population. The ownership of vehicles in Delhi and Bangalore is as 30 vehicles per 100 persons, which is highest among the six metros (Table 9.4). The growth of vehicles was highest (73%) in Bangalore followed by Chennai (51%)during 1997-2001[2].

**Table 9.4 :** Vehicle Ownership in Mega Cities, 2001

*(Vehicles per 100 persons)*

| Mega City | Mumbai | Kolkata | Delhi | Chennai | Bangalore | Hyderabad |
|---|---|---|---|---|---|---|
| Total | 6 | 5* | 30 | 21 | 30 | 17** |

*Source* : Motor Transport Statistics of India, 2000-2001

* Relates to 1998.

** Relates to 1999.

Table 9.5 shows the car ownership in different mega cities. Delhi has recorded the highest car ownership as 72 cars per 1000 persons followed by Bangalore 41 and Chennai 36 cars.

**Table 9.5 :** Car Ownership in Mega Cities, 2001

*(Cars per 1000 persons)*

| Mega City | Mumbai | Kolkata | Delhi | Chennai | Bangalore | Hyderabad |
|---|---|---|---|---|---|---|
| Car | 20 | 18 | 72 | 36 | 41 | 14 |

*Source* : Motor Transport Statistics of India, 2000-2001.

The share of two wheelers (motor-cycle, scooter, mopeds) in respect of Delhi is again at the top (38%) followed by Bangalore (20%) and Chennai (16%) of the total vehicles. Bangalore has 22 scooters per 100 persons followed by Delhi and Chennai with 18 and 16 scooters per 100 persons respectively (Table 9.6). The increasing number of scooters has serious implication in determining the accidents and emission of air pollution, etc.

**Table 9.6 :** Scooters Ownership in Mega Cities, 2001

*(Scooters per 100 persons)*

| Mega City | Mumbai | Kolkata | Delhi | Chennai | Bangalore | Hyderabad |
|---|---|---|---|---|---|---|
| Scooter | 3 | 2 | 18 | 16 | 22 | 14 |

*Source* : Motor Transport Statistics of India, 2000-2001.

## Road Density

The country as a whole has got 3.3 million km of total roads, of which national highways (NH) constitute only 58112 km account for 1.76

per cent and manage about 40 per cent of the total road traffic. The dismal picture of road connectivity in India received a major boost with introduction of National Highway Development Project (NHDP), which envisages 4/6 laning of existing high density highway corridors linking four mega cities and twelve port cities in the country with overall length of 14,162 km at a cost of Rs. 580 billion including Golden Quadrilateral portion of 5,846 km having cost of Rs. 240 billion[3]. The land under transport use and length of roads has not gone up to the desired level in different mega cities. Major road networks and PCUs per km are shown in Table 9.7. It is observed that large number of arteries and sub-arteries have less than 30 ROW, without segregation of lanes. The Delhi road is most congested having as much as 1450 PCU, per km[4].

**Table 9.7 :** Road Length in Mega Cities

*(Cars per 1000 persons)*

| Mega City | Mumbai | Kolkata | Delhi | Chennai | Bangalore | Hyderabad |
|---|---|---|---|---|---|---|
| Road length per 100 sq km | 121.10 | 62.20 | 107.55 | 141.89 | 93.82 | 59.52 |
| PCU per km | 567 | 838 | 1450 | 616 | 553 | 806 |

*Source* : Comparative Transportation Profile: Mega Cities.

## Travel Demand

The size of urban travel demand is constantly increasing with the increase of urban areas. Approximately 89 per cent of Traffic volume is shared by intra-city trips and 11 per cent by inter-city trips. Most redeeming feature of travel scenario is that high percentage of traffic is carried by public transport modes like buses and trains. The commuters have taken significant turn towards personalized modes, which is not necessarily linked with income but is often linked with non-availability of dependable public transport choice. Largest percentage of trips is performed on account of work followed by education, social and other purposes. Due to unorganized transport system available in the cities, the average per capita time spent in travel is constantly increasing which takes away significant share from per capita income of commuters. The metro system will thus be able to save the time significantly.

The trip is uni-directional having a serious strain on public transport system. We have to be better cautious about Tri Nagar–Rithala Section of first phase of MRTS where Rohini, which is planned for one million population, is devoid of any major industrial centres/work centres. The proposal for shopping complex, district centre has not come on the ground. It is most likely that capacity of metro train remain unutilized especially Rithala bound trip in morning hour and Tri Nagar bound trip in evening hour.

### *Travel Supply*

In spite of the fact that India has one of the most extensive railway system (63,140 km) with 14000 trains per day, transporting 13 million, passengers per day and 1.3 million tonnes of freight per day, the passenger's movement in the cities barring Kolkata and Mumbai are mainly road based[5]. Kolkata is the only city to have largest completed metro, 70 km of tramways and 90 km of waterways. Mumbai too has sub-urban rail system to provide commuters' services. In Mumbai, Rail Vikas Corporation has been set up to execute metro rail project with 51:49 joint venture between Indian Railway and Maharashtra Government. World Bank has approved the loan of $ 542 million and the first phase is scheduled to be completed by December, 2007. In Delhi, the city bus transport system is the predominant mode of public transport. In current situation, Delhi Transport Corporation (DTC) has 3,166 fleets inclusive of 841 fleets for inter-state against the total authorized fleet of 5,000[6]. The DTC buses are able to carry 1.61 million trips daily. Most interestingly, out of 50 million passengers (May 2003) carried by DTC, 47 per cent are pass holders putting severe strain on the DTC budget. The employees have great dissatisfaction due to continuously increasing burden on DTC. Rest of travel demand is met by Stage Carriage Buses popularly known as Blue Line, which are normally overcrowded, ill behaviour of crew and the operators are least bothered about safety and comfort of passengers.

Many bus owners are reluctant to go with Compressed Natural Gas (CNG) system in the buses, which is made mandatory following the directives of Supreme Court; thereby reducing the number of buses considerably. With, whatever the number, the services provided by these buses are highly dissatisfactory and unreliable. And in present set up the demand (public) and supply (services) has yawning gap.

The contract carriage buses do provide services to school children and office goers especially upper middle class.

## Previous Efforts in Making MRTS

India has very poor track in putting the efforts in making MRTS, except few like Mumbai, which introduced sub-urban system when its population was less than a million, and Kolkata in 1960s. In Delhi we missed the train and now the trains are missing us. The delayed decision in conceiving the implementation and slackness in completing the projects on time has resulted in cost over-run on one hand and tremendous increase in magnitude of problems on the other hand. In Delhi, the first MRTS related project was conceived in 1957 by TCPO (Box 9.1), since then dozens of studies were conducted, but the project

**Box 9.1** : Details of MRTS Related Study

| | Study | Agency | Year |
|---|---|---|---|
| 1. | Origin Destination Suvery for Delhi | TCPO | 1957 |
| 2. | Traffic and Transportation Proposal for Master Plan for Delhi | DDA | 1962 |
| 3. | Bhagawan Sahay Committee Report, | Govt. of India | 1963 |
| 4. | Interim Report on Traffic and Transportation | Planning Commission | 1967 |
| 5. | Report on the Working Group on Metropolitan, Transport Services | Planning Commission | 1970 |
| 6. | Comprehensive Traffic Transportation Planning, Greater Delhi | CRRI | 1971 |
| 7. | Reports on MRTS | TCPO | 1973 |
| 8. | Rapid Transit Corridors for Delhi | Planning Commission | 1974 |
| 9. | Land use Traffic and Studies-Concept Plan MRTS Network and Traffic | TCPO | 1974 |
| 10. | Delhi Urban Territory, Conceptual MRT Network-2001 | TCPO | 1974 |
| 11. | Transport Development Progamme for Delhi | Planning Commission | 1975 |
| 12. | Report on MRTS/Delhi (Network and priorities) | MTPR | 1975 |
| 13. | MRTS/Delhi-Project report on Sub-Urban Area | MTPR | 1975 |
| 14. | MRTS/Delhi-Report on Connaught Place, Rajouri Garden, UG Corridor | MTPR | 1975 |
| 15. | Rapid Transit System for Delhi | CRRI | 1975 |

*(Contd.)*

| | | |
|---|---|---|
| 16. MRTS Delhi Feasibility Report for Sahibabad Tuglakabad Surface Corridor | MTPR | 1975 |
| 17. Project Report-Sub-Urban Services for Delhi Area | MTPR | 1975 |
| 18. Report of Working Group on Public Mass Transport System for Delhi | WG (W&H) | 1977 |
| 19. Urban Railways with regard to Delhi | DDA | 1983 |
| 20. Running of EMU, Rail Services in Delhi area (Dalvi Committee) | Planning Commission | 1983 |
| 21. Mass Trasport Rapid System for Delhi by IBCOL, GMBH, West Germany | Govt. of Delhi | 1985 |
| 22. Master Plan for Delhi-2001 | DDA | 1990 |
| 23. IMMRTS for Delhi | RITES | 1995 |
| 24. Improvement of Transport Facilities in Delhi Metropolitan Area | RITES | 1991 |
| 25. Integrated Study of MRTS for Delhi | Northern Railway | 1994 |
| 26. Utilization of Ring Railway in Delhi for Running of EMU Trains | Planning Commission | 1994 |
| 27. Delhi High Speed Tram Project | Govt. of Delhi | 1995 |
| 28. Intra-Urban Train Services in Delhi | RITES | 1997 |

could arrive only at the end of previous century. High capital cost was the major deterrent in introduction of MRTS. Besides the resource limitation, Railway Act 1899, which empowers the railway to take up any inter-city and intra-city transportation project, was equally major hurdle. In the mean time estimated cost and transport problems increased manifold.

Similarly, the concept and plans to provide rapid transit systems was conceived in 1960s in Kolkata, but the project started only in 1970s, which took 22 years to complete. Ever since start of Kolkata Metro, it is still reeling under financial impact of the project. Now, Kolkata's endowment of mass transit option stretches from underground metro to muscle powered cycle rickshaw.

The approach to adopt MRTS in Chennai can be traced back to Metropolitan Transport Team of Planning Commission, which was constituted in 1968. The Metropolitan Transport Project Railways (MTPR) was set up in 1971 to assess the travel demand and to recommend a suitable Rapid Transit System (RTS) in Chennai. Inordinate delays were due to financial, legal, political and institutional constraints, which led to move the project in an elusive manner. With a result, the initial capital cost which was worked out to Rs. 436.5 million in 1983 rose to Rs. 2600 million in 1997 [7]. The project includes Phase I from Chennai Beach to Tirumalai (8.97 km) with estimated cost of Rs. 2600 million and Phase II from Tirumalai to Velacheri (10.8 km) with estimated cost of 7,330 million, which is to be borne by Railways and Government of Tamil Nadu in the ratio of 33 : 67. The potential use of the project after completion is likely to be underutilized as the project instead of passing from highly dense area; it passes through canal where there is no scope for development in eastern side.

Similarly, the Government of Karnataka commissioned several studies to find an acceptable solution to meet the travel needs, besides the first study conducted by CRRI (1963). This was followed by constitution of study group in 1982 to suggest the improvement of the transport system. The government was almost agreed to construct ring roads, great separators, improvement of bus system and construction of MRTS in 1993. But later in 1994, M/s. Infrastructure Leasing and Financial Services (IL&FS) in its study concluded that railways had no plan for running sub-urban services or for building circular railways. The MRT as recommended was not financially viable. Hence, a fresh proposal of ELRTS covering a route of 90 km over 6 lines as an integrated network to be built in 4 phases between 1997 to 2006 was recommended with a project cost of Rs. 42,000 million (at 1994 prices) inclusive of interest during construction and inflation. This includes (i) Yesvantpur to Kanakapura—24.14 km, (ii) Krishna Rajendra Circle to HAL Airport and beyond–15.16 km, (iii) Yesvantpur to Mayo Hall—10.50 km, (iv) Jayanagar to Mayo Hall—9.40 km, (v) Chord Road to Kanakapura Road—14.75 km and (vi) Ulsoor to Mekhri—15.70 km[8].

Hyderabad followed the LRTS, based on recommendation of the South Central Railway, which provided new rail services and rail links (1978) between the city and industrial centre in Hyderabad Urban Area (HUA)[9]. The RITES in association with SOFREV (1994), a French consultant proposed the introduction of LRTS, phase I from Balanagar to Kheratebad (16 km) with project cost of Rs. 7,070 million having 19 stations and Phase II from Afsalganj to new bus station, Malakpet and Dilsukhnagar (6 km), with project cost of Rs. 2,650 million having 7 stations. The project floated on BOOT basis. The

Hyderabad Light Railway Transit Corporation (HLRTC) is responsible for supervising the construction.

## DELHI'S CASE OF METRO SYSTEM

(a) Delhi, the capital city of India adopted rail-based transit system to meet the traffic demand up to the horizon year 2021. The metro network inclusive of underground, elevated and surface corridors will stretch to the length of 245 km in full system (Table 9.8, Table 9.9) shows the details of first phase of MRTS, which covers three lines spanning 61.8 km, with completed cost of Rs. 105.7 billion (at 2005 price level). The project, implemented by Delhi Metro Rail Corporation (DMRC) will be completed by 2005, when about 2.2 million commuters are expected to use the system[10].

**Table 9.8 :** Details of Full System of MRTS

| | UG | Elevated | At Grade | Total |
|---|---|---|---|---|
| Phase I | 12.21 | 44.62 | 5.42 | 62.16 |
| Phase II | 8.7 | 39.4 | 3.6 | 51.7 |
| Phase III | 6.4 | 53.0 | 2.8 | 62.2 |
| Phase IV | — | 67.7 | 1.1 | 68.8 |
| Total | 27.22 | 204.72 | 12.92 | 244.86 |

(b) The eco-friendly MRTS project will be facilitated with latest technical know-how available in metro systems worldwide, which will result in time saving for commuters, reliable and safer journeys, reduction in atmospheric pollution, reduction in accident rates, reduced fuel consumption, reduced vehicle operating costs and increase in the average speed of road vehicles[11]. The strategies to restore the traffic services (diversion, by-pass, traffic control, etc.), utility services (water supply line, sewer line, electricity cables, telephone lines, gas pipe and petrol pipe, etc.), and rehabilitating the affected people and religious structure, monument/place of historical importance during the construction period has been adopted to ensure minimum inconvenience to the public.

(c) *Financing:* The 64 per cent of project cost will be met by Japan Bank for International Cooperation (JBIC), Japan, 28 per cent by Equity Contributions subscribed equally by the Central Government and the State Government, 5 per cent interest-free subordinate loan to cover the cost of land acquisition by Central and State Governments and balance 3 per cent will be met by raising money through property development. JBIC has committed funds for phase II as well.

**Table 9.9 :** Details of First Phase of MRTS

*(length in km)*

| Section | Length | Under-ground | Elevated | At Grade | Stations |
|---|---|---|---|---|---|
| **Line No. 1** Shahdara–Barwala | 28.0 | Nil | 17.5 | 10.5 | 21 |
| **Line No. 2** Vishwa Vidyalay-Central Secretariat | 11.0 | 11.0 | Nil | Nil | 10 |
| **Line No. 3** Connaught Place-Dwarka | 22.8 | 1.1 | 21.7 | Nil | 22 |
| **Total** | 61.8 | 12.1 | 39.2 | 10.5 | 53 |

## PROGRESS AND ACHIEVEMENT

### Shahadara-Barwala Section

In a landmark development, two stretches namely Shahdara–Tis Hazari with 8.3 km length having 6 stations and Tis Hazari-Tri Nagar Section-4.5 km with 4 stations have started operating even before completion of the project (Fig 9.1). The civil works of Trinagar–Rithala Section is almost completed. Metro corridor will have ultimate carrying capacity of 60,000 commuters phpd. Interchange of commuters between Metro corridor and Rail corridor will be at ISBT station.

### Vishwa Vidyalaya-Central Secretariat

The most difficult task of underground section has been started. The utilities services identified are diverted and tunnel construction from Patel Chock end has been completed. Details are given at Phase II in Table 9.10. With completion of this system the number of buses may be reduced to the extent of 2600 along with increase of average speed

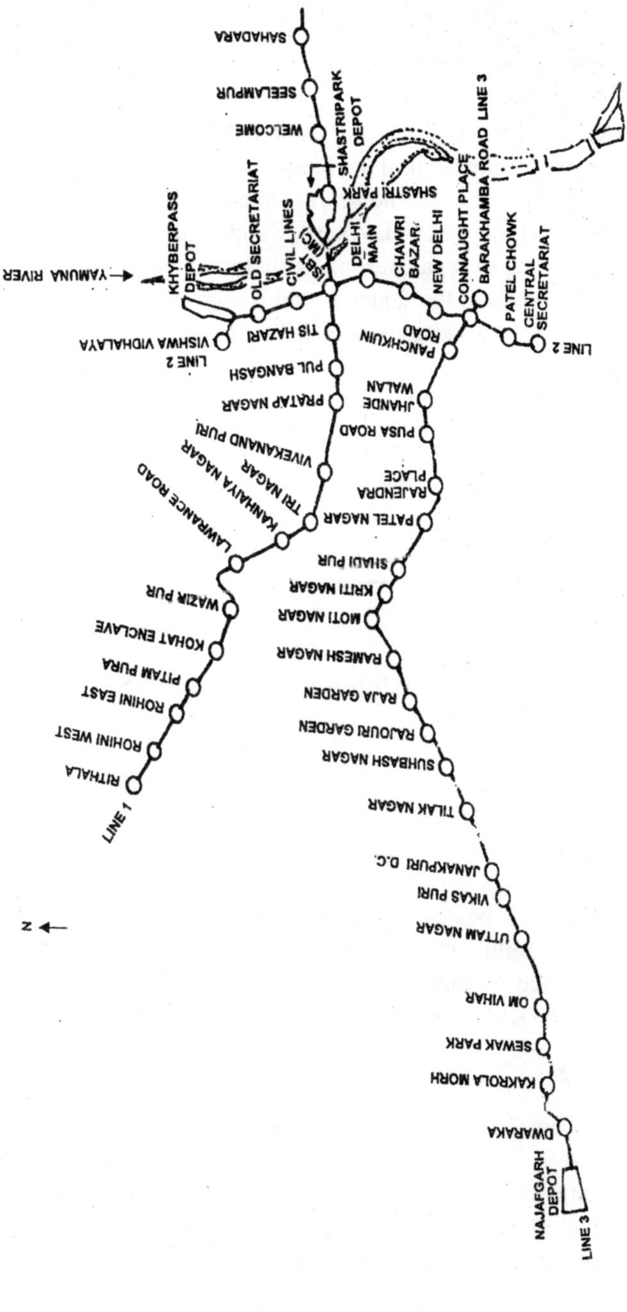


**Fig : 9.1:** Delhi MRTS—Phase I

of buses from 10.5 km/hr to 14.0 km/hr, saving of fuel and reduction in journey time.

The design for signalling and train control, power supply and electric traction, automatic fare collection systems etc., is likely to be completed soon. The underground section of the metro project between Delhi University and Central Secretariat in a length of 11 km with 10 stations will pass through the heart of the city carrying 0.45 million passengers everyday. M/s. Dyckerhof and Widmann AG, Germany and M/s. Kumagi (Japan) along with Indian partners have been assigned to complete the underground works. A maintenance depot for the underground metro corridor will be located in the Khyber Pass area.

**Table 9.10 :** Details of Phase II

*(length in km)*

| | | |
|---|---|---|
| (i) | Vishwa Vidyalaya-New Azadpur-S.G. Transport Nagar | 8.6 |
| (ii) | Central Secretariat-Vasant Kunj | 18.2 |
| (iii) | Barakhamaba Road-Indraprastha-NOIDA | 15.3 |
| | Total | 42.1 |

## MAJOR ISSUES AND STRATEGIES

### (i) Pollution

The contribution of motor vehicles on total pollution in Delhi has increased from 23 per cent in 1970-71 to 64 per cent in 2000-01. Among the major sources of pollution in Delhi, motor vehicles accounts for 64 per cent followed by power plants 16 per cent, industries 12 per cent and domestic 8 per cent. Of the total vehicular pollution, two wheelers take the highest share (77.7 %) followed by cars 11.5 per cent. The CNG operated buses in Delhi have shown good sign of decrease in pollution level.

### (ii) Parking

About one-fourth of valuable road space in our cities is being taken away by parked vehicles. The rapid urbanization, acute concentration of white-collar jobs, improved income and rise in the level of ownership of private vehicles in the city has given rise to enormous parking demand. The major challenges being faced are due to absence of sound parking policy and enforcement of parking tools for environmental improvement. Most of the parking provisions have been made on off-street surface parking lot and they are so located that it can be more economical for the purposes other than the parking. Development of parking space is not very spectacular and on-street parking is more noticeable on the road of right way. Collection of parking charges for off-street parking is more of *ad-hoc* nature. There is no metered parking. This needs to be more seriously addressed and dealt by the city authority.

In the existing scenario of MRT, the concept of 'park-n-ride' needs to be adopted with integration to metro rail to help reduce the number of private vehicles on the urban roads. Rationalization of parking charges may improve the parking turnover rates as well as higher mobilization of resources for upgradation of parking infrastructure. The Parking Information system also needs to adopt for easy accessibility. The community parking will have to be encouraged which is practiced in United States where people park their vehicles and walk about 200-300 metres. to reach their homes.

### (iii) Accident

The fatal accidents are increased due to speeding of vehicles, poor enforcement of traffic rules, poor road geometrics, prevailing transportation system, traffic behaviour, driving habits and increasing number of vehicles on roads. We have designed and specification for almost every thing, but what about footpaths? People find no good footpaths so walk on the road. Nearly 60 per cent of deaths on roads are that of pedestrians and cyclists irrespective of any causative factor.

### (iv) Commuter Rail Services

The study on commuter travel in NCR and Delhi by Northern Railway concluded that rail services are able to cater to only 20 per cent of the existing 2 million inter-city trips. The Intermediate Public Transport system (IPT) including mini buses, rural transport vehicles (RTV), Kids Care, and Phatphat is not able to provide comfortable services to the commuters. The auto rickshaws are most limited as they are hired for personalized transport. If corrective measures are not taken, it is likely that vehicle has to wait for multiple signal cycles to cross the intersection, thereby forming long queue. This will lead to severe energy crisis and time consumption giving enough room to pollution. In addition to MRT, commuter ring rail services should be more popularized, keeping in view the near saturated road traffic situation.

## STRENGTHENING MRTS SERVICES

### (a) Accessibility to Commuters

To facilitate the movement of commuters, it is needless to say that accessibility should be provided to large residential areas. Delhi has almost completed a year since the metro services have commissioned on one segment *i.e.,* Shahadara–Tis Hazari. The system, though it is early to have a word, is not able to use its full capacity, which is evident from Table 9.11.

**Table 9.11 :** Ridership in Shahadara-Tis Hazari Section

| Line 1 Shahadara-Tis Hazari | Speed km/hr. | Headway in minute | Ridership km/hr. |
|---|---|---|---|
| Designed | 80 | 3 | 60,000 |
| Operational | 30-40 | 10 | 20,000-30,000 |

*Source* : Based on observation.

With extension of this segment from Tis Hazari to Trinagar, the ridership has gone up to 40,000-50,000 passengers km/hr and speed has improved a bit.

Out of 41 stations in first phase, 10 stations are operational in line 1, including one interchange at ISBT. A total of 115 bus feeder services ranging in length from 1.7 km to 8.9 km have been proposed but unfortunately bus feeder services have not yet been strenthened to facilitate the commuters. Once these services are improved the commuters from Nand Nagri, Yamuna Vihar, Bhajanpura and Trans Yamuna area can be facilitated with metro stations located at Shahadara, Welcome and Seelampur. The train fare has not been integrated with the bus fare. Why a commuter living in Yamuna Vihar having work place at ITO would pay Rs. 5-7 to reach Shahadara by bus and from Shahadara to ISBT by Metro by paying Rs. 7 as a fare and again from ISBT to ITO by bus with fare of Rs. 5. Instead, he would prefer to travel by bus from Yamuna Vihar to end of the journey point just by paying Rs. 10. Other options are monthly DTC pass or route pass, which are consideration for small income group people. If a commuter requires to take two or more rides in order to reach the work place, it should be ensured that total fare paid for travel by MRTS is not more than alternative fare paid over travel by bus[12]. Most likely, if the fare is not integrated, the commuters will prefer to travel by bus rendering the metro semi/under utilized. Table 9.11 shows the world scenario where half a dozen metros are utilizing less than 50 per cent of its capacity; Delhi will be appended at the bottom of the list.

**(b) Pedestrian and Cyclist Facilities**

With the increase in trips of rapid transit system, the walking and cycling trip is also likely to be increased. These groups are most sensitive groups. Hence, require special treatment. The interchange at ISBT attract large number of pedestrians, incidentally there is no segregated path, which provides safety to this group. The metro station under construction at Madhuban Chowk (Rohini) will be most vulnerble which has combination of underpass costing to Rs. 230 million in a length of 550 metres on outer ring road constructed by Delhi Tourism Department with AFCONS Infrastrucre Ltd., as consultant and elevated metro rail system. With non-provision of any sub-way or segregated paths for pedestrians, the entire traffic bottleneck is going to be created. How to access the metro as a safe pedestrian is a big question. There is no evidence that operation of metro system on its own would result in reduction of accident, congestion and abatement of pollution. The equilibrium between special measures of traffic calming, speed reductions for public transport system part on one hand and providing better facilities for cyclists and pedestrians with actuated signalized intersections on the other hand, to be maintained.

### (c) Provision for Handicaps

Provision for accessibility is made within the metro, at the station along with parking facility for physically handicapped persons. But how to reach to parking place or metro station is challenging job for the disabled persons. A disabled person is confronted with series of problems right from the origin of his journey *i.e.* walking through the narrow street boarding the bus, travelling within the bus, and alighting from the bus and finally reaching to the destination.

**Table 9.12 :** Utilization Rate of Selected Metros

| City | Capacity | | Volume of Passenger/ Peak Hour | Utilization %age |
|---|---|---|---|---|
| | Train | Line | | |
| Berlin | 1182 | 47820 | 40000 | 85 |
| Caracas | 1668 | 66720 | 28700 | 43 |
| Hong Kong | 2250 | 90000 | 60000 | 67 |
| London | 814 | 32560 | 23000 | 71 |
| Montreal | 1440 | 57600 | 20000 | 35 |
| Nagoya City | 1508 | 60320 | 43697 | 72 |
| New York | 2200 | 88000 | 68000 | 77 |
| Osaka | 2750 | 110000 | 62696 | 57 |
| San Francisco | 800 | 32000 | 15086 | 47 |
| Santiago | 1000 | 40000 | 14925 | 36 |
| Toronto | 1800 | 72000 | 15166 | 49 |
| Washington D.C. | 1400 | 72000 | 31900 | 44 |

*Source:* [13].

Delhi MRTS would not solve all the problems associated with movement of disabled persons in the city. A conducive environment has to be created in the city beyond MRTS. Proper coordination is needed among DMRC, DSRC and Road Transport Authority in adopting the provisions for disabled persons at different transport system levels, keeping in view the access to "Total Environment"[14].

### (d) Integration of Different Transport Modes

The experience of CIDCO approach in developing a New Mumbai with initial population of about 2 million and employment of 0.7

million as a counter magnet to Mumbai is a classic example of covering different modes of transport *i.e.* Commuter Railway Sub-system, Bus Sub-system, Para Transit Sub-system, Private Transport Sub-system and Water Transport Sub-system. The large part of Delhi which is not served by metro, high capacity bus system can be run taking few lessons from Curitiba (Brazil) where planning the public transport system at a fraction of cost (5% to 10%) involved in metro system. CIDCO, which is responsible for planning, development, financing and management of all modes of transport virtually, enjoys the benefit of Unified Metropolitan Transport Authority (UMTA), though it is not enacted with legislation. The attempt should be taken to integrate metro rail, bus transport system especially the DTC and high capacity bus system, commuter ring rail and water transport (partially by Yamuna river and existing drain).

**Recommendations**

(i) The feeder bus services need to be strengthened giving adequate services to metro stations and interchanges in order to provide convenient and quick transfer of passengers from bus to rail and *vice-versa.* The feeder bus service to radial roads of outer/inner ring roads needs to be looked afresh.

(ii) All the commuters using the metro rail system will not have origin and destination within the affordable walking distance. Therefore, special care should be taken in facilitating the movement of most vulnerable group of our society *i.e.* children, old aged/ handicapped, pedestrians and cyclists, so as to offer convenient mobility between the two systems.

(iii) The logic to depend upon single technology of CNG for urban transport, which has massive demand supply deficit, need to have a relook. The fuel crisis and shortage experienced during Gulf War has raised serious doubt regarding continued dependency on petroleum fuel based transportation system. Therefore, mix of alternative fuels such as petrol, diesel, CNG, electricity, alcohol fuels and LPG as used in the US and European cities should be given as second thought besides actions to check engines, technology, availability of fuels, etc., in order to protect the public health.

(iv) Appropriate coordination among transport related agencies need to be strengthened. There is exigency to come out with legislation like Delhi Metropolitan Transport Authority (DMTA) for planning, management, implementation and monitoring of the urban transport projects.

(v) Indian cities have complex network of utilities spread throughout the cities, where planning authorities and utility providers are often clueless. The adoption of the GIS based technology and mapping of various underground utilities is required to be taken up urgently in the cities.

(vi) In a situation where traffic volume has increased so much and the transport is under tremendous pressure, it would seem necessary to decentralize the population of Metropolitan area and NCR and develop next order towns with all supporting infrastructure. There is also need to have multi-pronged efforts to strengthen the economic base of small and medium towns/ satellite towns with appropriate integration of land uses and transport to reduce the pressure on transport infrastructure of mega city.

(vii) The Transport System Management (TSM) including low cost traffic engineering measures such as removal of encroachment and stray cattle from the carriage way, improvement of traffic rotary and geometric designs, improvement of traffic control devices and Travel Demand Management (TDM) such as car pooling, peripheral parking scheme, parking restraints, road pricing etc., need to be adopted as short-term measures.

(viii) The public participation and planning, implementation and monitoring of the projects need to encouraged.

(ix) To enhance the implementation of energy efficient and environment friendly options of mass transit system for major metropolitan cities, a substantial amount of finance is required, which can be raised through combination of funding arrangements like Public-Private partnership, concession agreement BOT, BOOT, etc., foreign assistance and found from Urban Transport Development Bank of India as recommended by the Working Group on Urban Transport.

(x) The Intelligent Transport System (ITS) need to be encouraged in order to manage parking, bus transport, and interchanges, etc. in metropolitan cities.

## CONCLUSION

As planner and transport professional, we plan and build the cities for tomorrow. Our job becomes easy when we anticipate how our society's expectation will shift and take a new shape in the coming days. So, in this scenario, recent bringing of MRTS, though costly, is wise step in improving the movement of commuters in Indian cities, but most wisest approach is to have better coordination among metro rail, sub-urban rail and transport departments to make the system sustainable. Probably putting every thing under one umbrella like DMTA for timely effect is wisest step among all.

### NOTES

1. Census of India, 2001.
2. Government of India, Ministry of Road Transport & Highways, Motor Transport Statistics of India, 2001-02.
3. A.K. Lal, "Nation-Building Through NHDP", *Yojana*, Vol. 47, No. 10. Oct. 2003.
4. Government of India, TCPO. (1999), Report on "Comparative Transportation Profile: Mega Cities.
5. *Indian Infrastructure,* Vol. 6, No. 1, August 2003.
6. Delhi Transport Corporation, GNCT, Delhi, Operational Statistics, May 2003.
7. Government of India, TCPO (1996), Report of the Working Group on the Urban Transport.
8. Government of India, TCPO (1996), Report of the Working Group on the Urban Transport.
9. Subramanian, K.P. (1999), "Urban Railways", *MRTS in Chennai* : Lessons Learnt, Vol. 2, Issue II.
10. Government of NCT, Delhi, (1995)," Integrated Multi-Modal Mass Transport System for Delhi.
11. News Letter of DMRC, August 2003.
12. Ratna Udit (formerly Ram Ratan), (1999), "Civil Engineering & Construction Review", (1999), *Delhi MRTS : A Sustainable Transport Development in the Next Millennium,* Vol. 12, No. 6.
13. Amsler Yves, (1996), *"Greater Metropolis Development* & Transportation Policy", Proceedings of CODATU VII.
14. Ratna Udit, (1999), "Urban Railways", (1999), *Issues, Options and Challenges in Making MRTS"* Vol. II, Issue II.

# 10

# Technologies for Sustainable Urban Development

## A Study of the National Capital Region

S. MOHAN

## INTRODUCTION

India is considered to be a land of villages, and in most of the developmental literature the continuing growth of the cities in this country has been considered an undesirable feature. But India has always had a distinguished urban profile as well; as witnessed by the Mohonjodaro civilization, which was primarily urban. All through history, development has meant increasing urbanization, and today, most of the developed countries are 70–80 per cent urban, and only about 3–5 per cent of the labour force works in agriculture, though a significant number of people continue to stay in rural areas due to lifestyle preferences. In the growth of developing countries, there is no doubt that the thrust of the development pattern is towards greater urbanization. This is because urbanization has major positive features. The greater density of population facilitates human interactions, and this in turn leads to greater exchange of goods and services. The dense agglomerations reduce per capita costs for transport, infrastructure and most other essential services. In a densely populated but resource rich environment, economic activities can diversify into a network of mutually symbiotic activities, just like the activities of living organisms in a natural ecosystem, and as in an ecosystem, economic activity also require a dense network and large species diversification for stability. Due to these reasons, cities are a natural hub of economic activity, and even in countries considered predominantly rural, contribute a greater share to the national GNP both relatively and absolutely. In predominantly rural Asian countries, the contribution of urban areas to GDP ranges from 32 per cent in Bangladesh to 53 per cent in the Philippines.

But despite their positive contributions to human development, urban conglomerations also impose great costs on the ecosystem. By drawing on resources beyond their boundaries (and often using them inefficiently), they deplete the surrounding areas. The pollution and other loads that they impose fall beyond the natural capacity of ecosystems to handle. Traffic and other services become over-stretched. When such problems accumulate beyond a certain level, life in the city becomes unhealthy and stressful. Cities must find means of carrying out their functions while reducing the environmental and human stress burdens that they pose. A measure of the environmental load that a city poses is captured in the term "ecological footprint" which is the area that a city needs to use to generate the inputs that it needs. This usually exceeds the city area by a large margin: in the example of London, it is only marginally smaller than the land area of the whole of UK ! A typical city of one million people in the West daily uses 625,000 tonnes of water, 2,000 tonnes of food, 10,000 tonnes of fuel and generates about 1,100 tonnes of human waste, 500,000 tonnes of waste water, 1000 tonnes of air pollutants and 1,000 tonnes of other solid wastes. The amounts of inputs and wastes may be somewhat smaller in the Indian cities, especially of water, but nevertheless they also need substantial inputs and generate large amounts of wastes.

As can be expected, provision of the inputs and disposal of the wastes generate environmental problems, which are not shared evenly, but are more heavily borne by the poor. Lower income groups are more likely to be situated near polluting industries or near waste dumps or polluted waterways etc. and have problems disposing of their waste, especially human waste. This leads to significant health problems. Though technology can make a contribution to the solution of these problems, but usually it is neither lack of technology or lack of money that prevents solutions from being developed, but lack of legal titles and other institutional support. As cities develop, that is, as they become more economically productive and sophisticated, some environmental problems diminish, but others become more important. At low income levels, the issues are that of dense squatter settlements, access to sanitation, disposal of wastes, provision of safe drinking water and other health related issues. As income levels increase, these give way to pollution from manufacturing industry, traffic congestion etc. At still higher levels of income, the issues may be concerned about general quality of living. But typically, in a developing country context, all three types of problems occur simultaneously, due to widespread income disparity. As incomes increase, people devote more money to solving their environmental problems, but usually all that occurs is a problem shift. For instance, installing sewer lines improves the sanitation in project area, but at the cost of greatly increasing water needs, increasing pollution of waterways, and incurring of infrastructural costs. Sustainable development requires that all three sets of problems be addressed simultaneously and comprehensively.

## THE NATIONAL CAPITAL REGION

Since cities require land much beyond their boundaries, it makes sense, while planning the environmental development of cities, to carry out city planning in conjunction with the planning of a large adjoining area. This is the concept of the metropolitan developmental region, which is essential for planning the sustainable development of any large city. Delhi is fortunate in having established a National Capital Region (NCR) around itself as far back as 1985; some developmental efforts have also begun. It now remains to integrate them into a sustainable pattern. Some of the essential features of the NCR are presented below (NCR PB 1996).

The NCR covers an area of 30,242 sq. km centered around the NCT of Delhi and comprising parts of the states of Haryana, Rajasthan and Uttar Pradesh. The constituents of the NCR are :

1. The NCT of Delhi (1,483 sq. km)
2. The Haryana subregion, comprising the districts of Faridabad, Gurgaon, Sonepat and Rohtak, the Rewari and Bawal Tehsils of Mahendragarh District, and the Panipat Tehsil of the Karnal district (13,413 sq. km)
3. The Rajasthan Subregion, comprising the six tehsils of the Alwar district, namely Alwar, Ramgarh, Behror, Mandfawar, Kishangarh, and Tijara (4,493 sq. km)
4. The Uttar Pradesh subregion, comprising the districts of Meerut, Ghaziabad and Bulundshahar (10,853 sq. km).

The Delhi NCT with an area of 1,483 sq. km is composed of 6 towns and 231 rural settlements or villages. The contiguous towns of Ghaziabad, Loni, and NOIDA in Uttar Pradesh, and the Faridabad-Ballabgarh complex, Gurgaon, Kundli in Haryana and the extension of the Delhi ridge falling outside the Delhi UT, Gurgaon or Faridabad are considered part of the Delhi Metropolitan area. Together they cover about 1,696 sq. km and are being extensively developed. The rest of the NCR comprising of an area of 27,063 sq. km is predominantly rural in character and have 83 urban centres and 6,046 villages. Due to the strong pull of Delhi, the population growth rate in the urban areas outside the DMA has been lower than the national average urban growth rate.

**Physical Features**

The region is characterised by the Ganga skirting along its eastern boundary, the Yamuna crossing it north-south and the sand dunes and low hills of the Aravalli range in the West. To the South West it is enclosed by the hills of Aravalli range, enclosing fertile lands and high tablelands. Rolling plains dominated by rain fed gullies form the southern portion and the rest of the area is generally plain. The NCR can be divided into two regions, (a) the Ganga-Yamuna Doab and (b) the area west of the Yamuna. The Doab region is covered by new alluvium ('Khader') and old alluvium ('Bhanger'). Due to the presence of fertile soil, level land and canal irrigation, the area is intensely cultivated and supports a dense population. The region west of the Yamuna is enclosed by the outliers of the Aravalli which are extensively eroded. The rainfall is sparse (around 80 cm a year) in the Delhi NCT, and the Haryana region, somewhat higher in the UP subregion, and significantly less in the Rajasthan subregion. But because of the presence of the Yamuna, there is in general adequate water supply, and groundwater, if not depleted can also contribute. The soils are mainly alluvial, ranging between hard clay-clayey, loam-sandy loam, and sandy soils. The Uttar Pradesh subregion has rich loamy soils which are very fertile. The natural fertility is very poor in the Rajasthan subregion, and Delhi and Haryana subregions are moderately fertile. Due to extensive cultivation and the pressure of population, very little of the natural vegetation survives, and the forest cover is under two per cent, as compared to a national average of 20 per cent. The forest cover is of the tropical thorn type, ranging from open stunted forests to xerophytic bushes on both plain and hills. The tree types are acacia, Dhak, Kikar, and Babul. The forest in the NCR is useful more as a source of fuel and fodder than as a source of timber. In the NCT, the scanty rainfall and gravelly substratum of the soil cannot support a perennial vegetation. The reported 1.8 per cent of the forest is due to the Ridge area, and the recreational parks in the urban area.

The mineral resources of the region are negligible, consisting mainly of construction material. China clay, fire clay, silica sands, kaolin etc., also occur but generally are minor deposits. About 7.54 million tonnes of fire clay occur in Delhi and Gurgaon, 15.32 million tonnes of copper in Faridabad and Gurgaon, 0.31 million tonnes of copper in Alwar district.

## Demographic Profile

From a population of 2.5 lakh in 1911, the population of Delhi has grown to 94.2 lakh in the 1991 census. There has been a corresponding growth in employment, energy generation and consumption, industrialization etc. The population of the Delhi NCT has increased by 115 per cent in the last two decades and that of the NCR by 65 per cent. The total population of the NCR in 2001 was estimated to be 3.25 crores. Decadal growth rates in the Delhi Union Territory were 90.18 per cent (1941-51), 52.46 per cent (1951-61), 52.91 per cent (1961-71), 52.98 per cent (1971-81), and 47.8 per cent (1981-91). The decadal growth rates in the NCR as a whole were 32.89 per cent (1961-71), 36.48 per cent (1971-81) and 32.7 per cent (1981-91). These must be compared with the national average of about 25 per cent per decade. The growth in population has been mainly by immigration especially from the nearby states. Of the inflow, 48.2 per cent has been from Uttar Pradesh, followed by Haryana (15.5%), Punjab (9.8%), Rajasthan (7.6%), Madhya Pradesh (2.4%) and others, including from outside India (16.5%). There is a significant element of illegal immigrants from Bangladesh as well. The growth rate in population can be expected to keep up for the next two decades despite a slowdown in national population growth because of the pull of the metro. In which case the population of the NCR would be around 550 lakhs in 2020 AD. An increase of the same order of the last two decades may not be manageable in the case of the Delhi UT by itself, but in the NCR as a whole, it should be possible to accommodate the expected population. The key question is to see whether it can be done in a sustainable manner, and if not, what elements of sustainability can be built in and what resources need to be brought in from outside.

## Water Resources

The region is endowed with three perennial rivers, namely the Ganga along the eastern boundary, and the Yamuna and the Hindon traversing it. In addition, there is the Sahibi which is ephemeral, arising from the Aravalli range and flowing in a north easterly direction before losing itself in sandy region in Haryana. In exceptionally good monsoons it drains into the Najafgarh depression and joins the Yamuna. There are also a number of seasonal streams in the Rajasthan region. The districts of Karnal, Rohtak, Faridabad, Bulandshahar and Ghaziabad are served by canals providing water for irrigation and domestic consumption. Other districts depend on sub-surface water extracted through handpumps, motorised tubewells and wells. The groundwater resources to the west of the Yamuna are however insufficient due to the scanty rainfall, and the water is brackish. The tubewells often go dry in the summer as the watertable sinks.

Out of the 94 urban centres in the region, 67 have well organised water supply systems. The per capita supply ranges from 17 litres to 240 litres per capita per day. Water treatment is complete in only 20 per cent of the urban centres, and in the others it is partial. The rural regions have to depend on wells and tubewells, as organised water supply systems are available only in about 12 per cent of the total villages. More than half of the villages have either water scarcity or poor quality water.

A reliable and adequate supply of clean water is therefore the most important issue facing the NCR. The water resources are inadequate even now; in the future the expected populations cannot be accommodated without a drastic improvement in the availability of water. Water treatment and reuse therefore becomes the most urgent priority.

## Industrial Sector

Since independence, Delhi, which was mainly a centre of administration in pre-independence days has emerged as a major centre for light industry. Large scale industries are restricted due to the land zoning regulations. Significant industrial activity also exists in the national capital region, but statistics is deficient. In 1996, the NCT of Delhi had 1,26,000 number of industrial units. A wide variety of industrial products are made in Delhi, as profiled in Table 10.1.

### *The Role of the Informal Sector in Industry*

Urbanisation of India involves the informal sector in substantial measure. On the one hand, it pulls in migrants from the countryside,

**Table 10.1 : Comparison of Various Types of Mass Transit Options**

| Transit System option (Dual Track or major road) | Capital cost (in Million US$ per km, (1987 prices) | Capacity per hour per direction (Thousands) | Operating speed (Kmph) | Flexibility |
|---|---|---|---|---|
| Buses in mixed traffic | Nil (uses existing roads) | 10-15 | 12 | High |
| Bus lanes | Less than 1 | 10-20 | 15-20 | High |
| At Grade busways/High capacity bus systems | 2 | 25-30 | 17-25 | High |
| Light rail transport (LRT) at grade | 8.27 | 20-25 | 17-25 | Low |
| Metro elevated | 22-60 | 50-75 | 28-37 | Low |
| Metro underground | 50-165 | 50-75 | 28-37 | Low |

*Source* : Saraf (1998)

creating tremendous pressure on the city infrastructure and services. The migrant initially finds shelter in some slum cluster and employment in some ongoing economic activity, or takes up some self-employment, generally petty trading, handicrafts etc. His requirements have not been included in the projected growth rates of the infrastructure and services. Very often, he does not pay for the utilisation services such as water, sanitation or electricity, or when payment is unavoidable such as in public transport, the quality of the services soon deteriorates due to the additional unanticipated demand. Hence most planners and urban policy makers view the informal sector with disfavour. On the other hand, this sector absorbs a substantial fraction of the economic migrants, and in the absence of any concerted policy for regulating migration from the countryside to the cities provides an essential safety valve. The economic activity generated by the slum clusters and informal sector is also a significant fraction of the total economic activity. Over a time period, a fraction of those employed in the informal sector move into the formal sector of the economy, and set up their own enterprises. For these reasons it is necessary to take these sectors into account for planning the infrastructure, and to upgrade the facilities and services in the locations where they exist.

There is no consensus on what constitutes a unit in the informal sector. The number of employees per unit (ranging from 5-25), the non-applicability of labour laws, the existence of highly unorganised and unhygienic working conditions, the type of activity, etc. have all been considered for a definition. Contrary to commonly held opinions, about half the units appear to be registered with some agency or other. It may not be possible to apply some rigid definition and hence the definition should be location specific, and situation specific especially when the aim is to assist decision making.

With some inputs of finance and infrastructure, the informal sector can become a powerful component of the city economy. The requirements of the sector should be taken into account to provide minimum basic services and amenities such as water supply, street lighting, drainage, sewerage, housing, health services, open space, security etc. With this, the informal sector units can be upgraded into small and medium scale industries, and the workers too can be upgraded in their skills. The informal sector was found to make a significant contribution to the industrial production of Delhi and of the adjoining regions of the NCR. Seven informal sector clusters in the NCR were identified in a study some years ago (Lall, 1989), namely Alwar (Rajasthan), Sonepat and Faridabad (Haryana), Ghaziabad and Khurja (Uttar Pradesh) and Tri Nagar and Vishwas Nagar (NCT of Delhi).

The financing of the informal sector industrial projects seem to be primarily from the savings of the entrepreneur or his relatives, loans from the banking sector were small. The forward and backward linkages are closely controlled by middlemen, who either supply the raw materials, or purchase the final articles, or both. Less than one-third of the units have their own linkages beyond 5 km. Production is mostly on an order linked basis and inventory holdings are very small, approaching the "just in time" concept favoured by modern management techniques. The profitability is comparable with the formal sector and may well be higher. The growth in investment is about 10 per cent per annum, which compares well with the formal sector.

## Pollution Problems in Delhi

### *Water Pollution*

Water in Delhi and adjoining regions is thoroughly polluted. Most of the pollution arises from domestic sewage, though industrial pollution is also increasing. At present, Delhi generates about 1900 million litres per day (mld) of raw sewage, as against a treatment capacity of 1270 mld (Biswas and Trivedi, 1996). The treatment is only partial in much of the cases. Hence about 630 mld of untreated and a significant quantity of partially treated water is discharged into the Yamuna every day. The water in the Yamuna in the summer season is very less, and therefore its self cleaning capacity is very limited. Nearly 80 per cent of the water extracted form the river is returned as domestic or industrial sewage through 19 drains which also serve as storm water drains. The problem of domestic waste is exacerbated by the absence of sewerage systems in most of the unauthorized and resettlement colonies, insufficient capacity and poor maintenance in existing sewage systems, and the termination of sewers into what formerly were fresh water channels. The coliform counts in the Yamuna water are orders of magnitude above permissible limits, being above 20,000/100 ml in most of the Delhi stretch and 5,000-20,000 for about 70 km downstream (Parivesh, 1995). Industrial pollution, although less in quantity than domestic waste, poses its own problems, with non-biodegradable and toxic chemicals including cadmium, chromium, zinc, cyanide etc. (Priyadarshini and Kalia, 1993). Groundwater contains fluoride and nitrates in excess of safe levels and there is considerable leach off from fertiliser applications.

### *Air Pollution*

Health problems related to air pollution in Delhi have been estimated to be one of the highest among Indian cities. Delhi has also been considered to be the fourth most polluted city in the world. The number of excess deaths attributed to the poor air quality run into several thousands per year. The major contributors to air pollution in Delhi are motor vehicles (64%), thermal power generation (16%), and industry (12%). The transport sector is thus the largest polluter, and it is responsible for 97 per cent of the hydrocarbons (HC), 76 per cent of the carbon monoxide (CO), and 48 per cent of the nitrogen oxides (NOx) emissions into the atmosphere (Pandey 1998). The effects of air pollution on health vary in severity depending upon the age, physical condition and previous medical history of the persons concerned. Most of the conventional air pollutants are believed to directly affect the cardio-vascular and central nervous systems. High levels of sulphur oxides (SOx) and suspended particulate materials (SPM) are associated with lung diseases and a variety of illnesses like asthma and shortness of breath. Lead particles in the air, emitted from mainly petrol vehicles prevents haemoglobin synthesis in the bone marrow, damages liver and kidney function and causes neurological damage. It is especially associated with impaired intelligence and development in children.

Among the Indian metros, Delhi has the largest number of vehicles, more than the other three metros put together. As of 1996, there were 26.29 lakh motor vehicles in Delhi, of which nearly 70 per cent were two wheelers. The overall growth rate in the vehicles was 10.86 per cent in the 1971-95 period, with the passenger fleet growing at a faster pace (10.98%) than goods vehicles (9.05%). The emissions are increased substantially during acceleration, and in general lower cruising speeds adds to the air pollution. A study in 1993 by the Tata Energy Research Institute suggested three options to reduce transport related air pollution in Delhi : (1) Improvement in the vehicular speed from an average of 20 km/hr to 40 km/hr. This will reduce emissions of total suspended particles (by 43%), sulphur oxides (38%), nitrogen oxides (35%), carbon monoxide (16.5%), hydrocarbons (17%) and lead (15%). (2) Increase in the number of diesel fueled buses, which will cause a decrease in the number of petrol fueled personal transportation, thus reducing pollution loads per passenger substantially, and overall reductions in hydrocarbons (19%), carbon monoxide (19%), and lead (24%). (3) The introduction of the mass rail transit system (MRTS) to cater to about 25 per cent of total passenger transportation demands, which will reduce CO, NOx, HC, SOx and TSP by 25 per cent, and lead by 23 per cent.

## TECHNOLOGIES AND PRACTICES FOR SUSTAINABLILITY IN THE URBAN CONTEXT

To achieve sustainability, new technologies and practices have to be developed and implemented in a number of areas. The most important of the areas of concern in the urban context are in (1) City planning including design and layout, (2) green cover enhancement, (3) water supply, (4) human waste disposal, (5) industrial production including pollution control, (6) transport and telecommunications, (7) energy and power generation, (8) housing, (9) health care, and (10) rural urban linkages. Needless to say, these issues will have to be faced in a holistic manner as there are significant synergies in the operation of systems in these areas; it will not be possible to implement fragmentary solutions covering a single area, as efforts in any one area will affect all. Hence care must be taken to integrate the systems from the inception stage; even when solutions are being retrofitted to existing infrastructure, as will inevitably be the case in most occasions, it is necessary to think of overall synergies, opportunities and impacts. In what follows, an effort is made to identify technologies and practices in some of these areas that can contribute to sustainability in an integrated manner.

### City Planning

One of the most important parameters of sustainability is proper city planning. A city does not become sustainable merely on the basis of well provided infrastructure for energy, waste disposal, manufacture etc. It should also be a place where one can live in peace, interact harmoniously with neighbours, and where children can grow up with happiness and learn useful skills. Some of the most pathological manifestations of social breakdown in Western societies, are now known to be partially at least caused by the architecture. The large housing estates of Britain and US, notorious as breeding grounds for crime, provide no means of safe interaction with strangers. In India also, the city of Chandigarh, built according to Le Corbusier's specifications, was unlivable until it had been humanised by the illegal accretions of markets and street commerce. Corbusier said that a building is a machine for living in, but his buildings and city seem to be designed for machines to live in, rather than for humans. The complex requirements of human life have to be kept foremost in mind while designing buildings and neighbourhoods, and it must be remembered that spatial cultures that is the way people use space differs from culture to culture and is strongly influenced by climate, community practices, religious requirements and so on. Indian cities have always had a mixture of activities of residence, commerce and small scale manufacture at every locality, and there is no great segregation between the rich and the poor. This has provided a measure of security and convenience, as well as low transportation requirements. Social tensions are also kept down. This facet of organisation should be preserved in so far as feasible if we are to provide stable living spaces.

A social region, whether residential area or otherwise, is an integrated system composed of buildings and social organisations: that is, a physical system and an abstraction. The commonality between the two is the idea of space. Space is "the machine for living in" in Corbusier's terms. The relationship between humans and the space is governed by two basic types of laws: the laws of spatial emergence in which the larger configurational properties follow as a consequence of the local physical structures, and secondly the laws of generic function, in which constraints are placed on space by the contained human activity. These activities will tend to differ with the individuals and social groups concerned; particularly children and adults tend to use space quite differently. Normal, well occupied adults are space users, that is they use the space for specific activities. Children are space explorers, they are interested in discovering the space potential for its own sake, and they quickly find the lacunae in the adult movement system. Both over regulation and under regulation of children's space can cause problems. Another set of problems is caused by dysfunctional adult elements (junkies, muggers, burglars etc.) who exist in every society. They are also space explorers, and they need to be constrained rather than encouraged. All of these requirements impose a pattern which has to have a proper mix of centrality and linearity, *i.e.*, a mix of internal and external interactions.

Relatively simple changes in building layout and design can often contribute substantially to the needs of sustainability. Merely the refusal to cater to the current high fashion by creating environmentally undesirable designs such as all glass walls for office buildings can make a difference. A design with large glass windows, in the climate of Delhi, by collecting and trapping sunshine in the summer, raises inside temperatures to intolerable levels in the absence of high levels of air conditioning, which often may not be available. It would make much more sense to orient the buildings carefully, to reduce the insolation on the walls, to use smaller windows which are openable, and to use wind and air channelling structures for interior cooling as was used in old *havelis* in Rajasthan and elsewhere.

In order to design a stable and sustainable urban system, we may have to discard many of the concepts that currently operate in this paradigm. One of the concepts that seems due for drastic change is the idea that cities are clearly organised, simply ordered and thus predictable entities; therefore they should be capable of being planned minutely, with master plans and a full set of regulations covering every aspect of life in them. But even in countries where the resources existed for full and complete planning and implementation, (which is far from being the case in India) urban planning seems to have been incapable of prediction and has not yielded the expected results. Thus in the West, the shifts to the suburbs, the emptying and subsequent decay of the inner city and many of the social malaises in residential areas were not predicted. Equally unpredicted has been the change in city forms such as the "edge city", and the emergence of the "network city" which focusses on information and communication technologies. The rise of the global megalopolises were also neither predicted nor managed. Detailed planning stifled economic growth and hindered the ability of society to respond fast to emerging technological and globalisational challenges, and transport system planning everywhere yielded only momentary respite and generated ever greater pollution and congestion in the long run.

A response to this dilemma has been derived from the idea of complex systems. Complex systems are built of simple systems, but the rules governing them are such that their behaviour is completely unpredictable, even in principle. The weather and stock market are often seen as classic examples of inherently unpredictable complex systems, Even if all initial conditions and positions were known, slight random perturbations would push their behaviour into unpredictable forms. They show discontinuities in their behaviour, marked by many bifurcations, and a very large number of possibilities, only a few of which may be realised. Just as a football game or chess game is essentially unrepeatable if it is played a second time even by the same set of participants in the same conditions, so too the behaviour of complex systems is unrepeatable except in a large overall sense. Most systems in the real world (city growth, geomorphology, ecology, social organisation) take on this characteristic. One way of taking into account the complex nature of city growth is to consider it as being governed by the theory of fractals (Batty, 1998). Fractals are forms which are self-similar, that is there is a regular motif or design which repeats itself as the structure increases in scale. Patterns emerge in a dynamic response to need, rather than as a result of prior planning, as exemplified by trees, river branchings, blood vessels and nerve growth etc. The fractal idea of the city therefore recommends that "seeds" structures of different types be provided to act as cores of growth, and the city allowed to develop naturally around them in response to requirements. The "seeds" can be of different types to provide for a dense growth to put maximum functions in minimum space or they can be made to grow in open structures that would cover space efficiently but would provide for gaps inside them which can be made into parks, gardens etc. These are called diffusion limited aggregations (DLA). Formal planning would be avoided in favour of the structures growing in response to actual requirements, their forms being determined by the initial core and the type of interactions provided.

An interesting suggestion has been made that urban congestion and transportation bottlenecks can be significantly reduced by adopting innovative layouts (TIFAC, 1996; Indiresan, 1989). Instead of the conventional rectangular layout, connected by a mesh of roads, an annular layout is suggested, whereby the city will be developed in an annular manner, along a ring of a few kilometres in diameter. Along the centre of the ring runs a mass transportation system (which can be either underground mass transit, surface light rail, elevated track, bus corridor etc.) and for one kilometre on either side, the city is allowed to develop, while the central portion of the ring is developed as a parkland or green area. This is claimed to have significant advantages as compared to the conventional rectangular city matrix. In conventional designs, there is a tendency to concentrate various activities more and more at the core, which will cause a spiralling increase in land prices at the core, and increased needs for transportation since everybody will need to get to the centre. By contrast, the annular town tends to distribute activities uniformly around the ring, and congestion is avoided. Since the CBD is distributed, all residential neighbourhoods will lie within walking distance of some section or other, and hence commuter traffic is drastically reduced. There would be only one major thoroughfare, and the needs for intersections eliminated and entry and exit to the major arterial road is also simplified. The overall road-length is cut to nearly half of that of the conventional design. The annular does not have to be perfect circle or oval, any closed loop will do. This gives an opportunity to link pre-existing villages and townships in the new scheme.

In areas outside the dense urban scheme, whether conventional or annular, that is in the relatively rural areas of the national capital region, it is suggested that every family be provided with a single storey residential structure located in 500 sq, metre plot of land (Indiresan, 1992). The residence will be integrated with water harvesting facility, vegetable plot, and sanitation unit. A biodigester will ferment all waste and clean the water to be used for agriculture in the vegetable/fruit tree plot. Most of the water requirements will be met by rainwater harvesting. This will make a sustainable and decentralised living possible in almost any rural area, especially if teleconnectivity is assured. The city and the surrounding hinterland should be integrated, with the city concentrating on communication intensive, pollution free, service related activities, and the rural areas going in for the industrial aspects.

### *Enhancing the Green Cover*

An urgent need is to increase the green cover in the city. Cities can be eight to twelve degrees hotter than the surrounding countryside because the paved areas absorb heat and reradiate it. Planting trees and plants around buildings, at street corners and intersections etc. can bring down the overall heat levels and significantly enhance comfort levels. Hedge rows instead of street dividers will absorb a lot of vehicular pollution. Many evergreen plants, trees and shrubs have high levels of air pollution tolerance, and will absorb carbon monoxide and trap and contain dust. A city with high levels of greenery will be a much more livable place than a concrete jungle, simply because of the variety of environments and contrasting visual appearance that it will possess. The living organisms that a functioning plant life will attract such as insects, butterflies and birds will also have very positive influence. The rooftops can also be used for greenery, provided weights can be kept down by using some soil substitute instead of soil. Shredded paper, polystyrene and many other materials can be used along with drip irrigation or nutrient film techniques (see later section) too have both urban greenery and if required, urban farms. Enhancing the green cover is also intimately linked to improving the water supply.

Some work is already on-going. The green cover in Delhi is less than 2 per cent, as against a national average of 20 per cent. However, this is to be substantially enhanced by a "tapovan" of half km length on both sides of the Yamuna. About 40 lakh saplings will be planted in the site over a four year period. The project will have a mixture of fruit bearing and other trees, such as jamun, arjun, salix, jungle jalebi, keekar, peepal, mulberry, kadam, gulmohar, babul and so on. The entire 35 km stretch of river from Wazirabad to Okhla is to be demarcated, and fenced off for plantation work. The advantages are said to be checking of soil erosion and flood control. The water trapped in the root system will be released during the lean season, enhancing the ground water level.

## Augmenting the Water Supply

### *Rainwater Harvesting*

With an annual rainfall of about 80 cm, rainfall in the NCR would be generally adequate though on the lower side for agriculture. But the heavy municipal demand from the National capital territory is difficult to fulfil from local sources and Delhi at present demands almost entirely on the Yamuna. Due to demands from other areas, the water in the Yamuna, is over committed and decreasing in availability. There is a significant water shortage for most outlying areas of the city.

Supplies for Delhi can be substantially improved through rainwater harvesting. The techniques used for rainwater harvesting can also be useful for recharging the groundwater. Rainwater harvesting with relatively low additional costs is possible for all built up areas, especially roofs. By leading the roof drain through a filter (Gravel/ sand trap of about a cubic metre) into an underground cement lined tank and installing a small (100-150 watt) pump, about 30-40 per cent of the water requirements of a household could be met, assuming 50 per cent collection efficiency and 50 per cent storage efficiency. This will be a significant input, especially in the summer months. A well constructed tank could hold water against seepages and evaporation for more than an year, so storing the monsoon rainfall till the next summer is feasible. The only trouble will be in the periodic cleaning of the tanks. Such cleaning could be avoided if the water is used to augment groundwater supply, in which case, the filter can be dispensed with, and the requirement reduces to a percolation tank and a pump. However the soil has to be suitable, so that the water does not leak away.

Delhi has large areas of paved roads and parking lots, and these can be turned into water storage mechanisms at low cost. The sides of the roads will be contoured so that the water can run off and collect in a soil trap which can be planted with grass and herb type plants to protect the surface. The soil below the soil trap (about a metre below) should be compacted by pounding or it should be asphalt covered. It is necessary to avoid trees, as their roots will break through the impermeable layer, and anyway, they are very water hungry, whereas the grass and herbs can be allowed to dry out in the summer. An additional advantage is that the grass can be mowed and used for cattle-feed in the monsoon and winter. Around large parking lots, if the contour is right, sand-traps or dry wells can be constructed. They can also be constructed in other areas also, wherever a depression is surrounded by sloping land. Dry wells are depressions or wells, filled with sand, gravel and small rocks, into which the rain water is guided.

If sloping land is not available all around or if situated on a hill side, a check dam can be constructed on one side. Water permeates and is held in the pores of the sand and gravel. The dry well or sand trap should have impermeable sides and bottoms. The water can be pumped out when required from a small percolating area through small pump. Evaporation losses are reduced by as much as 90 per cent. If larger areas are needed for water collection, they can be made by making impermeable a suitable area through asphalting or covering with plastic sheets. Plastic sheets will have to be covered by some gravel which will protect it against damage by ultra-violet light as well as wind, and impacts. With proper construction and maintenance such catchment systems have projected lifetimes of 20-30 years. Such areas will have to be protected from people, cattle and vehicles through fencing, otherwise the places where the soil is broken will start eroding. Impermeable layers can be made also by wax spraying, the use of sodium salts, or through chemicals such as silicons, but such methods are likely to be expensive.

The soil itself can be the storage medium, by reducing evaporation and runoff losses. By covering with a mulch of leaves, twigs, small branches, plastic, paper etc., rainwater is slowed down and percolates into the soil. Evaporation losses are substantially reduced and runoff is almost eliminated. In a couple of years, mulch covered soil will dramatically increase its water holding capacity and fertility, it will also recharge the groundwater. In regions with suitable topography, the slopes can be covered by series of check dams, the bottom of the higher one being at the same level as the top of the lower one. With some provision for overflow, so that the water doesn't dig its way around the dam, the whole hillside can be made into a water storage medium, from the bottom of which substantial quantities can be extracted through a perforated PVC or concrete pipe. Check dams can be also used for groundwater recharging, they are particularly effective over aquifers, since they would slow down floodwater during the monsoon to allow the aquifer to recharge. Groundwater can be increased also by forcing water by powerful pumps in the monsoon into borewells.

A beginning has been made in water harvesting in Delhi. The President's Estate is to go in for water harvesting systems. It is estimated that the area of the estate receives about 850 million litres of rain water annually. If trapped and used, it will fulfil the requirements of the entire demand of the 17,000 people living in the estate. Harvesting rainwater in a two hectares area alone will meet the requirements of water for the Rastrapati Bahavan's 300 residents. Initially, the water will be stored on roof tops and specially made wells and ponds in the area. Some of these structures will be constructed in the Mughal Gardens to show the visitors how they can store rain water. Water harvesting in all major buildings must be made (*Times of India*, 98).

### *Water Storage*

Water can be stored in storage tanks, pools, lakes etc. A proposal to augment Delhi's water supply by turning the exhausted quarries at Asola Bhatti into a series of water reservoirs has been made. The quarries overall are around 2 km long, half km broad and several hundred metres deep. The total storage volume when developed will be of the order of 100 million cubic metres, which will make it one of the largest water supply reservoirs in India. The proposal will involve the construction of several kilometres of feeder canals from the Yamuna and installation of significant amounts of pumping power to pump surplus water from the Yamuna during the monsoon and store it so as to use in the lean season. The relatively large depths suggested in this particular case will keep surface evaporation losses down to a relatively small fraction of the water stored, but in smaller and shallower reservoirs, evaporation losses can be considerable. Several methods have been experimented with for reducing evaporation losses. Aliphatic alcohol monolayer such as cetyl alcohol reduce evaporation losses and are non-toxic to fish, and are permeable to oxygen so that the aquatic life is not disturbed. Its main disadvantage is that since it does not reduce the sunshine penetrating into the water, the heating of water is not reduced and evaporation occurs at accelerated pace at places where the monolayer is broken by wind or wave action. Wax blocks can be floated on water, in hot climates such as Delhi in summer, the wax melts and forms a continuous film which retards evaporation by as much as 80-85 per cent. The wax layer can keep going for years, though annual replenishments, about 10-15 per cent of the original charge are recommended. Floating blocks of polystyrene rubber or even lightweight concrete can cover large areas of a water pool and reduce evaporation losses. The exposed surfaces should be white to maximize reflection, the bottom coated with bitumen to prevent fouling and for durability. The slabs should have rounded corners to allow the water body to "breathe" properly. Foamed rubber can also be effective; initial high costs are offset against long life, in excess of 10 years.

### *Gray Water Utilization*

Gray water, that is waste water from bathing, dishwashing, laundry etc. is a neglected resource in most cities today. Unlike toilet waste water it does not require major treatment, and can be a significant source of plant nutrients such as phosphates. While not as much water is used for this as for toilet flushing, it can be significant, amounting to 30-40 litres per person per day. With provision of a small tank, filter and pump in every household, this water can be used for toilet flushing or irrigation of urban garden plots, vegetable plots etc., putting it to productive use.

### *Disposal of Human Waste*

One of the most important needs for any urban system is to provide a safe, cheap and reliable method for the disposal of human excreta. Inadequate and unhygienic excreta disposal practices as well as contaminated and leaking water mains lead to an enormous disease burden especially in developing countries such as India. These include water borne diseases such as diarrhoea, dysentery, cholera, gastroenteritis and typhoid, water related vector borne diseases such as malaria, dengue fever, filaria and schistosomiasis, parasitic diseases including hookworm and other helminthic diseases and many other viral and bacterial diseases. It has been estimated that more than half of all disease burden in the country is based upon faeco-oral contamination.

Regarding sewerage, we are unlikely to be able to afford the level of water supply needed to operate a fully water borne sewage disposal system. It should be possible to consider systems which do not use so much water, where the organic manure can be recycled, or gas generated. It is estimated that Delhi in 2001 would require about 5100 million litres of water per day, of which about 4000 millions would be for sewage disposal. If the sewage water could be treated and recycled, it can be used for agriculture, industrial requirements, fire fighting etc. It will be much cheaper than providing fresh water for the whole use.

Conventional sewerage uses approximately 200 litres per day per person of water. It uses large diameter pipes at a suitable depth for the main sewerage lines which are connected to households by smaller pipelines. The sewers should be laid at an angle sufficient to prevent accumulation of deposits, and the water flow should be sufficient to allow the sediments to flow to the treatment plants. The capital costs of the treatment plants is also considerable. All this means that conventional sewerage is the most expensive option for human waste disposal. While the costs would vary depending upon construction material costs and labour costs, it is generally beyond the reach of most urban administrations in developing countries.

A number of alternate systems are available, either on site (the excreta is disposed close to the point of generation) or off-site (where the excreta are conveyed to a distant point for processing. The off-site systems are conventional sewerage, simplified (or shallow) sewerage and settled sewerage. The on site systems would include ventilated pit latrines, septic tanks, pour flush toilets, leach pits etc. Shallow sewerage refers to basically conventional sewerage stripped down to basics, smaller pipes, shallower gradients etc. It receives all domestic waste water without settlement in tanks, and is suitable for high density housing. The disadvantages are lack of the safety and reliability associated with conventional sewerage, and possible leaching problems. Settled sewerge describes a system in which the waste water from one or more households is discharged into a single compartment septic tank, which functions to intercept solids and settle them. The settled solids free water is disposed of into shallow small bore gravity sewers. While the cost of the onsite systems does not depend upon density of settlement, the cost of off site systems falls sharply with settlement density and reaches a stable value at around 200 persons per hectare. The cost of onsite systems (as well as simplified sewerage and settlement tanks) has been estimated to be around 50 dollars per household per year, while that of conventional sewerage is around 75 dollars. The capital costs of VIP and pour flush toilets is around 10 per cent to that of conventional sewerage (Mara, 1996).

Onsite systems require periodic emptying. If the VIP and pour flush toilets are of the twin pit variety (where the excreta are held for more than two years in a dry condition before emptying) the risk from excreted pathogens is very small, since all except a few Ascaria eggs will be dead. Manual removal which is cheap and efficient can be employed here. In other systems, *e.g.*, wet disposal tanks, sludge removal from septic tanks or settlement tanks etc., manual removal is dangerous to workers. In Western countries, vacuum trucks have been developed for this purpose, which can suck the liquid sludge by powerful vacuum pumps into hermetically sealed tank which are taken away and poured into treatment tanks. While the tanker and associated equipment are of high costs, costs per household need not be high, since a tanker and crew can service around 2000 pits per year, which in normal terms can serve a community of around 20,000-30,000.

The residue from twin pit alternating ventilator dry systems, or composting systems or from twin septic tanks is essentially pathogen free, so that they could be used in a vegetable garden, or off site in a farm, treebelt or forest, or sanitary landfill. But the sludges from single septic tank or solid settlement tank is not pathogen free and hence they have to be treated before use in composting, treatment tanks or other systems.

An onsite system that does not use water for faecal transportation and hence drastically reduces water pollution is the composting toilet. One of the available designs, namely the Clivus compost reactor, was developed in the West and hence assumes the use of toilet paper. If the organic materials including soiled toilet papers were mixed with the toilet wastes, it would make an ideal compost material with favourable balance between carbon, nitrogen and phosphorus, and trace minerals such as sodium, iron, magnesium, zinc etc., the composted material could be used as fertiliser.

The Clivus compost reactor works on the principles of gravity, capillary action and ventilation. The system consists of an airtight sloping chamber which is connected to toilet and kitchen refuse openings by two chutes. The bottom of the chamber contains soil, with a rising portion about one-third from the bottom. The faeces and kitchen refuse accumulate in two chambers above the sloping chamber which communicate with the chamber by air ducts (or perhaps perforated sheeting). A vent provides a means of escape for the gases produced by the decomposition process. Urine is drained off down the sloping bottom to be decomposed by the soil bacteria into nitrates and carbon dioxide. As the urine drains out of the excrement chamber, air is able to reach the aerobic organisms that break down faeces. As the kitchen refuse decomposes, the high proportion of the cellulose present in the material produces heat, which helps to evaporate the liquids, thus reducing the volume. The first stage, in which the larger particles are broken down and the greatest heat is produced, is quite rapid. The secondary process, the mineralization of the material, takes months or years. The ventilation duct is high and can extend into chimney. Because the inside of the converter is kept at a lower pressure than the outside, there will be no seepage of gases into the latrine or kitchen when the covers are opened. When material is not to be put in the two chutes have to be kept closed by airtight covers at the bottom. The total amount of finished compost per person per year is about 30 litres. The final product contains no E. Coli because of the inhospitable nature of the environment where the composted soil slowly emerges. The compost is removed from the bottom of the sloping chamber through an opening normally closed airtight. This material is almost completely mineralized and can support only the soil bacteria. They also consume most pathogens.

A single dwelling unit has a sloping chamber about 3 metres long, 52 cm in diameter and kept at a slope of about 60 degrees. The system is practically failsafe because there is no turning or stirring in the pit, uses no extraneous energy, slow turnover speed (about 2-3 years for the soil particles to run through the reactor) and the construction makes it almost impossible to take out material that is not fully mineralised. The present design has been installed in about 1,300 Scandinavian homes. A multi-apartment project is carried out in Finland in a two storeyed, four apartment house. The main concerns are capacity and end product. It is not clear whether the system will cope with the water that is normally used in India for cleaning up after defecation. The temperature changes that are part of the Delhi climate may also cause problems.

In the long run, for sustainable city development, a system has to be developed which is able to recover the plant nutrient value of human excreta in a hygienic and cost effective manner. We must move from a policy of human and other waste disposal to one of waste utilisation. In much of Western literature, the traditional Indian practice of anal cleaning with water is thought of as an obstacle in the development of waste utilisation and recovery systems. But in fact it can be better integrated with a high-tech and efficient cost effective system. For instance, consider an individual household or small community (or apartment block) in which a pour flush system removes human waste and cleaning water into a hermetically sealed tank. Here, the liquid is evaporated off under low pressure, with an electric heating coil. After the water is evaporated, the coil heats the remainder to sterilisation. The water is condensed and reused, and the offgases from the sterilisation are filtered and made odour free before release to the atmosphere. When the residue is dry, (sensed by an automatic moisture sensor), a large heating coil is turned on and the residue is burned in a stream of oxygen or air (provided by pipes), releasing carbon dioxide, nitrogen and water vapour, which can be pumped out. The remaining residue will be ash amounting to only one or two grams per day per person, which falls into a containment chamber. The containment chamber may be emptied and cleaned once in several years. With such a system, all the water, gases and minerals may be recovered and reused in an efficient and hygienic manner. The waste disposal system will be integrated with the design of the apartment and will be an appliance much like the others, and its cost may be only a small fraction of the cost of apartment, with energy utilisation amounting only to a few tens of kilowatt hours per capita per annum. When the land cost and treatment costs of other systems is taken into consideration, the overall costs may be found to be highly affordable. Alternative individual household systems such as chemical toilets will not be useful in India as it cannot deal with the water used for anal cleaning, and the frequent (once every few months) emptying will be a nuisance. It may be also possible to deal with the human waste in a community system, where the excess water is recovered by means of semi permeable membranes and the concentrated residue is either dried and burned off as in the previous example, or oxidised under water at the triple point. (At the triple point of water, any organic residue can be burned off under water with excess oxygen, precipitating any inorganic material as insoluble ash. A strong reaction chamber will be needed. The advantages are very small land requirements as compared to traditional methods, as well as the ability to deal with large amounts of material at the same time. It may however be costly compared with the traditional systems. But the cost may be affordable in the future.)

Alternatives to the traditional water seal in lavatory pans have been designed, consisting of either heavy mineral oil or expandable polystyrene beads coated with special chemicals. As these are less dense than water, they will float back after passing the faecal matter, urine and cleaning water. Coupled with proper lavatory pan design, the use of special super smooth finishes for the pans and if necessary, a vacuum assist to pull the flushed material out into storage or treatment chambers as previously mentioned, the system could be made to function with the use of only a few litres per day per person, thus alleviating water requirements substantially.

Domestic water consumption could be reduced substantially in other areas as well. Buckminster Fuller has devised a "Fog Shower" for bathing, in which a highly pressurised spray of water, broken up into tiny droplets, cleans a person effectively even without the use of soap using only about a litre of water at a time. Special non-foaming detergents have been developed which greatly reduces the water requirement for washing clothes. Ultrasonic cleaning devices for both clothes and utensils can also be developed which will able to do the job with very little water. If effectively implemented, these technologies can reduce the requirement for water in the domestic sector to a few percent of what is used today, and all this water and waste materials can be fully recycled and reused.

### *Municipal Solid Waste*

A pilot scheme to compress municipal solid waste and burn it so as to produce energy had failed in Delhi because the designers (a foreign design was used) had omitted to take into account the high water and vegetable and other organic material content of Indian city municipal waste. Drying it so as to be able to burn will consume much more energy than it produces. At present, plastics, metal and other residues in municipal solid waste are separated out by rag-pickers. While it gives employment to many, it is a very unhygienic and extremely poorly paid employment, and certainly cannot be relied upon in the long run. Plastic bags especially have become a significant problem in many metros and other urban areas. They are not biodegradable, clog drains, and cause death among cattle. Being so thin, a very large number have to be collected before a saleable weight can be reached, so rag-pickers are not interested in picking them up. At present there seems to be no option but to ban the use of these bags unless they are reusable and above a certain thickness, when they might be interesting for recycling. A long-term alternative is to develop biodegradable plastics for carrybags, the versions at present available are not strong enough or waterproof, and are costly. Also in the long run, some relatively automated system has to be designed which can handle mixed municipal wastes, as rag-picking etc. will not be renumerative enough for even poor people as economies improve. Present day municipal waste processing are either landfills, or incineration both of which cause adverse environmental impacts, and proposed techniques for collection and recycling will require careful sorting of plastics, metals etc. to separate them from the organic wastes. A possible system can be visualised where the solid wastes are first shredded, and mixed with a water stream on a wet pathway/channel (Very poor quality water, grey water or perhaps settling tank supernatant water can be used). The plastic and wood come to the surface and are skimmed off. The fats, which are high in energy content are recovered and made into soap or grease or burned for fuel, the plastic and wood go back into the machine and are pulverized. Metals and other inert matter sink to the bottom. They are pushed out, washed down with clean stored water and put back. Iron can be mangnetically separated, the other metals are collected and when enough have accumulated, they can be processed. The paper and other biodegradables are left as a slurry in the middle, roughly in a ten to one ratio, as compared with the solid contents in sewage. This can be processed by biodigestors. The water and slurry can be used on the land for yielding crops, and soon an agro-industrial complex can develop. Integrating waste treatment with agro industry results in economies of scale, and maintains the fertility of the land.

### Waste Water-Biomass-Food Linkages

An essential aspect of sustainable city development is the productive use of all waste water and plant nutrients. The city wastes can be closely linked to biomass and food generation. (Mohan S., 1992). Domestic waste water and sewage would be an excellent input to agriculture if it could be decontaminated adequately. Industrial waste water should be kept away from it as it contains toxic chemicals that would kill the bacteria used in domestic waste treatment and also seep into groundwater. Without going into very high tech waste disposal even, the on site and off site waste treatment methods discussed above could be integrated into a reliable agro industrial system. The domestic waste would be treated by fermentation in sealed tanks, with the off gases being collected and used as fuel. The liquid effluent goes into settling tanks, and the top layer (supernatant) would be pumped out and put into fishponds as they still contain an appreciable amount of nutrients. The fishponds could be small, about a hectare or less, interspersed with farm lands. It would be useful to grow plants which are directly edible by fish such as carp. Plants such as duckweed and many types of algae suit these criteria. The water from the fishponds would be pumped out and used to grow vegetables and fruits by the nutrient film technique (NFT) or drip irrigation. Both of these would minimise water needs as opposed to conventional agriculture. In NFT, the plants are grown in triangular gullies, coated with a thin layer of polythene sheet. The plants actually do not come into contact with the soil at all, and all their nutrient needs being met by the fertilised water circulating around their roots. Therefore, any kind of soil or even small rocks or gravel could be used to lay the gullies in; the soil provides only a means for holding the troughs in which the plants grow, and to provide area for solar energy collection by the plants. Water circulates in a thin (1 mm layer) in the troughs. Being from the treatment ponds, they would contain nutrients, but more could be added when necessary. There would be no runoff losses, and the fertilisers can be applied just when needed. Hence their total quantity would be very small, as would be that of pesticides, fungicides etc. which can also be supplied along with the water. Water losses are essentially confined to evapo-transpiration losses, at present water needs are at about 5 per cent of those in conventional agriculture. Even these could be reduced drastically by the use of the special genetically engineered plants. Yields are very high in the NFT system, and reliable yields in excess of 100 tonnes (wet) per ha. have been reported. This would mean that the needs of about 300 people could be satisfied from the produce of one hectare. If the NFT system is considered too expensive (polymer sheeting, pumping costs, monitoring), drip irrigation can be used, with the additional advantage of being able to use the residue from the sewage settling tanks, after treatment for pathogen removal. An integrated domestic waste water treatment-cum-horticultural system would be able to meet most of the requirements of fruits and vegetables in the city. The inedible portions of horticultural plants could be used as cattle feed or used in biogas generation.

If NFT or drip irrigation is used for horticulture, some water would be left over. This can be used for tree cultivation, including fruit trees. In the relatively dry parts of the NCR, special trees and plants used for wasteland rehabilitation could be grown with this water. In areas with slightly more rain fall, treated sewage water could be used for supplementary irrigation for fodder crops. It might also be possible to grow plants that could directly yield liquid hydrocarbons, which after suitable concentration and treatment can be used to drive diesel engines. Latex bearing plants for rubber production would be an additional possibility. Bamboos and quick growing trees may be used to make furniture and wood products. Many quick growing softwoods can be processed to hardwood strengths and finishes by chemical impregnation. Cultivation of even high quality hardwoods like teak may be possible if the plants can be acclimatized to the climate of the NCR and if the harvesting cycles were sufficiently long. Optimal combinations of plants for horticulture and biomass applications would have to be worked out according to water availability, location, availability of other resources etc., but there seems to be little doubt that a well organised waste water-biomass system could make the city along with its surroundings largely self reliant in food energy and materials.

### *Energy Options*

Of late, Delhi has been going through an acute electricity shortage, especially in summer, with power cuts lasting for 3-5 hours on the average, but extending to breakdowns for days in many areas. This has frayed tempers and caused acute social as well as economic problems. The main reason is that the city is entirely dependent on electric power from thermal power plants, with some electricity purchases from the national power grid. Electricity demands is also increasing exponentially with population growth, purchases of energy consuming new appliances by the middle class, and increasing industrialization. The only long- term solution is to use the resources that are freely available in the city and the NCR, namely direct use of solar energy and biomass. Wind power is not a particularly reliable option for Delhi, because of the relatively low windspeeds.

### *Direct Use*

Direct use of the sun's energy is the ultimate aim of any renewable energy programme, since the sunlight which falls on any country exceeds by far any human use, and is available without cost forever. Delhi is particularly well placed to use solar energy, since it is hot and sunny, with about 250-300 clear days per year. There are two possible routes: Direct use of solar heat in solar thermal appliances and photovoltaic electricity generation. Cost has been a major deterrent for photovoltaic applications, which currently run at around Rs. 18.00 per KWh (*Frontline* 1998). Breakeven costs for competition with coal is estimated to be around Rs. 4.00/KWh, so there is still a long way to go. By 2010, overall system costs for thin film solar cells integrated with buildings is expected to drop to around US $ 1.50 (1994 Dollars) per peak watt. (Frankl, 1998). But when the pollution control costs and greenhouse gas mitigation costs for coal are taken into consideration, perhaps a higher breakeven cost should be considered.

### *Solar Thermal Energy*

Solar thermal energy is suitable for many medium temperature industrial and agro-processing applications, which in the context of the NCR can be service to alleviate the pressure on energy, especially electricity resources. The temperature ranges which can be generated by solar thermal devices have been classified into three (i) Low grade thermal energy below 100 °C for water heating, air heating for drying fruits and vegetables etc., and desalination. (ii) Medium grade thermal energy between 100 and 300 °C for applications such as cooking, industrial process heat, low pressure steam, refrigeration, water pumping etc. (iii) High grade thermal energy above 300° C for power generation and materials processing. As a result of R&D efforts over the last two or three decades, a very large number of appliances for low and medium grade applications have been made. Typical applications include solar water heaters, solar air heaters and driers, solar cookers and solar stills. Other applications include solar dryers for fruits, vegetables and spices, solar desalination units (only demonstration units so far) and passive solar architecture using shape, orientation and shading devices in building to produce cooling in summer and greater warmth in winter. R&D efforts in the solar thermal area include solar ponds (non-convective ponds which can generate temperatures upto 80-90° C at the bottom used as low cost, large area collector), solar/biomass hybrid systems for drying of agricultural produce, low temperature multistage distillation units, solar energy based refrigeration systems using zeolite/water absorption cycle. Sustainable integrated industrialization of the NCR shall certainly make full use of this free resource. If there are significant economies of scale in manufacture of solar thermal systems, using lightweight composite materials, the overall costs can become competitive with that of coal, especially when transport, and pollution related costs are taken into consideration.

### *Improving Efficiency of Coal Utilisation*

Till the biomass, solar thermal and photovoltaic costs come down, coal will remain the major source of energy. But its efficiency has to be increased and pollution levels brought down. A number of options are available and are being implemented. These include coal beneficiation, fluidised bed combustion, coal water slurries, micronised combustion, combined gasification cycles and so on.

### *Biomass Utilisation*

The use of advanced techniques such as gasifier/gas turbine systems for electrical power generation and fuel cells for transportation would make it possible for biomass, preferably cultivated using the waste water from water and waste treatment plants.

A reappraisal of biomass as a source for energy and materials is important because of its potential for (a) Contributing to sustainability by reducing the ecological footprint of the city by meeting a major portion of energy and material requirements locally, (b) Reduction of urban air pollution, (c) Contributing to reduction in emission of greenhouse gases since biomass is generated without any increase in net atmospheric carbon dioxide, (d) Promoting rural/near urban industrialization and employment generation, and to provide for income stability for farmers, (e) Rehabilitation of degraded lands, and (f) Reducing dependence on imported petroleum and hence improving the balance of payment for the nation. There are some difficulties for using biomass for energy or materials. Part of it arises from the low bulk density and high moisture content of wood and other biomass. Freshly cut wood has typically an energy density of 10 GJ per tonne, as compared to 25-30 GJ/T for various grades of coal and more than 40 GJ/T for oil. Hence to be useable on a large scale biomass needs to be densified and dried thoroughly. Sun drying, though sufficient for use in fireplaces, does not provide the dryness needed in industrial applications and for economic transportation. It may be possible to adapt a modification of charcoal making process and compression by machines to provide the required degree of densification and dryness.

Cultivation of biomass using city waste water would lead to a variety of industrial products. Three major approaches can be adopted for this : pyrolysis, organosolvent processing, and stem explosion of wood in pyrolysis, biomass materials are heated in deficiency of air (*i.e.,* less air than that required for full combustion). The products are formed : gas (a mixture of carbon monoxide and hydrogen), pyroligneous acid and charcoal. The gas can be used for household cooking, running of small foundries and furnaces, and after cooling, filtering and compression, for the running of Sterling cycle engines which can be used for motive power, water pumping etc. Pyroligneous acid can be used as a source of many organic chemicals such as furfural, butadine and methanol. Charcoal can be used as a high quality transportable fuel (useable for making producer gas for motive power engines), as a good quality reductant, source for carbon black and activated charcoal, for making graphite electrodes, in vulcanization of rubber and many other uses. It can also be used in the manufacture of many metal matrix composites. In organic solvent processing, hot aqueous phenol is passed through coarsely ground wood chips and other biomass materials, lignin is dissolved, and the hemicellulose hydrolyses. On cooling, a water rich layer contains the sugars from the hydrolysis, and an organic (phenol) rich layer contains the lignin. Full recovery of the phenol is essential for the economies of the process. Hot formic acid can also be used, which is somewhat cheaper. The final traces of formic acids remaining in the organic layer extract can be neutralized to water soluble salts. The recovered cellulose can be used for paper or rayon, and the lignin for adhesives for particle boards, fibre boards etc. The sugars recovered can be further fermented to alcohol or further processed to other organic chemicals. In the steam explosion technique, high pressure steam impregnating wood chips in a pressure chamber is suddenly allowed to expand suddenly. This disintegrates cellular structure of the wood. The sugars are leached out by a water wash, and the lignin by an alkali wash. The cellulose produced by this method is not strong enough for paper, but can be used in other applications and for cattle feed, it is possible to produce good quality cattle feed from otherwise unusable materials (Mohan, S., 1992).

Biomass energy appears to be cost effective even now, much cheaper than the current costs of photovoltaic power, and comparable to diesel. Coal, of course has an edge at present, but it must be remembered that it is a depleting resource, and if the pollution control costs and its contribution to greenhouse warming are taken into account, biomass energy appears quite attractive costs can be expected to come down further, as gasifier and Sterling cycle engine costs come down due to mass production. Currently, the best costs for biomass cogeneration are expected to be about Rs. 2.25/KWh, as compared with 1.80-2.00 for coal, and 3.5-4.0 for diesel. (*Source:* National Institute of Ocean Technology, quoted in *Frontline*, September 25, 1998.) The data is of 1997, and not adjusted for inflation.

## Materials

Materials technology is considered to be among the three major driving forces of the last decades of the twentieth century, the others being biotechnology and information technology. All three have strong implications for sustainability. New materials enable us to do "more with less" carrying out more functions while being less energy and materials intensive. Advanced ceramics, composites, polymers, matrix materials etc. are changing the face of industry in advanced countries and these will surely make their contributions in India also. But in addition, there are a number of technologies which need to be developed specifically in India to meet with the goals of sustainable development. Especially important are material technologies which will convert a hitherto unused or underused material into high value products or meet basic needs. Among these can be considered low cost cements using fly ash, development of poymeric binders for imparting greater strength to clay and mud build structures, macrodefect free cement for high strength low cost structures, break resistant pottery and glassware, new methods for compressing clay and ceramic powders to nearly theoretical maximum densities to have high strength defect free materials, higher durability plastics, hydrogels for conserving water in agricultural applications, new methods to use naturally occurring substances such as lignin to polymers, and so on (Mohan, S., 1995). New materials are constantly being developed, for instance a recent report suggests that glass can be made almost completely shatter proof (*Times of India,* 1999). Glass, especially tempered glass breaks catastrophically when the strain exceeds a certain limit. Researchers have found a way to temper glass to break more evenly, with cracks developing and propagating ion a stable manner. In the usual process of tempering, sodium ions on the surface are replaced by potassium ions. The potassium ions, being larger, make a tighter fit among the glass molecules and the glass is compressed enabling it to withstand greater stress. In the new process, potassium ions are added throughout the body of glass, and sodium ions are added back on the surface only. The glass has compressed layers within. A crack that develops at the surface propagates to the compressed layer and then stops. Many cracks can develop and propagate in this manner before failure occurs. Similar opportunities may be available in many areas, especially important are techniques which should be developed to impart high strength and crack resistance to clay products.

### *Materials in Buildings and Construction*

The building and construction industry is one of the most dynamic in the industrial sectors in any active economy. It has significant feedback and feedforward effects, and in many cases is a sensitive barometer of the health of the economy. By its very nature, it is very large and resource intensive. In Britain it is estimated that the building sector is responsible for 50 per cent of the materials taken from nature, 40 per cent of all energy consumption (including energy in use over the lifetime of the building for heating, cooling, water supply etc.) and over 50 per cent of the wastes generated by society. The reduction of energy and materials intensity should, therefore, begin with the building sector, where there is a great scope for it.

Previously we have referred to the city as an 'organism'; the same can be said about the buildings as well. Because their life cycle is somewhat longer than ours, we tend to think of them as permanent, but they too are subject to decay and need to be replaced. With the speeding up of all human activity in industrial society, the life of buildings have also become significantly shorter, and they need to be rebuilt or replaced at ever faster intervals. In Hong Kong it is said that any building over 40 years of age tends to be looked upon as a "Heritage Site' and the average age of buildings in the CBD is less than 20 years. Because of their large sizes, dependence on materials and energy brought from long distances and increasingly shorter life cycles, buildings cause significant impact on the environment. We need, therefore, to look at the environmental impact of a building during its whole life, with special attention to materials extraction, and disposal of materials after demolition. The environmental costs incurred during life cycle of a building consists of the following : (1) Quarrying and preparation of materials including aggregates, (2) Production of raw materials, (3) Manufacturing of materials and components, (4) On site construction, (5) The energy and materials expenditures concerned with the building in use, and (6) The demolition and disposal of the building after its useful life is over. A Life Cycle Analysis (LCA) of the different contributors to the environmental impact can be done, although it is quite data intensive. To reduce the impacts we must minimise the energy and materials use in the construction of the buildings, minimise through better design the energy and materials in use during the lifetime, and build the components in such a way that they can be reused after the building itself is demolished. The ultimate aim is to provide an integrated system in which all materials are used in a closed loop, mirroring the natural processes such as the carbon cycles. This will mean that all the construction materials can be made to undergo only reversible operations, including chemical reactions so that everything can be remanufactured. In the meanwhile, we can provide useful check points towards sustainability by maximising the use of renewable resources, minimizing the use of nonrenewables and using them more efficiently, and choosing materials with the least environmental impact. Changes in construction techniques are necessary which would pay attention to the problems of dismantling and refitting, just as any machine is built out of components which can be taken apart and put together again, so should a building. Only the worn-out parts should be discarded, others should be reused. Prefabricated modules such as floors, frames, walls etc. with plumbing, electrical wiring and fixtures attached which are attached to a mainframe and which can be de-assembled and reused can go significantly towards reducing overall environmental impacts. The waste product produced at the demolition of a building (*"malba"* in Hindi) should be ground up and used to make concrete. Technology now exists to grind up used concrete, and the resulting powder can be mixed with additional cement so as to make more concrete. Door and window frames should be made of chemically impregnated wood, or metals such as aluminium, and plastics that they could simply be taken off and refitted elsewhere. Treated wood would be fire and insect proof. Components which are unfit for reuse in the same form should be capable of being ground up and used as mix in a remould. A Californian company has developed a method of grinding up old wood, newspapers, cardboard boxes etc., into a material called "Grindcore" which is then moulded to make beams, panels etc. (Maf Smith *et al.,* 1998). Another possibility is particles boards, laminated sheets, hardboards etc. which can be made from wood chips, old newspapers and so on. Such products greatly reduce the need for wood, which is increasingly in short supply. Processes are also available to use straw to produce bonded boards and blocks using heat and pressure only. They could be used for all partitioning and other applications where load bearing is not called for. They can be made insect proof and fire proof. Straw is completely renewable and fast growing, and millions of tonnes of it are available. Bricks, which are energy intensive can also be reused. Formerly, bricks used to be fixed with lime mortar so that when the building is demolished, they could simply be knocked off and the mortar removed. The bricks could then be reused. But nowadays cement mortar is used so that the bricks will be broken if they are separated. There is a need to go back to older practice with a modification, so that the building is constructed with load bearing pillars and the bricks in the separating walls etc. are fixed with less bonding mortar so that they can be reused. One of the major requirements in the Delhi climate is for buildings of high thermal mass, which can stay cool in summer and warm in winter without the need for artificial cooling or heating. Old style buildings with appropriate ventilation used to provide this, but concrete buildings of the present day have become unbearably hot in summer and cold in winter, with the use of thin walls. This exacerbated by the lack of any vegetation around many residential colonies. In principle, these problems can be solved by going back to traditional styles of construction using mud, with appropriate modifications to accommodate modern requirements such as indoor toilets, electrical appliances etc. Rammed earth and mud uses a material that is abundant and cheap, and available at the housing site. Above all, after the buildings has served its purpose, the materials melt back into the soil and can be reused indefinitely. Earth and mud building is done by rammed earth construction using frames or the use of extruders (ref: Balram, from Development Alternatives, New Delhi) which manufacture earthen blocks on site. The embodied energy estimates of such blocks vary, but are generally considered to be more than on order of magnitude lower than concrete or bricks. They can certainly be tried out in applications where multi-storey buildings are not needed. There is a need to develop new and cheaper building materials, and significant research is ongoing in this area in India. Cement has been manufactured from fly ash, rice husk ash, and clay cement mixtures can be used instead of pure cement in many applications. Building materials can also be generated from low quality clays, industrial waste etc. as well. New roofing materials and techniques, micro-concrete roofing tiles, cement fibre and bitumen fibre composite etc. need to be tried out along with techniques such as geodesic domes for durable, light and cheap structures. There is especially a need to get away from the multi-storey constructions except where they are unavoidable such as city centres, since these are often far too expensive on a unit area covered basis. High density and sustainable buildings and structures can be created using a variety of techniques and styles as well as materials and there is a need to intensively investigate them.

## Improving the Transportation Sector in Delhi and the NCR

In planning the transportation sector and pollution control, one has to keep in mind the fact that India is a low income country and is likely to remain one for a considerable time. Solutions that are suggested should cater to India's specific conditions. The main reason that pollution control and other measures in the country have not succeeded is due to the fact that the suggested measures are based on patterns prevalent in the advanced countries and not of our own.

Most Indian cities, including Delhi are characterized by high density of population, intensely mixed type of land-use, and a high share of walking and non-motorized transport, especially bicycles. There is also a high density of poor people and of animal drawn vehicles for goods transport. Delhi has in fact a fairly good road network in comparison with other Indian cities and even in comparison with international standards. Delhi has a road network of 20,487 km. (1990) of which 800 km. was broader than 30 metres. The road length per person was 2.17 metres, higher than Singapore (1.0), Hong Kong (0.2), Tokyo (1.9) and London (1.9) (Saraf, 1998). The transport pattern is very mixed, with large buses and good vehicles sharing the roads with cycles and pedestrians. Not surprisingly, the accident rates are high, and pedestrians, cyclists and two wheelers account for 65 per cent of the fatalities, generally caused by buses and trucks.

In Delhi, more than 57 per cent of all trips are less than 5 kms., 20 per cent of 5-10 kms., and the rest more than 10 kms. The average speed in city areas are less than 10-15 kms. per hour [*Source* : ORG Household Travel Survey in Delhi (Final Report 1994)].

About 70 per cent of the motorised fleet consist of two wheelers, which take up less space than cars or buses, and have an inherently high passenger moving capacity. Delhi also does not have too many ups and downs in its natural topography. All this means that a viable system could be built around dedicated lanes for bicycles and scooters, and segregated lanes for buses.

In the present proposals for traffic planning, there is provision for a large number of flyovers and subways. These do not take the actual reality of traffic in the city into account. Flyovers may be useful for cars but not other traffic. After the construction of a flyover, bus users have to walk for additional distances upto a kilometre to change buses. Cycles, autos, and other low speed/non-powered transport find the gradients difficult, and people find it difficult to cross the road at locations near the subways, but they would cross anyway, increasing accidents. The large number of subways in central New Delhi are also not very useful, especially to the handicapped, people carrying loads, old people etc. A comparison of the cost and capacity of different modes of transportation is given in Table 10.1.

The proposed massrapid transit transport system (MRTS) for Delhi also may not be very useful. At the proposed lines, the MRTS will carry less than 10 per cent of all work related trips, and hence the traffic density or pollution may not be substantially reduced. The MRTS is not flexible, and is very costly. The Calcutta metro costs around Rs. 4 per passenger-km, far higher than competing modes unless subsidised. Worldwide experience shows that Metros will be successful only in countries with a per capita income of around $ 3000 or higher. Our average incomes are around one tenth of this. Hence metro construction should be deferred until experience has been gained of lower cost intermediate transport solutions, including high capacity bus systems, tramways etc.

High capacity bus systems (HCBS) provides dedicated bus lanes on crowded sections of arterial roads, with priority for buses at some junctions. The buses are run in platoons wherever possible, with special boarding platforms. The schedules are optimised by on line communication facilities. A dual lane HCBS system can be built at much lower costs than a single track MRTS, is functional in much less time and can be altered to meet changing requirements, unlike the fixed structure of the MRTS. The capacity of the two parallel corridors of an HCBS system will have passenger capacity of around 60,000 per hour compared to 40,000 for a MRTS. Altogether, this appears to be a more feasible and useful option for Delhi than the proposed MRTS (Saraf, 1998). The city of Curitiba in Brazil has long been held up to be role model for other cities in developing countries. The key features of the Curitiba system are reserved lanes for buses, priority for buses over other traffic at junctions, a hierarchy of frequent interconnecting routes, machines for ticket sales to passengers at stops before boarding to minimise stopping times and good bus shelters. The buses are mostly privately owned, operating under licence from the municipality (Rabinovitch, 1992).

Recently, compressed natural gas was tried out as an option for city transport, but results at the moment do not appear to be clear cut. Certainly there is a reduction in pollution, but there are significant safety concerns, and high refitting costs. Though demand for CNG at present is being partially met, the situation could change as demand increases. Right now, private vehicles, which contribute significantly to the pollution load are prevented from using the CNG option.

As we have seen, the best way of reducing transportation problems is by intelligent design so as to reduce commuting requirements by providing distributed CBD functions, mixed high density neighbourhoods, commercial, and employment facilities. Where commuting is unavoidable, it should be organised as far as possible by public transportation or bicycles, scooters and other low impact vehicles. High and medium speed buses, dedicated bus and cycle corridors, tramways, innovative street design etc. can also serve useful purpose in reducing congestion and increasing speed and comfort of transport. As explained in a previous section, underground MRTS systems do not appear to be cost effective under the present circumstances, but they could be developed when the per capita income rises above a certain limit. Electric vehicles are certainly an option for the future, but at the present time, their costs are high, especially since the present day batteries have limited capacity. Disposal of lead acid batteries after their stipulated lifetimes will also impose significant environmental costs. Many other options suggested such as fuel cells etc, though causing much less pollution, will impose considerable cost burdens. Ethanol and methanol, derived from biomass or agricultural products will be a long-term option if costs can be brought down by about a factor of two to three. Hydrogen as vehicle fuel poses problems of storage, embrittlement of containers, low bulk density necessitating larger transport costs and shorter ranges as compared with present day fossil fuel vehicles, but is certainly a clean fuel. Another drawback is dependent on abundant electricity supplies for its generation, though the thermochemical route is being intensely investigated. Another option is that of photosynthetic (algal) hydrogen production, but economies of this is also uncertain at the moment. In the next two decades, hybrid elctric vehicles (internal combustion engines charging batteries for short range urban journeys) with lightweight composite bodies are expected to be available which will significantly reduce urban pollution and increase fuel efficiencies. A number of options are thus available, which will have to be investigated and cost analyses made.

## THE SUSTAINABLE CITY : A LOOK AT THE FUTURE

In the sections above we have discussed some of the technologies that will contribute to sustainability. The emphasis has been on available or almost available technologies, such as biomass processing, water-biomass linkages, solar energy, building materials and so on.

Even if a technology is not available right now, what has been suggested is a straightforward extrapolation. No cognizance has been taken of futuristic technologies, such as advanced fusion techniques, major breakthroughs in photovoltaic energy, new forms of engineering plastics for low cost membrane filtration, intelligent buildings etc. There are some good reasons for this : if we can demonstrate that a sustainable city is possible with the current technology options, then we can be sure that as technology advances further, sustainability becomes an even more realizable goal.

But technologies are only one part of a sustainable society; far more important are the community and social structures. The traditional society in India, whether urban or rural, was one which provided for sustained and effective interaction with others, and thus provided security and community satisfaction. We are in serious danger of losing these advantages, in Delhi as well as many other urban areas. More and more, "gated" communities are coming up, in which people of similar income categories congregate, and the poor are physically kept out. Although it has not reached American proportions because of our inherent lack of capital, there is also a tendency for sub-urbanisation and long commuting distances. These are all absolutely antithetical to sustainability. The sustainable city is one where people can live and work comfortably in communities which are accessible on foot or low powered forms of transport such as bicycles. It would be densely inhabited, and catering strongly to public places such as parks, squares, shopping areas, *maidans* etc. where sporting and religious events can be held. The need is for relatively decentralised multiple core areas around which viable communities could be built and which in turn could be integrated into the overall city by high speed efficient transportation such as light rail, bus, trams etc. In general all needs of shopping, medical care except for specialies, and entertainment should be available within walking distance, so should most of the work opportunities. This means mixed use neighbourhoods, where industry, trade, residences, educational institutions etc. all mingle; any problems of waste disposal whether industrial or domestic should be dealt with by adopting clean technologies and not by segregating the activities. Equally if not more important is to provide a proper human mix, that is people of differing income levels and religions etc. should live together and not form *ghettos*. The interactions provided by such a mix would generate the social capital which alone would keep a community together, by constantly seeing and interacting with each other, the rich and poor would be motivated to work with each other rather than to exclude each other. This would lay the basis of a living community; with low levels of crime and high levels of harmony, and with real problems to solve, so that people's lives would remain purposeful.

It would be interesting to look at what a well designed city could look like. The business of a city is to facilitate human interaction. As such every city needs a core, a central business district, where interaction can be concentrated. The dominant urban activity centre may be of varying types, such as government, financial, trade, business office, cultural, medical, residential, entertainment or many of these in combination. But they should be compact and concentrated, hence it is necessary to restrict the size of the core. If the activity centres are allowed to spread outward along the radial traffic ways, they soon dissipate in strength, and leave a dilapidating core. It may, therefore, be necessary to restrict the ultimate size by physical barriers, such as a ring park, waterway, ring road etc. Major cultural, governmental and business facilities should be within this ring, and proposals to spread such activities outside should be resisted. As a guide, it is proposed that a thriving CBD (Central business district) should cover an area of about 300 acres, or within a radius of about 2000 feet, walkable at normal pace within about 10 minutes. Except for passenger buses moving along well defined rights of way, and goods transportation vehicles confined to subsurface tunnels, no private automobile will be permitted within the CBD. Instead, multilevel garages will be provided at the edges to provide parking facilites, and rapid transit systems, bus routes etc. will have their stations at the edge of the ring. Goods will be delivered from points outside the CBD to internal distribution points through underground passageways, preferably through electrically operated vehicles or pneumatic tubes.

The city of the future will be a multilevel garden city, rising in terraced decks above its service and utility levels. Its modular, interlocking base extending horizontally and vertically in response to need and topography, will support the office towers, domes and other structures. All will be served by the transit system and will be interconnected by escalators, flying walkways and high speed lifts. Concentrations will be much greater than at present because of the removal of space consuming streets, and parking facilities. Instead, the offices will look down upon a pleasant park and interconnecting networks of malls, garden walkways, fountains etc., which can be roofed for weather protection if necessary. Some routes should be preserved for evolving forms of local transportation such as monorail, moving chairs, beltways etc. In addition to the primary central area functions, the plans and zoning will encourage the inclusion of speciality shops, boutiques, restaurants, cafes, entertainment facilities etc. that will enhance the quality of life. Centralised facilities will range from energy, waste disposal to computerised accounting and information facilities to subsurface storage and goods distribution.

But initially we must start with what we have. As technology and economic levels improve, we can build in further elements of sustainability and comfort.

## REFERENCES

Ayres, R.U. "*Turning Point: The End of the Growth Paradigm*" Earthscan Publications 1998.

Ayres, R.U. "*Industrial Metabolism*" in Jackson (1993) pp.165-188.

Ayres, R.U. and Weaver, P.M.(Eds). "*Ecorestructuring : Implications for Sustainable Development*" United Nations University Press and Vistaar Publications, New Delhi, 1998.

Batty, M. and Longley, P. "The Fractal City" *Architectural Design Profile* No. 129 (1998), pp. 74-83.

Biswas, D. and Trivedi, R. C. "Delhi's Water Crisis, Recycling and Reuse" Seminar on Water Resources of the National Capital Region PHD House, Nov. 22-23, 1996.

Campbell, T. "Urban Development in the Third World: Environmental Dilemmas and the Urban Poor" in H.J. Leonard (Ed.) *Environment and the Poor; Development Strategies for a Common Agenda* " Overseas Development Council, Washington D.C. and Transaction Books (USA), 1989.

Castells, M. (Ed.) *High Technology, Space and Society,* Vol. 28, Urban Affairs Annual Reviews, Sage Publications (1985).

Central, Pollution Control Board, Government of India : Inspection Report of Polluting Sources of Yamuna River and Western Yamuna Canal (1997) (Internal Report).

Cohen, M.J. "Risk Society and Ecological Modernisation : Alternative vision for post-industrial nations" *Futures* Vol. 29, No. 2, pp. 105-119, March 1997.

Frankl, P. "Photovoltaics" in *Ayres and Weaver,* 1998, pp. 223-256.

Gardner, G. and Sampat, P. "Mind over Matter : Recasting the role of Materials in our lives" World Watch Paper 144, World Watch Institute, Washington D.C. (December 1998).

Gielen, D.J. 'Towards integrated energy and material policies? A case study of $CO_2$ reduction in the Netherlands.' *Energy Policy,* Vol. 232, No. 12, 1995, pp. 1049-62.

Gowariker, V. (Ed.) : "The Inevitable Billion Plus : Science, Population and Development, an exploration of Inter-connectivities and action possibilities in India "Unmesh Publications, New Delhi, 1992.

Ground Water Board (1996): Data presented at the Seminar on Water Resources of the National Capital Region PHD House, November 22-23, 1996.

Hall, P. "Modelling the Post Industrial City" pp. 311-321 *Futures* Vol. 29, No. 4/5 May-June 1997 (Special Issue "Time and Space: Geographical Perspectives on the Future").

Hamm, B. and Muttagi, P. (eds.) *Sustainable Development and the Future of Cities*, Intermediate Technology Publications Ltd (1998).

Hillier, B. "Space is the Machine: A configurational theory of Architecture" Cambridge University Press (1996).

*India Today*, October 19, 1998, pp. 87-88. "A New Lease of Life".

Indiresan, P.V. Guided Urban Development : A Report prepared for the Housing and Urban Development Corporation and TIFAC, 1990.

Indiresan, P.V. *Population and Quality of Life in Gowariker* (1992) pp. 307.

Jackson, T. *Material Concerns : Pollution, Profit and Quality of Life*, Routledge (1996). pp. 77-78.

Jackson, T. (Ed) *Clean Production Strategies–Developing Preventive Environmental Management in the Industrial Economy*, Stockholm Environmental Institute and Lewis Publishers (1993).

Jacobs, J. : *The Economic Life of Cities*, Random House (1969).

Jacobs, J. : *Cities and the Wealth of Nations*, Viking (1984).

James, J. and Bhalla, A. "Flexible Specialisation, New Technologies and Future Industrialisation' *Futures*, Vol. 25, No. 6, pp. 713-732 (July/August 1993) (Special, Issue : Future of Industrialisation, Guest Editors: Sam Cole and Richard Florida).

Lall, V.D. *Informal Sector in the National Capital Region*, B.R. Publishing Corporation, 1989.

Leitman, J. "*Rapid Urban Environmental Assessment*" World Bank (1994), Vol. I.

Lindstorm, C. "Water free waste disposal" in *Strategies for Human Settlements*, Gwen Bell. (Ed).

Madan, V.L. 'Master Plan Compulsions—As per Master Plan of Delhi–Perspectives 2001'. Lallyma Publishers. 1993.

Mara, D. (Ed.) *'Low Cost Sewerage'* John Wiley & Sons, 1996.

Mara, D. *'Low Cost Urban Sanitation'*, John Wiley & Sons, 1996.

Marvin, S. "Environmental Flows, Telecommunications and the dematerialisation of Cities "*Futures*, Vol. 29, No. 1, pp. 47-65, February 1997.

McDonough, W. and Braugart, M. "The Next Industrial Revolution", *Atlantic Monthly* October 1998.

Meltzer, J. "Metropolis to Metroplex : *The Social and Spatial Planning of Cities*" John Hopkins University Press, 1984.

Mittlin, D. and Satterwaite, D. "Sustainable Development and Cities" in *Sustainability, Environment and Urbanisation* Cedric Pugh (Ed). Earthscan Publications (London) 1996.

Mohan, R. : "*Population and Urbanisation* : Strategies to cope with city growth" *in Gowariker*, 1992, pp. 244-272.

Mohan, S. "Industrialisation of Near Urban Areas—A Conceptual Framework' in P.S. Lamba and S.S. Solanki (Eds.) *Impact on Urbanisation and Industrialisation on Rural Society*, Wiley Eastern, New Delhi (1992).

Mohan, S. "New Materials–Impact on World Development and Culture" in A. Rahman (Ed.) *Science, Technology and Development"*, Vol. II, New Age International Publishers and Wiley Eastern, 1995.

Munro, D.A. "Sustainability : Rhetoric or Reality?" in *Trzyna* (ref. 19).

National Capital Planning Board *"National Capital Region : Growth and Development"*. Har Anand Publications 1996.

National Commission on Urbanisation, Government of India, 1988, Vol. I, pp. 17-18.

National Academy of Sciences, Washington D.C. "More Water for Arid Lands, 1974.

Newland, K. "City Limits : Emerging Constraints on Urban Growth" Worldwatch Paper 38 (August 1980) Worldwatch Institute, Washington D.C.

Pandey, R. Fiscal Options for Vehicular Pollution Control in Delhi, *Economic and Political Weekly*, November 7, 1998, pp. 2873-2880.

Parivesh : *Newsletter of the Central Pollution Control Board*, Vol. II, No. 2, September 1995. (special issue on biomonitoring. pp 5.).

Persistent Poverty in Developing Countries : Determining the causes and closing the gaps. A report of the Aspen Institute Conference on Peace and Security. 1998.

PHD Chamber of Commerce and Industry, "National Capital Region—A Critical Review". In collaboration with Ministry of Urban Development, Government. of India and NCR Planning Board, New Delhi, 1996, Proceedings of the Seminar on "National Capital Region—Need for a Critical Appraisal" on 16 May 1992.

Portugali, J. "Self organising cities" pp. 353-379, *Futures*, Vol. 29, No. 4/5 May-June 1997 (Special Issue " Time and Space: Geographical Perspectives on the Future").

Priyadarshini, M. and Kalia. K.N. "Pollution Level in the Yamuna" *STEPS Quarterly*, Vol. 3, No. 1, 1993, pp. 23.

Rabinovitch, J. Curutiba—Where the buses hold sway (Extracted from Environment and Urbanisation Vol. 4, No. 2 (1992) quoted in *Hindu Survey of the Environment* 1998, pp. 163-167.

Reddy, A. K. N. and Goldemberg, J. Energy for the Developing World Scientific American (International edition), September 1990, p. 64.

Renn, O., Goble, R. and Katzenholz, H. "How to apply the concept of sustainability to a region." *Technology Forecasting and Social Change*, 58, 63-81. 1998.

Saraf, R. "Third World Traffic—Alternate Approaches" *The Hindu Survey of the Environmment*. 1998, pp.153-161.

SEARO Health Paper No. 4 "Low cost water supply and sanitation technology, World Health Organisation, 1984.

Simmonds, J.O. *"Earthscape : A Manual of Environmental Planning and Design"* VNR Publications, New York, 1978.

Singh, K., Steinberg, F., and Einsiedel, von N. *Integrated Urban Infrastructure Development in Asia*, Intermediate Technology Publications, London, 1996. [Proceedings of the International Seminar on Integrated Urban Infrastructure Development, Feb. 1995, New Delhi].

Smith, M., Whitelegg, J. and Williams, N. *"Greening the Built Environment"* Earthscan Publications. 1998.

Socolow, R., Andrews, C., Berkhout., F., and Thomas., V., (Eds) *Industrial Ecology and Global Cange* Cambridge University Press, 1994.

Technology Information, Forecasting and Assessment Council (TIFAC), Department of Science and Technology, Government of India (1996): Technology Vision 2020: Driving Forces, Impedances (1996). (TIFAC: V:08:X: ESDR) Report Coordinator: P. V. Indiresan) *Times of India* (*Delhi Times*), March 24 and April 1, 1999.

Tryzyna, T.C. (ed). "A Sustainable World–Defining and measuring sustainable development" ICUN-World Conservation Union and International Centre for the Environment and Public Policy, California. 1995.

Wallace, D. "Sustainable Industrialization" The Royal Institute of International Affairs – Energy and Environmental Programme and Earthscan Publications Ltd., London. 1996.

Water, B., Arkin, L. and Crenshaw, R. "Sustainable Cities–Concepts and Strategies for Ecocity Development" *Eco Home Media,* 1992.

Winger, A. R. "Finally : A withering away of cities?" *Futures,* Vol. 29, No. 3, April 1997.

Wizacker, von E., Lovins, A., and Lovins, H. "Factor Four: Doubling Wealth, halving resource use" Earthscan Publications (1998). (From Interview with Amory Lovins, Resurgence, No. 190, Sept./October 1998, pp. 22-25).

# 11

# Urban Land Transformation in Relation to Distance

## A Case Study

**SHAHAB FAZAL**

United Nations' figures have indicated that in the new millennium, for the first time in history, a majority of the world's population will live in cities. By the year 2025 almost 61 per cent of world's population would live in urban settlements. Significantly, most of this explosive growth will occur in the cities of developing world. India known as land of villages but here also a steady trend of urbanisation is observed since independence. There was increase in the size and proportion of the urban population as well as number of urban centres. India's urban population in the last fifty years has more than tripled (62.4 million to 217.2 million) at an average rate of 3.09 per cent per annum. In India, urban population is increasing through migration of population to urban centres from rural areas. The main reason for this migration is lack of employment opportunities in the rural areas. The main occupation in rural areas of India is agriculture, which is unable to bear the burden of increasing population in rural areas. The agricultural land remains the same while the dependent population is increasing leading to low land-man ratio. Demographic growth stimulates structural change through multiplier effects and behavioural changes attract immigrants but the basis of urbanisation is economic change and in particular the growth of large-scale production and expansion of infrastructure. Urban areas have become centres of all the activities they are exploding in size, land use is changing quickly and constantly intensifying urban lands and large-scale land transformation is taking place due to substantial increases in urban land value.

Urbanisation in any region is the result of three components:

(i) Natural increase,
(ii) Increase due to migration, and
(iii) Appearance of new urban centres.

The migration is also the outcome of "centripetal forces". These forces attract the population towards the urban centre. Some of the main attractions are:

1. Employment opportunities.
2. Regular and higher wages.
3. Fixed working hours.
4. Better amenities of living.
5. Better education facility.
6. Socio-cultural activities.
7. Attractive life style.

Because of the above-mentioned factors the population increases in the urban centre and urban expansion because of 'centrifugal forces' take place, which pushes the population to the outer periphery of the city. Some of the main reasons are:

(i) Availability of land,
(ii) Over crowded and congestion in the city region,
(iii) Lower cost of land, and
(iv) Congenial environment.

As the population increases in urban areas the demand for land for various urban activities also increases. This results in change in urban land-use and expansion of urban areas. This expansion of urban areas is termed as 'urban sprawl'. The present study is to study the land use pattern of Saharanpur city, to find out the change in land-use of the city with respect to distance from city centre and to measure the urban sprawl. Saharanpur city was chosen as the study area, which is one of the class I (population of more than 1,00,000) city of western Uttar Pradesh (India) having nodal location between plain and hill districts. It acts as the service centre for nearby towns and hilly districts and more significantly this city, which had traditionally an agrarian dominated population. But lately because of the emergence of several industries, the city has lost its agrarian fabric and more and more of its population now shedding agrarian sector and switching to secondary and tertiary sector. This development in secondary and tertiary occupation sector is luring the population not only from the city's hinterland but also from far of places for providing better job opportunities.

## STUDY AREA

The study area lies between 29° 55′ to 30° north latitude and 77° 30′ to 77° 45′ east longitude. It is situated in western part of Uttar Pradesh

(India), in the fertile tract of Upper Ganga-Yamuna doab (inter-riverine plain). Saharanpur City is the district headquarters and second largest city in Meerut division. It is well connected by several state road highways to the important cities. City is having nodal location between the hilly district (in the north) and plain region (in the south) of Uttar Pradesh. The city is spread over 4,030 hectares (Municipal boundary). But, since it has expanded beyond this limit, so we have also extended our study area, which deals with 7,745 hectares. The present city is divided into two parts by the railway line, the northern part is the older part while southern part is newer, where most of the institutional and industrial development has taken place. The population of the city is 0.37 million according to 1991 census. The city has the population density of 239 persons per hectare. The projection by the Town and Country Planning Department of Saharanpur city has indicated that by the year 2001, the population of the city will increase up to 0.6 million and the city needs another 64,000 houses to the existing figure of 60,575 houses.

## DATA AND METHODOLOGY

The present study is based on secondary data including the remotely sensed data (satellite imagery). This data along with extensive field checks and surveys provided accurate and up-to-date. The advantages of these data are many, because urban areas are very dynamic and complex in nature and conventional data source were unable to cope with these data. The information was far too much and they too get changed in a very short period of time. On the other hand their collection took a very long period. So remote sensing is a strong tool for urban studies. Now IRS lC is providing 5.8 metres resolution, which makes the urban studies even more fruitful.

The study is spread over a time span of sixteen years (1982-98). The urban sprawl mapping was done with the help of Saharanpur City Guide Map, prepared by Survey of India (1982) on 1:20,000 scale, IRS 1C geo-coded panchromatic satellite analogue imagery on 1:12,500 scale, acquired in 1998. The minimum delineation unit for both the maps was 0.5 cm × 0.5 cm. The satellite imagery was first visually interpreted with the help of separate interpretation keys to identify various land-use classes. Some of the land-use classes could not be distinguished by visual interpretation of satellite imagery. Especially, the differentiation between residential and commercial land-use classes. These classes were identified during the field checks and demarcated afterwards. Subsequently, the details of these final maps were transferred on Base map, bringing both the maps on same scale. Thereafter, these maps were digitized for analysis. Further the study was done in GIS environment because the use of GIS techniques, coupled with remote sensing would be essential elements for the rapid production of accurate and up-to-date databases. The inherent flexibility of GIS techniques can make important contribution for improving the speed and qualitative performance of urban and regional planning. GIS techniques allow quite complex quantitative and spatial relationships to be made and displayed in graphical form and improve the clarity of the planning and decision making process. The present work has been carried out using ILWIS software (The Integrated Land and Water Information System) 2.2 windows version developed by ITC, The Netherlands.

**Discussion**

Traditionally Saharanpur has agro-based economy. It lies in the fertile land between two master streams of India, the Ganga and the Yamuna. Initially the development of Saharanpur City was also because of its agrarian background. It had well-developed market for agro based products. It also played the role of service centre for nearby towns and hilly region of Uttaranchal. But in the last 25 years several industries have also come up and changed the fabric of the city's economy. The city has well known paper, straw board, tobacco and cigarette industries. Besides these big industries several medium level agro-based, motor transport, hosiery industries are flourishing in the city. The city has also excelled in wood sculpture and its products are exported to several countries. That is why the city and its surroundings have undergone radical changes.

## URBAN LAND-USE OF SAHARANPUR CITY

Saharanpur City is named after one Sufi Saint Shah Harun Chisti. It was ruled by Mughals, but the development of city took place only under Britishers who in 1903 made this city as district Headquarters.

In 1926 when the city received electric supply its economic development got a boost and city started to develop at a faster speed. After independence a good number of refugees came to this place and settled here. The present city is divided into two parts by the railway line, the northern part is the older part while southern part is newer, where most of the institutional and industrial development has taken place (Fig. 11.1).

Although the municipal area of Saharanpur City is only about 4,030 hectares but due to the objectives of our study we are dealing with 7,745 hectares of land. It includes the changes and urban expansion of the city, which have occurred in the city during the study period. From the perusal of Table 11.1 and Fig.11.2, it is clearly evident that land-use of Saharanpur city is not very well planned. With time, the older part of the city has become more and more congested while on the other hand the city has expanded outward in a haphazard manner and swallowed the agricultural land in the fringe area. The urban land-use of Saharanpur city is dominated by residential class, which occupies more than 23 per cent of the study area (42 per cent of municipal area). However, most of this residential area is unplanned and only 2.2 per cent are planned having open spaces and comparatively better basic infrastructure facilities. The second largest area is occupied by vacant land (12.2 per cent), which is the outcome of rapid transformation of occupational structure and emergence of secondary and tertiary activities. The main reason for the increase of vacant land in the city was that initially when industrialization took place, there was shortage of open land for construction. This demand has led to increase in the land value and owners of land started to get more money instantly, which they were not getting in agricultural sector. So, in anticipation more and more people started to offer their land for construction resulting in phenomenal transformation of land from agricultural uses to vacant land. But later this demand due to stagnation and saturation subsided, resulting in increase of vacant land that is neither used for urban development nor it is useful for agricultural sector. Similarly, area under plantation (tree crop) is also spread over 6 per cent of the study area. This again is mainly due to two reasons, firstly, rich people are protecting their lands (in city area) from encroachment by planting trees and they are waiting for increse in land value. Secondly, it is also quite remunerative as well as assured market in the city itself and these factors helped in increase of area

**Table 11.1 :** Saharanpur City Area Under Different Land-Use (1982-98).

| Land-Use | Year 1982 | | Year 1998 | | % age Change 1982-98 |
|---|---|---|---|---|---|
| | Area | % | Area | % | |
| Residential | 1024 | 11.9 | 1790 | 21.8 | 78.6 |
| Commercial | 44 | 0.6 | 125 | 1.6 | 184.1 |
| Institutional | 144 | 0.8 | 170 | 0.8 | 18.05 |
| Industrial | 122 | 1.5 | 216 | 2.9 | 77.04 |
| Agricultural Land | 5178 | 66.8 | 3495 | 45.2 | –33.5 |
| Tree Plantation | 395 | 5.2 | 459 | 5.9 | 16.2 |
| Vacant Land | 306 | 3.9 | 948 | 12.2 | 209.8 |
| Restricted Area | 402 | 5.2 | 402 | 5.2 | 0 |
| Others | 130 | 1.6 | 140 | 1.7 | 00.7 |

*Note*: Area in Hectares.

*Source*: Based on Saharanpur City, Guide Map and IRS, 1C Satellite Imagery.

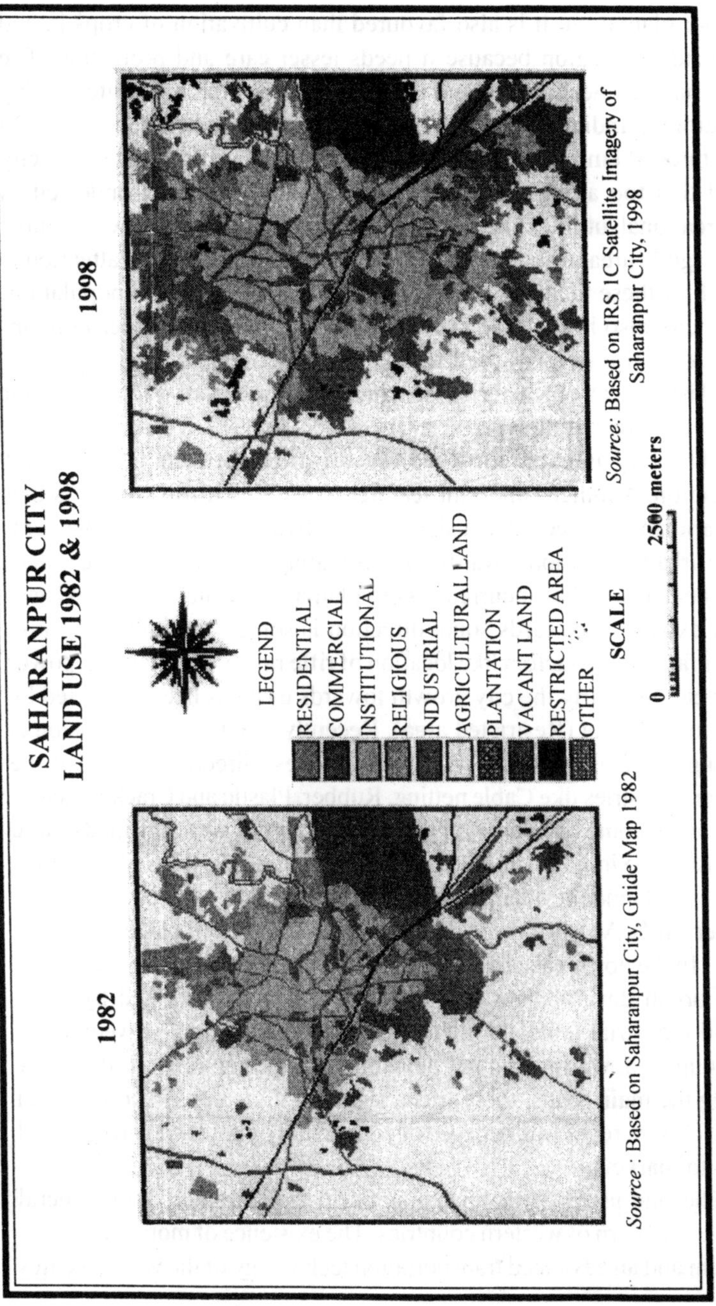


*Source* : Based on Saharanpur City, Guide Map 1982

*Source:* Based on IRS 1C Satellite Imagery of Saharanpur City, 1998

**Fig. 11.1 :** Land-Use of Saharanpur City, 1982 and 1998

under plantation. It is also favoured than cultivation of crops in and around city region because it needs lesser care and protection. The city has 123 hectares of land under industries, which is quite high by traditional Indian standard. Commercial area in the city occupies 125 hectares of land. These areas are mainly in the central part of the city and that too along the major roads. Interestingly area under city's recreational, utilities and services (categorized as others) covers almost negligible area of study area. This indicates that, not much attention is paid for these facilities despite the significant increase in population. The city also has a good share of land (5.2 per cent) under remount depot (restricted area) used for defense purposes.

The salient characteristics, which emerges from Table 11.1 and Fig.11.2. are as follows :

The city is expanding mainly towards north and south-west direction. Another important feature of city's land-use change is that vacant land has recorded a significant increase of about 250 per cent. The urban expansion towards north is mainly by industries (rice mills). This expansion has incurred loss to plantation, which earlier existed. The expansion towards south direction is somewhat limited because of unfavourable factors like location of rifle range, high-tension power line etc. Similarly the city growth towards east has been restricted by Remount Depot (Restricted area). Recently rapid urban expansion is taking place along Delhi road in south-west direction. Some of the major industries like Cable netting, Rubber, Plastic and Cracker factory etc., have come up. Some unplanned residential area surrounds these industries. Similarly in south-east direction along the railway track some unplanned residential area has come up. It is extended up to Star Paper Mills. Most of these developments have taken place on vacant land. In the north-eastern direction, along the Dehradun road, a ribbon like urban development is taking place, which is marked by some small industrial units along the Dehradun road and in between these built up area, vacant land has developed. In the central part of the city along the main roads, there was a significant increase in commercial area. This increase was because of conversion of unplanned residential area to markets.

The land-use pattern of Saharanpur city is different from the general land use pattern of western countries. The existence of mono-economic system and an advanced transportation technology of the western cities

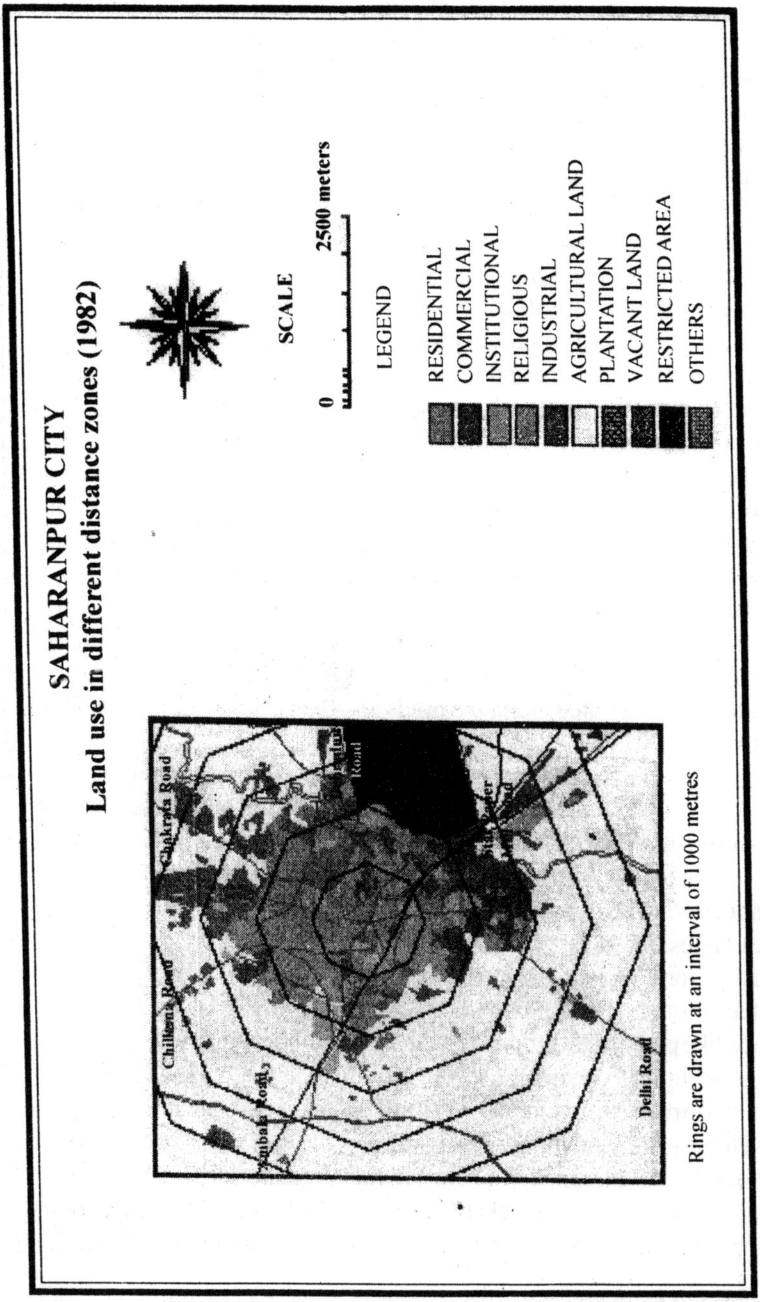


**Fig. 11.2 :** Land-Use in Different Distance Zones (1982) of Saharanpur City

had led to a maximum specialization of land-use which has most frequently taken the form of concentric circles of relatively homogeneous economic usage. From the perusal of Fig. 11.2, no such clear zonation characterizes the land-use pattern of Saharanpur city. It is hard to generalize about the patterns of residence. The rapid growth of population of the city associated with the soico-economic changes, which are creating an emergent middle class. This has caused a proliferation of squatter settlements in the interstices and fringes of the city. At present Saharanpur city shows little conformity with the western cities where direct relationship is observed between social class and distance from the centre of the city with working class living closest to the city core and upper class in the city fringe. The pattern of residence in Saharanpur city includes a mixture of poor and rich elements of the city in both the core and outer areas. It represents some transitory phase, which is developing between the patterns of pre-industrial and post-industrial. There was only one distinct commercial zone in Saharanpur city. This zone has peculiar radial dimension along the main roads from the Ghanta Ghar (located almost at the centre of the city). It is the central economic zone, which consists of shops and showrooms of reputed products ranging from machinery, consumer goods and warehouses etc. Other commercial areas are scattered, but located along the roads and their concentration declines with distance. These commercial areas are crowded and picture of congestion and traffic jams and to the western observer, this is a place of noise and colour. The industrial land-use of the city resembles the western location in some way. The larger industrial units are located in the fringe area but the main difference from western cities is that it is not confined to specialized estates but are scattered. The other land-use classes like vacant land and plantation (tree crop) are governed by local factors. The same trend is not necessarily found in other cities of India. Another significant feature of Saharanpur city is lack of public space like parks, play ground etc., and even public utilities and services have negligible occupance in the city. It indicates lack of planning and co-ordination among various government authorities for developing these facilities, which are under severe stress from rapidly increasing population. The overall spatial organization in Saharanpur city represents indigenous characteristics, which stem from indigenous living conditions and the indigenous ways of adaptation with them.

**Table 11.2:** Saharanpur City Land-Use in Different Distance Zones (1982-98)

| Land-Use | 0– km. | | 1–2 km. | | 2–3 km. | | 3–4 km. | | 4–5 km. | | 5–6 km. | |
|---|---|---|---|---|---|---|---|---|---|---|---|---|
| | 1982 | 1998 | 1982 | 1998 | 1982 | 1998 | 1982 | 1998 | 1982 | 1998 | 1982 | 1998 |
| Residential | 230 | 199 | 511 | 581 | 171 | 542 | 41 | 589 | 22 | 114 | 50 | 65 |
| Commercial | 18 | 49 | 13 | 42 | 9 | 30 | 4 | 4 | -- | -- | -- | -- |
| Institutional | 11 | 11 | 31 | 31 | 19 | 21 | -- | -- | -- | -- | -- | -- |
| Religious | -- | -- | 19 | 15 | 35 | 35 | -- | -- | 3 | 3 | -- | -- |
| Industrial | 4 | 4 | 30 | 30 | 28 | 28 | 29 | 48 | 25 | 84 | 6 | 22 |
| Agricultural Land | -- | -- | -- | -- | 805 | 509 | 1613 | 844 | 1706 | 1292 | 1054 | 850 |
| Tree Plantation | -- | -- | 4 | 4 | 148 | 86 | 179 | 209 | 58 | 107 | 6 | 53 |
| Vacant Land | 13 | 13 | 113 | 18 | 178 | 132 | 10 | 478 | 8 | 214 | -- | 72 |
| Restricted Area | -- | -- | 5 | 5 | 216 | 216 | 178 | 178 | 3 | 3 | -- | -- |
| Others | 54 | 84 | 144 | 173 | 137 | 70 | 12 | 22 | -- | 8 | -- | -- |

*Note*: Area in Hectares.

*Source*: Based on Saharanpur City, Guide Map and IRS, 1C Satellite Imagery.

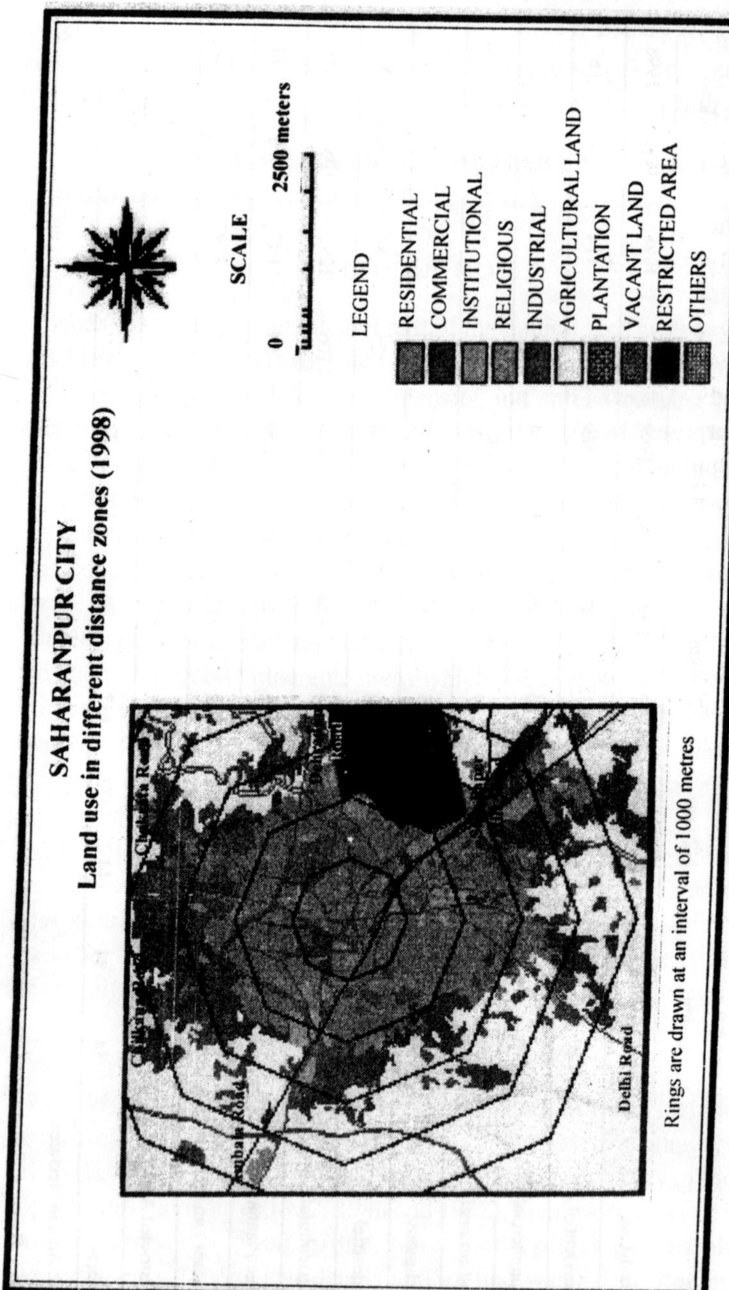


**Fig. 11.3 :** Land-Use in Different Distance Zones (1998) of Saharanpur City

This pattern confirms the Gerald Brees's opinion for Indian urbanization where he termed it as subsistence urbanization (Breese, G.,1969).

**Urban Land Transformation in Different Distance Zone**

The study further investigates the trend of urban land-use change in different distance zones. These distance zones were made from the city centre (*Ganta Ghar*). The distance zones were at the interval of one kilometre radius. From the perusal of Table 11.2 and Figure 11.3 and 11.4, we observe that in the *First ring* (city centre to one kilometre radius) most of the land is part of older city and was used for residential purposes. However, during the study period a large share of it was captured for commercial use. This change in land-use is mainly due to very high land value in this zone. High land value and demand for commercial place has resulted in transformation of residential areas to commercial uses.

The *Second ring* (1-2 kilometre radius) again was dominated by residential class which consumed the available vacant land of this zone during the study period. There was also some change in commercial and utilities and services (land-use class others) as the area under these categories have increased to provide services for increasing population.

The *Third ring* (2-3 kilometre radius) has recorded significant increase in residential class during the study period. This zone was the urban limit in 1982 and that is why most of the new urban expansion is on the agricultural land and agricultural land has lost about 300 hectares of land.

The *Fourth ring* (3-4 kilometre radius) where in 1982 residential class was almost negligible now has swallowed a very substantial area from agricultural land. This zone represents newer part of the city. This zone is also characterized by substantial vacant lands, which are speculative land holdings.

The *Fifth ring* (4-5 kilometre radius) again shows significant loss of agricultural land. It is captured by vacant land and tree plantation and will be used for future urban expansion.

The *Outer ring* (5-6 kilometre radius) shows lesser change in the land-use as this zone is not under much influence of urban expansion.

**SOCIO-ECONOMIC URBAN STRUCTURE MODEL**

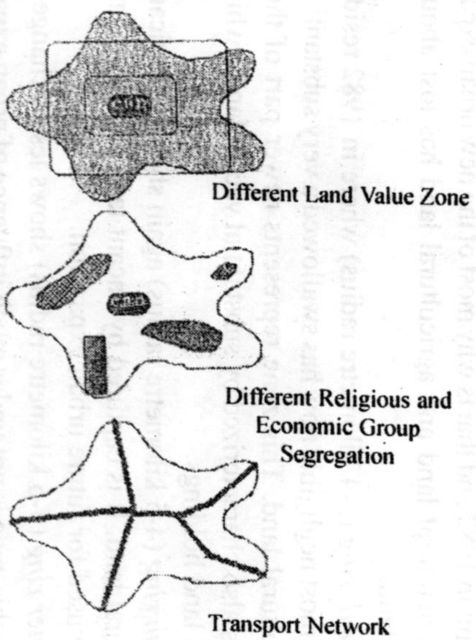


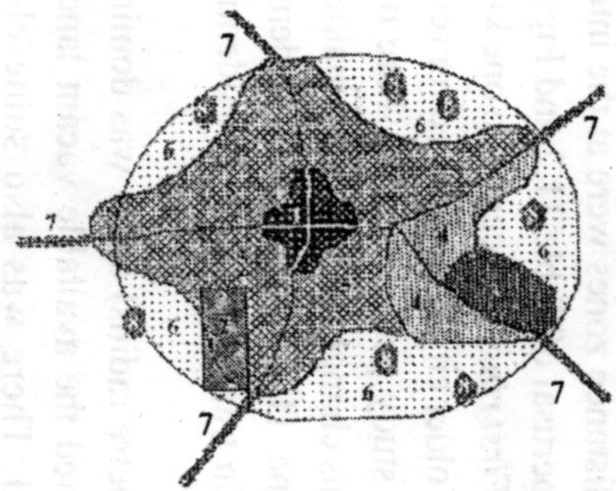


1 = High intensity, high land value commercial and residential
2 = Planned residential (wealthy and educated society)
3 = Industrial
4 = Squatter settlement (poor, unskilled workers)
5 = Unplanned residential (mixed population representing different economic, social and religious group)
6 = New extensions (scatter and mixed land use)
7 = Transformation of agricultural land to vacant land, along main roads (speculative land holdings)
8 = Vacant land or plantation, in between recently developed area (speculative land holding)

**Fig. 11.4 :** Socio-Economic Urban Structure Model

However this zone has also showed loss of agricultural land, which is captured mostly by vacant land.

The above discussion can be depicted by a generalized *Socio-economic Urban Structure Model* (Fig. 11.4), which broadly represent urban land-use of Saharanpur city. This model incorporates the dominating physical aspect (transport network), social aspect (religious, caste and economic group segregation) and economic aspect (different land value zones). These three aspects were superimposed to generate Socio-economic Urban Structure Model and it highlights the main characteristics of land-use pattern of Saharanpur city. The model shows that a *chowk* (intersection of streets) occupies the city centre (C.B.D.) around which shops and business establishments as well as the old houses of rich and people of high status have developed. This region characterizes by intensive land-use and high land value. This is surrounded by unplanned residential area. It consists of population from different economic, social and religious group settled in separate pockets, but the overall physical appearance remains more or less same. The wealthy and educated population because of congestion and lack of basic amenities have moved outward and formed a new separate block of planned residence. This is an island of very high land value despite the fact that it is away from city centre. Industrial areas are located away form the city but along the main roads. This is surrounded by squatter settlements occupied by poor and unskilled workers and labourers. The model also points towards ribbon like urban development along main roads in Saharanpur city. The urban expansion takes place in three phases. In the first phase agricultural land is replaced by tree crops or converted into vacant land along the main roads.

In second phase this land is used for constructing buildings. During the third phase the intervening peripheral land between the roads is used for urban development, that is why, the newly developed areas have patches of vacant land or land under plantation. This process of urban development can be termed as frontal expansion, which is characterized by piecemeal accretion of the built up areas.

## CONCLUSIONS

Some of the main findings of the present study are as follows:

— Built up area has expanded in all direction but it was more pronounced in west direction than in eastern part of the city, where restricted area has blocked the growth.

— The study area has recorded a significant increase in residential area to accommodate the rapidly growing population of the city, but this increase was more pronounced in case of unplanned residential area rather than in the planned residential area.

— Agricultural land is being converted into non-agricultural land (built up and non-built up urban expansion) because of rapid expansion of Saharanpur city.

— The urban expansion is taking place in peculiar way. In the first phase agricultural land is replaced by tree crops or converted into vacant land along the main roads. In second phase this land is used for constructing buildings. During the third phase the intervening peripheral land between the roads are used for urban development. This process of urban development can be termed as frontal expansion, which is characterized by piecemeal accretion of the built up areas.

— There was massive increase in residential area but not much change has occurred among utilities, services and recreational facilities etc., which indicates haphazard city expansion.

— Commercial areas have increased in the central part of the city, that too along the main roads. These areas are in very high land value zone, and that is why commercial areas have pushed residential area away to the outer part of the city.

— The land transformation in Saharanpur city is clearly the outcome of the operation in the urban land market. It has many dimensions but the most important and relevant in present study was land value and land transformation in Saharanur city which is basically the outcome of competitive bidding among various land use classes. However, in India social factors are still quite influential and they act as barrier in land transformation.

— The characteristic feature of urban land-use in Saharanpur city (like most of the Indian cities) is its high mix and it is very difficult to make out any pattern out of it. Specialization of activities in a specific area, so common in the western cities, does not exist here. The spatial organization in the Indian towns and cities is distinguished by the diversified occupance of space. The Indian towns and cities have evolved this peculiar way of adaptation with space, is not based on economic interdependence and segregation.

The Socio-economic Urban Structure Model very appropriately shows the land-use of Saharanpur city as a chowk (interesection of streets) occupies the city centre (C.B.D.) around which shops and business establishments as well as the old house of rich and people of high status have developed.

This region is characterize by intensive land-use and high land value. This is surrounded by unplanned residential area. It consists of population from different economic, social and religious group settled in separate pockets, but the overall physical appearance remains more or less same. The wealthy and educated population because of congestion and lack of basic amentities have moved outward and formed a new separate block of planned residence. This is an island of very high land value despite the fact that it is away from city centre. Industrial areas are located away from the city but along the main roads. This is surrounded by squatter settlements occupied by poor and unskilled worked and labourers.

Lastly, we can say that urbanization pattern of Saharanpur city is characterized by poverty, acute shrotage of housing and civic amenities, dismal filth and diversified occupance of space, which resembles like a large village. Herein lies the major departure of the urbanisation pattern in Indian cities from the western cities. Urbanization may be an indicator of development in western countries but in India, especially in growing small towns it is difficult to accept. Here, the population is increasing raidly, the demand for land also increases. But civic authorities have little control over urban development and expansion, which results in violation of basic rules and regulations in municipal area.

## REFERENCES

Alam, M. (1965) : *'Hyderabad-Secundrabad : A Study in Urban Geography'* Asia Publishing House, Hyderabad.

Alam, M. and Pokshishevsky, V.V. (1976) : *Urbanization in Developing Countries*, Asia Publishing House, Hyderabad.

Borah, J. (1985) : *Spatial Structure of Urban Influence in the Neighbouring Areas of Gauhati City,* Concept Publisher, New Delhi.

Breese, Gerald (1969) : *Urbanization in Newly Developing Countries,* Prentice-Hall of India Pvt. Ltd., New Delhi.

Buksar, J.F. (1964) : *Problems of Rapid Urbanization in India,* Bombay.

Deshpande, C.D. *et al.* (1980) : *Impact of a Metropolitan City on the Surrounding Region,* New Delhi.

Prakasha Rao, V.L.S. (1983): *Urbanisation in India: Spatial Dimensions,* Concept Publishing company, New Delhi.

Fazal, S. (2001): 'The Need for Preserving Farm Lands—A Case Study from a Predominantly Agrarian Economy.' *Landscape and Urban Planning,* Vol. 55, No.1, Elsevier Science Publication, U.K., pp. 1-13.

Fazal, S. (2001): 'Land Reorganization Study Along Major Roads'. *Land Use Policy,* Elsevier Science Publication, Vol. 18, No. 2. United Kingdom. pp. 191-199.

Fazal, S. (2001): 'Application of Remote Sensing and GIS Techniques in Urban Sprawl and Land Use Mapping—A Case Study of a Growing Urban Centre in India.' *Asian Profile,* Vol. 29. No. 1, Canada, pp. 45-62.

Fazal, S. (2001): 'Dynamics of Urban Land Transformation in Developing Economy'. *Indian Journal of Regional Sciences,* Indian Institute of Technology, Kharagpur, Vol. XXXIII, No. 1, pp. 98-111.

Surekha, Pandit (1988): 'Urbanization the Indian Way' ed. Yadav, C.S. *Perspectives in Urban Geography,* Vol. 3, Concept Publishing Company, New Delhi.

# 12

# Environmental Impact Assessment of Tanneries in Dindigul Town, Tamil Nadu

**N. D. MANI**

Human life is intricately linked with the environment. The demand for intensive use of the environment is increasing manifold due to the rise in population, increase in standard of living and growing industrial activities. This has led to decreasing natural resources and the use of the environment for waste disposal. The disposal of pollutants has contaminated the environment, especially the soil, water and air. Though initially this phenomenon was restricted to the developed countries, it is now increasing at an alarming rate in developing countries also. India is not an exception to this phenomenon.

## ENVIRONMENT

The word 'environment' is a broad term. It has been defined by scientists drawn from different disciplines under different references. The Global 2000 report states "Literally the environment is the physical and biological surroundings... of human species. Human kind depends on his life-supporting environment... and the distinction between individual and environment blurs."[1] According to Boland (1993), the environment is the total of all social, technological, biological, physical and chemical elements which compose the surroundings of man[2]. Thus the environment is the surroundings of human beings with all its life supporting elements. It performs three basic functions *viz.,* providing living space, storehouse of resources and dumping ground of waste materials.

## ENVIRONMENTAL POLLUTION

The word 'pollution' is derived from the Latin word '*pollutionem*' which means defilement of soil[3]. Environmental pollution is the unfavourable alteration of our surroundings, wholly or largely as a result of man's actions, through direct or indirect effects of changes in energy patterns, radiation levels, chemical and physical contribution and abundance of organisms[4]. In other words, it is the presence of extraneous materials in high concentrations that are harmful to flora and fauna in a particular environment.

Among the major pollutants, industries come to the fore, mainly due to advances in technology and rapid industrialization. Among industries, the tanning industry is one guilty of polluting the environment for long.

## Tanneries in India

Tanneries are concentrated only in a few states, although the basic raw material is available throughout India. According to a report of the Central Leather Research Institute, Chennai, there are 1,083 tanneries in India with a total installed processing capacity of 62.05 million hides and 161.345 million skins[5]. They are mainly concentrated in Tamil Nadu, West Bengal, Uttar Pradesh, etc.

### *Tanneries in Tamil Nadu*

The leather industry plays a pivotal role in the state of Tamil Nadu. It exports 55 per cent of the total leather exported from India, while 70 per cent of the hides and skins produced in the country are tanned and finished in Tamil Nadu (Leather and Leather Products Report 1989)[6]. In this state, they are clustered in places like Chennai urban agglomeration, Ranipet, Ambur, Vaniambadi and Pernampet in Vellore District, and Dindigul Town.

### *Tanneries in Dindigul Town*

Tanning is one of the important industries in this drought prone district. The tanneries function in most parts of Dindigul Town. They are located here mainly because of the elevation and the natural drainage system with a number of tanks (Figs. 12.1, 12.2 and 12.3). The first tannery was established by Mr. Mohammed Ismail in 1936. At present, there are 68 units in and around Dindigul Town, *i.e.* 10 per cent of the total tanneries in Tamil Nadu. All these tanneries together process about 120 MT skins and hides daily and in the process, discharge 3,168 $m^3$ of waste water.

The present study is aimed at assessing the impact of tanneries on environment in Dindigul Town, in Dindigul District of Tamil Nadu. The assessment is based on the data collected from the local farmers about the impact of tanneries on their land, underground water and consequential changes in land-use and crop pattern.

Out of the 26 affected villages in the vicinity of the tanneries, only seven villages have been selected for the study. Among the 586 affected farmers, the required data were collected from 59 farmers (*i.e.* 10 per cent). The data were collected through a per-tested interview schedule. To understand the intensity of pollution, water and soil samples were subjected to chemical analysis and mapping.

## Findings

### *Changes in Land-use*

- The net area cultivated was 150.65 acres in 1984 and it had declined to 31.6 per cent by 1994. The percentage change in area is--79 per cent.
- Of the total respondents, 85 per cent now possess uncultivated land because of soil pollution.
- Ninety per cent of the respondents have not cultivated their lands in the past while 4 per cent have not cultivated their lands, for more than 15 years.
- Tannery effluents directly flow into 52.5 per cent of the respondents' land and pollutants have indirectly damaged the lands of 47.5 per cent of the respondents.
- All of them maintained that, their lands were not suitable for cultivation as the tannery effluents had continuously damaged their lands and water sources.
- The major reasons for the unsuitability were: (1) retarded and inhabited germination of seeds (91 per cent), (2) accumulation of salt in soil and water (100 per cent) etc.
- According to the respondents, the soil and water resources of these villages have been completely damaged by the tannery effluents. The water available in the wells is suitable neither for drinking nor for irrigation.

### *Changes in Cropping Pattern*

In 1984, 74 acres of land were under paddy cultivation, this has declined to 20 acres in 1994. It is clear that areas under paddy have declined by 73 per cent. During the same period the land under bajra and cotton have shrunk to 78 per cent and 83 per cent respectively and the same is the condition of oilseeds. Vegetable cultivation has been completely wiped out.

### *Crop Yield*

- Due to soil and water contamination, the yield of paddy, bajra and cotton has declined by 91, 98 and 93 per cent respectively between 1980 and 1994. Of the total respondents, 94 per cent said that the yield has gone down due to the tannery effluents.
- The reasons for poor yield and reduction in net area cultivated, as stated by the respondents, include (1) water pollution, (2) infertile and salty soil, and (3) poor germination of seeds.

### *Water Source*

- Wells are the chief source of irrigation for 88 per cent of the respondents. Now the density of water well is high. It is salty, and has a strange colour and odour. All these factors have made the underground water unsuitable for domestic/industrial use.
- It is reported that all of the respondents used water from their own villages in 1980 and that, now (in 1994) none of them use the local water for drinking purposes. Now 29 per cent of the respondents depend on water available in nearby villages and the rest use water supplied by the Dindigul Municipality. When the respondents tried to use local water for domestic purposes the results were (1) food got spoiled, (2) the colour of cooked food changed, and (3) a sensation of stickiness was felt after bathing/ washing of clothes.

### *Livestock*

- The number of livestock-owning respondents have declined by 29 per cent.
- The cow population has declined by 52 per cent. Buffalo, sheep, goat and poultry birds have declined by 63 per cent, 98 per cent, 93 per cent and 100 per cent respectively.
- The respondents' use of fodder has declined considerably by 29 per cent in the case of corn straw, by 35 per cent in the case of grass, by 32 per cent in the case of paddy straw and marginally in the case of oilcake between 1980 and 1994.

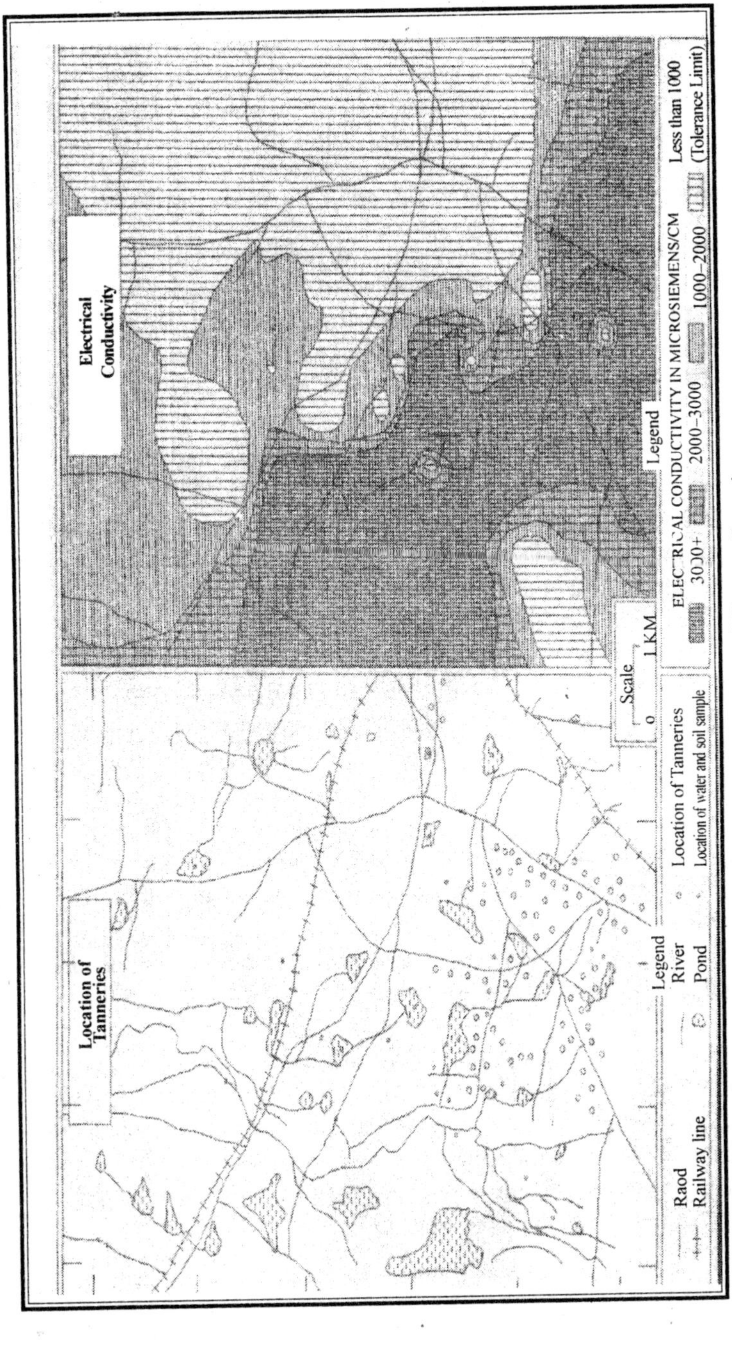


**Fig. 12.1 :** Poullution of Water by Tanneries

- The availability of fodder within the village has decreased by 93 per cent and fodder obtained from outside has increased by 91 per cent by 1994.
- By 1994, the majority of the cattle have become impotent and milk yield has decreased.

### *Intensity of Water and Soil Pollution*

For the purpose of estimating the intensity of the problem of pollution, 26 water and soil samples were collected. Water samples were tested for estimating the quantity of pH, electrical conductivity, total dissolved solids, chloride, fluoride, alkalinity and hardness. Soil samples were tested for sodium and potassium. The details of the chemical analyses have been presented in Figs. 12.1, 12.2 and 12.3.

Fig. 12.1 presents the location of tanneries and the water and soil samples and electrical conductivity (EC). The EC is more than 30,000 microsiemens/cm in and around the tanneries and it is rapidly decreasing in the south, the west and the north-east of Dindigul Town. Potable groundwater with less than 1000 microsiemens/cm of EC is available in the north-eastern part of the town.

Fluoride, alkalinity and chloride hardness are depicted in Fig. 12.2. The fluoride is more than 20 mg/*l* in the central part of Dindigul Town and that the southern part has between 1 and 1.5 while in the northern part of the town, it is below the permissible limit of less than 1 mg/*l*. Hardness is more than 650 in the entire region, except a small pocket in the north-east.

In the north-east, alkalinity is between 100 and 200 mg/*l* and, in all the other parts of the region, alkalinity is more than 300 mg/*l*. The entire region has alkalinity above the permissible limit (vide Fig. 12.2). Chloride is high only at a few places near the tanneries and the tanks. About half of the area has groundwater within the tolerance limit of less than 250 mg/*l*.

Total Dissolved Solids (TDS) and pH in water and potassium and sodium soil are presented in Fig. 12.3. The tolerance limit of pH is 7.5 to 8.5 the pH level is between 7.8 and 8.5 in the north-east and the south-west. In the remaining areas it is less than 7.5. TDS is more than 1500 mg/*l* in the entire region. There are very small pockets of groundwater within the tolerance limit of less than 500 mg/*l* at a few locations.

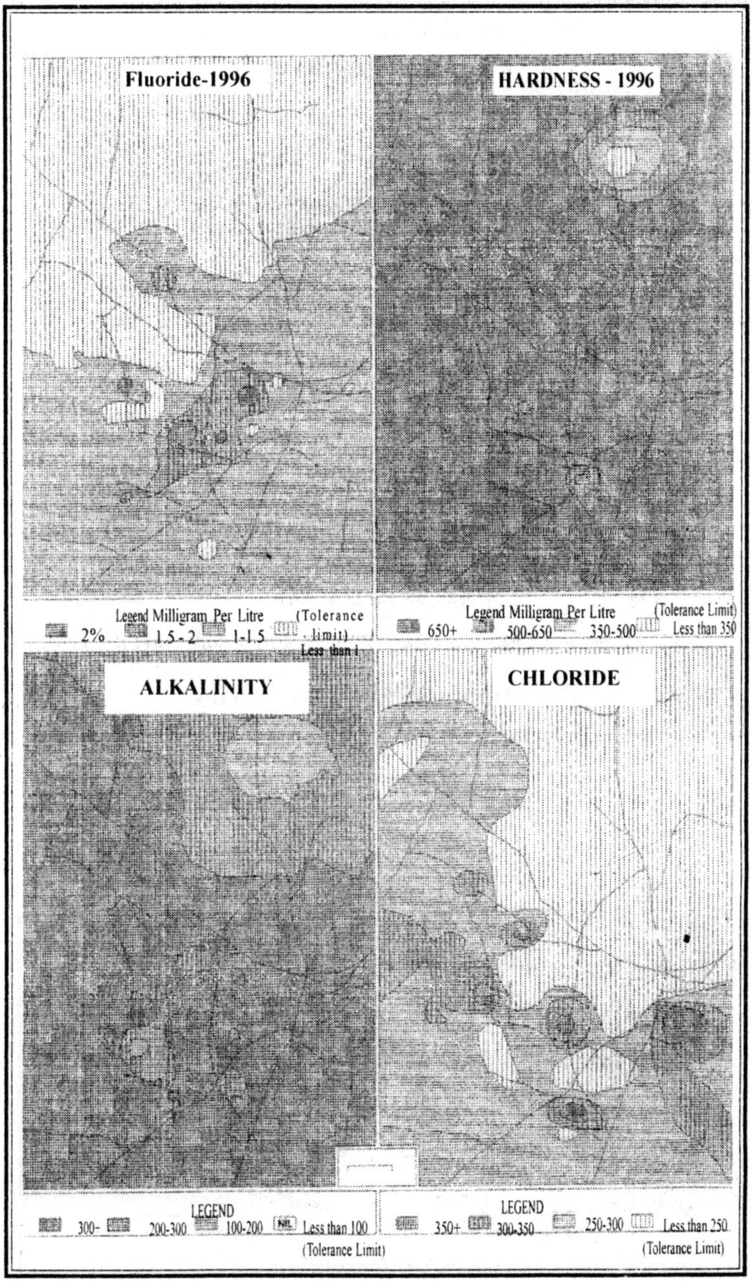


**Fig. 12.2** : Pollution of Water by Tanneries

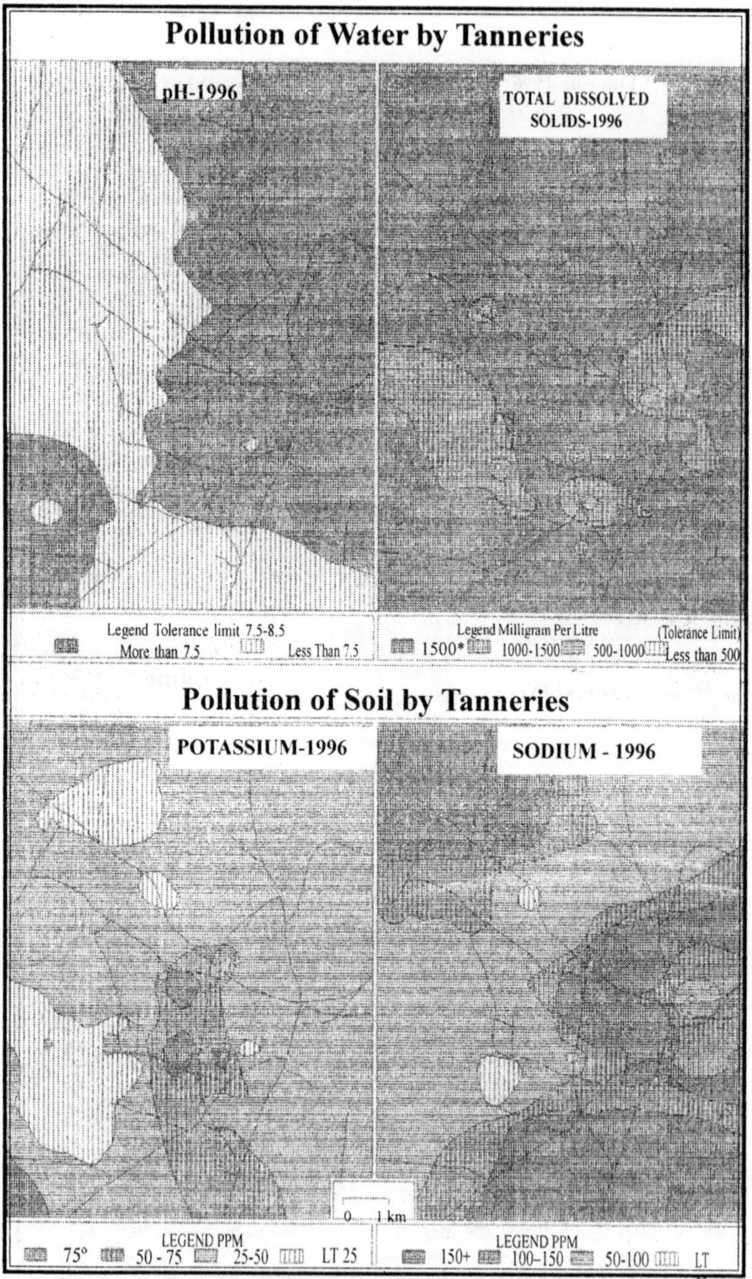


**Fig. 12.3 :** Pollution by Tanneries

The north-eastern part of Dindigul Town has groundwater with permissible quantity of chloride, EC and fluoride. The north-western part has water with fluoride and pH within the tolerance limits. The southern part of the region has all the chemicals above the tolerance limits .

Fig. 12.3 shows the impact of tannery effluents on soil. Potassium in Fig. 12.3 shows that it is more than 75 ppm in the centre of the region, while in the entire region potassium is more than 25 ppm. In the south-west and in the north-east it is less than 25 ppm.

The presence of sodium in the polluted area is more than 50 ppm. In the north-west and the south-east it is more than 100 ppm. The above analysis shows that sodium content in the soil is less than 50 ppm in and around the tanneries while potassium is more than 50 ppm.

The study reveals that tanneries have completely polluted the land and water sources of the surrounding areas of the tanneries. This has led to changes in land-use, crop pattern and yield of crops, animal husbandry etc. Therefore, the local villages are badly in need of intervention by the Government short-term remedial actions like compensation, supply of water and provision of alternate employment and long-term measures like reclamation of lands.

NOTES

1. The Global 2000 Report to the President : Entering the 21st century, Penguin, 1982, pp. 227. In: *Population Resources, Environment and Quality of Life.* R.C. Sharma ed., Dhanpat Raj & Sons, Delhi, 1984, pp. 441.
2. Boland, G. A. (ed) (1993); *Environmental Management Training,* Sterling Publishers Pvt. Ltd., New Delhi pp. G 1.5.
3. Sharma, R.C. (1984) *Population Resources, Environment and Quality of Life,* Dhanpat Raj & Sons, Delhi, pp. 451.
4. Katyal Timmy and Satake, M. (1991). *Environmental Pollution,* Anmol Publications, New Delhi, 1988 as quoted in M. Karpagam, *Environmental Economics*, Sterling Publishers Ltd., New Delhi, 1991, pp. 63.
5. CLRI, Report (1990) Capacity Utilisation and Scope for Modernisation in Indian Tanning Industry, Central Leather Research Institute, Madras, pp. 13.
6. *Leather and Leather Products, Report of the Working Group of VIII Five Year Plan for Tamil Nadu,* paper presented in a workshop on 'Perspectives for Industrialisation in Tamil Nadu during VIII Five Year Plan,' Madras Institute of Development Studies, Madras.

# 13

# Infrastructure in Arunachal Pradesh, India

## An Exploration into Development and Distribution

**RAVI S. SINGH**

## ORIENTATION

The importance of infrastructure in the development process needs no elaboration. Precisely speaking, infrastructure refers to the flow of services, out of a stock of facilities (like road, electrification, and so on) created during a specific time period, utilized to attain some level of development. It is generally agreed upon that economic development has a significant and direct (positive) correlation with the level of infrastructure. Similarly, it is equally worthwhile to mention that every specific type of infrastructure-creation requires different time length. Actually, the very process of creating infrastructure is broadly speaking a function of the degree of physical/natural hindrance, technological (viability), and politico-economic factors, along with the contemporary concern of environmental/ecological suitability (!). For example, lying of new railways (particularly in difficult terrains) or construction of a multi-purpose dam could prolong for decades, but telecommunication network may require a few months only.

Development studies are clear about the positive impacts of infrastructure on development. In numerous ways a chain of cumulative causation is energized by the infrastructural growth that converges to create 'economies of agglomeration'. This situation in due process of time, attracts varied enterprises and thus, concentration of economic activities emerges at a specific place spilling out into the micro-region. Later on, these economic processes occurring over space are expected to accelerate the optimal resource utilization and enhance the productive capacity of the region.

At the broader level, it is felt that though perceptible sea-change(s) have taken place in our economy still larger populace and geographical areas remain deprived in the politico-economic context and process too. The 'island of growth' (compare with the 'suction-points' and 'enclaves' of the colonial era) grow at the cost of (receding) 'waterbodies' that surround them. The everyday realities and experiences in this context in North-East (NE) India, especially Arunachal Pradesh (AP) are precarious. Other bare truths which are inseparable elements of the saga of planned development are either overlooked in the euphoria of achievements (?) or deliberately kept in dark to illuminate the victory ! The NE India is important to us not only for its geo-strategic location, but in terms of resource endowment it is also vital for the Indian economy.

This chapter attempts to highlight the state of infrastructure in AP on the premise that understanding the economic (under) development of this state and the NE region at large depends on the analysis of infrastructural framework developed so far. In this exercise mainly the physical infrastructure is considered which in its totality has a deciding effect on the nature and level(s) of a region's economy. The methodology adopted here incorporates statistical tools and the conventional geographical tool—maps.

The study area—AP is located in the far north–eastern corner (26°28′N–29°31′ N latitudes and 91° 31′ E–97°30′ E longitudes) of India. The state is divided into 13 districts as per the SAAP, 1997. The total geographical area (of 83743 km$^2$) is, predominantly mountainous (80 per cent area is above 600 m altitude), inhabited by 8,64,558 persons (1991 census). Over 87 per cent of it lives in villages. The (scheduled) tribal population forms nearly 64 per cent of the total population. The people of AP could be further disaggregated into 31 ethnic communities who are permanent inhabitants. This social plurality is better understood with reference to the languages (dialects) in use and the (indigenous) faith systems professed. AP shares international boundary line with Bhutan, Tibet (China), and Myanmar (Burma); whereas Assam and Nagaland surround it in south-west and south directions, respectively. It attained full statehood in 1987 prior to which it had the Union Territory status since 1972. In the past, it was called as North-East Frontier Tract (prior to 1954) and North-East Frontier Agency (NEFA) during 1954-1972.

## CHOICE OF VARIABLES AND INDICATORS

Main hurdle in the way of meaningful assessment and understanding of the level(s) of infrastructure is the availability of data on relevant variables that could be used directly. This limitation is alarming in the case of states like AP which do not generate substantial data base at different (spatial) levels. In this study too, acutely insufficient data in the state government published *Statistical Abstract of Arunachal Pradesh (SAAP)* has deprived the researcher from adding more meaning to the dimensions of interpretation. At the same time, lack of clarity in the different heads under which numerical figures are given is another significant problem faced by researchers. Further, gross inconsistency in the general framework within which data is pulished in the several volumes of the SAAP forbid the temporal comparisons.

Five of the available informations, are selected for current analysis. These variables are: (i) total road length, (ii) number of telephone connections, (iii) total number of post offices, (iv) number of bank branches, and (v) rural electrification. Here the assumptions behind selection of these variables must be clarified. It is assumed that the road length represents physcial spatial accessibility, the telephone connections and post offices together represent existing communication facilities, the bank branches indicate capital transaction facility, and the village electrification reveals electricity distribution network. As the variables themselves are meaningless for analytical purpose, they should be converted into indicators (see Kundu, 1980 : 30-32). In order to convert the selected variables their density has been worked out as specified at relevant places.

## GROWTH OF INFRASTRUCTURE : SOME GENERAL OBSERVATIONS

The rate of growth, in planned economies like India, has been predominantly decided by the successive governments and their policies. Till yesterday it was through public finance and investment alone that major infrastructural bases got created all over the country. Of course, recent governments seem welcoming private investment; the conventional understanding, that for the longer gestation period and uncertain return of the (invested) capital private entrepreneurs hesitate stepping into infrastructural projects, remains valid even today. For several reasons, some of which incompletely understood and some others grossly misunderstood, the fate of marginal (frontier) regions has been precarious. In the case of AP, we find this territory lying in administrative doldrum for fairly long period of time. It has affected the overall development process. Evidently it is clear in the discussion to follow how slow has been the growth of infrastructure and minor regional variations, with respect to the select indicators, reflecting the general underdevelopment of the state as a whole.

We find the British taking least interest in development particularly in this part of India. For the necessary movement they depended on bridle paths and porter tracks. Naturally, during the first fifteen years after independence in the total road length; bridle paths, mule paths and porter's track together had larger share, *e.g.* in 1951-52 out of 223.69 km of all kinds of roads/paths/tracks, proper roads measured merely 62.76 km (a meagre 28 per cent only!). The local government and the Union Government did feel the need to systematize and strengthen transportation network for which construction of roads was the primary task. The local Forest Department (FD) took first initiatives and later supported by the Public Works Department (PWD), the Border Roads Task Force (BRTF), and the Rural Works Department (RWD). As a result, within 20 years period more than forty-fold increase(!) in road length was registered. In this context one may mention the greater need felt by the Union government to connect this region with the national mainstream and bitter realization of its geo-strategic significance in the aftermath of Indo-China war in 1960-61. All said and done, still we find the progress of road construction in AP too slow if compared with other parts of the country. In 1989-90 the total road length was reportedly 9295.96 km and it increased to 12900.059 km in 1996-97. We must remember more than fifty per cent (of the total road length) is of *kuchcha* (non-metalled) roads.

Expansion of postal services in this state has been slower than road network. Even seven years after the independence there were five odd post offices in 1953-54 and the then Tirap Frontier Division had none at all! Little by little, this number grew to 23 in 1960-61, 55 in 1965-66, and 70 in 1970-71. In the next 15 years there was a tremendous growth of postal services and in 1985-86 there were 274 post offices, 35 of them having telegraph facility. In 1996-97 this number increased to 283; however, telegraph facility was available at only 20 of them. Similar slow growth may be found in the case of other infrastructural facilities that we are considering here, with the exception of telephone connections.

## Spatial Distribution of Infrastructure

### *Roads*

Construction of roads and their maintenance in AP is done through four important agencies/departments, *viz.*, the PWD, the RWD, the BRTF, and the FD. Table 13.1 (a) reveals that around 50 per cent of the total road length has been created by the APPWD to be followed by other agencies. Yet, we cannot forget the role played by Forest Department in the early days after independence, as mentioned earlier. As far as the types of road are concerned, on the basis of categorization

**Table 13.1** (a) : Road Length by the Construction Agencies, 1996-97

| Agency/Department | Total Road Length | % |
|---|---|---|
| 1. Arunachal Pradesh Public Works Department (APPWD) | 6647.189 | 49.98 |
| 2. Border Roads Task Force (BRTF) | 3719.303 | 28.83 |
| 3. Rural Works Department (RWD) | 1683.000 | 13.05 |
| 4. Forest Department (FD) | 1050.567 | 8.14 |
| Total | 12900.059 | 100.00 |

*Source* : *SAAP*, 1997.

by the APPWD and the RWD some sub-types of generally accepted *pucca* (metalled/black-topped) and *kuchcha* (non-metalled) major types

**Table 13.1** (b) : Arunachal Pradesh : Road Classification*, 1996-1997

| | Road Type | Length** (km) |
|---|---|---|
| 1. | Black-topped/Metalled *(Pucca)* | 2873.805 |
| | (a) District Roads | 2112.417 |
| | (b) Station Colony Road | 761.388 |
| 2. | Non-Metalled *(Kuchcha)* | 5256.384 |
| | (a) Water bound Macadum | 1248.577 |
| | (b) Unsurfaced | 4007.807 |

*Note* : * It is based on the APPWD and the RWD data.

** Roads constructed by the BRTF and the Forest Department are not included here.

*Source* : *SAAP*, 1997.

could be recognized [see Table 13.1 (b)]. Almost half of the total road length is *kuchcha* which indicates they are not quite reliable for vehicles plying during rainy season when even the black-topped roads are often in bad shape.

Distribution of roads is highly imbalanced in this state. As far as the absolute road length is concerned, East Siang (with Upper Siang), West Kameng, and West Siang are the first three districts having 1512.5 km, 1488.88 km and 1366.72 km, respectively. Thus, more than 33 per cent road length concentrated in three districts alone! But if the road density is a considered a different picture emerges (*cf.* Table 13.2). The first three districts, identified on the basis of absolute road length, do not find place among the developed districts in terms of road density (RD). How to explain this condition? Undoubtedly, the RD index is better measure than the simple road length. However, at least, in the case of AP, we find the districts having smaller geographical area performing well in terms of RD. Hence, we tentatively conclude that the smaller districts have better road connectivity.

It will not be out of place to see whether some kind of general spatial pattern is emerging. If we take the average road density of A.P. as yardstick, clear regional picture is evident (*cf.* Table 13.2). The western part (including Tawang, West Kameng, East Kameng and Papum Pare districts) and the south-eastern part (Changlang and Tirap districts) are well above the state average and the central region, from Lower Subansiri to Lohit is below the average (except West Siang district). Here, a conclusion may be drawn that larger area of this state has below average RD (which itself is as low as 15.40 km/100 km$^2$). We had noted earlier that almost half of the total road length is constituted by non-metalled (*kuchcha*) roads which cannot be accepted as effective with reference to development process; rather they are liabilities. Therefore, it is proposed to find out the concentration of metalled (*pucca*) roads. The simple method of 'location quotient' (LQ) is employed here in this regard.

Table 13.2 also illustrates that out of the 12 districts, only five have 50 per cent or more of their roads black-topped. While looking at the composition of black-topped road (constructed by different agencies) one may find the BRTF road affecting the performance of districts in this regard. For example, in Tawang the BRTF road is longest (517.61 km) and in Changlang it is the shortest (54.7 km only); probably due to this reason the former ranks at the top in terms of *pucca* road and the latter is one among the laggards. If the spatial

**Table 13.2** : Arunachal Pradesh: Distribution of Road, 1996-1997

| District | Area ($km^2$) | Total Length (km.) | %age of the State | Road Density ($km/100 km^2$) | Metalled Roads (%) | LQ |
|---|---|---|---|---|---|---|
| 1. Tawang | 2172 | 812.31 | 6.3 | 37.399 | 77.26 | 1.51 |
| 2. West Kameng | 7422 | 1488.88 | 11.54 | 20.060 | 46.60 | 0.91 |
| 3. East Kameng | 4134 | 715.33 | 5.54 | 17.303 | 45.42 | 0.89 |
| 4. Papum Pare | 2875 | 661.17 | 5.12 | 22.997 | 41.87 | 0.81 |
| 5. Lower Subansiri | 10135 | 1247.04 | 9.67 | 12.304 | 47.71 | 0.93 |
| 6. Upper Subansiri | 7032 | 946.94 | 7.34 | 13.466 | 51.55 | 1.00 |
| 7. West Siang | 7643 | 1366.72 | 10.59 | 17.881 | 49.77 | 0.97 |
| 8. East Siang** | 10875 | 1512.5 | 11.72 | 13.908 | 40.88 | 0.79 |
| 9. Dibang Valley | 13029 | 884.55 | 6.86 | 6.789 | 66.94 | 1.30 |
| 10. Lohit | 11402 | 1358.53 | 10.53 | 11.914 | 54.30 | 1.06 |
| 11. Changlang | 4662 | 1002.23 | 7.77 | 21.498 | 43.94 | 0.86 |
| 12. Tirap | 2362 | 903.84 | 7.00 | 38.266 | 57.84 | 1.13 |
| Arunachal Pradesh | 83743 | 12900.04 | 99.98 | 15.404 | 51.10 | |

*Note* : * Only PWD and BRTF roads considered and here expressed as percentage of total road length.
** It includes Upper Siang district.

*Source* : Computed by the researcher.

patterning of (concentration and dispersal of) metalled road is taken into account, the LQ values reveal somewhat different picture than the general road density pattern. The general feature emerging out is majority of the districts have highly dispersed *pucca* roads. Three districts—Tirap, Lohit and Upper Subansiri appear to have moderate concentration; whereas Tawang has highest concentration followed by Dibang Valley.

### *Telephones*

Like other parts of India, the telecom facilities in AP expanded mainly in the 1990s; thanks to the successive governments, unchanged support to the policy of making telephone connections available to commoners, taken up more vigorously by the former Prime Minister Late Rajiv Gandhi's regime. It is clearly understood, therefore, needs no elaboration, that the expansion of telecom is more associated (or correlated) with the government policy decision rather than other infrastructural network. We shall take up correlation issue between the select indicators used in this study at a later stage.

**Table 13.3 :** Telecommunication Facility in Arunachal Pradesh, 1996-1997

| District | Population | Telephone Connections | % age of the State total | Telephone Density* |
|---|---|---|---|---|
| 1. Tawang | 28287 | 473 | 4.02 | 16.72 |
| 2. West Kameng | 56421 | 752 | 6.39 | 13.33 |
| 3. East Kameng | 50395 | 209 | 1.78 | 4.15 |
| 4. Papum Pare | 72811 | 4224 | 36.79 | 59.39 |
| 5. Lower Subansiri | 83167 | 489 | 4.16 | 5.88 |
| 6. Upper Subansiri | 50086 | 491 | 4.18 | 9.80 |
| 7. West Siang | 89936 | 638 | 5.42 | 7.09 |
| 8. East Siang** | 99463 | 877 | 7.46 | 8.80 |
| 9. Dibang Valley | 43068 | 695 | 5.91 | 16.14 |
| 10. Lohit | 109706 | 1278 | 10.87 | 11.65 |
| 11. Changlang | 95530 | 680 | 5.79 | 7.12 |
| 12. Tirap | 95508 | 846 | 7.20 | 9.89 |
| Arunachal Pradesh | 864558 | 11752 | 99.97 | 13.59 |

*Note* : * Number of telephone connections per 1000 persons.
** It includes Upper Siang too.

*Source* : Computed by the researcher.

In comparison to other states the number of telephone connection holders is of course quite small in AP. And, even this number is not uniformly distributed. The largest concentration of telephone connections is found in Papum Pare district with more than one-third of the state's total. It could be explained by simply referring to the fact that the capital urban complex of Itanagar falls within this district. Due to this reality, which indirectly suggests larger concentration of urban population and overall better per capita income conditions, abruptly highest concentration is found in this small district. The other two districts to follow Papum Pare are Lohit and East Siang respectively (*cf.* Table13. 3). If we tentatively assume that the urban population percentage and telephone connections are positively correlated, at least in the case of AP it would be highly valid; as Papum Pare, Lohit and East Siang districts have highest concentration of urban populace and the telephone subscribers too. One may try to find out the relationship between per capital income and telephone connection's concentration through a separate exercise.

The pattern of telephone density, however, is somewhat different. Except Papum Pare, Tawang, and Dibang Valley districts all other parts of the state have very low density of telephone connections. The worst three districts in this regard are East Kameng, Lower Subansiri and West Siang (*cf.* Table 13.3).

### *Post Offices*

The system of post offices has been very important in the communication network. Even in the days of electronic mail today, post offices remain important medium of sending and receiving messages within a country and also abroad. Liberalization has resulted into entrance of many private courier agencies giving specialized and better services in comparison to the government owned postal department. But such services link important urban centres only where a small proportion of Indian population lives. Further, as the private courier agencies charge higher rates, which are unaffordable for people belonging to lower middle strata of the society and below, their clientele is limited.

In AP, new mediums of communication are extremely limited, dependence on postal services is more. Of course, at some places (like Itanagar) people enjoy access to alternative means of communication. As mentioned earlier, with a humble beginning immediately after attaining independence, some 283 post offices existed in 1997. During these years, by all measures the growth was quite slow yet steady. Of the existing 283 post offices, more than 80 per cent are the extension and distribution branch offices (EDBDs), and merely 20 reportedly have the telegraph facility.

More than 35 per cent of the post offices are found in Lohit (14.84%), East Siang (12.01%) and Tirap (10.60%) districts. One may identify inter-district disparity in terms of post offices distribution. The six western districts (Tawang, West Kameng, East Kemeng, Papum Pare, Lower Subansiri, and Upper Subansiri) together contain around 35 per cent of post offices of the state and the eastern region has rest of the 65 per cent. Of course, this pattern of regional distribution changes a little with reference to the density of post offices (*cf.* Table 13.4). The state's average density is 3.27. The district-wise

**Table 13.4 :** Arunachal Pradesh: Distribution of Post Offices, 1996-1997

| District | No. of Post Offices | %age of the Total | Density* |
|---|---|---|---|
| 1. Tawang | 12 | 4.24 | 4.24 |
| 2. West Kameng | 19 | 6.71 | 3.37 |
| 3. East Kameng | 14 | 4.94 | 2.78 |
| 4. Papum Pare | 22 | 7.77 | 3.02 |
| 5. Lower Subansiri | 19 | 6.71 | 2.28 |
| 6. Upper Subansiri | 12 | 4.24 | 2.39 |
| 7. West Siang | 29 | 10.24 | 3.22 |
| 8. East Siang** | 34 | 12.01 | 3.41 |
| 9. Dibang Valley | 22 | 7.77 | 5.11 |
| 10. Lohit | 42 | 14.84 | 3.82 |
| 11. Changlang | 28 | 9.89 | 2.93 |
| 12. Tirap | 30 | 10.60 | 3.50 |
| Arunachal Pradesh | 283 | 99.96 | 3.27 |

*Note*: * Density of Post Offices is number of post office(s) per 10,000 persons.
** It includes Upper Siang too.

*Source* : Computed by the researcher.

performance, if measured with reference to this average, will emerge interesting. Six districts each are on either side of this dividing line forming two categories–first being better ones and the other of the worsts. The region formed by the clustering of East Kameng to West Siang represents the latter. The better districts' cluster is somewhat fragmented; however with greater continuity in the eastern part (*cf.* Table 13.4).

### *Banking Institutions*

The function of banking institutions is very important in any economy, as it not only facilitates general money lending/deposit but also boosts economic growth through financial loans and many other schemes meant for developmental projects. In AP historically speaking, the market economy entered through the colonial (capitalist) economy that found its way in the second half of the nineteenth century. However, the transition, from pre-capitalist tribal economy to colonial (–capitalist) economy and finally, and market economy, has been extremely slow. Though to a great extent the economy of AP is a market, economy, today the remnants of tribal economy are still found simultaneously; of course, in the remote interiors. The banking institutions played laudable role in the economic integration of the

**Table 13.5 (a) :** Arunachal Pradesh: Growth of Banking Institutions

| Year | No. of Bank Branches | Population per Bank Branch ('000)* |
|---|---|---|
| 1970 | 2 | 234 |
| 1975 | 7 | 67 |
| 1980 | 19 | 25 |
| 1985 | 47 | 13 |
| 1989 | 84 | 8 |
| 1994-95 | 98 | 9 |
| 1996-1997 | 99 | 9 |

*Note* : * Calculation of this average for 1970, 1975 and 1980; 1985 & 1989; and 1994-95 & 1996-97 is done on the basis of the total population figures of 1971, 1981 and 1991, respectively.

*Source*: Das, 1995 : 91, and the *SAAP*, 1995-1997.

state along with other hill states of the NE region. The beginning of systematic banking activities in the state is the outcome of the preliminary survey undertaken by the State Bank of India (SBI), following recommendations of study groups and committees, under the Lead Bank Scheme (1969) formulated by the Reserve Bank of India (RBI). In December 1970, the SBI opened two branches one each at Pasighat and Bomdila; this marked real beginning of banking services in the state. Later on, other nationalized banks, like the United Bank of India, United Commercial Bank, Vijaya Bank, etc. opened some branches. In order to promote banking activities and expand this network, the state government floated the Arunachal Pradesh Co-operative Apex Bank (APCOAB) in 1979-80 and the Arunachal Pradesh Rural Bank (APRB) in 1983 (Das, 1995 : 91). As revealed in the Table 13.5 (a) major expansion of banking network, took place during 1980s; this welcome development was possible due to the floating of APCOAB and APRB. The branches of these two banks outnumber the nationalized bank branches here (*cf.* Table 13.5b).

The distribution pattern of bank branches suggests concentration in Papum Pare and East Siang districts (see Table 13.6). These two districts contain more than one-third of the total number. Whereas, in East Kameng and Upper Subansiri we find 3.03 per cent and

**Table 13.5 (b) :** Arunachal Pradesh: Existing Banking Institutions, 1996-1997

| | Name of Bank | No. of Branches |
|---|---|---|
| 1. | State Bank of India (SBI) | 42 |
| 2. | Arunachal Pradesh Cooperative Apex Bank (APCOAB) | 31 |
| 3. | Arunachal Pradesh Rural Bank (APRB) | 19 |
| 4. | United Bank of India (UBI) | 2 |
| 5. | United Commercial Bank (UCB) | 2 |
| 6. | Vijaya Bank (VB) | 2 |
| 7. | Central Bank of India (CBI) | 1 |
| | Total | 99 |

*Source : SAAP,* 1997 : 83.

**Table 13.6 :** Arunachal Pradesh : Districtwise Distribution of Bank Branches 1996-1997

| District | Total Number of Bank Branches | % age of the Total | Bank Density* |
|---|---|---|---|
| 1. Tawang | 5 | 5.05 | 1.77 |
| 2. West Kameng | 8 | 8.08 | 1.42 |
| 3. East Kameng | 3 | 3.03 | 0.60 |
| 4. Papum Pare | 17 | 17.17 | 2.33 |
| 5. Lower Subansiri | 8 | 8.08 | 0.96 |
| 6. Upper Subansiri | 4 | 4.04 | 0.80 |
| 7. West Siang | 11 | 11.11 | 1.22 |
| 8. East Siang* | 16 | 16.16 | 1.61 |
| 9. Dibang Valley | 5 | 5.05 | 1.16 |
| 10. Lohit | 9 | 9.09 | 0.82 |
| 11. Changlang | 7 | 7.07 | 0.73 |
| 12. Tirap | 6 | 6.06 | 0.70 |
| Arunachal Pradesh | 99 | 99.99 | 1.14 |

*Note*: * Bank density is defined as number of bank branches per 10,000 persons.
** It includes Upper Siang too.

*Source* : Computed by the researcher.

4.04 per cent respectively. Half of the districts (East Kameng, Lower Subansiri, Upper Subansiri, Lohit, Changlang and Tirap) do not have even one branch per every 10,000 persons! That is how considerable intra-regional disparity in this regard is evident. Whether the general weaker economic conditions could be held responsible for such a scenario is issue of separate investigation.

### *Rural Electrification*

In order to understand expansion of electrification network, rural electrification is better an index, as generally the urban centres are assumed to be electrified. In AP, trend of electrification, particularly rural electrification, has been slow but steady. During 1974-1997, massive expansion is seen in this regard. By the end of 1974, only 55 odd villages (2%) were electrified (Das, 1995:147) compared to 1950 villages (53.32%) by March, 1997.

This development experience apparently has not been shared by all districts equally. In Tawang (100%), Tirap (96.15%), and West Kameng (89.41%) commendable level of rural electrification has been achieved; in contrast to these first three districts, the performance of East Kameng, Upper Subansiri and West Siang with 25.55 per cent, 29.90 per cent, and 33.99 per cent village electrification respectively, indicates big gap (*cf.* Table 13.7). Larger percentage of electrified villages are found in Lower Subanisiri, Changlang, Papum Pare, and Lohit districts. Nevertheless, if one considers the LQ values, concentration is highest in Tawang (1.88) followed by Tirap (1.80), West Kameng (1.68), Changlang (1.61), and others (see Table 13.7).

## Infrastructure Development Levels

The description and discussion presented in the above paragraphs demonstrate how the chosen infrastructural facilities have grown in the process of time and what is the existing pattern of their spatial distribution. Interesting conclusions have been drawn at respective

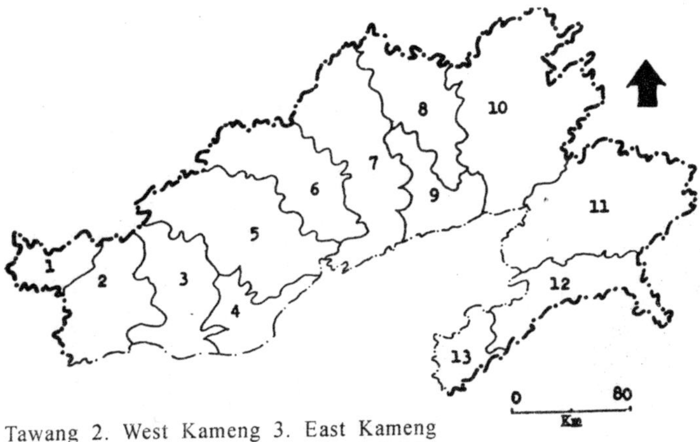


1. Tawang 2. West Kameng 3. East Kameng 4. Papum Pare 5. Lower Subansiri 6. Upper Subansiri 7. West Siang 8. Upper Siang 9. East Siang 10. Dibang Valley 11. Lohit 12. Changlang 13. Tirap

**Fig. 13.1(a) :** Arunachal Pradesh: Districts' Location

**Table 13.7** : Arunachal Pradesh : Rural Electrification Scenario, 1996-1997

| District | No. of Inhabited Villages | No. of Electrified Villages | %age of the Total | Electrified* Villages (%) | Location Quotient |
|---|---|---|---|---|---|
| 1. Tawang | 163 | 163 | 8.36 | 100.00 | 1.98 |
| 2. West Kameng | 170 | 152 | 7.79 | 89.41 | 1.68 |
| 3. East Kameng | 274 | 70 | 3.59 | 25.55 | 0.48 |
| 4. Papum Pare | 263 | 201 | 10.30 | 76.43 | 1.43 |
| 5. Lower Subansiri | 595 | 256 | 13.12 | 43.03 | 0.80 |
| 6. Upper Subansiri | 408 | 122 | 6.26 | 29.90 | 0.56 |
| 7. West Siang | 409 | 139 | 7.12 | 33.99 | 0.63 |
| 8. East Siang** | 204 | 161 | 8.26 | 78.92 | 1.48 |
| 9. Dibang Valley | 237 | 91 | 4.67 | 38.40 | 0.72 |
| 10. Lohit | 493 | 200 | 10.26 | 40.57 | 0.76 |
| 11. Changlang | 285 | 245 | 12.56 | 85.96 | 1.61 |
| 12. Tirap | 156 | 150 | 7.69 | 96.15 | 1.80 |
| Arunachal Pradesh | 3657 | 1950 | 99.98 | 53.32 | |

*Note*: * Electrified Villages/Total Inhabited Villages × 100.
** Includes Upper Siang too.

*Source* : Computed by the researcher.

places and now it is justified to look into the overall development scenario on the basis of indicators considered here. Several methods are available today to develop composite index to measure development level(s) (*cf.* Kundu, 1975, 1980; Pal, 1975; Ghosh and De 1998; Banerjee and Ray, 1998). Since the number of observations is too small, therefore compositing is done using the ranking method.

Table 13.8 once again reveals a very low level of general (cumulative) infrastructure development. Even the top ranking districts do not have perfect concentration of infrastructural facilities. More so, it appears that their better performance over other districts is not more than a myriad-function of their smaller geographical area [see Fig. 13.1(b)]. To a great extent under development is distributed with thin edges which separate, intra-regionally, the so-called developed and under-developed districts. This picture is the outcome of a combination of intrisically woven several factors. One may expect some breakthrough by looking at existing correlation between the selected indicators.

The existing correlations between the five indicators selected do not provide any noteworthy dimension. None of the correlations are significant at 1 per cent level. However, the positive correlation

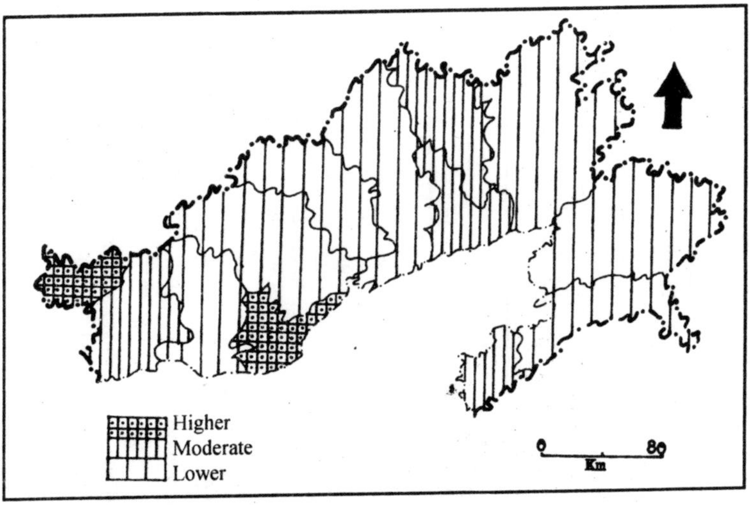


**Fig. 13.1(b) :** Arunachal Pradesh: Level of Infrastructure Development (*cf.* Table 13.8)

**Table 13.8 :** Arunachal Pradesh : Concentration Index of Infrastructure Development, 1996-1997

| District | Road Density | *R* | Tele Density | *R* | PO Density | *R* | Banks' Density | *R* | Electrified Villages' Density | *R* | CIDI* |
|---|---|---|---|---|---|---|---|---|---|---|---|
| 1. Tawang | 2.47 | 2 | 1.23 | 2 | 1.29 | 2 | 1.55 | 2 | 1.88 | 1 | 9 |
| 2. West Kameng | 1.33 | 5 | 0.98 | 4 | 1.03 | 6 | 1.24 | 4 | 1.68 | 3 | 22 |
| 3. East Kameng | 1.13 | 7 | 0.31 | 12 | 0.85 | 10 | 0.52 | 12 | 0.48 | 12 | 53 |
| 4. Papum Pare | 1.53 | 3 | 4.37 | 11 | 0.92 | 8 | 1.04 | 1 | 1.43 | 6 | 19 |
| 5. Lower Subansiri | 0.80 | 10.5 | 0.43 | 1 | 0.70 | 12 | 0.84 | 7 | 0.80 | 7 | 47.5 |
| 6. Upper Subansiri | 0.87 | 9 | 0.72 | 7 | 0.73 | 11 | 0.70 | 9 | 0.56 | 11 | 48 |
| 7. West Siang | 1.20 | 6 | 0.52 | 10 | 0.98 | 7 | 1.07 | 5 | 0.63 | 10 | 38 |
| 8. East Siang** | 0.93 | 8 | 0.65 | 8 | 1.04 | 5 | 1.41 | 3 | 1.48 | 5 | 29 |
| 9. Dibang Valley | 0.47 | 12 | 1.19 | 3 | 1.56 | 1 | 1.01 | 6 | 0.72 | 9 | 31 |
| 10. Lohit | 0.80 | 10.5 | 0.86 | 5 | 1.17 | 3 | 0.71 | 8 | 0.76 | 8 | 34.5 |
| 11. Changlang | 1.40 | 4 | 0.52 | 9 | 0.90 | 9 | 0.64 | 10 | 1.61 | 4 | 36 |
| 12. Tirap | 2.53 | 1 | 0.73 | 6 | 1.07 | 4 | 0.61 | 11 | 1.80 | 2 | 24 |
| Cumulative Density | 15.46 | | 12.51 | | 12.24 | | 12.34 | | 13.83 | | |

*Note*: R-Rank, * Composite Infrastructure Development Index,
** It includes Upper Siang too.

*Source* : Computed by the researcher.

between (i) road density and rural electrification, (ii) telecommunication and post offices, and iii) telecommunication and bank-branches, are significant at 5 per cent level (*cf.* Table 13.9). One may conclude that such correlation realities suggest two things. Firstly, rural development is influenced by roads development that is strongly associated with electrification. And, secondly, facilities like telephones and bank branches being indicator of development in a natural way promote each other. Being basically urban biased, their higher concentration in urban areas and/or administrative headquarters (of different level) results into significant positive correlation between them.

## Towards Basic Conclusions

Previous sections have briefly been attempted to unravel the distribution of facilities in AP which are required for the kind of development any region desires to have. The attempt by Ghosh and

**Table 13.9** : Correlation Matrix

| | RD | TC | PO | BB | EV |
|---|---|---|---|---|---|
| 1. RD | 1 | 0.26<br>(0.85) | 0.04<br>(0.12) | 0.14<br>(0.44) | 0.66<br>(2.78) |
| 2. TC | | 1 | 0.63<br>(2.57) | 0.60<br>(2.37) | 0.46<br>(1.63) |
| 3. PO | | | 1 | 0.32<br>(0.07) | 0.40<br>(1.38) |
| 4. BB | | | | 1 | 0.34<br>(1.14) |
| 5. EV | | | | | 1 |

*Notes* : RD–Road Density, TC–Telephone Connections, PO–Post Office, BB–Bank's Branches; EV-Village Electrification.

1. Parentheses values are computed '*t*' values.
2. The tabulated '*t*' values for 10 (12-2) degrees of freedom is 3.17 at 1%, 2.23 at 5%, 1.81 at 10%, and 0.700 at 50% levels.

*Source* : Computed by the researcher.

De (1998) aptly highlights how the physical infrastructural facilities determine regional income (of the Indian states) which in turn is responsible for other kinds of desirable development. No doubt, AP emerges as one among most disadvantaged ones. It is noteworthy that inadequacy in terms of infrastructure is considered to have plagued the Indian economy (Parikh, 1999 :1). Similarly, other scholars too take note of this problem and it is observed that low economic level, infrastructure, and social development are interdependent. And, the distribution of these all is highly inequal in regional terms (*cf.* Kurian, 2000).

These general observations come true in AP as well. This state is backward in terms of physical infrastructural facilities as proved by a very low cumulative density. That is why the gap between most advanced districts and the most disadvantaged districts is apparently very small. Such a situation may be a note of satisfaction to a regional analyst obsessed with regional disparities, but development researches will shade tears (at least pretend to do so) on the state of affairs. The final outcome of the study is that it identifies Tawang and Papum Pare as most developed districts while East Kameng and Lower Subansiri being the most disadvantaged ones in AP.

Before concluding may we ponder for a while on what to do and how to overcome this situation? The economist may straight way suggest the 'user should pay', as said by Parikh (1999); is this viable in this poverty stricken humble population? Obvious answer to such a complex yet important question is government should take genuine interest and public money be utilised rationally and on priority basis. Private investment is not possible at all in this sector. But, after all we do have some degree of responsibility towards peripheral and disadvantaged regions like AP, the people for whom, as the national obligation, we have to ensure 'greater freedom as development', to use Sen's idiom (1999). On top of all, quality of governance is crucial (Kurian, 2000 : 549).

## REFERENCES

Banerjee, Sarmila and Samik Ray, 1998. On Construction of District Development Index in West Bengal. *EPW,* XXXIII (47 & 48), pp. 3019-3026.

Ghosh, Buddhadeb and Prabir De, 1998. Role of infrastructure in regional development. *EPW,* XXXIII (47 & 48), pp. 3039-3048.

Government of Arunachal Pradesh, 1998. *Statistical Abstract of Arunachal Pradesh, 1997.* Itanagar: Directorate of Economics & Statistics,

Kundu, Amitabh, 1975. Construction of composite indices for regionalisation–An enquiry into the methods of analysis. *Geographical Review of India.* Vol. 37 (1), pp. 19-29.

———1980. *Measurement of Urban Processes : A Study in Regionalisation.* Bombay: Popular Prakashan.

Kurian, N.J., 2000. Widening Regional Disparities in India : Some Indicators. *EPW,* XXXV(7), pp. 539-550.

Pal, M.N., 1975. Regional Disparities in the Levels of Development. *Indian Journal of Regional Sciences, Vol. II (1),* pp.12-35.

Parikh, Kirit S., 1999. *Infrastructure, Public Goods and Market.* Mumbai : Forum of Free Enterprise.

Sen, Amartya, 1999. *Development as Freedom.* New Delhi, Oxford University Press.

# 14

# Pachmarhi

## The Trekker's Paradise

**GOVIND PRASAD** AND **BHOJRAJ SINGH**

### THE REGION

The region (Pachmarhi Hills) popularly known as 'PANCHAMARHI' is located between 22° 16′ 48′′ N and 22° 36′ N latitudes and 78° 10′ E and 78° 38′ E longitudes. From east to west, it is extended in 24′ longitude (about 41 km. of length and from north-south it lies in 19′ 12′′ latitude (about 35 km. of width). The maximum area of the region (about 770 sq. km.) is located in the south-eastern part of Sohagpur Tehsil of Hoshangabad District of Madhya Pradesh. A limited part marked in the north-east corner of Betul Tehsil of Betul district (about 33.50 sq. km.) and in the north-west portion of Jamai Tehsil of Chhindwara district (104.50 sq. km.) is also included along the southern boundary of the region. The total geographical area of the region is 908 sq. km. which falls in toposheet Nos. 55J/2, 55J/3, 55J/6, 55J/7, 55J/10 and 55J/11 of Survey of India (Fig. 14.1). The region is located in Malwa region in India.

### GLIMPSE OF ENVIRONMENTAL OUTLOOK

Pachmarhi is Madhya Pradesh's most verdant jewel, a place where nature has found exquisite expression in myriad enchanting ways. If on earth be an Eden of bliss, it is this and none but this. This saying is the most befitting for Pachmarhi—a hill resort and rightly called the queen of Satpura. In this era of hectic activity when you are strained and stressed to a point of seemingly no return, then a stay here, far from maddening crowd for a few days replenishes all your sapped energy and calms you down. This hill station is a religious place for the Hindus as lakhs of people visit this place to pay their homage to Lord Shiva on "Shiv Ratri" and "Nag Panchmi" and other auspicious days. This hill station is the most ideal place for the honey mooning couples where they can find lovely places and can be all alone except the pleasant winds and the melodies singing birds. After working hard throughout an academic year you may need a change. The little and

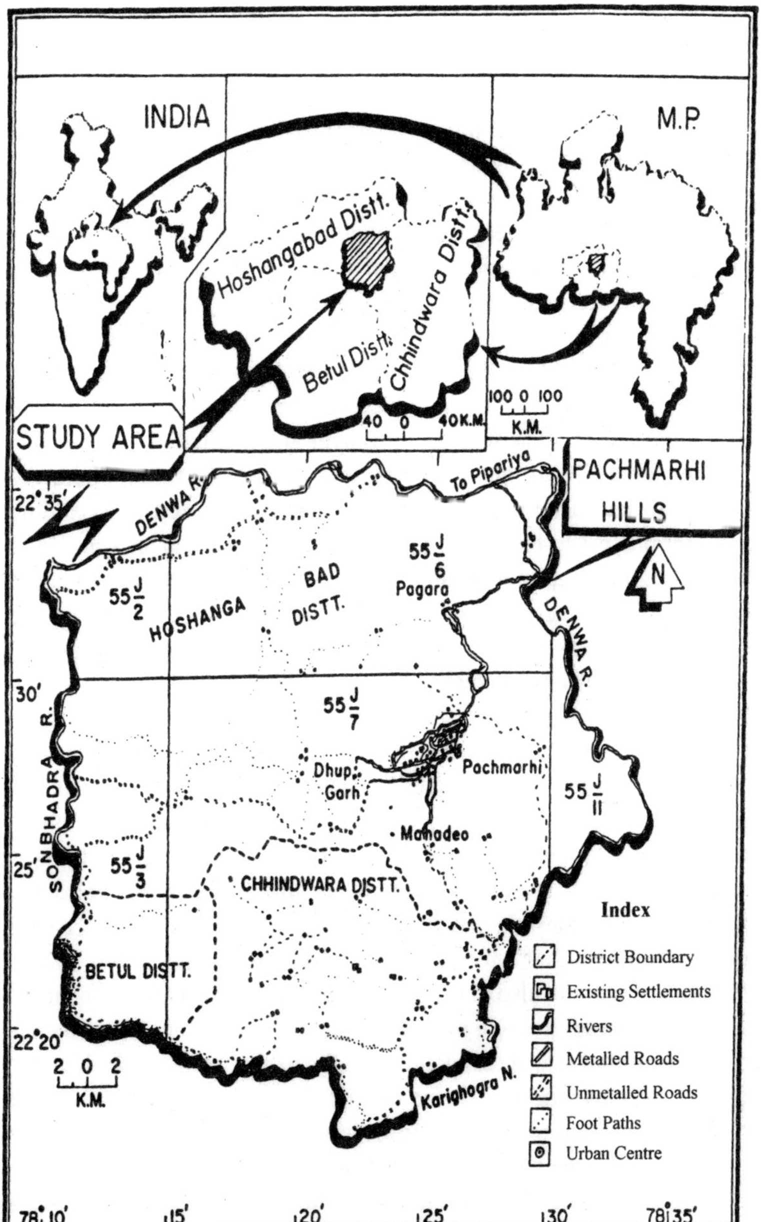


**Fig. 14.1 :** Location Map

great cascading waterfalls, glades valleys and hills and flashes silver lining in the sunshine. The deep valleys, ravines, maze of gorges sculpted in red sandstone by the winds and weather green forests, long winding roads and fall will certainly help to all in revitalizing themselves and preparing for the next higher step.

Panchmarhi has a national forest where people have their longings fulfilled. Even while coming to Panchmarhi, keep yourself awake at night lest you should miss a leopard, a bear, a bison or some other wild animals majestically across the road, and if you just want to do nothing and be in time with infinity, Panchmarhi would not fail you in this respect too. Just stroll along some distance away from your lodging and you get the environment, which had been described and longed for by '*rishis*' of ancient times for prayer and meditation.

Panchmarhi presents a nice picture of topo-features where the setting sun colours, the green leaves by its rays, scattered hills standing in silent prayers to the power unseen, waterfalls giving an allusion of bees, buzzing deep ravines and valleys to remind us how deep could be, dark silent covers, where we could feel the coolness of silence and rediscover ourselves. At night one can listen to the sight swaying tress.

The original name of Pachmarhi was' Panchmarhi' based on 'Panch Pandavas' which can be traced back to the period of Mahabharat. Historical evidences advocate that Panch Pandavas has passed their exile period in the Pandav caves of Pachmarhi. In Mahabharat, it was named as 'Khandav Van' the place of security of Pandavas and at that time it was well recognized as *'Agyat Bas'* Landmass of Pandavas.

Pachmarhi is a large plateau ringed by hills on the evergreen central Satpura ranges. Satpura may be defined as 'SATPURA' the seven sons of the Vindhyachal Mountain or 'SATPURA' (the seven folds). Pachmarhi hills are also know as Mahadeo Hills. The name 'Mahadeo' specially denotes a single peak 1336 metres high at the southern edge of the small but raised tableland of Pachmarhi at the feet of which are the sacred cave and the shrine of Mahadeo. The Mahadeo hills are originally applied to include the widermass of sandstone hills which is encircled by the Denwa and the Sonbhadra rivers, Now it includes the whole section of the Satpura mountain between the Chhindwara plateau and the Narmada valley.

Pachmarhi hills depict the assemblage of land forms. It is an uplifted land mass mostly showing massive sandstone. The raised tableland

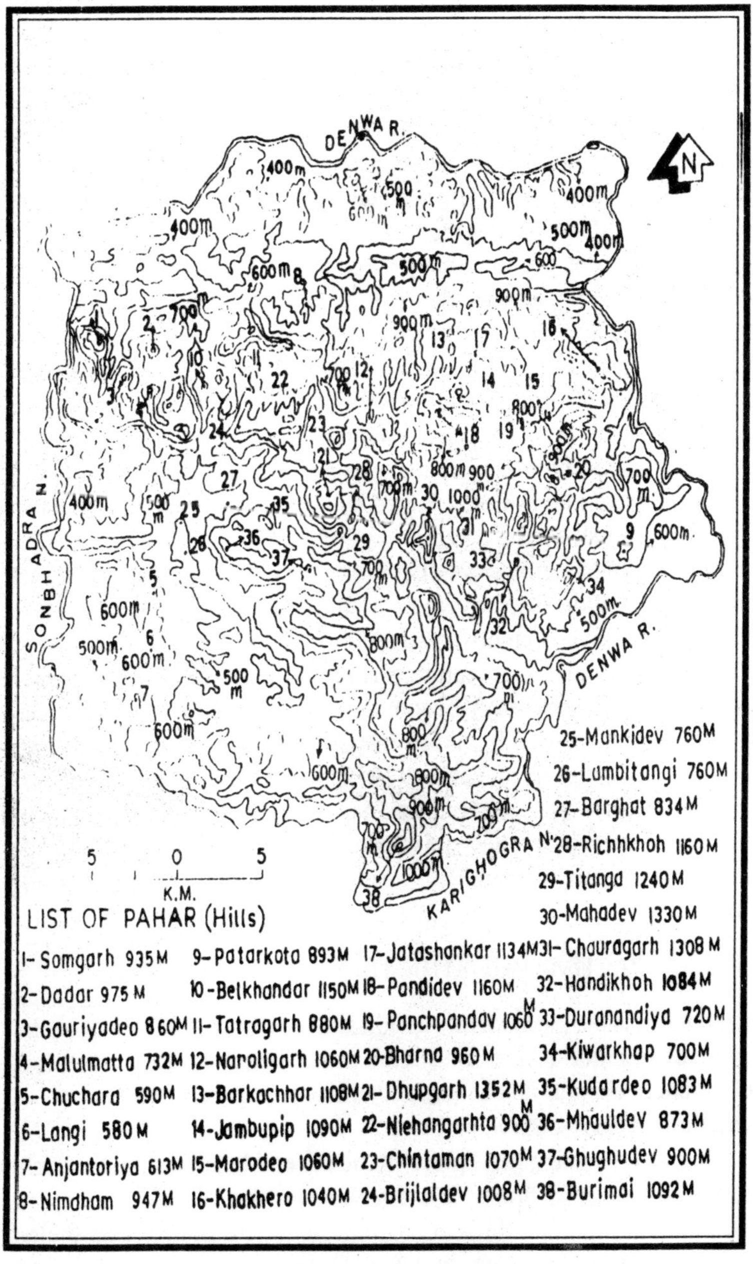


**Fig. 14.2 :** Pachmarhi Hills: Contours Map

(Plateau) of Pachmarhi is ornamented with table upon table topography, mesas and buttes, springs, caves, narrow cut deep gorges, deep drained rivers, typical ravines, rapids and waterfalls, isolated dissected hills from all sides and boulders controlled valleys. The topography of the region is very complex in nature. The plateau is highly dissected by Denwa River in the north and west and by Sonbhadra river in the west Dhupgarh (1352 m) is the highest point between the Nilgiris and the Himalyas except Mount Abu. The northern flank of the plateau is distinct from the plain by the sudden uplift. (Fig. 14.2) depicts the main contour lines and prominent hills of the region. (Fig.14.3) shows the cross section of major hilly country denoting the relief irregularities everywhere. According to Sinha (1994-1995) and Srivastava (1990); the region generally occupies the Gondwana rocks.

The Pachmarhi hills were the area previously covered by Satpura basin. The region was well affected by Narmada rift zone in the north and Asirgarh gap in the south.

The region experiences a dry climate except during the south-west monsoon season. The average annual maximum and minimum temperature have been observed as 26.6° C and 16.6° C respectively. The normal annual temperature is recorded as 21.76°C. The summer season (April and May) becomes pleasant. The average annual percentage of relative humidity ranges between 50 per cent and 60 per cent. According to Peltier (1950) and Wilson's (1973) test of geomorphic processes and climatic parameters, the region experiences minimum intensity of mechanical weathering and wind erosion while moderate intensity of chemical, weathering, mass wasting and running water impact.

## PACHMARHI—THE TREKKERS PARADISE

Pachmarhi is the pleasant hill station and most attractive tourist centre of Madhya Pradesh. The hill station is the shelter of peace, affection, ebullience, elation, emancipation, emotion, engagement, enjoyment, entertainment, excursion and excitement.

It is also the most ideal place for health and happiness and thought to be as the happy home of excitement for the all approaching the view. History denotes the fact that the Pachmarhi is the oldest shelter for the tourist as it is named and famed by Pandavas since Mahabharat times. Bison Lodge is the first building constructed in 1862 at

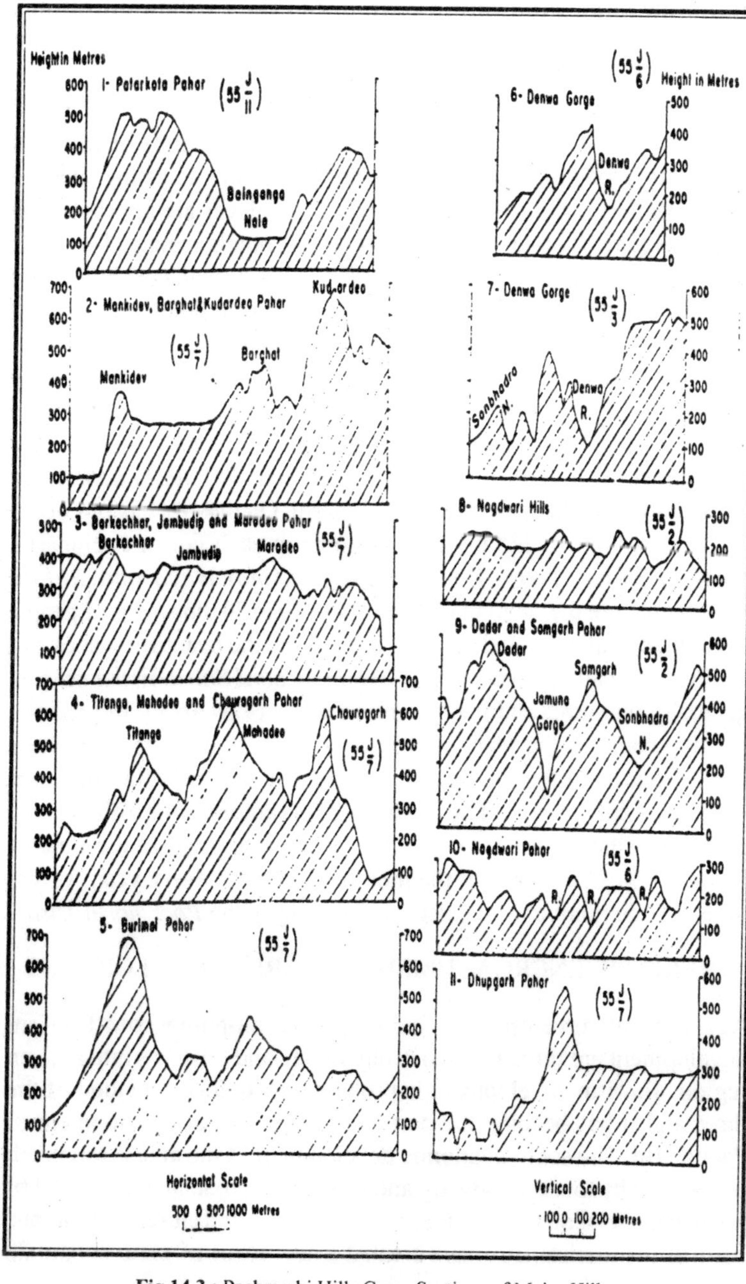


**Fig.14.3 :** Pachmarhi Hills:Cross-Sections of Major Hills

Pachmarhi. Nagdwari, Jata Shanker, Rock Doh, Lata Cambs, Chaura Garh, Jambu Dweep, Reechhgarh, Dhupgarh, Rajendra Giri and Apsara Vihar groups are the main sites of tourism development where hundred of places exist for tourists (Fig. 14.4.).

Pachmarhi has well developed markets and all kinds of facilities for fooding, lodging and transportation. The main interesting sites are also linked with metalled roads. The typical places are approachable with footpaths (Gupta, 1998). There are 10 hotels managed by M.P. State Tourism Development Corporation, 6 hotels managed by Special Area Development Authority (SADA), 25 private hotels and 11 well established restaurants for lodging and fooding facilities.

On the basis of the extensive field survey of the area and asking questions from the people of Pachmarhi, most of the respondents have indicated that Pachmarhi receives more than 20 lakh tourists in a calendar year. '*Shivratri, Nag Panchami*' and '*Raksha Bandhan*' are thought to be as the main fair of Pachmarhi. On these occasions about 5 lakhs fair tourists are believed to come in each fair of Pachmarhi. *Chaitra Nava Durga Pooja, Somvati Amavashya* and *Rohini Shankranti*' are the small fairs when about 10 to 20 thousands of people in each festival are noted to come here to see the beautiful places and for the holy bath in rivers and *Darshan* of *Lord Shiva*. In the season, generally one thousand people and in off seasons about 300 tourists per day come to the place. On festival times, the tourists generally come from the different localities of the country including the local people of M.P. State. The cultural programmes like folk songs, exhibition, dances etc. are generally to be organized at the time of *Pachamarhi Utsav* held in the month of October every year. At that time, a large number of tourists come to enjoy the *Pachmarhi Utsav.*

## TREKKERS ENCROACHMENT V/S AREA DEVELOPMENT

Agricultural development, industrial development and tourism development are three ways to bring money and business into a given region. Tourism development is probably the quickest method of the three and it has become the part and parcel of area development of Pachmarhi. The socio-economic development of the area is too much influenced by tourism industry and trekkers encroachment. The act of hotel management, taxi driving, managing open and closed restaurants, guiding the tourists, etc. have created a new sense of socio-economic

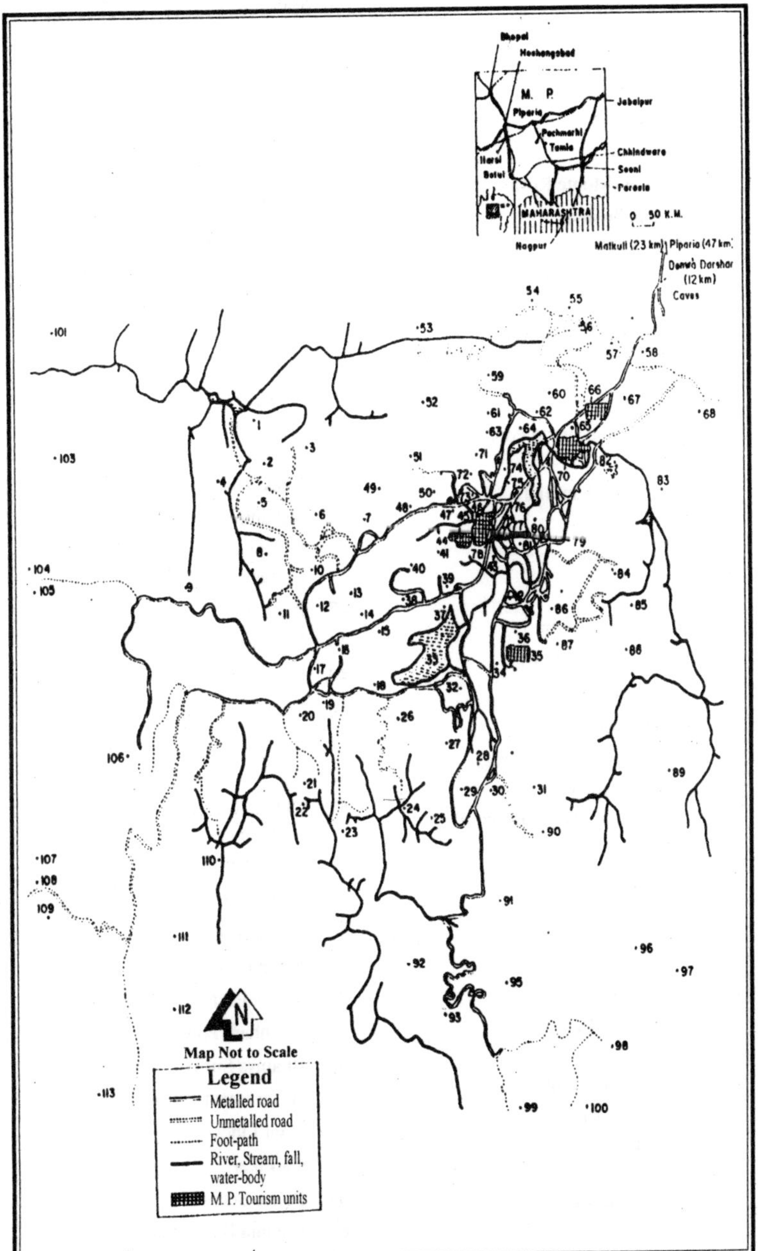


**Fig. 14.4 :** Pachmarhi Hills: Guide Map

1. Sunderkund (Saunder's Pool)
2. Jalawalaran (Duchess Fall)
3. Bharant Neer (Dorothy Deep)
4. Echo Point
5. Astachal (Monte Rosa)
6. Asanna Drishya (Belle View)
7. Asanna Khud (Fanshawe Khud)
8. Echo Hills (Pratidhwani)
9. Jal Gali (Fraser Gully)
10. Reechhgarh
11. Ramya Kund (Irene Pool)
12. Vatsalya (Jwynham Memorial)
13. Air Strip
14. Short Chakker
15. Polo Udyan
16. Christopher Corner
17. Dhoopgarh Foothill
18. Long Chakkar
19. Sangam Door
20. Sushma Sar (Crump Crag)
21. Vanshree Vihar, Patharchalla (Pansy Pool)
22. Sakree Gali (White Fish Gully)
23. Sangam (Fuller's Khud Waters Meet)
24. Agam Triveni (Fleet Wood Junction)
25. Shailanjali (Best View)
26. Lat Shring (Lansdowne Point)
27. Rajendra Giri (Panorama Hill)
28. Ekant Giri (Mount Morris)
29. Long Khakkar
30. Handi Khoh
31. Handi Khoh Pahar (3,659)
32. Bharat Scouts and Guides
33. Padmini Jheel (Lake)
34. Rock Climbing Institute
35. Satpura Retreat
36. Carmel Mount
37. Champak Bungalow
38. Vanasthali Cottages
39. D.I.B Amrak
40. Ravi Shankar Bhavan
41. Hog's Back (Vallabha Prastha)
42. New Hotel Block
43. Bison Public Lodge Gardens (Forest Museum)
44. Rock-Ena Manor
45. Nellamber
46. Panchvati Huts and Cottages China Bowl
47. PTO
48. Long and Short Chakkar
49. Lanji Giri (3,600)
50. Madhuban
51. Jamuna Prapat (Bee Fall)
52. Raj Giri (Club Hill)
53. Chhota Mahadev/ Jambudwip Nala
54. Jambu Dwip
55. Brindavan
56. Jata Shankar
57. Nimbu Bhoj
58. Octroi Post
59. Twynham Pool
60. Bhainsa Sur Hill
61. Government Hospital
62. Civil Lines
63. Karnikar
64. Police Station
65. Cinema Bus Stand
66. Holiday Homes

67. Chusul (Army Education Corps)
68. To Kanjighat Village
69. Bainganga Nala
70. Tourist Information Centre
71. Pachmarhi Club
72. Old Hotel Block
73. Raj Bhawan
74. Festival Ground
75. Christ Church
76. Suman Nandan Van
77. Youth Centre
78. Amaltas
79. Sahakar
80. Catholic Church
81. Prasthal
82. Pavas Prapat (Little Fall)
83. Sudrishya (Kitty Crag)
84. Poorva Darshan (Clematis Point)
85. Apsara Vihar (Fairy Pool)
86. Pandav Caves
87. Cemetery
88. Rajat Prapat (Silver Fall/Big Fall)
89. Bharna Pahar (2,772)
90. Chaura Darshan (Malcom Point)
91. Priyadarshini (Forsyth Point)
92. Mahdeo Pahar (4,360)
93. Bada Mahadeo
94. Denwa River
95. Gupt Mahadev
96. Bharna Village
97. Rocky Knob
98. Chauragarh (4,290)
99. To Nandiya
100. To Nandiya
101. Tamat Maidan
102. Nagdwari Nadi
103. Nandigarh Pahar
104. To Nagdwari Caves
105. To Kajri Village
106. Dhoopgarh (4,435)
107. To Kajri Village
108. To Bori Village
109. Ronghat Village
110. Tridhara (Picadilly Circus)
111. Reechhkhoh Pahar
112. Titanga Pahar
113. To Alimod Village

and business activities in the area. The business of arts and paintings and photography have been found most effective. The area is very rich in rock paintings since the ancient times.

Since long, Pachmarhi is thought to be as the tourist's place. It is used by the coming generations as the place of providing natural gift, glamour and enjoyment. Thus the beauty of the place have been stolen by the people day by day whenever they approach the nice campus of Pachmarhi. It is praised by all in various respective ways. It is the highness of Pachmarhi's landscapes that they have ever reflected virgin ideas of glamour in their sovereignty. Degradation is a common factor in an every state of landforms but it seems that changing panorama of Pachmarhi due to human interferences is increasing gradually.

Natural processes have caused the assemblage of land forms in Pachmarhi, but in view of associating groups of local people and tourists in the area, these erosional landforms are the attractive places fortifying the charms of the area. Thus, the changing attitude of the plateau due to destructive natural processes is the boon for Pachmarhi.

## ENVIRONMENTAL PROBLEMS AND THEIR MANAGEMENT

It is found that the interesting sites of Pachmarhi now encircled by dirty materials divorced by the tourists. People never follow the rule of making the environment neat and clean. The hotels and restaurants are smiling in western culture. The local culture is also badly affected by the tourists. Although the existing population of Pachmarhi never like this type of behavioural change but they are unfortunately related to tourists arrival directly or indirectly. They love Pachmarhi because tourists love Pachmarhi. Love is very common in both sides. We are enjoying Pachmarhi without any care of present and past leaving behind sorrow kits. None of them have been seen in a thinking to improve the nice picturesque of Pachmarhi.

Bansal (1991) have stated that modernity has in breed very little worth the natural spots and nature of Pachmarhi but the facilities provided by public sectors are not advance in nature. It is observed that the growth of the town and the sewage of the settlement cause too much pollution. The picnic spots, gardens and boating sites need further improvements. Even then the most interesting sites like Jata Shaker, Gupt Mahadeo, Bara Mahadeo, Dhup Garh, Chaura Garh and the sites of various interesting waterfalls have not proper facilities to reach and enjoy there. The nature of Pachmarhi has self decorated her beauty and charm. It is not a gift of peace by local people or through government efforts. Thus the proper management should be provided at public and government levels.

## REFERENCES

Bansal, S.C. 1991: *Pachmarhi: A Trekker's Paradise*, Kamal Kishore Dhool Publishers, Pachmarhi.

Gupta, K.L. 1998: Profile of process, form ecology and tourism development in Pachmarhi hills, Ph.D. thesis (unpublished) submitted to Purvanchal University Jaunpur.

Peltier, L. C. 1950: The *Geographical Cycle in Periglacial Regions as it is to Climatic Geomorphology*, Annals Association of American Geographers, 40, pp. 214-236.

Singh, A. M. 1994 & 1995 Madhya Pradesh, District Gazetteers, Hoshangabad & Chhindwara Gazetteers Unit Department of Culture, Government of M.P., Bhopal.

Srivastava, P. N. 1990: Madhya Pradesh District Gazetteers, Betul Distt. Gazetteers Unit, Dept. of Culture, Government of M.P., Bhopal.

Wilson, L. 1973: *Relationships between geomorphic processes and modern climates as a method in Palaeclimorphology* (ed. DerByshire, E.) Geographical Readings, Macmillan Press, London, pp. 269-278.

15

# Floods in Delhi

## A Geomorphological and Geological Perspective in an Urbanised Landscape

H. S. SAINI, S. A. I. MUJTABA AND A. K. GUPTA

### INTRODUCTION

Floods have become an integral part of the natural land-water system of Delhi. The event is repeated almost every year during monsoon (July-September) with varying intensity and spread causing heavy economic loss, health hazards and land-water degradation, thereby affecting the prosperity of society and the state. The actual losses in terms of money are difficult to assess. However, their dimension could be anticipated from the reports that about rupees 20 crore were spent on flood prevention during 1994 monsoon. This problem was not so acute few decades ago, because the areas affected were mostly open and less populated. With rapid increase in population, the urbanisation spread to the flood vulnerable areas which led to increasingly severe losses. Delhi, therefore, presents an example of spread of urbanisation without due concession for natural hazards. It shows how flooding becomes disastrous in an economically developed, politically sensitive and socially aware capital city.

It will be interesting to evaluate the geomorphological and geological setting of Delhi in the context of spread of urbanisation and problem of recurring floods as it may guide future planning of areas for human habitation and may also be taken as a necessary input for similar development in other cities.

### METHODOLOGY

The study included mapping of flood prone zones of Delhi including identification of Yamuna palaeobanks, using satellite imageries (IRS-1B, F.C.C. 1992 and landsat MSS, B6, 1972) and Survey of India toposheets (surveyed in 1932, 1946 and 1988). Field work was carried out to verify the flood prone zones and collect geomorphic measurements, lithological details and ground water data. Regional as well as local E-W and N-S geological cross-sections were drawn on the basis of topographic and field data.

## GEOLOGICAL SET-UP

A geological succession of lithologies exposed in Delhi is given in (Table 15.1)

Ajabgarh group which forms the northward continuation of a doubly plunging "Harchandpur-Delhi anticline" constitutes the oldest rock sequence (Prasad *et al.*, 1994). The Quaternary Group, unconformably overlying the Ajabgarh, consists of a thick (+210 m) sequence of clay and sand forming the Older Alluvium and a thin (+ 10 m) sequence of grey sand forming the Newer Alluvium (Fig. 15.1).

## GEOMORPHOLOGY

Delhi occupies a unique geomorphic position in the Indo-Gangetic Plain. It lies on the water divide between Ganga basin characterising south-easterly flowing perennial drainage in the east and the Haryana plains characterising southwesterly and northerly flowing ephemeral drainage in the west. The state is drained by a perennial, locally meandering but regionally straight, southerly flowing Yamuna river.

Three major geomorphic units have been identified in the study area (Fig. 15.1) Their landforms, lithology and land-uses are summarised in (Table 15.1).

### Denudational Hill Unit

This smallest unit covers 220 sq. km area and forms the highest surface consisting of NE-SW trending Delhi ridge. It is broad and prominent in the south (Max. height 318 m) and becomes narrow and subdued in the north (213 m). The surface is traversed by structurally controlled NE-SW, N-S and E-W water courses.

### Upland Unit

Representing the Older Alluvium sequence the upland unit is most extensive surface (925 sq. km.) developed west of hill unit. Regional surface has a gentle (0.4 m/km) southerly slope, though, local variations of slope are also present. In one such instance, the upland unit slopes south-west along the western flank of Delhi ridge while this unit in

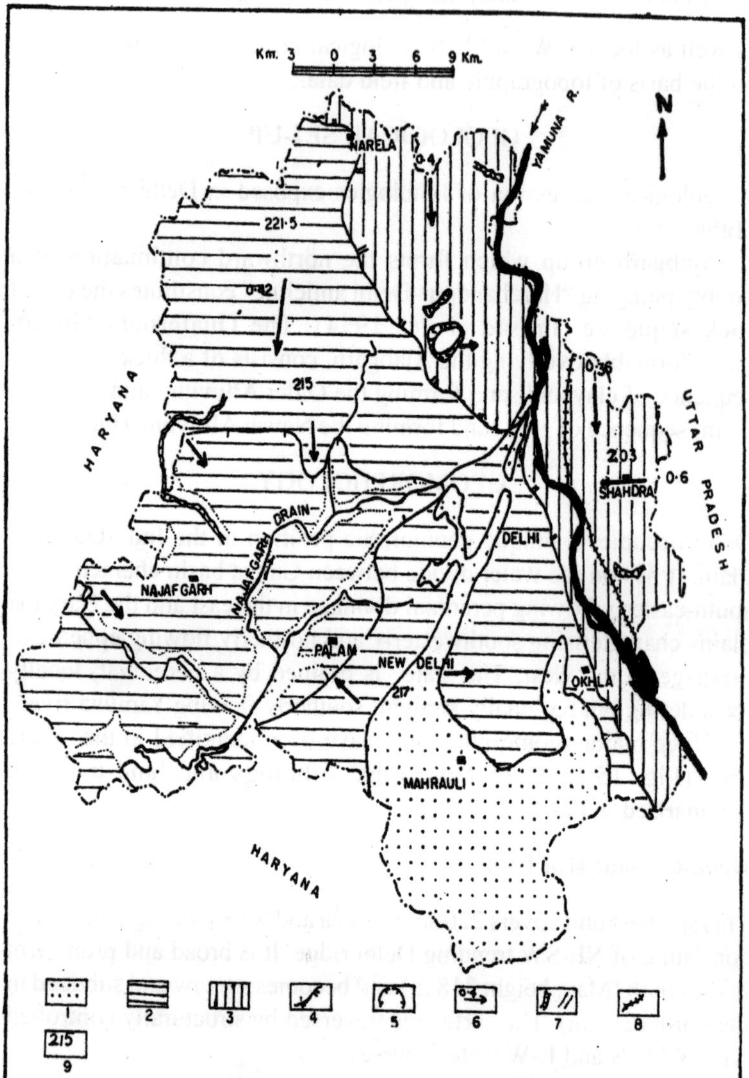


Geology : 1. Ajabgarh Group, 2. Older Alluvium, 3. Newer Alluvium.

Geomorphology : 1. Denudational Hill Unit, 2. Upland Unit, 3. Low Land Unit, 4. Palaeobank, 5. Depression, 6. Slope amount and direction, 7. Palaeochannel Depression, 8. Embankment, 9. Elevation in m.

**Fig. 15.1 :** Geological and Geomorphological Map of Delhi.

**Table 15.1 :** Geological and Geomorphological Setting of Delhi

| Age | Geology | | Lithology | Morphostratigraphy | | Land form | Land-Use |
|---|---|---|---|---|---|---|---|
| Holocene | Newer Alluvium | Recent Alluvium | Grey sand | Low Land Surface ($T_1$) | Active Flood Plain ($T_0$) (208-210 m) | Channel bars | Water course, barrage, built up area. |
| | | Terrace Alluvium | Grey fine sand & silt clay | | Abandoned Flood Plain (211-203 m) | Terraces, Abandoned channel, meander scars mounds. | Built up area, agriculture, water bodies. |
| ..............Disconformity... ........... | | | | | | | |
| Mid-Upper Pleistocene | Older Alluvium | | Brownish silt-clay, sand and kankar | Upland Surface (220-210 m) | | Alluvial plain depression, palaeochannel, tals | Built up area, agriculture. forest, water bodies |
| ... ...........Unconformity... ........... | | | | | | | |
| Lr.–Mid Proterozoic | Delhi Super Group (Ajabgarh Group) | | Massive Quartzite and pegmatites | Denudational Hill Surface (318 –213 m) | | Structural hills | Waste land, forest built up land, quarrying |

the south-western parts of Delhi slopes south-east. A gentle depression having a general elevation of 210 m exists in the south-west (Fig. 15.1).

### Lowland or Flood Plain Unit

North-eastern, eastern and south-eastern parts of Delhi lying 4 to 7 m below the upland unit along the Yamuna river constitute the "Low Land Unit". It covers around 300 sq. km. area and defines the flood regime of Yamuna river. The unit mainly comprises an upper $T_1$ terrace and a subordinate active channel surface ($T_0$), 2 m below the $T_1$. Presence of two well defined levels of flood regime signifies neotectonic movements and climatic changes during Holocene (Kumar, 1992).

The western limit of low-land unit is defined by a 5 to 7 m high, subdued and obliterated bluff representing the palaeobank. The eastern limit lies outside Delhi in Ghaziabad district of Uttar Pradesh where the flood plain of Yamuna merges with that of the Hindon (Fig. 15.2).

### Flood Prone Zones of Delhi

On the basis of geomorphic and geological considerations, three main flood prone zones *viz.*, eastern, northern and western, are identified (Fig. 15.3) whose vulnerability has been proved in recent time. In addition, a linear south-eastern zone along the Rajghat-Kalindi road and few random patches in southern Delhi are also flood prone (Table 15.2).

The eastern and northern zones lie within the Yamuna flood regime itself, whereas the western zone is flood prone on account of its low topography, centripetal slope and influence of Sahibi river. Brief description of these zones is given below.

#### *Eastern Flood Prone Zone (EFZ)*

The left flood regime of Yamuna covering around 100 sq.km. of eastern Delhi constitutes the EFZ. It includes a thickly urbanised $T_1$ terrace and a narrow, tortuous, partly encroached $T_0$ surface with average elevations of 205 and 203 m respectively. The $T_1$ has a poor natural drainage and is characterised by abandoned channel scars (around Shamaspur, Sharroli and Mandoli) and depressions (around Mandoli and Karkarduma). These landforms are now almost completely habitated.

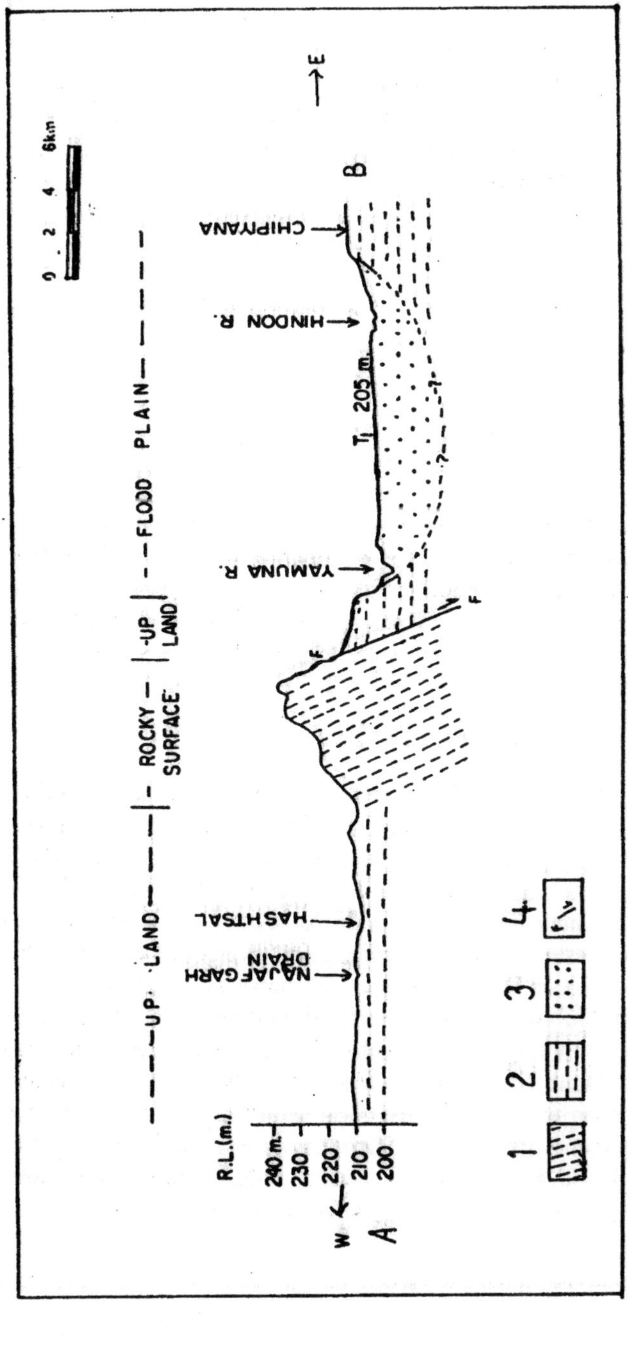


1. Quartzite, 2. Silt-clay (Older Alluvium), 3. Fine Sand (Newer Alluvium), 4. Fault.

**Fig. 15.2 :** East-West Geomorphological-cum-Geological Section Along Hastsal (Delhi)-Chipiyana (U. P.)

**Table 15.2** : Important Flood Prone Localities of Delhi

| Eastern Zone | Northern Zone | Western Zone | Others |
|---|---|---|---|
| Karawal Nagar, | Alipur, Adarsh Nagar, | Janakpuri, | Pitampura, |
| Dayalpur, | Libaspur, Model Town, | Vikaspuri, | Ranibagh, |
| Mukund Vihar, | Mukherjee Nagar, | Uttam Nagar, | Sarita Vihar, |
| Prem Vihar, | Jahangirpuri | Hastsal, | Kalindi, |
| Jagatpuri, | | Najafgarh, | Rajghat |
| Yamuna Vihar, | | Punjabi Bagh, | |
| Bhajanpura, | | Kakrola | |
| Sonia Vihar, | | | |
| Ashok Nagar, | | | |
| Sunder Nagri, | | | |
| Nand Nagri, | | | |
| Rajiv Nagar | | | |

The $T_1$ dominantly consists of stabilised grey, fine sand with minor clay intercalations. However, a 30 to 50 cm clay layer usually covers the sequence. The $T_0$ includes loose, slightly coarser, grey sand. In $T_1$ terrace, ground water occurs at shallow depths between 3 and 5 m. At some places in northern parts water logging also exists. The $T_0$ is a water logged region.

## Northern Flood Prone Zone (NFZ)

The right flood regime of Yamuna covering 150 sq. km. of north-eastern Delhi between Delhi-Panipat Railway line and Yamuna river constitutes the NFZ. It comprises a stabilised $T_1$ terrace lying 5 to 7 m below the upland unit (Fig. 15.3). Its elevation varies from 211 m in the north (Bakhtawarpur) to 205 m in the south (Adarsh Nagar) with a southerly master slope and a subsidiary riverward easterly slope. Remnants of older Yamuna course still occur as meandering scroll (Tikrikhurd, Bulswar, Jahangirpuri and Qudepur) and depressions (Jahangirpuri). A few of the abandoned channels are now converted into drains (Drain No. 6 and Dayalpur drain etc.) . This zone is less urbanised than the EFZ and has rural settlements in the north and urban settlements in the south. Ground water is shallow, generally between 3 and 5 m deep, but locally water logging conditions (Jahangirpuri) are also present. The geological set-up is same as in EFZ.

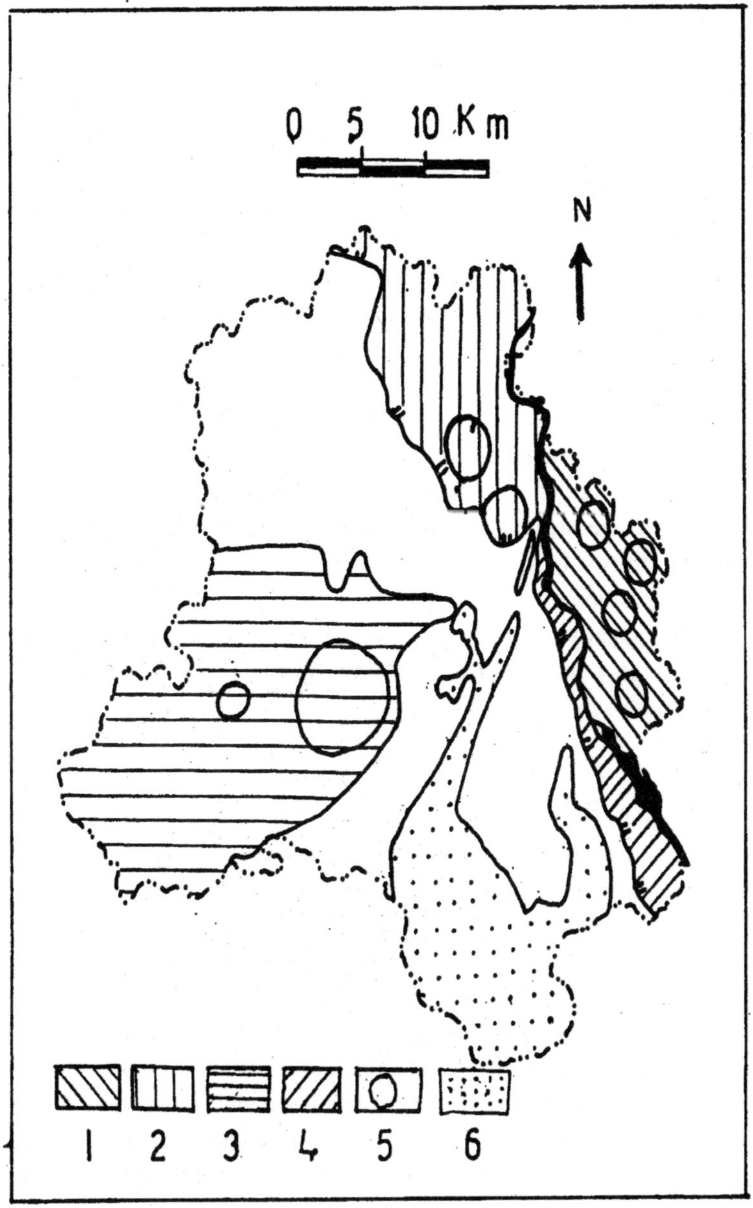


**Fig. 15.3 :** Flood Prone Zones of Delhi : 1. Eastern Flood Prone Zone, 2. Northern Flood Prone Zone, 3. Western Flood Prone Zone, 4. South-eastern Flood Prone Zone, 5. Perennial Flood Prone Area, 6. Quartzite Ridge.

**Western Flood Prone Zone (WFZ)**

A broad, subtle saucer like depression in the upland, imperceptibly sloping towards south-west, constitute the WFZ (Fig. 15.4). It includes about 350 sq. km. area of south-west Delhi. This topographic low represents a pre-Holocene palaeochannel zone which extends further south-west in Haryana and merges with the northerly sloping terminal fan zone of Sahibi river. A 700 feet contour, marked in 1922 edition of toposheet, tentatively defines the boundary of WFZ. The eastern periphery is comparatively steeper due to proximity with the hill unit. Several linear palaeochannel depressions (near Mundela Khurd, Pindwala Kalan and Dichawan Kalan) exist in the zone which become pronounced when rainwater accumulate. Some of these palaeochannels have been converted into drains, of which Najafgarh drain is most notable. It is largely a meandering palaeochannel loop artificially extended in the meandering palaeochannel loop artificially extended in the north-east to discharge flood-sewage water in Yamuna against the ground slope.

Lithologically the depression surface consists of a 3 to 5 m thick yellowish clay with 'kankar' of Older Alluvium and is overlain by brown loose sand heaps at places.

DISCUSSION

Foregoing description indicates that flooding in Delhi takes place due to natural conditions like presence of the Yamuna flood basin, poor drainage, complex surface slope, lithology and shallow watertable. The intensity and magnitude of flooding, however, is compounded by anthropogenic factors like urbanisation and silting of Yamuna channel. In EFZ and NFZ flooding is caused by Yamuna river and rains whereas in WFZ Sahibi river and rains are the main causative factors.

The EFZ and NFZ are flood prone as they are located on a terrace ($T_1$) surface which was earlier the active flood plain of Yamuna. Since this surface lies within the river domain, it is liable to flood in case river water rises above the $T_0$ bluff which is upto 2 m in height. On account of blocking of river water at both northern and southern extremities, it is difficult to ascertain the average flow level of Yamuna in Delhi. However, just downstream of Wazirabad barrage the average

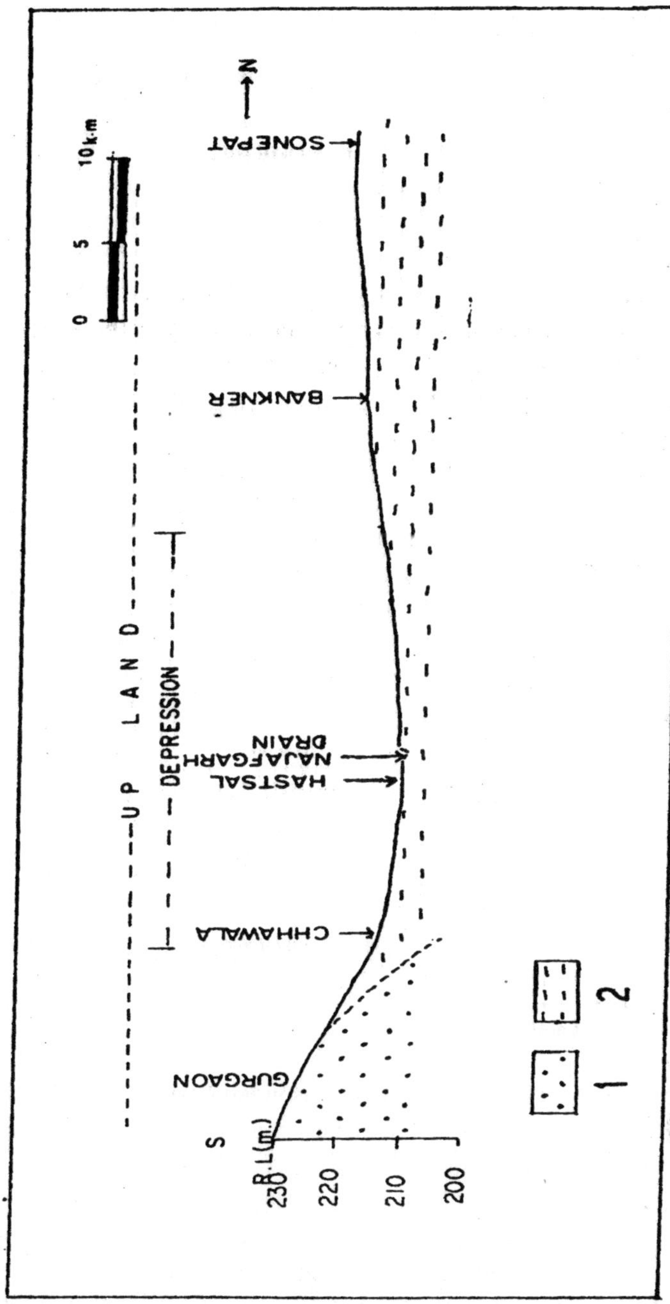


1. Quartzite, 2. Silt-clay.

**Fig. 15.4 :** North-South Geomorphological cum Geological Section along Sonepat (Haryana), Bankner (Delhi), Gurgaon (Haryana)

water level in Yamuna is 203 m and the flood danger level is 204.83 m. A difference of 2 m between the base level of urbanisation (*i.e.*$T_1$ surface) and river water level presents a potent flood hazard especially at the time of heavy rainfall or release of stored water from upstream barrages or impoundment of water at the downstream barrages. Some of the high flood levels attained by Yamuna river in Delhi are given in (Table 15.3).

Normally, extensive inundation of $T_1$ of EFZ is prevented by a 3-4 m high embankment. But hundreds of temporary settlements erected between Yamuna channel and embankment are regularly flooded. It must also be clearly understood that construction of embankment is only a temporary safeguard as increase in local base level of Yamuna will necessitate further higher embankment. Moreover, it does not help in preventing the seepage of water from upstream acquifers to which the sandy acquifers of EFZ are interconnected. Water logging in the northern part of EFZ as well as around Jahangirpuri of NFZ are caused due to this phenomenon which convert into flood during rains.

**Table 15.3 :** Major Flooding Events of Yamuna River in Delhi

| Date | Highest Flood Level in Metre |
|---|---|
| 9. 10. 55 | 205. 39 |
| 15. 10. 56 | 206. 44 |
| 10. 08. 71 | 206. 90 |
| 23. 09. 76 | 206. 59 |
| 06. 09. 78 | 207. 45 |
| 27. 09. 88 | 206. 87 |
| July, 93 | 205. 02 |
| 23. 07. 94 | 205. 30 |

Flood Danger Level = 204.83 m

The WFZ, being a topographic low, is vulnerable to flooding due to an ephemeral river Sahibi originating in Rajasthan. It is a typical desert river notorious for sudden and widespread flooding in the upper as well as lower reaches in Rajasthan and Haryana. Unlike Yamuna, it flows towards north along a shallow, ill defined course that becomes untraceable beyond Dadri in Haryana. In the terminal zone, the river water fans out towards north and one such arm finds its way in the

WFZ through Najafgarh Jheel. This has happened during 1978 flood (Srivastava *et al*., 1979). After that, however, Sahibi hazard has been considerably reduced due to the construction of a barrage at Masani in Rewari district, Haryana. Once the water enters in this zone, it tends to get impounded in local palaeodepressions and stagnates due to clayey floor and shallow ground water.

Silting of Yamuna is another important factor that has increased probability of flooding in EFZ and NFZ. In 1936, the $T_0$ was 3 to 4 m deep around Wazirabad and Okhla. Due to subsequent sedimentation in channel caused by encroachment of surface for multiple uses and construction of barrages, the $T_0$ depth has been reduced to 1 to 2 m in 1994. This has led to decrease in the water carrying capacity of $T_0$ channel, thereby, increasing the chances of its overflow. Now about one lakh cusec water is enough to overflow the danger mark. With the same channel width and an additional 2 m depth around two lakh cusec of water would have been required to overflow the channel. Coverage of $T_0$ causes shrinkage of channel width, which further reduces its capacity. The river at the time of excessive discharge causes embankment breaches as happened in 1978 when Model Town and Mukherjee Nagar were heavily inundated.

In EFZ and NFZ, prior to spread of urbanisation, major part of the flood water run-off used to either filter down or return to active channel, thereby, leaving only a small part to occur as stagnating water bodies in the abandoned channel parts. Older toposheets (surveyed in 1942) show several such marshy patches on the $T_1$. Now closely spaced buildings impose an artificial lithology of impervious concrete horizontally as well as vertically in these areas. The cover increases the surface run-off during rains by preventing infiltration, decreases lag time and ultimately increases the magnitude of floods (Lundgren, 1986). Studies have demonstrated that run-off in urbanised surface increases by 1.1 to 4.6 times of the pre-urbanised surface (Montogomery, 1989). Increases in the built-up area of Delhi from 1940 to 1991 is shown in Fig. 15.5. Presently, almost the entire EFZ, northern parts of WFZ and southern parts of NFZ are occupied by dense buildings where the natural ground lithology is rarely exposed. Once the river or rain water is trapped in such areas, its height and lateral spread disproportionately increases and also the intensity and magnitude of the event. In July, 1993 a mere 10 cm rain was able to produce 3 to 4 m high water columns in these areas.

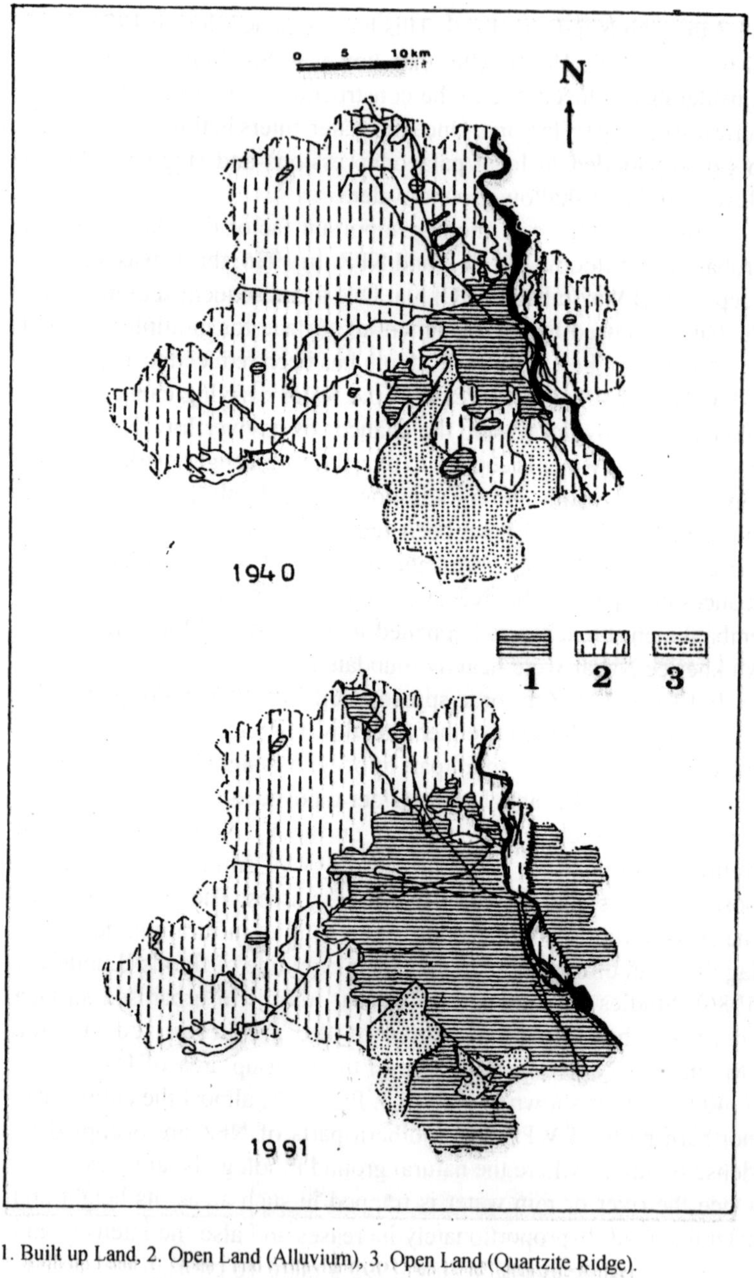


1. Built up Land, 2. Open Land (Alluvium), 3. Open Land (Quartzite Ridge).

**Fig. 15.5 :** Built up Land in Delhi in 1940 and 1991.

In Delhi, a rather peculiar factor in WFZ related to the adverse functioning of Najafgarh drain, compounds the flood problem. The drain is 44.5 m wide and 3.8 m deep in the south-western part while 28.95 m wide and 6 m deep in north-eastern part. Normally water level in the drain is around 208 m near Najafgarh and 203 m at the mouth. This 5 m level difference in around 27 km length appears to be insufficient to keep the drain flowing toward north-east as evident by nearly stagnant water around Najafgarh. During rains initially the water flows towards south-west; however, when water level rises in Najafgarh Jheel, the flow reverses towards north-east. In north-eastern part, while traversing the $T_1$ of NFZ, the bed level of drain comes close to 203 m which is the level of Yamuna bed. When Yamuna rises during flood, in order to maintain the hydraulic head, water rises in the drain and chokes its normal discharge. It leads to back flow in the drain and affects the secondary sewage drains which discharge in it at 2 to 3 m above its normal level. The drainage system of Delhi is designed to cope with half an inch of rain per hour, while the capacity of Najafgarh drain is 3000 cusec. During heavy spells, the system get choked at various points and causes spill over from manholes especially in the low lying areas, thus accentuating the flood problem even in the catchment area.

In the light of above, it is clear that the areas included in EFZ and NFZ were not suitable for massive urbanisation. These were rather most suitable for developing green belts and recreation centres. However, in view of the pressing housing demands in capital, if these areas were to be urbanised, then a thorough analyses of the geological and geomorphological conditions was necessary. This could have provided the planners inputs regarding flood hazards and guided them in evolving special architectural design, water draining system and demarcating vulnerable zones to avoid flood losses.

Flooding due to natural causes is a phenomenon that cannot be stopped. It could however, be considerably regulated. But, in post-urbanised scenario, the scope of flood prevention becomes rather less. Following suggestions are made for amelioration of flood hazards;

1. Detailed survey on intensity, magnitude, height and spread of flood water for flood zonation.
2. Channel modification including regular desilting to regulate flood water and increase carrying capacity of Yamuna.

3. Prevention of urbanisation near $T_0$ and as well as in the perennial water logging areas of NFZ and EFZ.
4. Construction of sub-surface barriers for preventing infiltration in NFZ and EFZ from upstream.
5. Regular desilting of existing drains.
6. Establishment of a flood forecasting system and evaluation of flood insurance schemes to spread the losses from few people to larger community. Some of these measures are given in details by Lundgren, 1986; Keller, 1988 and Montgomery, 1989.

## ACKNOWLEDGEMENTS

We are thankful to Sh. A.K. Raina, Director, GSI for his encouragement during the preparation of paper. We are also grateful to Dr. N.C. Pant, Geologist, who critically scrutinised the draft and offered useful suggestions.

## REFERENCES

Keller, Edward, A., *Environmental Geology*. 6th Edition, McMillan Publishing Co., New York, 1998.

Kumar, G., *Quaternary Event Stratigraphy and Evolution of Indogangetic Plain*, Uttar Pradesh, Group Discussion on Indo-Gangetic Basin, Department of Geology, Kumaon University. 5-7, 1992.

Lundgren, L., *Environmental Geology*. Prentice Hall, New Jersey, p. 576, 1986.

Montgomery, C.W., *Environmental Geology*. 2nd Edition, Wim, C. Brown Publication, Dubuque, Lowa, p. 476, 1989.

Prasad, S., Verma, K.P., Singh, R., Powar, M.M., Dasgupta, G., Kachroo, K. and Sharma, S. *Report on Stratigraphic Correlation and Regional Geochemical Appraisal of Delhi Supergroup in Southern Parts of Haryana*. Unpub. G.S.I. Report F.S. 1988-92. 1994.

Srivastava, A.K., Sinha, K.K., Gautam, G., Singha, A. K., Jalote P. M., Dasgupta, G., Ananthraman, S., Srivastava, M.C. and Gupta, S.K. *Progress Report on Geotechnical Project*, Delhi Unpub. G.S.I. Report, F.S. 1975-76 to 1978-79.

# 16

# Slums, Environment and Development in Metropolitan Cities of India

R. B. SINGH AND D. K. MISHRA

## INTRODUCTION

The environmental stress and socio-economic strains of urbanization are experienced both in the metropolises and their hinterlands. Metropolization, the dominant trend of Indian urbanization has been experienced in the second half of the twentieth century. This posed not only severe environmental problems like pollution but congested housing and slums also. There are widespread threat to health safety and environmental sustainability. The most challenging problem of present day urban metropolis particularly in third world countries is the maintenance of environment in the course of slum development. In metropolis the main threat which the environment is facing comes from increasing number of squatters and slums. The most important characteristics of slums of India is their location on illegal and unauthorised land. These settlements can be identified as informal housing structures, acute overcrowding, faulty alignment of streets, poor ventilation, inadequate lighting, paucity of drinking water, absence of toilet facilities, lack of garbage disposal and proper drainage etc.

As per an estimate, about 50 percent of population lives in marginalised environment of slums and squatter settlements. Slums, therefore should attract a major share of planning efforts, resources and involvement of planners. To assess the objectives to exempt the people from non-congenial environment a variety of policy options and tools are to be applied in national and regional context along with involvement of governmental and non-governmental organizations.

## SLUMS, ENVIRONMENT AND DEVELOPMENT

Historical enquiry and general survey of metropolitan cities reveals that urbanization and economic development is the most important cause of the slums and squatters. Better urban services attract the rural people who come to satisfy their livelihood and compound the existing urban problems and basic infrastructural facilities. The acuteness of the slum problem is more in industrially developed mega cities *i.e.* Delhi, Bombay, Calcutta and Madras etc. Table 16.1 reveals that the population of slums has increased considerably during 1981-91. It is likely that the growth would be more rapid in future (Fig. 16.1).

In Delhi, there are 929 Jhuggi-Jhopari clustres, 45 resettlement colonies and 1000 unauthorised colonies occupied by almost 2.63 million people. Over 50 per cent of urban population of Bombay lives in slums and on the pavements with hardly any access to sanitary facilities. Few have no toilets and legal water supplies. Dharavi, the largest slum of Bombay having more than 0.5 million population does not even have regular garbage collection system. A report based on a study done by Associated Industrial Consultants, a city firm in June 1994 estimated that at least 2 million persons in Bombay had no access to any toilet facility.

In Calcutta at least 33 per cent population constitutes the slum. As per record of the central government's–run Infectious Diseases Hospitals, at least 500 people die due to diarrhoea annually and 30 per cent of people suffer from cholera. Slums in Madras have developed mostly along the routes such as railway tracks and road sides. The waterways serve as open toilets. Though the Tamil Nadu Slum Control Board (TSCB) has provided one toilet for every 20 slum persons, most of them remain out of the order most of the times (Fig. 16.1).

The conditions of the slum colonies in Bangalore numbering over 400 is indeed pathetic, none of these is linked with sewerage system. During 1981-83 the Municipal Corporation of Hyderabad (MCH) mooted a proposal to provide minimum amenities *i.e.* drinking water and sewerage connections to 156 slums but due to paucity of funds the programme could not succeed. The second phase of programme known as Hyderabad Slum Improvement Programme (HSIP) was implemented during 1983-87 with a financial assistance of Rs. 15.57 crores from the Overseas Development Administration (ODA) of U.K. benefiting 48,521 families in 210 slums. About one-fourth population of Ahmedabad live in slums. Surat, the plague capital of India, is also occupied by rural migrants form the nooks and corners of India in search of bread and butter. According to the survey conducted by the Centre for Social Studies (CSS), Surat, 29 per cent of the urban population or 4.34 lakh people live in slums out of these roughly 80 per cent are migrants (Fig. 16.2).

**Table 16.1 :** Estimated Slum Population in Selected Metropolitan Cities of India (in million)

| Cities | Population | 1981 Identified Slum Population | | 1991 Estimated Population | | 2001 Estimated Population | |
|---|---|---|---|---|---|---|---|
| | | No. | % age | Urban | Slum | Urban | Slum Taking 1981 % age |
| Calcutta | 9.20 | 3.03 | 32.9 | 10.91 | 3.59 | 12.94 | 4.26 |
| G. Bombay | 8.24 | 2.83 | 34.3 | 12.57 | 4.31 | 19.18 | 6.59 |
| Delhi | 5.73 | 1.80 | 31.4 | 8.38 | 2.63 | 12.26 | 3.85 |
| Madras | 4.29 | 1.36 | 32.1 | 5.36 | 1.72 | 6.70 | 2.15 |
| Hyderabad | 2.55 | 0.50 | 19.6 | 4.28 | 0.84 | 7.18 | 1.41 |
| Bangalore | 2.92 | 0.31 | 10.4 | 4.09 | 0.43 | 5.73 | 0.60 |
| Ahmedabad | 2.55 | 0.54 | 20.3 | 3.30 | 0.67 | 4.27 | 0.87 |
| Pune | 1.69 | 0.27 | 16.3 | 2.49 | 0.41 | 3.67 | 0.60 |
| Kanpur | 1.64 | 0.61 | 37.5 | 2.11 | 0.79 | 2.71 | 1.02 |
| Lucknow | 1.01 | 0.29 | 28.3 | 1.64 | 0.46 | 2.66 | 0.75 |
| Nagpur | 1.30 | 0.42 | 31.9 | 1.66 | 0.53 | 2.12 | 0.68 |
| Jaipur | 1.02 | 0.30 | 29.1 | 1.51 | 0.44 | 2.24 | 0.65 |
| Surat | 0.91 | 0.23 | 25.4 | 1.52 | 0.39 | 2.54 | 0.65 |
| Coimbatore | 0.92 | — | — | 1.14 | 0.23 | 1.41 | 0.28 |
| Cochin | 0.69 | 0.17 | 24.8 | 1.14 | 0.28 | 1.18 | 0.47 |
| Baroda | 0.75 | 0.12 | 15.8 | 1.12 | 0.18 | 1.67 | 0.26 |
| Indore | 0.83 | 0.13 | 15.2 | 1.10 | 0.17 | 1.46 | 0.22 |
| Patna | 0.91 | 0.58 | 63.5 | 1.32 | 0.70 | 1.32 | 0.84 |
| Madurai | 0.91 | — | — | 1.09 | 0.22 | 1.31 | 0.26 |
| Bhopal | 0.67 | 0.06 | 8.5 | 1.06 | 0.09 | 1.68 | 0.14 |
| Vishakhapatnam | 0.60 | 0.15 | 25.2 | 1.05 | 0.26 | 1.84 | 0.46 |
| Varanasi | 0.80 | 0.26 | 32.6 | 1.03 | 0.34 | 1.33 | 0.43 |
| Ludhiana | 0.61 | 0.31 | 51.1 | 1.01 | 0.52 | 1.67 | 0.85 |
| Total | 50.74 | 14.27 | 28.12% | 70.66 | 20.20 (28.58%) | 99.77 | 28.29 (28.36%) |

*Source* : Town and Country Planning Organisation, Ministry of Urban Development, Government of India, New Delhi, 1994.

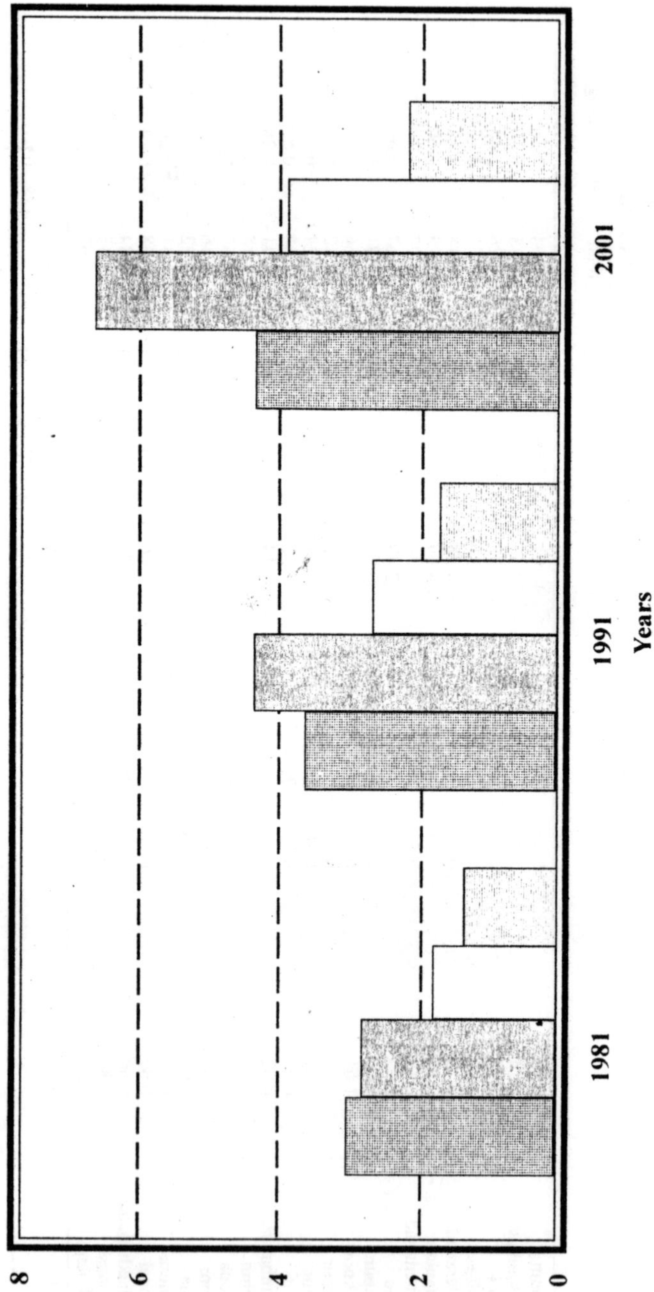


**Fig. 16.1 :** Trends of Slum Population in Mega Cities of India (Population in Million).

Thus, slum population is causing a very serious situation over urban environment of India threatening the process of social and cultural

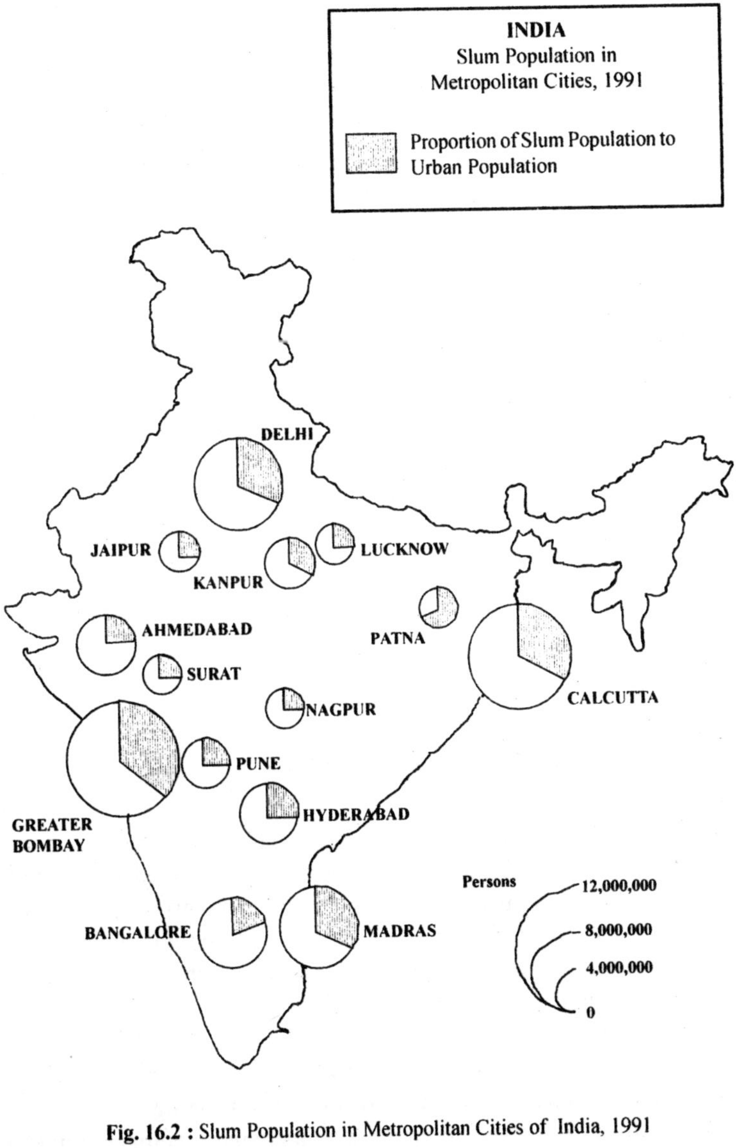


**Fig. 16.2 :** Slum Population in Metropolitan Cities of India, 1991

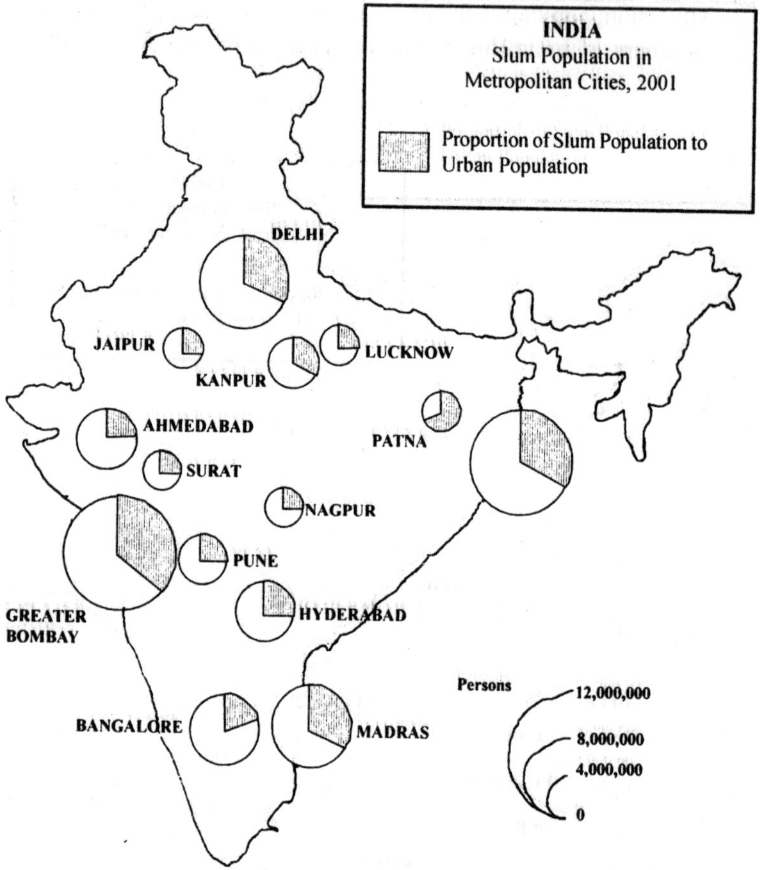


**Fig. 16.3 :** Slum Population in Metropolitan Cities of India, 2001

development. Somehow these metros are achieving economic growth but their social and cultural development is not taking place. Though, there may be several other causes of slum, poverty is one of the functional causes of the deterioration of socio-cultural environment. It is the result of the faulty development processes, growing population, poverty and inefficient utilization of resources.

The environmental situation in slums is very critical. The pressure of water supply is low throughout the year and is extremely inadequate during the summer months. The average water timing are about 4-5 hours in the morning and about three hours in the evening. During the four summer months most of the hand pumps are found dry and is likely to be contaminated because of its being unfiltered. Most of the latrines are of the dry type, even those of the flush type pose a problem for cleanliness in the absence of availability of water. The inadequate facilities for latrine and their over use by too many persons in the absence of their regular cleaning, made most of them not only unserviceable but also extremely unhygienic.

There are no sewerage system in the slum settlements. There exist only uncovered cemented drains which are led along the streets, lanes and bylanes. These drainage are not only insufficient but also improperly led with faulty gradients resulting the drains chocked with filthy water and refuse. The provision of street lighting is highly deficient and many settlements are facing complete darkness after the sunset. So it is understood that the environmental conditions in the urban slums are worst.

## INITIATIVES FOR SLUM IMPROVEMENT

Slum problems received attention in 1956, when the Slum Improvement and Clearance Act was passed. The Act provided the acquisition of slums, rehousing of families with low incomes, improvement of environmental conditions and construction of night shelters. Under this, a pucca tenement of 16.66 sq. metres of floor area, two rooms, a bath and a latrine, with a cost varying from Rs. 2700 to Rs. 4000, was also to be provided to each family. The amount for such construction was raised in 1971, varying from Rs. 5,380 to Rs. 7,000. As a result of the implementation of this scheme, nearly 89,000 tenements were constructed from 1956 to 1971. However, this covered only one-half per cent of the total slum households in cities with populations above 100,000. In addition to tenements, some plots ranging in size from 92.59 sq. metres to 111.11 sq. metres, were developed with an earthen platform for bathing and leaving the rest of the structure to be raised by the slum dwellers themselves. The size of the plots in subsequent years was considerably reduced because of the large-scale, illegal transfer of plots by slum dwellers. For instance, in Delhi it was reduced to 21 sq. metres by 1970. The programme was mainly adopted in Madras and Delhi. By 1970, Madras had provided 8,500 plots of 90 sq. metres and Delhi, 25,000 plots of 80 sq. metres and 21 sq. metres.

In April 1972 a Central Scheme for Environmental Improvement in slums was introduced whereby financial assistance was granted to state governments for undertaking slum environment improvement programmes in cities with population above 0.8 million. The cities thus identified were Calcutta, Bombay, Delhi, Madras, Hyderabad, Bangalore, Ahmedabad, Kanpur, Pune, Nagpur and Lucknow. This improvement programme made provision for water mains, sewers, storm water drains, community baths, latrines, water taps and street lighting. It also provided for widening the existing lanes, pavement of lanes, construction of roads, and land scarping and horticultural operations. The scheme further provided parks, playgrounds, community and welfare centres, police and fire stations, schools, hospitals and dispensaries on a non-profit basis (Table 16.2).

**Table : 16.2 :** Components Under EIUS Scheme

| Components | Norm for Facilities |
|---|---|
| Water supply | 1 tap for 150 persons |
| Sewer | Open drains with normal outflow avoiding accumulation of water |
| Storm water drains | For quickly draining out storm water |
| Community baths | 1 bath for 20-50 persons |
| Community latrines | 1 latrine for 20-50 persons |
| Widening and paving of existing lanes | For making room for easy flow of pedestrians, bicycles and handcarts on paved paths thereby avoiding mud and slush. |
| Street lighting | I pole for 30 metres distance |

*Source* : Ministry of Urban Development, Government of India, New Delhi.

This scheme also envisaged the construction of pucca slum dwellings, with water closets, bathrooms, water taps, either inside the premise or near the dwellings, conversion of a privy to a water borne system with connection to the main drainage providing smokeless hearths and sink in the kitchen, paved courtyards, electricity and enlarged rooms, windows and ventilations. Preference was given to slums located on public lands. Improvement of slums located on private lands was affected only by those areas where adequate legislation was in place to prevent landlords from claiming increased amount on account of improvement. In the Fifth Five-Year Plan (1974-79), this scheme was financed as a part of the minimum needs programme of the Government of India and was extended to all cities with a population of 300,000 and above (Nangia, 84).

In the Sixth Five Year Plan (1980-85), the slum improvement scheme focused on the 10 million people living below the poverty line in urban areas with population above 1,000,000. In addition to housing, basic amenities provided were water supply, sanitation, drainage, sewerage, transportation and recreation. The plan provided an outlay of Rs. 1505 million in the state plans to meet these objectives (Ministry of Housing, 1984) to be achieved at an expenditure of Rs. 150 per person. A mid-term appraisal of the Sixth Plan indicated that 3.77 million people had been covered during 1980-83 (Table 16.3).

**Table 16.3 :** Coverage of Slum Population in India

| Period | Fin. State | Outlay Central | Total (Rs. Crores) | Target (Persons million) | Achievement (Persons million) | Total Achievement (%) |
|---|---|---|---|---|---|---|
| Before | – | – | – | – | 6.73 | – |
| VI Plan | 151.45 | 20.97 | 172.42 | 10.00 | 9.34 | 93.4 |
| VII Plan | 269.55 | – | 269.55 | 9.00 | 3.97 | 44.1 |
| Upto | | | | | | |
| 31.3.87 | – | – | – | – | 20.16 | – |
| 1992-93 | – | 799.4 | – | 11.78 | 11.72 | 99.49 |

*Source* : Ministry of Urban Development, Government of India.

During 1990-91, the targeted number of beneficiaries was 1.54 million, against which the achievement was 1.93 million. The per capita expenditure was enhanced to Rs. 525 from 1991-92. During the Eighth Five Year Plan, the scope of the programme is being widened to ensure that the Environmental Improvement of the Urban Slums, the Urban Basic Services Programme, the Nehru Rojgar Yojana and the scheme of Liberation of Scavengers form a coordinated effort. Assurance of providing tenurial rights and evolving feasible cost recovery mechanism are important pre-condition for the success of the programme in a long-term context.

## SUGGESTED POLICY INITIATIVES TO IMPROVE THE SITUATION

Slum and squatter settlements require a renovation and *in situ* upgradation, provision of water supply, sanitation and other basic services and maintenance of amenities through community involvement. On the basis of various reports and studies, the following initiatives should be implemented on priority basis to improve the situation in the slums.

1. For implementation EIUS scheme, slum declared under slum Areas (Improvement and Clearance) Act, 1956 should be taken up.
2. Coordinated strategies for short-term and long-term new slum improvement programmes with particular reference to metropolitan cities while maintaining the improved slums.
3. Data collection in states, towns and cities on identified slums in order to develop slum information system.
4. To make efficient administrative and technical supports at local levels as well as maintenance of physical assets created in the slum.
5. Employment and income generating activities for unskilled persons.
6. Coordination among various agencies dealing with services like water supply, sewerage, electricity, health, etc.
7. Involvement of slum dwellers through self-initiative programmes, specially for women.
8. To link improvement schemes with security of tenures and assistance in house construction.
9. To provide coordination between government and NGOs and allocation of budgetary resources to local bodies and other implementing agencies.

## CONCLUSION

Urbanization is spreading in third world countries. The most regretful point is that approximately 50 per cent of the urban population is living in slums. The government and developmental agencies is not able to tackle the problems of slums dwellers and slum. These 50 per cent people access a meagre portion of budgetary portion of government resources needing more than other half population of the metros who are better off and still increasing their wealth and facilities. This comparison can be seen at two primary education centres, one of slum areas and other in income group localities. Therefore, to have sustainable environment, eradication of slums poverty and access to basic services such as water and sewerage etc. are very essential.

## REFERENCES

Dogra, Bharat. 1984, "Housing the urban poor Demolition by another Name," *Business Standard* (Aug.3).

Druijven, P. and Singh, R.B., 1995 " Environmental Degradation and its Impact on Livelihood Strategies in the Rural-Urban Fringe of Delhi : Some Theoretical Reflections and Research Experiences under Indo-Dutch Programme : in Disasters, Environment and Development, Editor: R.B. Singh, New Delhi, Oxford & IBH Pub.

Government of India, Ministry of Works and Housing, 1984, *New 20 Point Programme*, New Delhi, July 19, pp. 4-7.

Government of India, Ministry of Urban Development, 1994, 20 *Point Programme*, New Delhi.

Jagmohan, 1995, "Slums of India" *Hindustan Times* (12th April).

Meera, Bapat, 1995, Slums of Bombay, *The Hindu*—Survey of Environment.

Nangia, Sudesh, 1988, Slums of Urban India, Asian Urbanization: Problems and Process. Berlin: A Boritraeger, pp. 139.

Nangia, Sudesh, 1984, Innovative Approaches to Help Slum. Squatter and Rural Households Improve their Dwellings in India. Monogaraph prepared for ESCAP/UNIDO Division of Industry, Human Settlement and Technology, Bangkok, pp. 7 10.

Nangia, Sudesh, 1988, *Slums of Urban India, Asian Urbanization : Problems and Process Berlin :* A. Boritraeger, pp. 139.

Singh, R. B., 1995, "Urbanization, Environment Crisis and Urban Planning in India," Proceeding Int. Symposium on Urban Planning and Environment. Seattle, University of Washington.

Singh, R. B. and Pandey, B.W. 1995, "Spatial Planning through Landuse Environmental Zoing in Delhi Metropolis: Problems and Perspectives" Proceedings Int. Symp. on Urban Planning and Environment. Seattle, University of Washington.

# Groundwater Issues for Sustainable Water Supply in Delhi Area

P. S. DATTA

## INTRODUCTION

In urban areas, desire for adequate water supply and environmental quality have steadily increased in the past and will continue to increase in the foreseeable future with rapid growth in population and developmental activities. The quantity of water that can be economically developed in an area on a long-term basis being limited, water supply situation is likely to aggravate further, resulting in a multi-dimensional crisis, particularly when demand of water for different purposes increases dramatically as compared to not so elastic supply position. In some parts of Delhi region, the signs of such grim scenario has already creeped in. The solution apparently lies in search for an alternative approach for water supply within a framework of sustainable development, completely subservient to socio-economic issues and environmental considerations. However, knowledge of environmental issues remains tentative and insufficiently widespread along public. Creative interaction among science, engineering and society is, therefore, needed to ensure the lasting integrity of the water resource base, through systematic and enhanced research and monitoring of environmental problems, their patterns and remedies.

## WATER DEMAND-SUPPLY SCENARIO AND ASSOCIATED PROBLEMS

The current demand for water (770 MGD) far exceeds the installed capacity of Delhi's water works. The per capita water requirement (70 gallons/day) is almost double of the per capita water availability (40 gallons/day). By 2005 AD, the projected demand is expected to increase to 1151 MGD. The present availability of water fall short from the assessed requirement by about 150 MGD (36%), and the shortage is likely to increase further to 48 per cent by 2005 AD. Almost half of the total water consumption being non-metered, the unaccounted water is estimated to be as high as 60 per cent. Considerable zonal disparity in water supply is evident from the fact that there are areas which get 650 litres per capita per day, while some other areas receive as little as 25 *l*pc/day. River Yamuna, the only major source of surface water, is the main source of piped water, supplying as much as 68 per cent, according to the Government documents. The Ganga canal supplies about 20 per cent and groundwater tapped by tubewells and rainy wells supplies the remaining 12 per cent. However, the river Yamuna does not have always enough water to meet the requirements of the area, and the water being highly polluted is unfit for direct use. The available water treatment facilities are also not well equipped technologically to decontaminate the water completely from all toxic substances, due to high pollution load the systems remain closed many times in a year and maintenance cost of the facilities are quite significant.

## GROUNDWATER DEPENDENCY AND AUGMENTATION MEASURES

Therefore, it has become increasingly evident with time that to meet the daily requirements for agricultural, domestic and industrial purposes, direct or indirect dependence on groundwater is rapidly increasing. It is difficult to assess precisely the extent and share of exploitation for each purpose from the common groundwater reservoir. Agriculture being the main source of livelihood of the rural population, heavy dependence on groundwater is evident from the fact that 95 per cent of the total irrigated area receives groundwater irrigation. To meet the demand-supply gap, water users depend on water supplied through tankers by several companies, whose source of water is groundwater, most of which is unaccounted. Storage tanks and independent borewells are other well known examples of unaccounted waters. Water tariffs are very low for public supply and there is no mechanism of pricing for extraction of groundwater. The level of subsidy for domestic consumption being extremely high (79%) leads to more consumption and wasteful utilisation. This results in low level of revenue collection and hinderance in the investment capacities of the public utility as well as depletion in water reserve. To augment water supply, the main thrust of the short-term measures is on construction of more water-treatment plants, optimising production of water, water harvesting, artificial recharge and recycle. The long-term measures envisage augmentation of water through capital intensive, financially constrained inter-basin transfer projects, which may take more than 15 to 20 years to be completed. Therefore, the most critical problems facing the water managers in Delhi area are maximizing efficiency and minimizing cost of supply, while maintaining the satisfactory quality of water.

## URBAN ISSUES ON SUSTAINABLE WATER SUPPLY

Sustainability of water supply in an area is determined by growth in resource productivity, stability in its production and equatability in distribution. Past experiences indicate that water supply problems are essentially local or regional and engineering approaches alone result in more problems. Because, the water supply in different parts of a region is inextricably linked to the size and growth of the area, climate change, rainfall pattern and distribution, non-availability of adequate good quality water, availability of poor quality water in plenty, hydrology, fast expanding population and industrialisation, population density, settlement pattern, land-use, provisional basic social services, the degree of socio-economic development and public response to the need for environmental protection. Thus, the essential steps towards sustainable water supply are multi-dimensional, related to reliable assessment of available water from different sources, taking into account the interaction between land-use and water quantity and quality in groundwater aquifers and rivers, conservation of water, its scope for augmentation, distribution, reuse/recycling, its efficient use by reduction of demand and its protection from depletion and degradation. In this context, some of the important questions which the planners and decision makers are confronted with relate to the quantity and quality of groundwater; location of recharge intake areas; temporal and spatial variability of recharge; interlinkage between groundwater and surface water; existing hydraulic gradients and watertable situation, groundwater flow between different formations, etc.

## ASSESSMENT OF GROUNDWATER AVAILABILITY

Extensive hydrological investigations, undertaken by monitoring the spatial and temporal variations in the stable isotope signatures of rainfall, groundwater and surface water, provide a detailed and dynamic representation of groundwater in Delhi area. Occurrence of moderately to highly saline groundwater at all levels in more than sixty per cent of the area, mostly located in the north-western and south-western parts, suggests that the groundwater flushing is incomplete and that the amount of contemporary recharge is very limited or even absent at many places. Groundwater recharge from direct infiltration of rainfall shows a wide range (0.2 to 66.0%) of spatial variation, with most parts receiving less than 5 per cent recharge from rainfall. This fractional recharge being very small as compared to the groundwater withdrawal, there is a wide gap between groundwater demand and availability, leading to fast depletion in groundwater reserve in most parts of Delhi area, with an average rate of about 0.4–2.0 m/yr during the last decade. Very highly populated tail end areas (*i.e.*, Nangloi and Najafgarh blocks) of the water supply distribution system, receive relatively small amount of recharge from rainfall and face water supply problem, although located in the zones of high permeability and high yield. The potential recharge zones, having relatively higher infiltration from rainfall, are confined to a narrow strip (2-6 km. width) in small patches, along north to south, almost bisecting the area. But, in most of the zones, the thickness of the unsaturated soil available for recharge is very small, ranging from 0-2 m. Some of these recharge zones, particularly in northern parts, adjacent to the canal, are located in the aquifer zones of low permeability and relatively low yield.

In comparison to direct recharge from rainfall, indirect slow recharge through stagnant water pools, from high intensity rainfall contributed surface run-off, and lateral flow from surrounding areas in the west contribute 20-70 per cent recharge to the groundwater system. It has been computed that these surface water sources contribute to the extent of about 50 per cent to groundwater recharge upto 5-10 m depth in areas adjacent to the canal and Yamuna river in the northern parts of Delhi area. However, most of such water is of little practical utility, because, due to lack of civic amenities these water courses accumulate large amount of wastes and filth, thereby contributing to the groundwater pollution through lateral seepage along the water course, and the lateral flow water carries various types of contaminants alongwith it through indentified specific flow-pathways. Moreover, indiscriminate pumping of groundwater results in mixing of contaminated/saline water with fresh waterbodies through specific flow-paths. This leads to areal spreading of contamination salinization annually by 1-10 per cent and depletion of available fresh water potential, affecting the water supply.

**Nitrate and Fluoride Pollution of Groundwater**

Large part of the area to the west of the ridge, having very little recharge from rainfall and located at the tail end of the water supply system, is severely affected by nitrate and fluoride pollution of groundwater, exceeding the WHO prescribed maximum permissible limits (45 mg/*l* and 1.5 mg/*l* respectively) in drinking water. High nitrate plumes and high fluoride plumes from the west seem to have a tendency to migrate along specific flow-pathways towards the urbanised central parts in the city. The wide range in fluoride (< 1.5 to 16.5 mg/*l*) and nitrate (< 45 to 1600 mg/*l*) concentrations and highly skewed distributions in groundwater suggest contamination from both point and non-point sources. Very high nitrate and fluoride levels in some wells have resulted from point-source pollution, being located near drains/canal and industrial discharge sites. Infiltration of irrigation water/surface runoff water from the surrounding farm lands, alongwith fertilizer nitrate and chemicals containing fluoride salts in soils, leads to deterioration in groundwater quality. Levels of nitrate and fluoride in groundwater vary spatially and show an increasing trend during last 5-6 years, due to different degrees of evaporation/recharge, amount of fertiliser applied, anthropogenic activities, aquifer heterogeneity and hydraulics, adsorption/dispersion/denitrification processes in the soil zone and lateral mixing of goundwater. Yet, the extent of population affected by drinking polluted water is unknown.

## CONCLUDING REMARKS

The complexities of situation of groundwater occurrence in geological formations, presence of saline and contaminated groundwater at varying depths and locations, and growing urbanisation have influenced the groundwater availability in different parts. Groundwater has experienced major problems resulting from indiscriminate exploitation as well as combination of imprudent irrigation, diffuse pollution sources such as urban runoff, nitrogenous fertilisers used in agriculture, seepages from contaminated industrial sites and industrial discharges. Indiscriminate exploitation has led to widespread decline in groundwater-table in different parts of the region. Unplanned development of groundwater is leading to decline in productivity of wells, increasing pumping cost, more energy requirement, etc. More alarmingly, groundwater is getting severely contaminated with nitrate, fluoride, pesticides and heavy metals from anthropogenic activities, through slow leaching of water alongwith toxic contaminants present in landfills, agricultural areas and industrial discharge sites. Increasing groundwater use and pollution generation have crossed the sustainable limits in many parts. Hence, further exploitation of water resources must await more fundamental investigation of the spatial variation in the aquifer system and temporal variation in the replenishable groundwater resources, to evaluate the potential of the aquifers as a source of water for different purposes. Monitoring of aquifer responses to abstraction is also essential for efficient water supply from groundwater resources.

Enhancement in water availability and safe water supply will be always guided by the policies, plans and technologies at our disposal, in addition to political, socio-economical and other factors. Since, there is no single way to evaluate the maximum exploitable groundwater volume in advance or in absolute terms, because it depends on several factors such as energy, cost, criteria of profitability and quantitative and qualitative reaction of the resource to exploitation. It is imperative, therefore, to make public aware of various issues, to link water supply with changing water-use and to harmonise medium and long-term action, developing new principles in water resource assessment, based on detailed scientific information. Extensive regional survey is required on the groundwater system configuration, hydrogeological and hydrochemical characteristics, and the dynamic reaction of the system under natural and stressed conditions, based on efficient design and operation of a groundwater monitoring and surveillance system network. Assessment should be made of the causes of decline in watertable and balance groundwater extraction by time to time revision of recharge estimates with changes in land-use. Potential groundwater recharge zones should be delineated in relation to land-use changes, in order to restrict or eliminate waste disposal activities in these areas. Characterisation of contamination should be made by continued systematic research on the nature, dynamics and the attenuation capacity of the groundwater contaminants in the aquifer, the groundwater pathways and velocity between contaminant source and the water- supply well. Choices based on the best obtainable detailed scientific information, centred around the aspects outlined above, offer the best hope to assured sustainable water supply.

## REFERENCES


Datta, P. S., 1997. Stable isotopic investigations for groundwater management and sustainable environment. Nuclear Research Laboratory, IARI Report.

Datta, P. S., Bhattacharya, S. K. and Tyagi, S. K., 1996. $^{18}O$ studies on recharge of phreatic aquifers and groundwater flow-paths of mixing in Delhi area, *J. Hydrol.*, 176: 25-36.

Datta., P. S., Deb, D. L. and Týagi, S. K., 1996a. Stable isotope ($^{18}O$) investigations on the processes controlling fluoride contamination of groundwater. *J. Contaminant Hydrol.* 24 (1) : 85–96.

Datta., P. S., Deb, D.L. and Tyagi, S. K., 1997. Assessment of groundwater contamination from fertilizers in Delhi area based on $^{18}O$, $NO_3^-$ and $K^+$ composition. *J. Contaminant Hydrol.* 27 (3–4) : 249–262.

Datta, P. S.., Tyagi, S. K. and Chandrasekharan, H., 1991. Factors controlling stable isotopic composition of rainfall in New Delhi, *India J. Hydrology*, 128: 223-236.

Datta, P.S. and Tyagi, S.K. 1996. Major ion chemistry of groundwater in Delhi area: Chemical weathering processes and groundwater flow regime, *J. Geol. Soc. India.* 47: 179-188.

Rohilla, S. K. and Datta, P. S. 1998. Delhi's Water: Emerging Scenario, Vigyan Prasar Publication, New Delhi, (in press).

18

# Brick Kiln Industry as Drivers of Land-Use Change and Related Land Degradation in Rural-Urban Fringe of Delhi

R. B. SINGH AND JAG MOHAN

## INTRODUCTION

Land, whether it is inherited, allocated, bought or captured is the most basic resource of agriculture production. One of the most serious threats to food security is the increasing degradation of agricultural land from natural or human induced changes due to the physical, chemical, and biological processes. The word *'degradation'*, from its Latin derivation, means reduction to a lower rank. The term 'rank' relates to the present and possible uses, while reduction implies a problem for those who use the land. When land becomes degraded its productivity declines, unless steps are taken to restore productivity and check further losses (Blaike and Brookfield, 1987). The *rural-urban* fringe is "the zone which lies immediately outside the city area and has strong interaction with the city proper in terms of daily communication, exchange of goods and services and bears an urban reflection on the physical, occupational and demographic structure" (Nangia, 1976).

Brick, an essential feature of urbanization in the developing countries, is a heavy commodity and cannot be carried over long distances without an increase in costs. Thus, the industry is forced to locate itself near the market, that is the city. Fertile agricultural land having good amount of clay and loam is considered the best for bricks. The irony of the situation is that the soil which could have provided a fairly large amount of agricultural produce for many more years to come is quarried in a span of 3-4 years for about 1.2 to 1.5 metres in depth in order to cater to the developmental requirements of urbanization. Swelling urban population has necessitated vast lands to be quarried, so as to cater to the corresponding escalation in demand for brick and construction materials. Extensive areas are quarried for clay that is needed to mould the bricks. The kiln itself occupies approximately 0.8 hectares of land. The consequent land-use change has a telling impact on the land quality and land status. The quarried land often becomes degraded to such an extent that its restoration to a cultivable order is quite difficult. The issue of land degradation in Delhi's rural areas is one of the burning topics today as large stretches of agricultural land are being lost continuously to this irreversible developmental process.

## STUDY AREA

The *National Capital Territory* of Delhi comprises an area of 1,483 km$^2$. It is surrounded by the state of Haryana on three sides and to the east, across the river Yamuna, by the state of Uttar Pradesh. Delhi rural is divided into five development blocks *i.e.*, Shahdara, Alipur, Kanjhawala, Najafgarh and Mehrauli. Kanjhawala block is one with the maximum concentration of brick kilns. It is situated in the north-west part of the city. The whole block consists of 39 villages with total area of 17, 420.79 hectares. Kanjhawala block comes under the *Banger* or the old alluvium tract consisting of sandy loam and fine loamy soil (Fig. 18.1). The soil is fertile with high moisture.

## URBAN DEVELOPMENT AND METROPOLITANISATION PROCESS

The history of urbanization in India reveals, broadly, four processes of urbanization at work. These include the socio-cultural process, politico-administrative process, economic and geographical processes (Ramachandran, 1989). Since 1900, however, there has been a slow but steady upward trend in the level of urbanization. It has never been higher than 12 per cent or lower than 5 per cent of the total population. By 1991, India's urban population of 217.61 million constituted about 26 per cent of total population. Currently, every year about 3 million rural people migrate to the cities, and this flow is also showing a steady increase (Ramachandran, 1989).

Delhi, the capital city of India, has not been left devoid of the urban and metropolitan processes. Delhi, which in the pre-independence period, was limited within the Walled City, spread to the boundaries of Uttar Pradesh and Haryana in the post-independence period. The Delhi Master Plan of 1990, plans to include the neighbouring districts of Uttar Pradesh, which are Ghaziabad, Loni and NOIDA in the Delhi Metropolitan Area (Ministry of Urban Development, 1990). This is the consequence of the increasing population pressure on the scarce resources of Delhi.

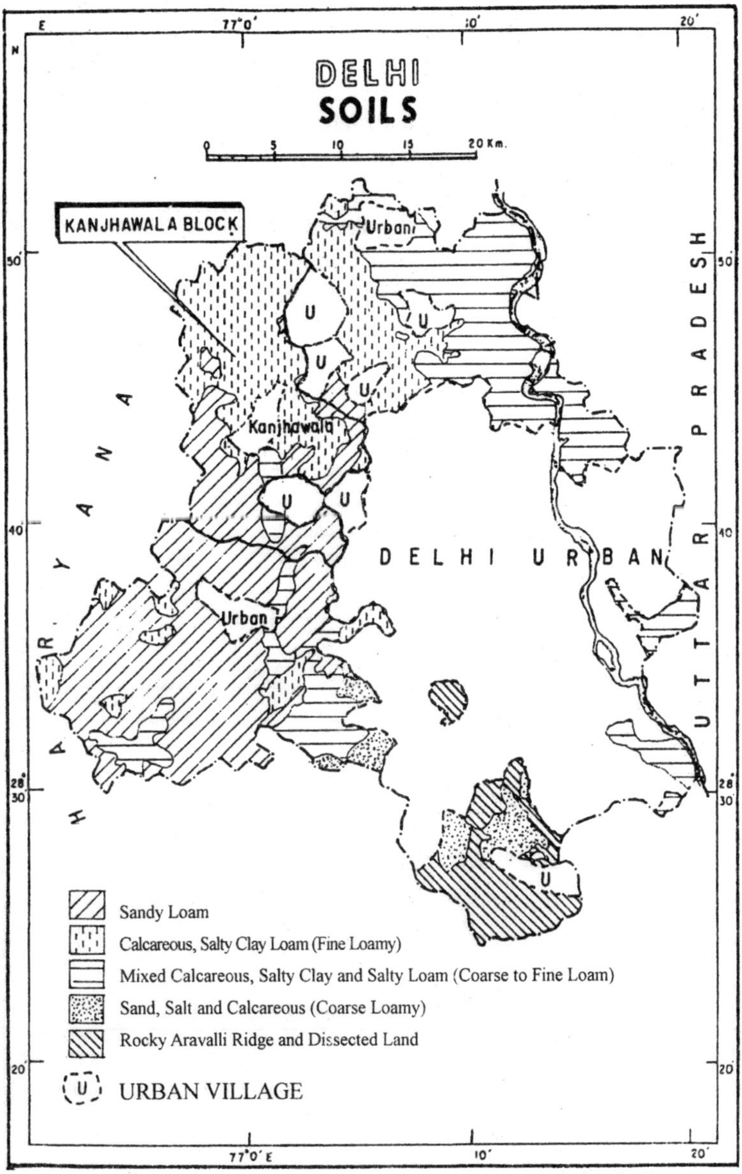


*Source* : Delhi Census Atlas, 1981 and Delhi Census, 1991(DCH)

**Fig. 18.1 :** Soils of Delhi

Urban Delhi, in 1981, accommodated about 1.15 million households. The next two decades would add another 1.3 million households. At present also, there is a shortage of 0.3 million houses. About 1.62 million new housing units would be required during the period 1981-2001 (Table 18.2).

In order to cater to the increasing housing demands in the past two decades, the Delhi fringe area saw the emergence of a number of brick kilns so as to fulfil the demands of construction materials and bricks. The bordering villages, which were earlier engaged only in agricultural

**Table 18.1 :** Delhi at a Glance

| Geographical area (km$^2$) | Years | |
|---|---|---|
| | 1980 | 1995 |
| Total | 1485 | 1483 |
| Rural | 1039 | 798 |
| Urban | 446 | 685 |

| Population (in Millions) | Years | | |
|---|---|---|---|
| | 1981 | 1991 | 1996 |
| Total Population | 6.22 | 9.42 | 11.224 |
| Rural | 0.45 | 0.95 | 1.13 |
| Urban | 5.77 | 8.47 | 10.09 |

*Source* : Delhi at a Glance, Directorate of Economics and Statistics, Government of National Capital Territory of Delhi, 1996.

**Table 18.2 :** Housing Requirements in Delhi

| Years | New Housing Required ('000) | Average per Year ('000) |
|---|---|---|
| 1981-1986 | 323 | 65 |
| 1986-1991 | 379 | 76 |
| 1991-1996 | 434 | 87 |
| 1996-2001 | 483 | 97 |

*Source*: Ministry of Urban Development, Master Plan for Delhi, 1990, DDA.

activity, underwent a radical land-use change catering to the urban as well as rural demand for bricks, in order to house the thousands immigrants into the city. These immigrants live mainly in slums and form 40 per cent of the Delhi's total population and requiring housing facilities in the cities. The process has, thus, begun for the metropolitanisation of the rural villages.

## CONTRIBUTION OF RURAL-URBAN FRINGE TOWARDS URBAN REQUIREMENTS

Urbanization, to manifest itself, requires intrinsic transformation in rural land-use and occupational structure. Changing agricultural land-use in the village is the first sign of impact of urban demands on village economy. "The city offers a market for products that a village is in a position to supply, such as milk, vegetables, flowers and fruits. A few enterprising farmers in the villages may perceive and take advantage of this opportunity, leading eventually to daily contact with the city." (Ramachandran, 1989). Besides the food, other products supplied by the area are the heavy construction materials like bricks, stone, timber, sand and gravel etc. Being heavy, these cannot be carried over long distances, without adding to its price. The industries processing these goods are located just outside the city limits in the villages. The brick industry is one of the most prominent of these.

The whole of Kanjhawala block is dotted with brick kilns which are the most integral part of these rural villages. The fertile land of villages provides a good resource base to brick kilns. Agriculture is the basic activity in which most of the villagers are participating. As the social norms keep on changing the joint family system is disintegrating leading to a change in economic activities. The young generation is unable to continue the agricultural activities and they lease out their good fertile and productive land to the brick kilns on a 4-5 years contract basis at the rates varying from Rs 0.2 million to 0.4 million, all paid at the beginning of the lease in cash. Once the lease is over they are left with barren, unlevelled and unproductive land devoid of all top soil and humus. On the other hand, the older generation is still continuing with agriculture to produce good qualities of wheat, rice, other foodgrains and vegetables.

## STATUS OF BRICK KILN INDUSTRY

At present there are 150 brick kilns located in 20 villages of the block. The maximum growth period was of 1980-85 in which 55 brick kilns were set up (Table 18.3). The industry saw a decline in the 90's decade due to the non-renewal of licensing to brick manufacturers, as the industry had been classified as one of the air-polluting industries. In order to fulfil the growing demand of bricks new sites are captured. But due to rapid urbanization and high demand of land for residential purposes, brick kiln spread has been abruptly halted. From 1990-95 only 14 brick kilns came up and there is no hope for the brick kiln owners to get new land sites for soil quarrying. This stagnation of brick kilns industry in the Kanjhawala block can end only by shifting this industry further towards the Haryana border.

**Table 18.3 :** Growth of Brick Kilns in Kanjhawala Development Block

| Years | No. of Brick Kilns | Total Established |
|---|---|---|
| 1970-1975 | 16 | 16 |
| 1975-1980 | 40 | 56 |
| 1980-1985 | 55 | 111 |
| 1985-1990 | 25 | 136 |
| 1990-1997 | 14 | 150 |

*Source*: Delhi Brick Kiln Association.

## IMPACT OF BRICK KILN ON LAND AND LAND-USE CHANGE

To know the impact of clay quarrying on land and land-use change, six villages were selected in the Kanjhawala Development Block. Only those villages were selected in which five or more brick kilns were operating. There are at present 63 brick kilns in the six selected villages. Each brick kiln, on an average, requires at least 2.2 hectares of land at any given time; of this 0.8 hectares are taken up by the kiln itself and the rest is required for clay quarrying. Thus, every kiln, in a span of four years, removes top soil from at least 1.4 hectares of land. To date, 513.2 hectares of land has already been quarried, while 333.2 hectares is at present leased by brick kilns for quarrying purposes and is under a severe threat of soil erosion and land degradation. With Honourable Supreme Court ordering the closure or shifting of brick kilns from the city limits, the question of areas most likely to be the potential sites of re-location has also arisen. The adjoining states of Haryana and Uttar Pradesh located in the National Capital Region, are the areas bearing an immense potential for setting up of brick kilns from the point of view of distance from the market as well as availability of raw materials.

The most visible economic impact of land degradation is on agricultural productivity. Any reduction in productivity of land resources has an enormous effect on the socio-economic conditions. The immediate effects of land degradation includes reduced crop yields, increasing need for agricultural inputs, decreasing profits and reduction in the value of land.

Standard of living, which depends upon the farmer's income, greatly declines with decrease in the per capita availability of land. Increasingly less remunerative farming systems force the peasants to leave the land uncultivated which then tends to becomes barren. All the above reasons ultimately result in shifting the land resources from agriculture to other uses including industry which results in environmental degradation. This is more common in Kanjhawala block where there were 150 brick kilns operating till September 1997 (Table 18.4).

The decrease in agricultural land is complemented by an increase in cultivable wasteland in the decades 1971-91. The decrease in agricultural land was more than 13 per cent while increase in cultivable wasteland, which includes common land and pastures, was 63.08 per cent. Area not available for cultivation decreased by 23.21 per cent from 1971 to 1981 and after a decade it increased by 49.38 per cent in 1991. After mid 70's various agricultural development programmes initiated by the government reduced barren and fallow land. But as a result of the spread of urbanization processes the area not available for cultivation increased by approximately 50 per cent. This area includes settlements as well as brick kilns and land under quarrying. Table 18.5 clearly depicts the relationship between growth of brick kilns and the simultaneous decrease in agricultural area.

**Table 18.4** : Consumption of Land in the Study Area

| Number of Brick Kilns | Total Land Consumed Till Date (in hectares) | Land Under Quarrying (in hectares) |
|---|---|---|
| 63 | 513.2 | 333.2 |

*Source*: Personal Survey.

**Table 18.5** : Land-Use Pattern in the Study Area (1971-1991)

| Year | Agricultural Land | Cultivable Waste | Area not Available for Cultivation (in hectares) |
|---|---|---|---|
| 1971 | 2706.6 | 460.52 | 426.11 |
| 1981 | 2788.8 | 500.8 | 327.2 |
| 1991 | 2350.59 | 751.03 | 494.78 |

*Source* : District Census Handbook, Census of India, 1971, 81, 91.

## LAND MANAGEMENT AND RECLAMATION RELATING TO BRICK KILN AREAS

Like all the other big development issues, brick industry also remains in controversy and poses a big question mark on the sustainability of its surrounding physical and cultural environment. The traditional method of moulding bricks by hand requires good-quality clay. This initiates the process of land degradation. The lack of awareness and financial constraints, mean that alternatives are not in regular operation in the study area.

Fly ash utilization is a national problem and has attained serious proportions. "The thermal power generating capacity in India is around 40,000 MW disposing of about 35 million tonnes of fly ash per annum. For every tonne of coal consumed, 0.2 - 0.4 tonne of fly ash is produced from thermal power stations in India. If the thermal expansion programme in the next decade is also taken into consideration the production of coal ash is likely to be about 130 million tonnes per year. This indicates the enormity of the problem, which the country has to face in disposal of the coal ash, which is an environmental hazard. This problem has to be fought on a war footing and fly ash put to proper use to reduce surface and air pollution (Roy, 1993). Developed countries in the West utilize as much as 30 per cent of the fly ash they generate by converting it into useable building products. Although much has been talked about utilization of fly ash in this country not even 3 per cent of the total ash generated here is utilized today. So it becomes necessary to utilize this ash to produce some useful materials. One of the established way is to produce new and alternative building materials like fly ash bricks. Sand-lime bricks consume about 70-80 per cent fly ash in their manufacturing process.

## CONCLUSION

In this study an effort has been made to study the present status of brick industry, its role in development as well as degradation of the environment and capability to cope with the future scenario, in a sustainable manner.

The fringe, which was meant to be an area of mixed land-use outside the city, is slowly losing its rural character, while catering to the urban requirements. Thus, there is urgent need to look into these urban needs and their fulfilment as an issue of morality and responsibility towards the environment, of which we are a part. The brick industry has played a significant role in altering the land-use pattern of the fringe area, from agriculture and related activities to quarrying and consequent renouncing of the land as barren and uncultivable.

### REFERENCES

Blaike, P. and Brookefeild, N. (eds.), 1987: *Land Degradation and Society*, Methuen Publication, London.

Government of India, *District Census Handbook*: Delhi, 1971, 1981,1991.

Government of India, Ministry of Urban Development, 1990, *Master Plan for Delhi*, pp. 115-122.

Government of NCT of Delhi, 1996, Delhi at a Glance, Directorate of Economics & Statistics, p.1.

Hajela, R.B. and Gupta, R.C. (*et al.*), 1991, "Manufacture of Improved Brick Utilizing Inferior Saline/Alkali Soils," *Brick and Tile News*, New Delhi, pp. 38-40.

Jain, A.K., 1988, "Urban Planning and Growth: A case study of Delhi" in Sharma, R.C. (ed.), *India's Urban Land Policy and Development Finance*, Seema Publication, New Delhi, pp.143-161.

Nangia, S., 1976, Delhi Metropolitan Region, *A Study in Setlement Geography*, K.B. Publication, New Delhi, p. 80.

Nusrat, A. and Mahadev, P. D., 1991, "Environmental Impact of Brick Loam Quarrying on Agricultural Soil" *The Indian Geographical Journal*, December, pp. 83-88.

Ramachandran, R., 1989, *Urbanization and Urban Systems in India*, Oxford University Press, New Delhi.

Roy, S., 1991, " Utilization of Fly Ash in the Brick Manufacturing Industry" *Brick and Tile News*, New Delhi, pp. 25-29.

# 19

# Size of the Household in India

## A Rural-Urban Perspective

RANDHIR SINGH SANGWAN AND SNEH SANGWAN

### INTRODUCTION

A household in the Indian census is a group of persons who commonly live together and would take their meals from a common kitchen unless the exigencies of work prevented them from doing so. A household may comprise of persons related with blood or of unrelated persons or having a mix of both (Census of India, 1991). On the basis of the principle of co-residence, it is a demographic unit composed of related or unrelated persons, who share some physically or socially defined space for everyday life (Curson, 1978). It must have a common kitchen as the nucleus as per requirements of the Indian census.

The household can be used in projecting the future population (United Nations, 1981) and is an important economic unit useful for planning purposes. The geographical significance of making a study of household lies in understanding the spatial variations in family organization ( relative representation of nuclear and joint families), mode of production (whether it demands pooling together of family resources or permits individual efforts), degree of modernization, represented by attitude towards family size and demographic situation in respect of natural increase, migration and marital status (Krishan, 1980).

Rural-urban differential in size of the household can be construed as an index to the relative level of modernization of traditional societies. A higher differential would indicate that the urban society has moved distinctly ahead of the rural in imbibing the modern trends in family formation and regulation. A small differential, on the other hand, would reflect that urban places of the region retain a high degree of rural life style. This hypothesis subsumes that the rate of change in urban places would be faster than that in rural areas of developing countries (Krishan and Rana, 1980).

## LITERATURE CITED

Indeed, the household is an important demographic unit in its own. Investigation of the household is perhaps the least developed of the demographic fields in India. Whereas leading geographical journals of the country, for instance, *Annals of NAGI, Transactions of IIG* and *Geographical Journal of India* are replete with research papers on fertility, mortality, migration, sex ratio, urbanization, etc., the household is left virtually untouched. It may find explanation among other things, in the way data on the household have been presented in the censuses. Another reason could be that the importance of the household as a demographic unit in its own right is often overlooked (Bose *et al.*, 1977; United Nations, 1980). There has been a long standing interest in the Indian household by sociologists, but not by demographers and geographers. The notable contribution made by demographers and geographers are a few to count and mainly belong to Burch (1970), Shan (1974), Curson (1978), Krishan (1980), Krishan and Rana (1980) and, Vos and Murty (1985).

## OBJECTIVE OF THE STUDY

The present study aims at examining the size of household, its rural-urban differentials and the trend of rural-urban differentials in size of the Indian household in the post-independence era because of the availability of data for this period.

## DATA BASE AND METHODOLOGY

Size and composition are two dimensions of a household. The Census of India normally provides data only on the size of the household. Information on composition of households (number of families/ generations in the household, age-sex structure of the family members and relationship of each member to the head of the household) is generally not given. Hence, any study of the household based on census data has to confine itself to the aspect of size alone.

For calculating rural-urban differentials in size of the household, Census of India (1991) provides most of the data required for the study. Some relevant data meant for the purpose have also been obtained from previous years publications of the Census of India. The data for Census of India (2001) on size of the household could not be published till date.

Decadal variations in rural-urban differential have been discerned from 1951 to 1991. These variations were calculated by simple deduction of the data of previous decade from the data of later. The trend of rural-urban differentials was computed by subtracting the rural-urban differential of 1991 from that of 1971. The census map of India (1991) has been adopted as the base map. Finally, to ensure accuracy and to save time, the use of computer has been made.

## INDIA: AVERAGE SIZE OF THE HOUSEHOLD, 1951-1991

According to 1991 census, a total of 846 million population of India is found to be distributed over 152 million households. Therefore, the average size of a household comes to 5.57 persons per household. Whereas the rural size of household is 5.63 persons with a population of 629 million persons residing in 112 million households, the urban size of household stands at 5.38 persons with 218 million populations living in 41 million households. A comparison of the average household size in India for 1991 census with those of previous decades reveals that the average size of the Indian household is gradually increasing over time. Since independence in 1947, it is observed that average size of the household has increased from 4.88 persons per household in 1951 to 5.57 in 1991 (Table 19.1 and Fig. 19.1). The maximum increase is witnessed for the period 1951-71. The recent decade shows some signs of stabilization.

Seen as rural-urban break-up, average size of the rural household is continuously increasing since 1951. The maximum increase in rural areas could be witnessed during 1951-71 when the average size of household registered an increase from 4.91 to 5.52 which was similar to the increase in total size of household during the same period. However, 1971-91 period has seen a small increase in size of the household of rural areas.

On the other hand, in case of urban size of the household, the maximum increase was during the decade of 1951-61. Between 1961-81, the size of household increased at slow rate, but, it declined during 1981-91 (Table 19.2). It shows that the urban household size reached its culmination point because many migrants were forced to take residence

**Table 19.1:** India: Average Size of the Household, 1951-1991

| Census Year | Size of the Household | | | Rural-Urban Differential |
|---|---|---|---|---|
| | Total | Rural | Urban | |
| 1951 | 4.88 | 4.91 | 4.71 | + 0.20 |
| 1961 | 5.16 | 5.19 | 5.07 | + 0.12 |
| 1971 | 5.46 | 5.52 | 5.23 | + 0.29 |
| 1981 | 5.55 | 5.59 | 5.45 | + 0.14 |
| 1991 | 5.57 | 5.63 | 5.38 | + 0.25 |

*Sources:*

(i) Krishan, G. (1980), "Size of Household in Rural India" in Singh R.L. & Singh R.P.B. (eds.), *Rural Habitat Transformation in World Frontiers*, Table 4, NGSI, Publication 30, Varanasi, p. 359.

(ii) Computed from, Census of India (1991), *Primary Census Abstract: General Population.* Series I, India, Part II-B (i), Vols. I & II, Office of the Registrar General and Census Commissioner, India, New Delhi.

in their peripheral villages rather than within the cities themselves to avail themselves of the lower cost of living, including rent. Secondly, the frequency of the territorial extension of existing towns was less visible during the 1980's. The net addition of towns/urban agglomerations during 1981-91 was only 390 as compared with 788 during 1971-81. Thirdly, rural development and the associated decline in the incidence of rural poverty appear to have had a moderating effect on rural-urban migration (Krishan, 1993). All these factors account for the slowing down of urban growth and the resultant slow rate of increase in size of the household.

## INDIA: RURAL-URBAN DIFFERENTIALS IN SIZE OF THE HOUSEHOLD, 1951-1991

The rural-urban differential has not been consistent but varying from decade to decade. It was 0.20 persons in 1951, 0.12 in 1961, 0.29 in 1971, 0.14 in 1981 and 0.25 in 1991 (Table 19.2). It shows that the overall gap between size of the rural and urban households has widened. The increased differential is because the size of rural household has increased constantly at a faster rate than the urban one. The rural household size increased continuously between

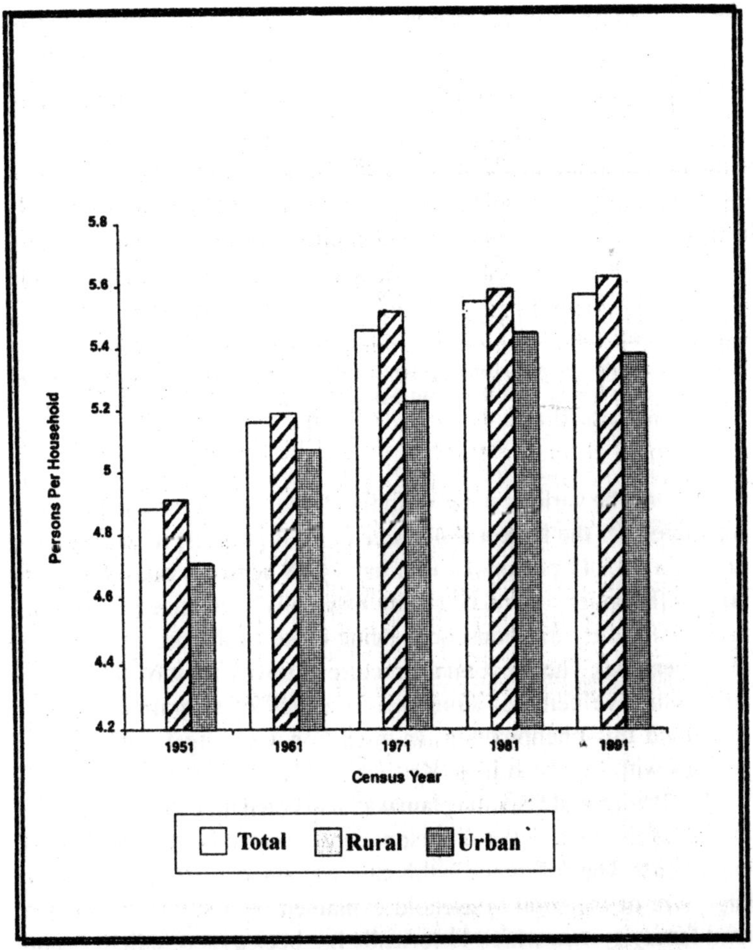


**Fig. 19.1 :** India—Average Size of the Household, 1951-91

1951-91 but this increase shows a declining trend since 1971. The increase in the size of household was 0.28 points in 1951-61, it reached 0.33 in 1961-71 but thereafter it declined to 0.04 points in 1981-91 (Table 19.2 and Fig. 19.2).

Its urban counterpart also displays a continuous increase except in the decade of 1981-91 where it is showing a decline in size of the household. The increase in household size was more in urban areas in comparison to rural both in 1951-61 and 1971-81 decades. During 1961-71, the rural household size recorded maximum increase.

**Table 19.2** : India—Decadal Change in Size of the Household by Rural-Urban Residence, 1951-91

| Census Decade | Decadal Change in Size of Household | | Trend of Change |
|---|---|---|---|
| | Rural | Urban | |
| 1951-61 | + 0.28 | + 0.36 | – 0.08 |
| 1961-71 | + 0.33 | + 0.16 | + 0.17 |
| 1971-81 | + 0.07 | + 0.22 | – 0.15 |
| 1981-91 | + 0.04 | – 0.07 | + 0.11 |

*Source* : Computed from Census of India (1991), *Primary Census Abstract: General Population*, Series-I, India, Part II-B(i), Vols. I & II, Office of the Registrar General and Census Commissioner, India, New Delhi.

Among the various states of India (Table 19.3), Himachal Pradesh was noted for the largest difference (+ 1.30 persons) in average size of its rural (5.48 persons) and urban (4.18 persons) household. The large differential was related to an unusually small size of the urban household, the rural household being close to the national average (5.57 persons). The functional structure of towns, most of which were administrative centres, along with recency of migration to them, explained this phenomenon. In-migration was largely of educated persons with small families (Krishan and Rana, 1980).

The Punjab and Haryana plain was also noted for a large differential in size of the rural (over 6 persons) and urban (about 5.50 persons) households. The difference in this case was associated with a distinctly large size of the rural household explained by a strong tradition of joint family system which historically has been a more salient feature of joint villages (with a joint tenure of land) as previously typical of north-western India (Powell, 1972). The region's urban community with predominance of the Punjabi-Hindus in service, trade and modern industry, had a lower proportion of joint families.

In Assam and Arunachal Pradesh also, with an average size of rural households as 5.92 and 5.02 persons and urban households as 5.18 and 4.37 persons respectively, wide rural-urban differential exists. These states experienced a rapid growth of population due to a decline in death rate accompanied by a stable high birth rate and sizeable in-migration.

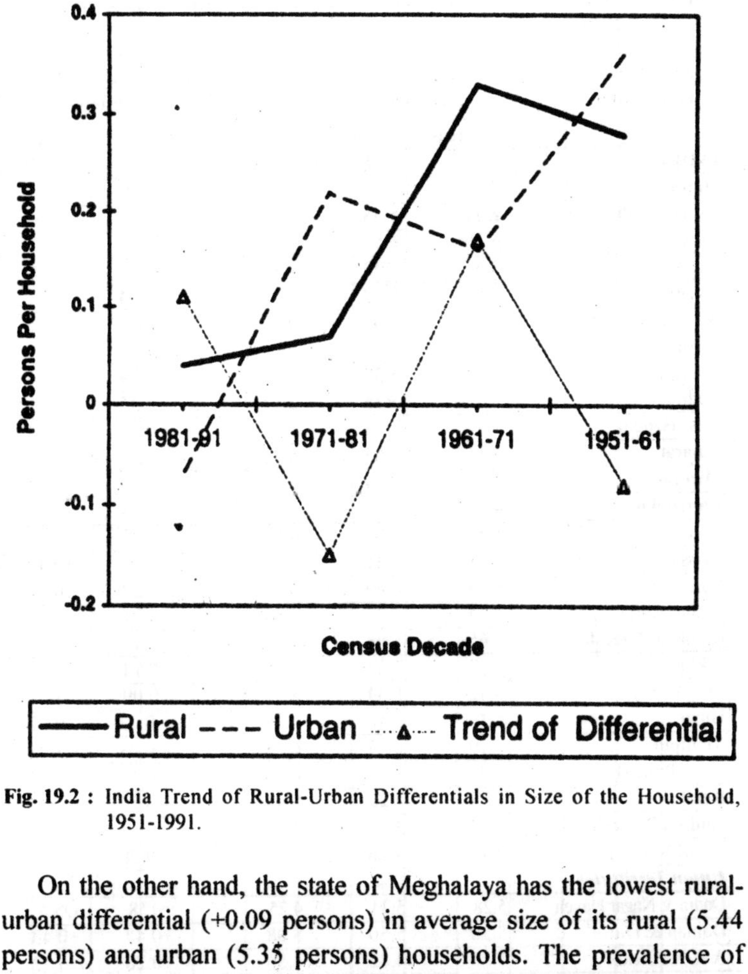


**Fig. 19.2 :** India Trend of Rural-Urban Differentials in Size of the Household, 1951-1991.

On the other hand, the state of Meghalaya has the lowest rural-urban differential (+0.09 persons) in average size of its rural (5.44 persons) and urban (5.35 persons) households. The prevalence of nuclear family system kept its rural as well as urban households small (about 5 to over 5.50 persons), and the resultant rural-urban differential index was also small (0.007).

Nine out of 31 states and union territories have urban household size bigger than rural. These in ascending order are Chandigarh (–0.86), Lakshadweep (–0.35), Pondicherry (–0.32), Tamil Nadu (–0.28), Andhra Pradesh (–0.24), Kerala (–0.22), Uttar Pradesh (–0.15), Manipur (–0.08), and Bihar (–0.02). The factors of local endogamy and prevalence of joint family system in urban areas play

**Table 19.3 :** India—Average Size of the Household by Residence and its Rural-Urban Differential, 1971-91

| Country/State/ Union Territory | Number of Persons per Household in 1991 | | | Rural-Urban Differential | |
|---|---|---|---|---|---|
| | All Areas | Rural | Urban | 1991 | 1971 |
| **INDIA*** | 5.52 | 5.58 | 5.34 | +0.24 | + 0.29 |
| ***States*** | | | | | |
| Himachal Pradesh | 5.34 | 5.48 | 4.18 | +1.30 | +1.39 |
| Haryana | 6.30 | 6.59 | 5.54 | +1.05 | + 0.22 |
| Nagaland | 5.57 | 5.73 | 4.92 | +0.81 | − 0.14 |
| Assam | 5.83 | 5.92 | 5.18 | +0.74 | +0.52 |
| Arunachal Pradesh | 4.93 | 5.02 | 4.37 | +0.65 | +0.85 |
| Punjab | 5.92 | 6.07 | 5.60 | +0.47 | +0.76 |
| Tripura | 5.24 | 5.30 | 4.91 | +0.39 | +0.04 |
| Delhi | 5.02 | 5.35 | 4.98 | +0.37 | +1.08 |
| West Bengal | 5.44 | 5.54 | 5.19 | +0.35 | +0.55 |
| Gujarat | 5.51 | 5.63 | 5.30 | +0.33 | +0.29 |
| Mizoram | 4.75 | 5.84 | 5.55 | +0.29 | +0.35 |
| Karnataka | 4.99 | 5.60 | 5.37 | +0.23 | − 0.33 |
| Goa | 5.52 | 5.08 | 4.86 | +0.22 | +0.18 |
| Orissa | 5.28 | 5.31 | 5.09 | +0.22 | +0.43 |
| Rajasthan | 6.04 | 6.09 | 5.87 | +0.22 | +0.20 |
| Maharashtra | 5.14 | 5.23 | 5.02 | +0.21 | +0.49 |
| Madhya Pradesh | 5.65 | 5.68 | 5.54 | +0.14 | +0.27 |
| Sikkim | 5.33 | 5.34 | 5.20 | +0.14 | DNA |
| Meghalaya | 5.42 | 5.44 | 5.35 | +0.09 | − 0.04 |
| Bihar | 6.16 | 6.16 | 6.18 | −0.02 | +0.32 |
| Manipur | 6.19 | 6.17 | 6.25 | −0.08 | − 0.50 |
| Uttar Pradesh | 6.22 | 6.19 | 6.34 | − 0.15 | +0.22 |
| Kerala | 5.28 | 5.22 | 5.44 | − 0.22 | − 0.43 |
| Andhra Pradesh | 4.77 | 4.71 | 4.95 | − 0.24 | − 0.08 |
| Tamil Nadu | 5.45 | 4.36 | 4.64 | − 0.28 | − 0.32 |
| ***Union Territories*** | | | | | |
| Dadra & Nagar Haveli | 5.28 | 5.33 | 4.75 | +0.58 | DNA |
| Daman & Diu | 5.30 | 5.50 | 5.08 | +0.42 | +0.43 |
| A & N Islands | 5.70 | 4.82 | 4.56 | +0.26 | +0.22 |
| Pondicherry | 4.97 | 4.77 | 5.09 | − 0.32 | − 0.53 |
| Lakshadweep | 6.23 | 6.04 | 6.39 | − 0.35 | DNA |
| Chandigarh | 4.38 | 3.63 | 4.49 | − 0.86 | +0.39 |

*Source* : Computed from Census of India (1991), *Primary Census Abstract: General Population.* Series-I, India, Part II-B (i). Vols. I & II. Office of the Registrar General and Census Commissioner, India, New Delhi.

* Excludes Jammu & Kashmir where census was not held in 1991.

***Notes*** **:**

(i) Data for the states/union territories of Sikkim, Dadra & Nagar Haveli and Lakshadweep are not available in 1971.

(ii) States and union territories are arranged in descending order of rural-urban differential in 1991.

their role in south Indian states. Joint family system and migration characterise the situation in north India. The overall differential ranges from –0.86 to + 1.30 persons per household.

## INDIA: TREND OF RURAL-URBAN DIFFERENTIALS IN SIZE OF THE HOUSEHOLD, 1971-1991

The trend in rural-urban differentials in size of the household has been observed using state-wise data for two-decades, from 1971 to 1991. The overall picture shows that the rural-urban differentials in almost half of India are squeezing but at a slow rate.

Some of the rural areas are adopting small size of household norms, under the influence of urban areas and many of the urban areas, while facing the housing and costly city life problems, are adopting joint family systems. Recent years have also seen a rise in the middle class families in urban areas with aptitude towards maintaining small, joint family system initially. These areas broadly fall under six categories (Table 19.4 and Fig.19.3).

| Category | Nomenclature |
|---|---|
| 1. | Areas where urban household size was bigger than rural with increasing differential trend. |
| 2. | Areas where urban household size was bigger than rural with declining differential trend. |
| 3. | Areas where rural household size was bigger than urban with increasing differential trend. |
| 4. | Areas where rural household size was bigger than urban with declining differential trend. |
| 5. | Areas where urban household size was bigger in 1991 but reverse was true in 1971. |
| 6. | Areas where rural household size was bigger in 1991 but reverse was true in 1971. |

### *1. Areas where Urban Household Size was Bigger than Rural with Increasing Differential Trend*

Only one state, *i.e.*, Andhra Pradesh (+0.16) falls in this category. The state is characterised by a high rate of natural increase of urban population (21.0 and 17.7 per 1000 persons in 1981 and 1991 respectively) which is more than the national average. Low mortality in urban areas (6.7 per thousand) than in rural (10.5 per thousand) and family migration to cities are other factors.

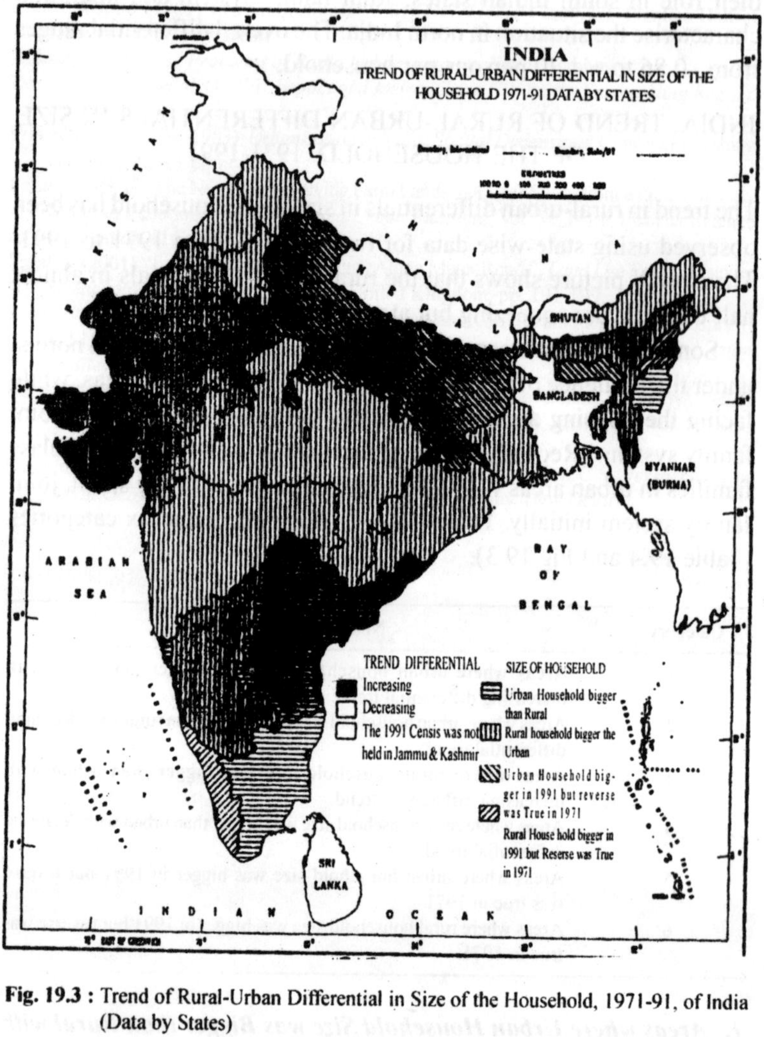


**Fig. 19.3 :** Trend of Rural-Urban Differential in Size of the Household, 1971-91, of India (Data by States)

The better employment opportunities through industrialization and modernization in the districts of Kurnool, Guntur, Krishna, Prakasam, Nellore, Hyderabad and Ranga Reddy, are able to attract majority of the scheduled tribes who migrate with families towards these urban centres (Reddy, 1996). Such types of migration trends have been helpful in increasing the urban size of household in Andhra Pradesh.

**Table 19.4** : India: Trend of Rural-Urban Differentials in Size of the Household, 1971-91

| Rural-Urban Differential Categories | | | | | |
|---|---|---|---|---|---|
| 1 | 2 | 3 | 4 | 5 | 6 |
| Andhra Pradesh (+ 0.16) | Manipur (– 0.42) | Tripura (+ 0.35) | Delhi (– 0.71) | Chandigarh (+ 1.25) | Nagaland (+0.95) |
| | Pondi-cherry (– 0. 21) | Assam (+ 0.22) | Punjab (– 0.29) | Uttar Pradesh (+0.37) | Goa (+ 0.55) |
| | Kerala (– 0.21) | Mizoram (+ 0.07) | Mahara-shtra (– 0.28) | Bihar (+ 0.34) | Megh-alaya (+ 0.13) |
| | Tamil Nadu (– 0.04) | Karnataka (+ 0.05) | Orissa (– 0.21) | | |
| | | Gujarat (+ 0.04) | Arunachal Pradesh (– 0.20) | | |
| | | Rajasthan (+ 0.02) | West Bengal (– 0.20) | | |
| | | | Haryana (– 0.17) | | |
| | | | Madhya Pradesh (– 0. 13) | | |
| | | | Andaman & Nicobar Islands (– 0.09) | | |
| | | | Himachal Pradesh (– 0.09) | | |
| | | | Daman & Diu (–0.01) | | |

*Source* : Computed from Census of India (1991), *Primary Census Abstract: General Population*, Series-I, India, Part II-B (i), Vols. I & II, Office of the Registrar General and Census Commissioner, India, New Delhi.

### 2. *Areas where Urban Household Size was Bigger than Rural with Declining Differential Trend*

Manipur (–0.42), Kerala (–0.21), Pondicherry (–0.21) and Tamil Nadu (–0.04) have urban household size bigger than rural but it is revealing a declining trend of differential. In southern states of Tamil Nadu and Kerala, high caste groups in urban places tend to have a larger proportion of joint families and display a greater degree of family solidarity. Besides it, local endogamy is also common (Karve, 1953). Now, the size of urban household is declining but it is still larger than the rural household size. The natural increase rate has declined considerably from 19.9 in 1981 to 12.3 in 1991 in Manipur.

Availability of job opportunities in rural areas motivate people to stay in their villages with their families and the male–selective migration towards urban areas decreased.

### 3. *Areas where Rural Household Size was Bigger than Urban with Increasing Differential Trend*

The rural-urban differential was maximum in Tripura (+ 0.35) followed by Assam (+ 0.22), Mizoram (+0.07), Karnataka (+0.05), Gujarat (+0.04) and Rajasthan (+0.02). Owing to the fact that the north-eastern states particularly have witnessed large scale family migration to rural areas from across the border in addition to high birth rate. In villages, cottage industries have been set up for young unemployed persons. Several districts in Gujarat and Rajasthan have been declared as industrially backward by the Government and qualified for special incentives and attracted considerable large-scale industries to their rural parts along the main transport routes, for instance, Panch Mahal in Gujarat and Alwar in Rajasthan. Such areas attracted significant migration to their rural areas in response to employment opportunities made available by new industry. So, a lot of rural-urban migration took the form of rural to rural migration (Krishan, 1993). Besides, a strong tradition of joint family system also worked in rural areas of Rajasthan and Gujarat. In Karnataka, the endogamous system of marriages between close kins and within the locality was typical.

North-eastern states witnessed large scale family migration in rural areas from across the border in addition to high birth rate. In Assam

Valley, rural household size is increasing due to stable birth rate in rural areas (33.8 in 1981 and 31.7 in 1991) and a fast fall in urban birth rate (33.2 in 1981 and 21.3 in 1991) accompanied by sizeable in-migration.

### 4. Areas where Rural Household Size was Bigger than Urban with Declining Differential Trend

Data for four states/union territories not being available, 11 out of 28 states/union territories fall in this category of declining differential trend with rural household size bigger than urban. The maximum differential exists in Delhi (– 0.71) which is followed by Punjab (– 0.29), Maharashtra (– 0.28), Orissa (– 0.21), Arunachal Pradesh (– 0.20), West Bengal (– 0.20), Haryana (– 0.17), Madhya Pradesh (– 0.13), Himachal Pradesh (– 0.09), Andaman and Nicobar Islands (– 0.9), and Daman and Diu (– 0.01). All these states have experienced high rate of rural-urban male-selective migration. The states particularly in the north-west and west have a strong hold of joint family system both in rural and urban areas. Also due to the impact of urbanisation, the rural household size is declining and male-selective migration is taking the form of family migration.

### 5. Areas where Urban Household Size was Bigger in 1991 but Reverse was True in 1971

The states and union territories which come in this category are Chandigarh (+1.25), Uttar Pradesh (+0.37) and Bihar (+0.34). Chandigarh being the capital of two states, attracted a lot of migrants with their families to work in administrative offices. In Bihar, predominance of single families among the tribals, coupled with a high mortality rate, explained the small size of the household in their predominantly rural habitats (Vidyarthi, 1977). In the hill districts of Uttar Pradesh, out-migration from rural areas had depleted the size of rural households. In north-western as well as in central Uttar Pradesh and north Bihar Plain also, the urban household size surpassed the rural household in 1991. Because many of the towns in these areas are overgrown villages characterised by large households associated with a high proportion of joint families, while out-migration from the countryside caused reduction in size of the rural household. A considerable number of the Muslim families in towns were also responsible for making the urban household large.

### *6. Areas where Rural Household Size was Bigger in 1991 but Reverse was True in 1971*

The states which falls in this category are Nagaland (+0.95), Goa (+0.55) and Meghalaya (+0.13). In these states, the urban household was bigger in 1971 but the rural household size surpassed it in 1991 and became larger than urban. Initially, the prevalence of nuclear family system in rural areas kept their household small (about 5 to over 5.50 persons). While the frequency of institutional household such as defence establishments, convents and boarding houses were responsible for raising urban household size (5 to 6 persons) in Nagaland and Meghalaya. But, now by facilitating rural areas with transport and communication and basic amenities like electricity, water supply, etc. rural-urban migration is checked to some extent and villages simultaneously rendered the attraction of urban facilities as less critical for rural migrants than before (Krishan, 1993). In hilly areas, incentives are given by government to unemployed youths for setting up of small scale and cottage industries. In Meghalaya and Nagaland, there is a stable high birth rate in rural areas. In Goa, the urban mortality rate increased to 6.4 in 1991 as compared to 4.3 in 1981 which was far more in comparison to rural one (8.0 in 1991 and 7.7 in 1981) while the birth rates were almost stable.

## CONCLUSIONS

A comparison of the average household size in India for 1991 census with those of previous decades reveals that the average size of the Indian household is gradually increasing over time which reached to 5.57 persons per household in 1991 from 4.88 in 1951.

Contrary to the popular notion that the rural household would be distinctly larger than the urban, the urban household in India is only marginally smaller than the rural suggesting a virtual continuation of the traditional family patterns in urban India as well. Ryan's assertion that urban atomization theory in regard of kinship has proven incorrect seems to be true in case of India (Ryan, 1975). In the urban as well as in rural areas, the incidence of joint family is very common resulting in only slight difference between the two. However, striking regional variations can be observed.

The size of household and its rural-urban differential did not show any consistent relationship. Regional differences in the urban household size are found to be more pronounced in comparison to rural household size. Thus, the rural-urban differential is determined more by urban size of household than the rural.

The rural-urban differential has not been consistent but varying from decade to decade. The overall gap between size of the rural and urban households has widened over the decades. The increased differential is because the size of rural household has increased constantly at a faster rate than the urban one.

Spatially speaking, there are wide regional variations in rural-urban differentials at the state level. Himachal Pradesh was noted for the largest difference (+1.30 persons) in average size of its rural (5.48 persons) and urban (4.18 persons) household. The large differential was related to an unusually small size of the urban household.

By contrast, the state of Meghalaya has the lowest rural-urban differential (+0.09 persons) in average size of its rural (5.44 persons) and urban (5.35 persons) households. The prevalence of nuclear family system kept rural as well as urban households small (about 5 to over 5.50 persons), and the resultant rural-urban differential index was also small (0.007).

The trend of rural-urban differentials in size of the household indicates that the rural-urban differentials in almost half of the India are squeezing but at a slow rate. Some of the rural areas are adopting small size of household norms under the influence of urban areas and many of the urban areas, while facing the housing and costly city life problems, are adopting joint family systems, resulting into the squeezing of rural-urban differentials in size of the household.

## REFERENCES

Burch, T .K. (1970), "Some Demographic Determinants of Average Household Size: An Analytic Approach", *Demography*, 7,1, pp. 61-69.

Census of India (1991), *Primary Census Abstract: General Population*, Series–1, India, Part II-B(i), Vols. I & II, Office of the Registrar General and Census Commissioner, India, New Delhi.

Curson, P. H. (1978), "Households and Household Structure in Auckland, New Zealand", *New Zealand Geographer,* 34, 2, pp. 97-104.

Karve, 1. (1953), *Kinship Organization in India*, Deccan College Monograph Series No. 11, Poona.

Krishan, G. (1980) "Size of the Household in Rural India", in Singh, R.L and Rana, P.B.S. (eds.) *Rural Habitat Transformation in World Frontiers*, National Geographical Society of India, Varanasi, pp. 354-363.

Krishan, G. (1993), "The Slowing Down of Indian Urbanization", *Geography*, 78, pp. 80-84.

Krishan, G. and Rana, P. (1980), "Rural-Urban Differential in Size of the Household in India", *Population Geography*, 2, 1 & 2, pp. 21-34.

Reddy, M.M.K. (1996), *An Introduction to Demographic Behaviour in india*, Kanishka Publishers, New Delhi, pp. 53 -70.

Shah, A.M. (1974), *The Household Dimensions of the Family in India*, Orient Longman, New Delhi.

United Nations (1981), "Estimates and Projections of the Number of the Households by Country 1975-2000", Department of International Economic and Social Affairs, New York.

Vidyarthi, L.P. and Rai, B.K. (1977), *The Tribal Culture in India*, Concept Publishing Co., New Delhi, pp. 188.

Vos,. S.D. and Murty K.R. (1985), "Some Reflections on the Demographic Study of the Households in India", *Demography India*, 14, 1, pp. 49-67.

# 20

## Social Dimensions of Urban Fringe

### Analysis of Living Conditions of Urban Poor with Special Reference to Basic Amenities

**ANOOP KUMAR** AND **H. M. KOTHARI**

This chapter is divided into two major parts. The first part deals with the theoretical analysis of the urban fringe and the condition of the urban poor. This part also discusses about the methodology and area of the study. The second part elucidates the major findings about the social dimension of the urban poor and conditions of the urban poor with the help of empirical data from two growing cities of Rajasthan *i.e.* Udaipur and Bhilwara. Some case studies have also been given which are about conditions of fringe area. Their anonymity has been kept by using abbreviated names.

### CONCEPT OF RURAL-URBAN FRINGE

The occurrence of the urban fringe is a rather recent phenomenon around Indian cities. It has been asserted that the urban fringe was non-existent even around the largest metropolitan cities in India before 1950. American land economist Wehrwein[1] was the first to coin the concept of rural urban fringe. According to him 'rural urban fringe is the area of transition between well recognised urban land-uses and the area devoted to agriculture.' Last three decades of the present millennium witnessed sharp increase in the urban population which further caused the much discussed tendency of outward growth of urban limits. Accommodating the added population mass required space and being already a congested area the core of the urban centre provided no encouraging picture. Thus, the mass shifted to the periphery of the urban centre and this swelling of the outer areas resulted into the concept of fringe growth. Rural area, surrounding the city region, inhabited by mostly poor villagers gradually gets converted into area inhabited by urban poor. Thus, the larger part of the fringe area is identified as a poverty pocket. In Indian context, the most befitting definition is given by Ramachandran[2]. He defined urban fringe as 'an area of mixed rural and urban populations and land-uses, which begins at the point where agricultural land-uses appear near the city and extends up to the point where villages have distinct urban land-uses or where some persons, at least, from the village community commute to the city daily for work or other purposes.'

Looking to the metro cities of Calcutta, Mumbai, Chennai and Delhi, above 40 per cent population is living in the slum and squatter areas. And about one fifth of the total urban population of India are slum dwellers. Though, Rajasthan doesn't face such an acute problem of unmanageable dimensions as in the other metro cities of India. Nevertheless, it has been found during the study that poverty pockets of slum dwellers in the fringe area is on increase. So there appears to be a need to realise the repercussions of consistency of this trend. One can visualise the shape of things to come. The point is that the poverty pockets in the rural-urban fringe area is on the increase. Poor people also dominate the *kuchchi busties* and *mohallas* of cities having no or very few civic amenities at their disposal.

The physical expansion of city brings in several changes in the social milieu of the fringe villages. The unskilled fringe people get one or the other job during the expansion of the city limits. Gradually, the fringe area people change their way of life and adopt several urban traits.

The delimitation of fringe area is a complex task to carry out. Several attempts have been made, getting mixed results. Posing proper conceptual framework for the task should be the initial step. Appropriate criterias are to be used, in order to have fairly good results.

## THE URBAN POOR

The urban poverty is that social condition in which a sizeable number of urban dwellers are found living on subsistence level of living. The general backwardness in the living standard is very much identifiable by the living conditions of people of the backward colonies, doing very low paid jobs to live. The meagre amount which they earn cannot allow them possess any property which further may provide them with another source of consistent income. Most of the poor people either remain unemployed for most of the period or they remain underpaid. This phenomena ensues what is called 'vicious circle of poverty'[3] encompassing elements of low income, poor health condition, low calorie food, poor living standard, poor level of education and so on. So the dictum goes 'poor people are poor because they are poor.' Numerical increase in the people who are poverty stricken particularly in urban fringe zone is very much conspicuous.

Noted Anthropologist, Oscar Lewis[4] gave the concept of 'Culture of Poverty' which is very much evident in the fringe area of the two cities. This concept has also been contemplated in depth.

One of the visible dimension of poverty is the housing. Thousands of people huddled in the unhygienic and suffocating accommodation with minimum of basic amenities is common sight in the fringe areas. This condition mostly leads to the adoption of a way of life which perpetrates the degradation of the local ecosystem too.

Among several perspectives of the poverty proliferation, one is the process of migration of rural unemployed to urban fringe area. It also signifies the transformation of rural poor to urban slum dwellers. The absorbing sector of urban structure is the informal sector of the city. The economic activities which are more dominating are the informal economic activities such as hawking, working as domestic help, repairing, carrying head load, rickshaw pulling and so on.

The major characteristics of urban poor are:

1. Urban poor are both the rural migrants to the urban fringe areas and the original urban dwellers.
2. Poor people first take up informal sector jobs and then gradually shift to organised sector, if get chance.
3. They live in slums and squatter settlements or *Kuchchi Busties* with very few civic amenities.
4. They are mostly engaged into menial jobs or low paid jobs.
5. The living conditions of fringe areas is most unhygienic, malnutritive, unhealthy alongwith prevalent illiteracy and ignorance.

Land absorbed by the fringe of the city was essentially agricultural in nature and was acquired by the government. This has created a new class of landless labourers who were farmers earlier. Having lost their source of income, these people shifted to low paid jobs and add to the poor people of the cities studied.

Among several repercussions of the expansion of the urban territorial limits into the fringe area, the enhancement of the urban poverty is the salient one. Processes which cause swelling of two city limits are also responsible for the increase in the urban poverty packets.

This concentration is much conspicuous in the fringe of Udaipur as well as Bhilwara. Rural folks migrate to fringe area searching for the employment and a better life in the city. Having no proper education etc. they are bound to engage in the low paid occupations. Accommodation, being the basic requirement, becomes very much hard to acquire and thus they occupy the fringe area. Another facet of this process is the transformation of fringe zone. Acquisition of agricultural land provides compensation to the farmer, who, having no business knack or farsightedness, loses the money to social customs and prodigality sometimes. Losing the only source of income forces them to take up jobs which are essentially low paid and hazardous too. Poor financial condition compels them to live in the squatter settlements in the fringe areas.

The study reveals that the average occupants of a room in fringe are five and anyone can visualise the kind of difficulties they face while living a hell-like life. Regarding basic amenities available, the situation is all the more alarming. Electricity, tapped water, sanitation, sewage etc. are really distant dreams for fringe poor. While the concept of basic amenities is very much subjective and ethnocentric too, here no contextual deviations has been made considering the international standards of basic amenities.

## STUDYING POVERTY: MEASUREMENT OR IDENTIFICATION?

Explanation presented by economist, regarding poverty, is based upon measurement. Help has been sought from data to provide a 'Poverty-line.' This approach, known as absolute approach, hold several loopholes. In most of the studies on poverty, the absolute approach have been used by Indian economist. Some of the pioneers are Rao[5], Sukhatme[6], Bardhan[7], Minhas[8], Ojha[9], Dandekar and Rath[10], and Costa[11]. The poverty line is a monetary fixture in rupees earned in a given period of time. It is very difficult to calculate the income of a poor as there exists no certainty as to his source of income throughout the time period. Countless variables are involved in the economy of a poor which cannot be explained by merely poverty line. Instead, the identification of poor is the potent approach which is viable one too. This methodology has been adopted by those scholars who prefer 'relative approach.' Leading workers of this approach are Gallbraith[12], Peter Townsend[13] etc.

Under the present study of two upcoming cities of Rajasthan, several case studies also have been undertaken adopting the relative approach to study poverty. Udaipur and Bhilwara, both cities' civic administration undertook acquisition movement in 1960s in the periphery of the city. These acquisitions turned out to be the turning point in the life of the land owners. In most cases, they utilised the compensation amount, on social customs and thus lost money very soon. Given here, in brief, is the crux of a few case studies which elucidates the transformation of economic as well as social status of people in the fringe areas.

**Case Study 1**

G.G. is an old man of 85. He lives in Malana Busti of Bhilwara city. He had 25 bighas* of irrigated land with 4 wells on it. Presently, he has only 3 bighas of irrigated land which he bought for Rs. 36,000 after acquisition at some other place. He got Rs. 20,000 as compensation amount and spent it on buying land and some other social obligations. Due to land buying and famine, G.G. is indebted to the tune of Rs. 20,000 and is a poor man now. He told "Fine days are gone, we are poor now. Earlier we used to get milk, and *ghee* etc. easily. But now keeping both ends meet seems impossible. It is really tough time ahead."

**Case Study 2**

U.R.J., 35 is living in Pula Basti, Udaipur and is *Dangi* (Agriculturist) by caste. He got Rs. 90,000 in lieu of acquisition of 18 bighas of irrigated land during land acquisition programme of Udaipur Municipality. The money was consumed in digging a well and *mritubhoj*** of his father. He resented the meagre productivity on the remaining land. In his words "My land, which was acquired by Municipality, annually yielded about 100 quintals of wheat along with sugarcane, cotton, *rachka* (green fodder for cattle). My land produced gold literally. Now I cannot manage even *dhan* and we are forced to

---

* 1 Hectare = approx. 5 Bighas.

** A social evil in the form of feast after the death, by his family to his acquaintance.

eat cereals from rationing." Presently, he is very poor fellow having debts to the tune of Rs. 25,000 and he is unable to pay even the interest of debt.

**Case Study 3**

U.C., aged 50, lives in Malan Basti of Bhilwara and *jat* by caste. His 20 Bighas of land was acquired by Bhilwara Municipality in 1960 and he was paid Rs. 7500 as compensation, which he spent paying some debts and on *mritubhoj* of his father. He said "we are illiterate farmers and our land is everything to us. It should not be acquired. Our land is our life. Acquisition crippled and killed us." UC told that they are four brothers and after acquisition their financial condition deteriorated. He cannot get balanced diet which led to poor health. Presently, he has a debt of Rs. 45,000 in his name.

**Case Study 4**

P.P., 42, lives in Tekri Basti of Udaipur, and is *poorbia* by caste. Out of his 40 bigha irrigated land, Udaipur Municipality acquired 15 Bighas of land and compensated him with Rs. 75,000. He bought some land and spent Rs. 40,000 on *mritubhoj* of his father. According to P.P. "Earlier my economic condition was good but now I am poor. I am now obliged to cultivate others' land on partnership basis for the want of finance." He told that during the acquisition of land, collective protest took place but the Municipality acquired the land with the help of police force. "The land acquired from us cannot be bought elsewhere", he maintained. The land had two wells on it. After acquisition., P.P. has become very poor.

Case studies given above reveal some basic findings which are, first, the land acquisition in the urban fringe areas results downward social mobility of farmers form upper strata to lower strata. Having poor farsightedness and negligible business tacts leads to irrational spending to the compensation amount which further makes them prone to indebtedness. Social evils like *mritubhoj* etc. being social obligation become more pressurising especially when farmer gets cash as compensation. This way these transformed poor folks dwell in the fringe area and adopts one or the other low paid jobs.

This way the physical expansion of the city limits outward into the fringe area also results into the transformation of rural farmers to urban poor and agriculturist to low paid menial job worker of the fringe area. This perspective of the problem is different from the migration of rural folks to urban fringe searching for employment and privileges of city.

## BASIC AMENITIES IN THE FRINGE AREA

Being the periphery of the city, the fringe area is generally considered suitable for those very activities which are prohibited or discouraged in the city core. The fringe is just like a dustbin for the city dwellers. Sewage and garbage piling up is a usual sight which is why epidemic generally erupt here. Garbage dumps also utilised as the site of *Kuchchi Busties* and Jhuggis in the fringe. Land-uses which are undesirable in the city are shifted to the fringe area of the city *e.g.* sewage treatment, butcheries, burial grounds, water tanks, garbage dumps and brick kilns. Relocation of slums to the fringe area is generally done. Industries, which are unhealthy to the environment, are established in the fringe area.

In fringe area, general scarcity of basic amenities is observed. Provisions of basic civic amenities is not properly met with. Protected and treated water, sewage disposal and proper drainage, garbage disposal, electricity, street lights, medical clinics and dispensaries, schools and colleges, paved streets are among the several basic amenities required for the proper development of healthy personality. Piped water supply, electricity, sewage, street light, school, dispensary etc. are a dream to fringe habitant.

The living conditions of fringe area of Udaipur and Bhilwara are miserable, to say the least. No proper sanitation is available to slum dwellers of Kishanpol harijan kachchi busti, Machla Mangara, Panerion ki Madri of Udaipur fringe and Dhandolai busti, Khawa Kheda busti, Kansipuri jhoparpatti of Bhilwara fringe. They either defecate in the open or have dry latrines which further spread unsightly open sewage in the streets. Defecating in the open is responsible for many endemic diseases, both contagious and infectious. Likewise, non-availability of safe and treated water is behind the dysentery, skin diseases, allergy and plethora of diseases, very common among poor people. Forced to drink the hand pumps water or tubewell water, people usually contact communicable diseases. Cheaper alternatives are not necessarily the safer ones. Power theft is common in major poverty pockets in both cities. Stealing power from street cables sometimes cause fatal accidents because open wire hooks, which slum dwellers use, are prone to electrocution. Living in limited space poses threat to the privacy of the inmates and incites premature sexual activities among children, which is why incest, rape, molestation etc. appear somewhat common. Drain water usually mixes with sewage and becomes breeding ground for mosquitoes, flies, further making the environment more conducive for epidemics. Lack of personal cleanliness and hygiene is another factor which gets accentuated when basic amenities become luxury to people. Such living conditions merit medical facilities close to the settlements. While the hospitals and dispensaries are generally a distant dream, quacks are found to be ruling the roost. Several casualties occur due to negligence of people and treatment by the quacks. Quacks are easily accessible; being illegal medical practitioners, they charge less fee and, therefore, are popular too. Location of *Kuchchi Busties* is usually near a drain, railway line, poorly drained land, garbage dump site and other undesirable areas. This very factor ensues several avenues for a tough life for the dwellers. City absorbs the peripheral area within itself but fails to provide due attention to ameliorate the living conditions of the slum dwellers.

## SUGGESTIONS

Awesome living conditions of our cities deserve immediate attention of planners and policy makers. Because the problem may soon attain unmanageable heights, thus it is pertinent here to present some viable suggestions, based upon the empirical work, in order to move towards a better and healthy urban fringe of future.

1. Foremost measure to be taken is to check the flow of unemployed masses from rural region to urban centres. Government should encourage cottage industries and small scale industries especially in the rural areas. Creating job opportunities within the village should be done on a consistent basis.
2. Adequate medical facilities alongwith cleanliness drive for fringe area poor should be made available through dispensaries and health centres.

3. Alternative sanitation facilities are a must as poor cannot invest. Sulabh Shauchalaya Complex is better option.
4. Personal hygiene and cleanliness is the key to good health. Safe drinking water should be available at least at the public places.
5. Power connections to slum areas of fringe at concessional rates should restrain the incidences of power stealing related hazards.
6. Non-Governmental Organisations if enters the scene, may make a big difference for the better. Educating the poor about each and every issue concerned to them should become a priority.
7. Educate poor masses, as their awakening will be achieved via this very route. Illiteracy makes poor susceptible to several problems.

## NOTES

1. Ramachandran R., *Urbanisation and Urban Systems in India,* Delhi, Oxford University Press, 1992, pp. 296.
2. Ramachandran, R., *Urbanisation and Urban Systems in India*, op. cit. 1.
3. Haralambas, M. and Robin H., *Sociology : Themes and Perspectives*, Delhi University Press, 1980, pp. 143.
4. Lewis Oscar, "The Culture of Poverty", *On Understanding Poverty,* (ed.), Denial P. Menihal, New York: Basic Books. 1968, pp. 187.
5. Rao, V. K. R. V. , *Food, Nutrition and Poverty* in India, Delhi: Vikas Publishing House, 1982.
6. Sukhatme, P. V., *Feeding India's Growing Millions,* London: Asia Publishing House, 1965.
7. Bardhan, R. K., "On the Minimum Level of Living and the Rural Poor", *Indian Economic Review,* Vol. I, 1970.
8. Minhas, B. S., *Planning and the Poor*, New Delhi, S. Chand, 1974.
9. Ojha, P. D., "A Configuration of Indian Poverty", *Challenge of Poverty in India* (ed.) A. J. Fonseca, Delhi : Vikash Publication, 1971, pp. 25-47.
10. Dandekar, V. M. and Rath, N., *Poverty in India*, New Delhi: The Ford Foundation, 1970.
11. Costa, E. P. W., "A Portrayal of Indian Poverty", *Challenge of Poverty in India* (ed.), A. J. Fonseca, Delhi : Vikash Publication. 1971, pp 48-59.
12. Galbraith, J. K., *The Affluent Society*, New York, New American Library, 1950.
13. Townsend, P. "The Meaning of Poverty" *British Journal of Sociology*: Vol. No. 2, 1954.

# 21

# Delhi : A Healthy City?

## It is a Distant and Wishful Dream

**H. R. SURI**

To think of Delhi as a healthy city may certainly be a distant and wishful dream primarily because Delhi has been drifting in the wrong direction and has been on the wrong track for many years now. There are varied reasons, but one simple reason is that we all are sleeping and that everyone of us has developed a knack for blaming someone else for this dreadful mess.

Delhi is an ancient town and has a long history. During the last few decades Delhi has transformed itself into a huge 'urban mass', and has spread itself over an area of 5000-6000 sq. km, provided we, for a moment, ignore the state and district boundaries. This total urban agglomeration today is a combination of many cities. It includes Ghaziabad spreading towards and upto Delhi Boundary apart from spreading towards Loni, Hapur and Bullandshahr, on the East; Noida and Greater Noida right upto Surajpur on the South-East have filled up the major gaps around Delhi, between District Gaziabad and Faridabad: This area has been made centre of the newly carved out District known as Gautam Budh Nagar. Faridabad and Ballabhgarh are packing up every inch of space upto Delhi border on the South. When we look at Gurgaon we find that well known colonizers have done their job by developing areas between Delhi border and Gurgaon and further spreading towards Sona and Daruhera. Along the North Western front we have Najafgarh, Bahadurgarh, Bawana including Badli and Narela exploding and are spreading right upto Kundli.

Due to tremendous pressures on this urban mass of Greater Delhi, the spaces and gaps left out in between and in the sorrounding areas of these numerous centres have been filled up by the spacious and luxurious farm houses as well as haphazard growth and is effecting this urban mass. The rich and neo rich are busy converting good agricultural land into large sized glorified palaces in the form of farm houses. They are leeching on the city services without paying for it, apart from evading Property Gains Tax/Income Tax as well as hood-winking the Authorities of the Urban Land Ceiling Act. As such there are no farms, no farmers and no farm product. This huge urban mass of Greater Delhi may be housing anywhere between 2 to 2.5 crores of population. Population in this area may touch 3.5 to 4.0 crores in next 2 to 3 decades. Further if we examine the actual position of housing in detail, we find that 65-70 per cent of population in Delhi has not been provided with any accommodation within the city. This population is forced to work everywhere and anywhere and live in the huge number of villages and other rural centres in and around Delhi. Major portion of this huge population has housed itself in unauthorised colonies and this has triggered haphazard spatial growth mushrooming all over the city. City today lacks basic infrastructure, services and amenities. Many times the squatters were cleared from the city but somehow because of the soft attitude of the authorities encouraged by the politicians, the problem of the squatters and unauthorised construction is increasing every day.

The first Master Plan for Delhi promulgated in 1962 was a well planned document and laid down clear cut guidelines for the development of the city. A detailed examination of the total development reveals that we have not been able to provide, even today, the level of infrastructure, required for this development as envisaged for in 1961 even after 35 years. The 1990 Master Plan not only blunted the influence of the 1962 Master Plan but also confused everyone concerned. The word land-use is under tremendous strain. It is being misinterpreted and misused. The new Master Plan has brought in many sub uses without any reason. We seem to have lost the sanctity of the word 'land use' which in fact has been introduced in this country only recently.

There are no budgeted funds earmarked specifically for the purpose of urban development in the State and Central Budgets. Financially local bodies are defunct and are unable to pay salaries and meet expenditure on their establishments.

As explained above the total urban fabric, spread over an area of 5000 to 6000 km consisting of many cities is being governed by many power centres, each operating in different directions.

The NCR plan 10,000 crores has failed to take off because the NCR authorities are waiting for the funds. Such funds I believe may never come. NCR has become another power centre. The numerous power centres operating in the 'Urban Mass' and that we are not prepared to unite every organisation within this urban agglomeration, under the umbrella of the 74th Amendment Act and help in establishing a Metropolitan Planning Committee, as envisaged in this important Amendment to the Act of the Constitution.

Therefore this Greater Delhi lacks a unified and cohesive urban management entity, administrative skill, and business like approach. A business like approach is the only alternative to achieve the desired results. This does not mean that urban development does not require funds. Urban development and finance are two sides of the same coin.

It is very interesting to note that every one in this 'urban mass' is pulling strings in different directions. Even the physical planners continue to get the total blame. Before we start fixing responsibilities we must examine the situation in detail to understand the reasons for this mess. Today the DDA may be a powerful body but a planner in DDA cannot even interpret or define land-use because it is the administrator who is required to issue NOC. Planners are not being used to monitor the development. There is no clear cut direction.

DDA is responsible for losing thousands of acres of land acquired for public purpose which was entrusted to them for development. Major portion of this land has gone into the hands of unscrupulous property sharks and has resulted into the bulk of unauthorised construction.

The housing programme has no link with the various economic groups in the area. For many years the Authority has been busy with self-financing schemes. They have not yet developed commercial centres as proposed in the First Master Plan. The commercial centre which have been developed are not responsive to the needs of the people in terms of area, quality of space, phasing, programming and monitoring. The district level needs are flourishing in the traditional markets, thereby, completely undermining the development plans for the various types of commercial centres planned by DDA. Stringent lease conditions and the system of two parallel economies operating in the country, people are hesitant to pay the right kind of price for the DDA plots/ready built spaces.

The slum department in Delhi has been shuttling from authority to authority. And is busy in making more slums. Lands in Delhi are in the control of DDA and others. Maintenance of the city is in the hands of MCD, NDMC and others. The squatters in the city located in about

1600 centres continue to stay wherever they are. They are occupying prime lands badly needed for the city. Now I understand that new locations for housing squatters are being planned outside the city of Delhi. Jauna Pur Village about 10 km from the urban limit of Delhi is one such example. Soon there may be many such centres. This will aggravate the problem further.

You may be very well aware that because of indecision Lutyen's bungalow zone area situated in the heart of the city comprising about 20-30 sq. km is lying dead for the last 3 decades.

As explained above, the Ghaziabad Development Authority (GDA) is busy filling up the gap between the city of Delhi and Ghaziabad. Some of the well known centres are Kaushambi, Vaishali, Indrapuram and Hustnapur etc. GDA had dumped huge accommodation in the form of multi-storeyed flats, commercial centres, and plotted development on the border of the city. For a long time there were no takers for these ready built flats. Ultimately all the investment has become infructuous and this built resource is now being dumped with the various institutions of the State and Central Government for their staff housing. Apartment buildings being developed by private developers are standing all over the place in half built condition. Large pockets of land in and around the area is growing into haphazard manner.

Noida has grown along the south-eastern border of the city. In addition to this, Greater Noida located about 7 to 10 km away from Noida has become part of this urban mass. Large multinational industries have come up in between. Whole thing has developed upto Surajpur. Greater Noida has already built roads, drainage system, lighting all complete and are waiting for the people and the multi-national business houses or national and international industries to come and construct buildings.

Faridabad authority with its 60 sectors and industrial areas today is packing up every inch of space right upto Delhi border. Today it has 29 km of length spreading along Delhi-Bombay highway and the railway track. The authorities in Faridabad are testing the delicate nerves of the citizens. They are issuing new orders every next day. This is apart from the action of the court and the Department of Environment/Central Pollution Control Board. This is creating havoc in the city. Values of the properties have gone to the bottom. Why

Faridabad is suffering in comparison to DLF/Unitech and Ansal areas, this is because these areas are in the hands of private agencies, who are looking after the needs of the people in their areas. The authorities of the Faridabad are not bothered about the city.

Gurgaon, in itself, is becoming a metropolis and today it boasts many cities. The well known developments with tall multi-storeyed apartments and commercial buildings all complete with well designed clubs, etc. are busy cornering the rich and the Non-Resident Indians (NRI) who are sending funds to grab areas near and around Delhi. The builders in this area are exploiting the proximity to the Delhi Airport. To add to this we have Dundahera. and Daruhera. Rajasthan too does not want to remain behind and is having a finger in the pie as well. Bhiwari, an industrial belt is coming up very fast and is attracting large number of new industries.

Urban development in our country seems to be the most relegated subject. Most of the politicians and administrators would like to take control of better power centres in the State and Central Governments. Urban development has some basic problems. The buildings and the cities are very bulky, these are finance consuming entities and once built cannot be shifted around. Very often the total mathematics can misfire.

Physical planners are not the only actors in the field of urban development especially if we go into the details of the urban mass under discussion. Politicians are often boosting the morale of unauthorised squatters to build up their vote banks. The administrators never reply any letter or query from a needy citizen. Their actions are many times contrary to the laid down objectives.

Ignorance of Urban planning technology alongwith lack of understanding of the needs of the people is creating havoc in the city. Engineering experts too have developed their own power centres as well and work within a set framework. The Physical planner, therefore, remains only a simple advisor and more often than not, his advice may or may not be accepted.

It is high time that the professional institutions and Government organisations together their technical resources and manpower so as to initiate research for the development of comprehensive data interpreting land-use, definitions, interpretations and ancillary functions, along with detailed research for establishing the planning standards on a firm footing.

If we want Delhi to be a healthy city we have to wake up and think afresh as to where we are and in what direction we are heading. We all have to work together, *i.e.* people, politicians, administrators, technocrats, every department, every organisation, every individual having any interest in the city.

Today our environment is degenerating. We have not yet developed many of our open spaces planned in the city. We have not made provision for playing fields. Our schools are undersized. The schools are insufficient in size for building in the basic necessities of the schools. Transport is suffering. Built up areas are disintegrating. The commercial areas are suffering, there is no parking. Even Authorities have been misusing lands designated for specific functions.

It may be ideal to combine all the forces and the power centres. With a unified force under the 74th Amendment to the Constitution and form M.P.C (Metropolitan Planning Committee). Under this programme it will be useful to convert DDA into a Technical Secretariat to plan and supervise and maintain at the highest level. Each area/ District to work within that framework. MCD, NDMC and every other local body within this framework to fall in line. This may necessitate to close down the NCR as well as the Slums Department.

We have to pool our resources together. We have to be business-men like. Use the physical planners as part of the total technical force for planning, phasing and monitoring of development. It is only then and that too with full determination and business like approach, we may be able to achieve our this distant and wishful dream. Otherwise it may remain a dream forever.

If we want Delhi to develop as a healthy city, a total spatial plan, transportation plan incorporating MRTS/Freeways, etc. water and power proposals with all the necessary infrastructure along with housing is a must, so that this huge 'urban mass' can be transformed to provide for the need of the citizens of this Greater Delhi to face the next century.

# Changing Population Structure of Jhajjar Town

## A Geographical Analysis

**S. HASAN ANSARI**

The changing population scene of the region is the statistical description and analysis of population, the numbers and description of people in a given area, spatio-temporal distribution, the age and sex composition, population occupation structure, the proposition of scheduled caste, the birth and death rates and their mathematical or social interrelation among these various qualities. The characteristics of population in an urban area derives its significance from the interaction of the quality or level of urban population with nature and level of urban amenity, but the culture of the people influence the size and the character of population which in turn, generates the demand for the urban land also. As high amount of demand of land, its availability and actual utilization results in destructive pattern of land-use in town. These are some burning questions arise before us, which needs thorough analysis for which a small city named Jhajjar now declared district headquarters of Jhajjar district has been selected as a case study.

### AIMS AND OBJECTIVES

The main aim of this chapter is to highlight the changing population structure of the town by analysing its rate and distribution of population, density distribution, spatial position of residential houses, sex ratio, education and occupational structure with special consideration of the scheduled caste population.

The objective of this research paper has been considered as a challenge to put up facts and figures of the actual problems of the town in relation to literacy, occupation, sex ratio of the town before the regional planner, administrator and the politician to eradicate above mentioned burning issues so that this newly created district headquarters *i.e.* Jhajjar town be developed in a planned way.

### METHODOLOGY

To achieve above aim and objectives, an attempt has been made to give more focus on the field work participation, observation of the

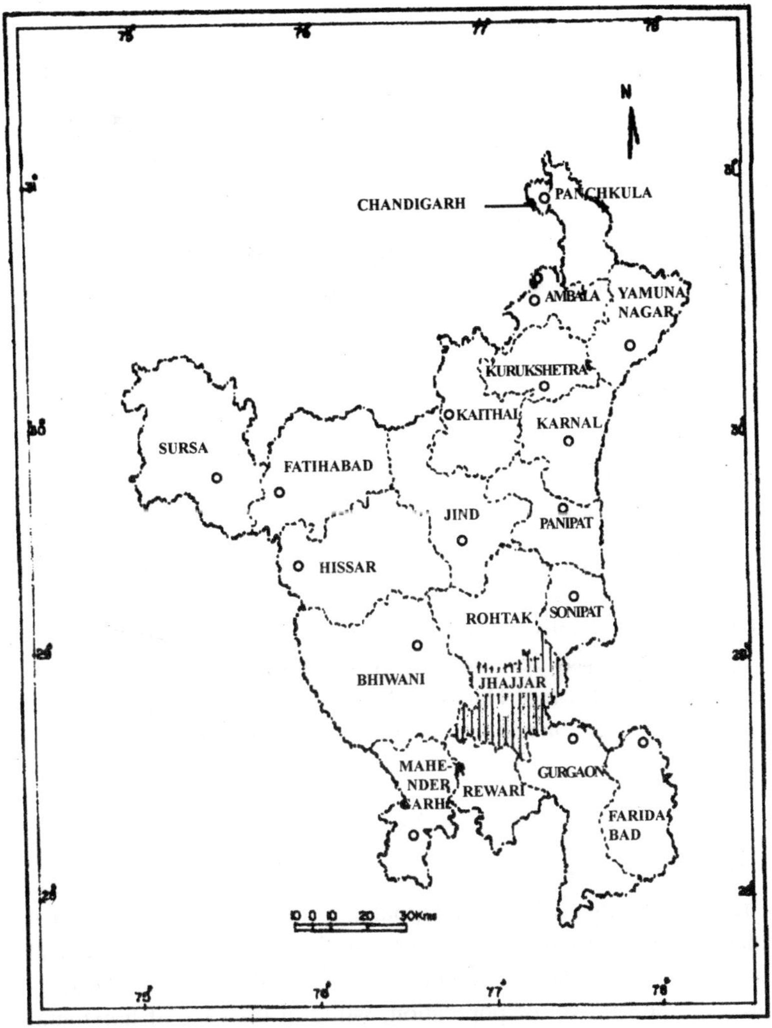


**Fig. 22.1 :** Jhajjar District in Haryana

area, put up questions before them and the censuses, statistical abstract of the town, gazetteers, settlements reports, maps of planner of the town etc. have also been consulted for detail analysis. The computer cartography, analysis of data by computer, and combinational analysis if needed may also be done for accurate analysis of data and the results. The occupational structure and the literacy of the area explain

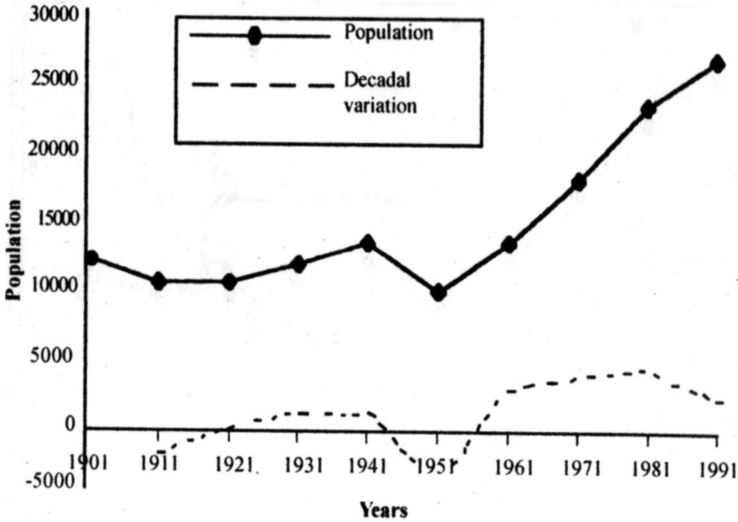


**Fig. 22.1a :** Population Growth of Jhajjar Town

themselves the status of the people, living style and the status of the region for planned development in the era of twenty-first century. Hence a small town of Haryana state has been selected for detailed analysis, observation and results of existing social problems of Jhajjar town.

## TEMPORAL CHANGE OF POPULATION

The population growth is one index of its economic development, social awakening, cultural background, historical events and political ideology. The urban growth can be studied in terms of its vertical growth or horizontal development. The vertical growth is related by an increase in level of population, while in the case of horizontal development, it is the study of growth of town and expansion rather than a fixed boundary.

Table 22.1 and Fig. 22.1(a) shows growth of population of Jhajjar town during A.D 1901 to A.D 2001. It has a very slow of population curve till A. D. 1941 which has two population brake *i.e.* A.D 1911 and A.D 1951 in which the growth of population has been decreased. It has been noted that during A.D 1901, the town contains a population of 12,227 persons which is declined in A.D 1911 and reached upto

10,617 persons. The growth rate of the population declined by 13.17 per cent due to famine and spread of epidemics. Then after the town has increased population in each decade as noted 10,800 persons in A.D. 1921, 12,232 persons in A.D. 1931 and 13,193 in A.D. 1941. During A. D. 1951, the population of Jhajjar town had been declined due to migration of huge population of Muslim to Pakistan. After that population growth of the town simultaneously rises up, but the town is experiencing decline growth rate from A.D. 1961 to A.D. 2001 by 35.38 per cent, 33.11 per cent, 27.97 per cent, 14.21 per cent, respectively. It has also been noted that the decline growth rate of Jhajjar is less than natural growth rate of 22 per cent, which reflects that the town is experiencing a net exmigration which is mainly due to lack of opportunity and other economical factors. Due to headquarters of Jhajjar district, a large number of offices including district administration and judicial complexes came up in this town. Moreover, the National Capital Region (NCR) Plan –2001 has proposed to be developed it as sub-centre, which will attract more and more population for employment and business from peripheral rural settlements and it is expected that the population of the town would reach upto the mark of one lakh by A.D. 2021.

**Table 22.1 :** Growth of Population of Jhajjar, Town Population

| Year | Population | Decadal Variation | Growth Rate in %age |
|---|---|---|---|
| 1901 | 12,227 | — | — |
| 1911 | 10,617 | –1610 | –03.17 |
| 1921 | 10,800 | 0183 | 00.72 |
| 1931 | 12,232 | 1432 | 03.26 |
| 1941 | 13,919 | 1687 | 03.79 |
| 1951 | 10,514 | –3405 | –24.46 |
| 1961 | 14,234 | 3720 | 35.38 |
| 1971 | 18,947 | 4713 | 33.11 |
| 1981 | 24,247 | 5300 | 27.97 |
| 1991 | 27,693 | 3446 | 14.21 |

*Source* : Computed from Town Director, Part IX-A, Series 8, Haryana, 1991.

**Fig. 22.2.** : Distribution of Population in Jhajjar Town, 1991

## SPATIAL DISTRIBUTION OF POPULATION

The term distribution refers the way in which people are spaced over the earth surface. The Fig. (22.2) shows that the distribution of population is uniformly distributed over the area but it differs at ward level. It has dense population in the interior part *i.e.* oldest part, which is situated on a mound enclosed by a boundary wall of 57′′ wide with 6 gate which are now famous by their name only. It accommodates 42.2 per cent of total population over 17.5 per cent of the total area. Another highly populated patch is closed to western part of wall town known as "Jabia Mohalla" comprising of high percentage of backward classes and Scheduled caste groups. There is 'camp area' situated on the south-west of the wall city established just after the partition of the country in A.D. 1947 which now has become a permanent residential area. There are two castes inhabited and dominated in 'Camp Area' *viz.*, Sikh and Sāini who inhabit in southern part and in the western part respectively. Other densely populated areas are along the main road. The outer peripheral area has been characterized by uniform distribution of population. It has also been observed that for the last three decades maximum expansion of the town is noticed towards western side which attracts high percentage of immigrants from nearby villages.

## STATUS AND QUALITY OF PEOPLE

The density of population is another important parameter to know index of measurement of population load which generates processes influencing morphology and functional attributes of an urban town. It has positive correction with quality of living. It means it is simply expressed as a ratio of population lived in unit area (built up area). Due to lack of open land and densely residential lots the average arithmetic density of the built up area of the town is three times more than the average density of the town noted as 14,051 persons per sq. km (56 persons per acre) and 4,615 persons per sq. km respectively. (Table 22.2) shows L.Q. of annual population of Jhajjar town, 1991.

There are 5 wards which records location quotient as less than one. In another 5 wards the location quotient has been noted in between 1 to 2 and 2 to 3 in ward No. 3 and more than 3 in ward No. 2 which clears that as the distance from the centre of the town increases, the population gradient is going down also as Simmon & Tennant (1963) supported the statement that the urban population density varies inversely with the distance from the city centre.

**Table 22.2** : Location Quotient of Annual Population, 1991

| Wards km² | Population | % in Total quotient | Area in | % in Total | Location |
|---|---|---|---|---|---|
| 1 | 2742 | 9.9 | .1924 | 9.8 | 1.01 |
| 2 | 1935 | 7.0 | .1088 | 5.5 | 1.27 |
| 3 | 1921 | 6.9 | .384 | 2.0 | 3.45 |
| 4 | 1956 | 7.1 | .1114 | 5.7 | 1.24 |
| 5 | 1703 | 6.1 | .570 | 2.9 | 2.10 |
| 6 | 1050 | 3.8 | .3277 | 16.6 | 0.22 |
| 7 | 2114 | 7.6 | .1552 | 7.9 | 0.96 |
| 8 | 1626 | 5.9 | .1393 | 7.1 | 0.83 |
| 9 | 1414 | 5.1 | .0663 | 3.4 | 1.5 |
| 10 | 1544 | 5.6 | .0384 | 2.0 | 2.8 |
| 11 | 1635 | 5.9 | .0424 | 2.2 | 2.68 |
| 12 | 2431 | 8.8 | .0544 | 2.8 | 3.14 |
| 13 | 1900 | 6.9 | .1128 | 5.7 | 1.21 |
| 14 | 1724 | 6.2 | .1459 | 7.4 | 0.83 |
| 15 | 1998 | 7.2 | .3822 | 19.4 | 0.37 |
| Total | 27693 | 100 | 1.970834 | 100 | — |

*Source* : Computed from Town Director, Part IX-A, Series 8, Haryana, 1991

The density of population of Jhajjar town has been shown in (Fig. 22.3). It has 4 category of density of population *viz*., (i) Very high density (more than 120 persons per acre), (ii) High density (80-120 persons per acre), (iii) Moderate density (40-80 persons per acre), (iv) Low density (less than 40 persons per acre). The very high density (203 persons per acre) found in ward No. 3, 5, 10, 11 and 12 fall into two category of population density which share 11.09 per cent area inhabited by 33.3 per cent of total population of the town which is the main old settlements of commercial activities. The second category of high density (80-120 persons per acre) has been found in ward No. 4 in which more than 80 persons per acre has been recorded.

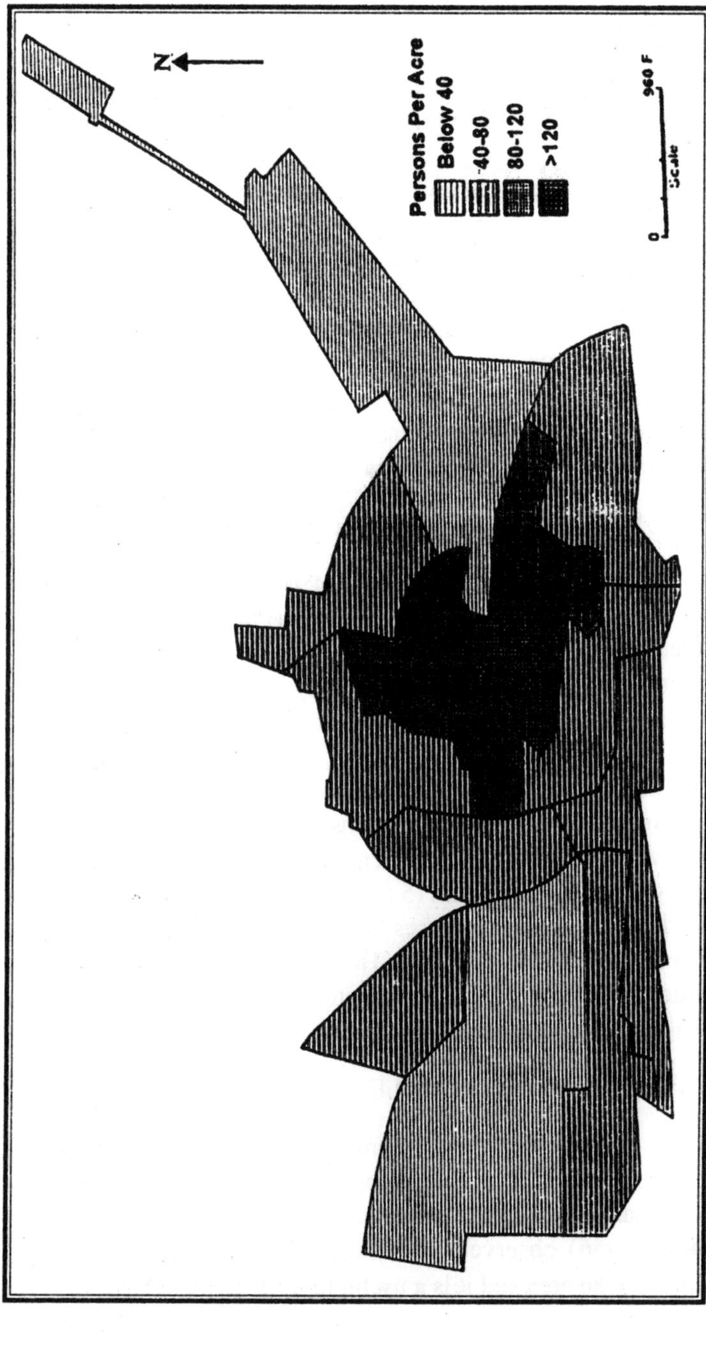


**Fig. 22.3 :** Density of Population of Jhajjar Town, 1991

The third category of moderate density is surrounded by the core/high density area found in the ward 1, 2, 4, 9 and 13. It contains 30 per cent of total area settled by 36 per cent of the total population. There is a decline trend of growth rate since A.D. 1981 in ward 2, 9 and 13.

The fourth category of low density has been recorded in ward 6, 7, 8, 14 and 15 lies in the peripheral or edge area of the town. There are two wards 6 and 15 where very few houses/residential quarters are built. During recent year a new residential area developed where private and public residential colonies proposed in ward No.15 and ward 6, which are minimum density area of maximum proportion (16%) of total land inhabited by minimum 3.08 per cent of total population. A tank, a tomb of Shah Ghazni Kanal (A.D. 1626) and main educational institutions are located in this zone also.

## SPATIAL POSITION OF RESIDENTIAL AREA

Figure 22.4 shows density of houses of Jhajjar town during 1991. It has four types of density of houses *viz*, (i) high density of houses, (ii) medium density of houses, (iii) low density of houses, (iv) very low density of houses. The first category of high residential density (more than 20 houses per acre of land) found in those wards lie in the core part of the town *viz*. 11, 12, 10, 5. This area has mature stage of evolutionary processes of the town where no vacant land is found. The second category of medium density of houses may be noted in ward 6 where 15 houses on per acre of land built. While in the third category of density of houses (5 to 10 houses per acre) has been seen in ward No. 15 where 5 houses built which shows more open land available for cultural activities. However, a bird view of the city indicates a concentric circle like structure where the density of houses decrease from core to peripheral area.

## CHANGING SCENE OF MALE AND FEMALE POPULATION

The term sex ratio represents number of female over per thousand male, which affects upon the demographic structure like population, growth, marriage rate and occupational structure of the region. As Franklin (1956) observed that sex ratio is an index of economy prevailing in an area and it is a useful tool for regional analysis.

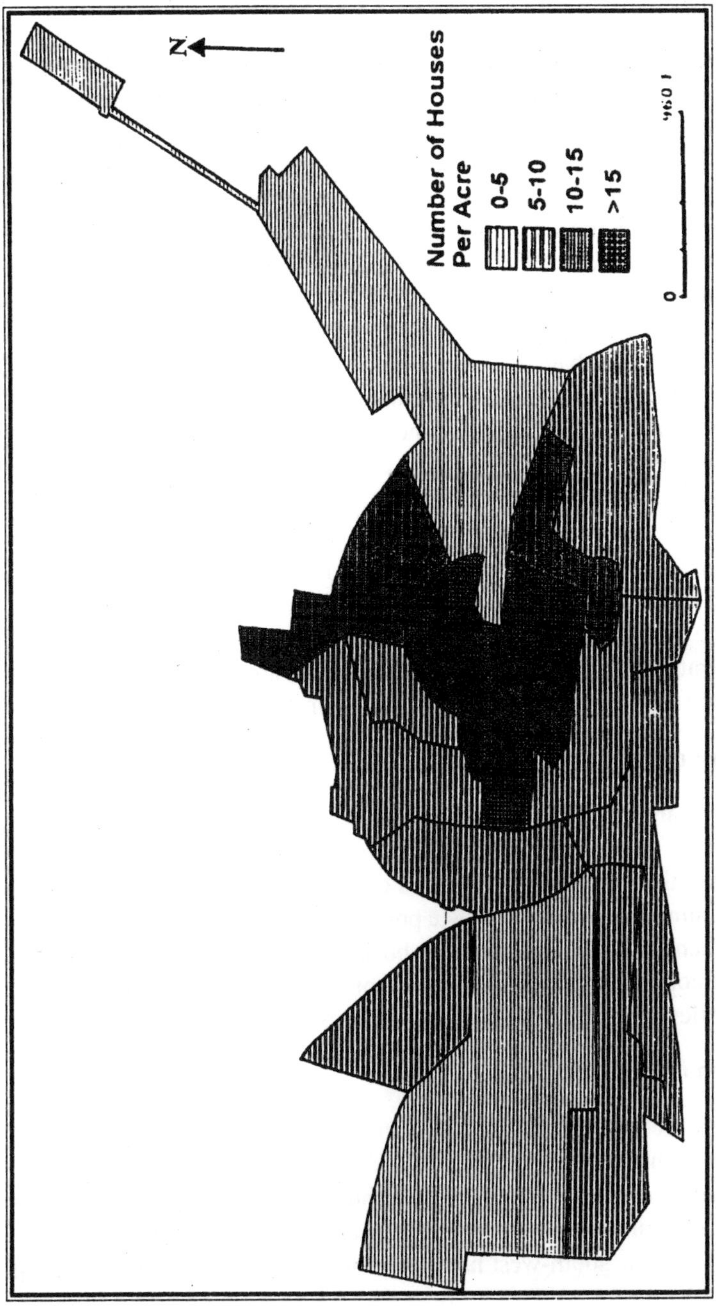


**Fig. 22.4** : Density of Houses of Jhajjar Town, 1991

Table 22.3 shows changing sex composition over time of Jhajjar town. There is an interesting point to note that sex ratio of the town has continuous declined after 1901 except some improvement has been noted during 1941 and 1991.

There was more number of female than the male till 1931 which was equalized during 1941 and then after the each census records more male than the females as Fig. 22.1a verified it. After independence, in 1951 the sex ratio was 930 which is continuously come down to 926 in 1961, 889 in 1971, 860 in 1981 but there is a little increase by 1.4 per cent (878) in 1991. However, it is higher than the district's urban sex ratio. Fig. 22.5 reveals trends of sex ratio of Jhajjar town which shows that there is a decline trend of sex ratio till 1981 but after then it has an increasing trend in sex ratio in the area under study.

## SPATIAL PATTERN OF SEX RATIO

Figure 22.5 shows the spatial pattern of sex ratio during 1991. It has four major categories *viz*, (i) very low sex ratio (< 858 females per 1000 males), (ii) low sex ratio (858-878 per 1000 males), (iii) high sex ratio (878-895 per 1000 males) and (iv) area of very high sex ratio (more than 895 female per 1000 male) in Jhajjar town.

### Area of Very Low Sex Ratio

There are three wards of the town comes in this category *i.e.* ward number 2 has very low sex ratio due to lowest literacy and huge population engaged in trade and commerce while in ward number 3 has minimum scheduled caste population and ward number 11 lies in the centre of town inhabited by business community engaged in trade and commerce. Due to these reasons a very low sex ratio *i.e.* 827 females per 1000 males recorded in this category.

### Area of Low Sex Ratio

There are four wards *viz.*, 1, 4, 6 and 14 marked as low sex ratio in the town. It has below from the average sex ratio of the town *i.e.* 875. All modern colonies, sectors (private and government) along the Jhajjar-Bahadurgarh road and some part of administrative area in the north-west and the south-west have also low sex ratio from the average of the town.

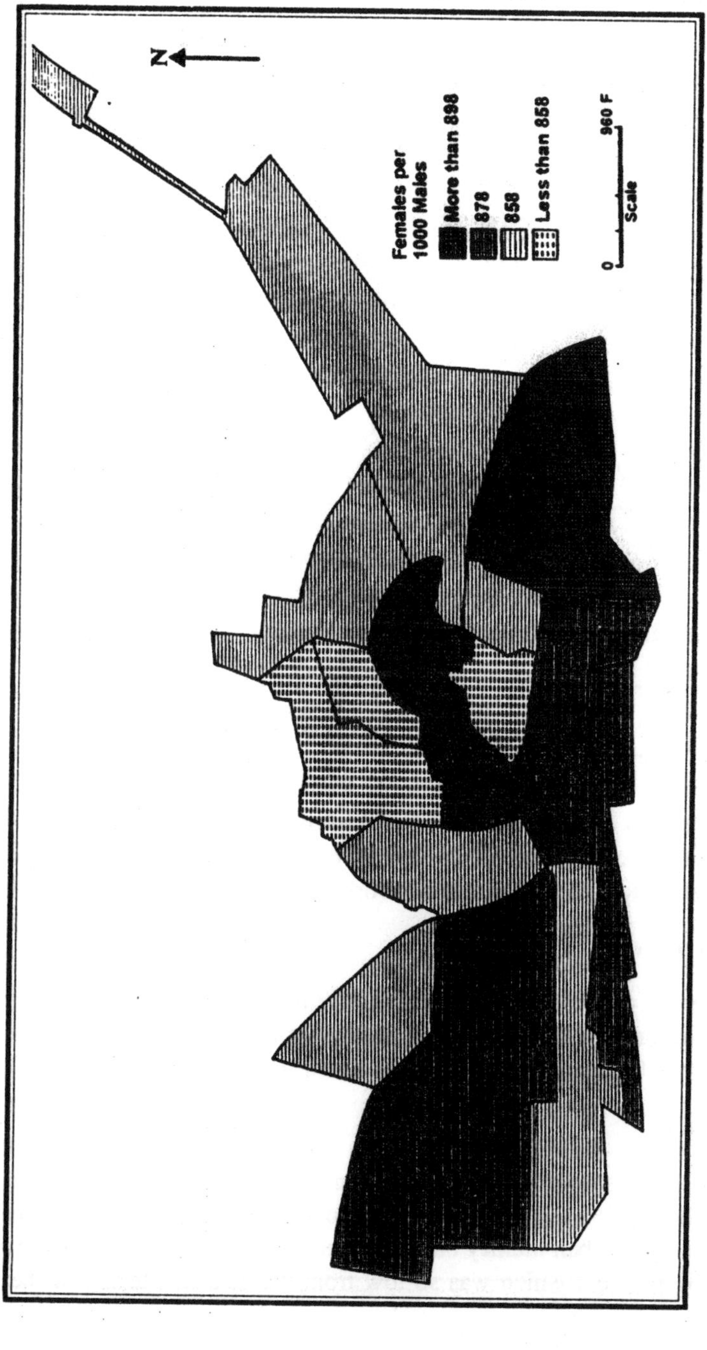


**Fig. 22.5 :** Sex Ratio of Jhajjar Town, 1991

**Table 22.3 :** Changing Sex Composition of Jhajjar Town, 1901-1991

| Years | Male | Female | Absolute Variation | Sex ratio | Decadal Variation in % |
|---|---|---|---|---|---|
| 1901 | 5955 | 6272 | 317 | 1053 | — |
| 1911 | 5182 | 5435 | 253 | 1049 | -0.37 |
| 1921 | 5364 | 5436 | 72 | 1013 | -3.43 |
| 1931 | 6266 | 5966 | -300 | 952 | -6.02 |
| 1941 | 6967 | 6952 | -15 | 997 | 4.72 |
| 1951 | 5447 | 5067 | -380 | 930 | -6.72 |
| 1961 | 7391 | 6843 | -548 | 926 | -0.43 |
| 1971 | 100229 | 8918 | -1111 | 889 | -3.99 |
| 1981 | 13031 | 11216 | -1858 | 860 | -3.26 |
| 1991 | 14746 | 12947 | -1799 | 878 | 2.09 |

*Source* : Computed from District Census Handbook, Part XII-A&B 1991.

## Area of High Sex Ratio

The western and the southern part of the town including three wards 8, 13 and 15 lie in this category. It has been noted that the ward 15 is a newly developed area where most of the population are immigrants from the nearby surrounding villages and it is one of the second highest literate area of the town. It has also been observed that most of the families who have migrated to the town belong to the old age (mostly female) who look after home on working time.

## Area of Very High Sex Ratio

There are 4 wards *viz.* 5, 7, 9 and 12 situated in the core area and south-eastern part of the town. The highest sex ratio may be noted in ward No. 9 and ward No. 7 accounted for 911 and 905 respectively.

### *Literacy*

Figure 22.6 shows spatial distribution of literate persons in Jhajjar town during 1991. The literacy of the town was 74.3 per cent close to the district's urban literacy *i.e.* 75.36 per cent. But the female literacy was 61 per cent which was so low from the general literacy of the

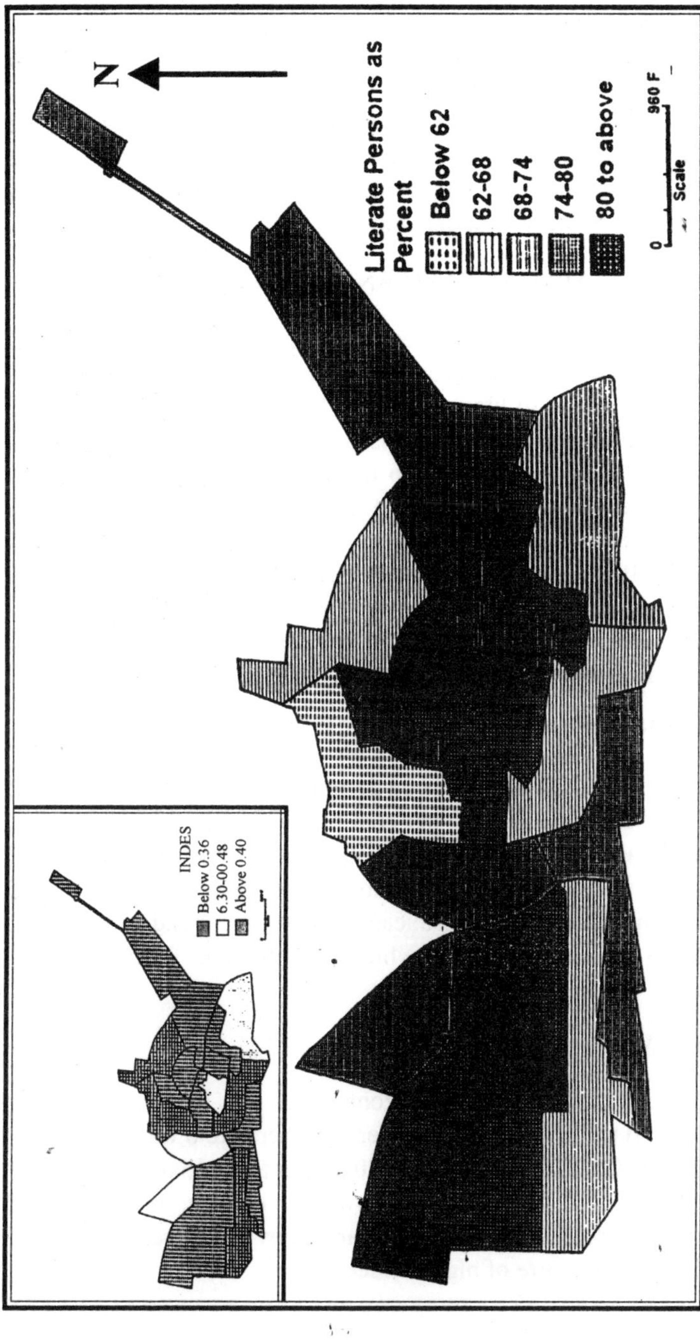


**Fig. 22.6 :** Literacy of Jhajjar Town, 1991

male literacy *i.e.* 86 per cent which reveals the fact that females have been mostly confined for long to the four walls as a dutiful home bride (Chandana, 1986). It has 10 high schools, 11 junior secondary schools and 14 primary schools provide grass root of education while for the higher and technical studies, there is one Arts and Science college, 2 vocational training institutes, 1 Polytechnic and 1 Women Arts College in the area under study.

## SPATIAL PATTERN OF LITERACY

There are many factors such as educational institutions, population of scheduled castes, persons engaged in tertiary activities and other which are directly related to literacy pattern. It has also been seen that the literacy declines with increasing distance but it is also related with the standard of the people. Fig. 22.6 reveals 5 categories of literacy of Jhajjar town, 1999. But for detail description it has been divided into three categories of literate population by clubbing I and II (into 1 category), III and IV (into 2 category) and V (3 category) respectively. Thus first category includes area of low literacy (<68%) followed by second category 68 per cent to 80 per cent and the third category (>80%). The detail analysis of pattern of the literacy is given as follows:

### Area of High Literacy

The area of high literacy has been designated in ward No. 5, 9, 11, 12 and 15 where more than 80 per cent people are literate. As the data denotes that there is high literacy rate with 94.2 per cent males and 74.3 per cent females due to very low percentage of scheduled caste population, concentration of educational institutions and most of them belong to high income group which become main factors for high literacy.

### Area of Moderate Literacy

This zone is known as transition zone which falls in the zone of high literacy and the low area of low literacy. There are 6 wards *viz.*, 1, 3, 6, 7, 8 and 10 where 68 per cent to 80 per cent people are literate. Due to existence of P. G. college, a polytechnic college, one Vocational Training Centre, Kendriya Vidyalaya and many private schools in ward No. 6 becomes centre of high literacy.

## Area of Low Literacy

It includes four wards namely 2, 4, 13, and 14 of low literacy area of the town. There are peripheral areas where agricultural labourers and cultivators are dominated. There is dominancy of scheduled castes population in ward No.2 in which lowest literacy *i.e.* 59.2 per cent with maximum literacy differential *i.e.* 0.56 per cent among males-females has been noted. In ward no. 4, 27.5 per cent of scheduled caste population inhabited which may be the highest proportion of the total population. Its male-female differential *i.e.* 0.56 per cent which shows 81per cent males and 45.5 per cent females are literate. The same proportion has also been noted in ward No. 13 and 14 where more or less same literacy differential is noted as 0.44 per cent and 0.48 per cent respectively. It may also be noted that these four wards have higher differential ratio of the whole town which indicates that the lowest literacy area lies in this region (Table 22.4).

**Table 22.4 :** Literacy of Jhajjar Town, 1991

| Wards | Male | Female | Differential by Sex | Total |
|---|---|---|---|---|
| 1 | 89.4 | 62.4 | 0.35 | 76.9 |
| 2 | 74.2 | 40.6 | 0.56 | 59.2 |
| 3 | 86.0 | 63.4 | 0.29 | 75.6 |
| 4 | 81.0 | 45.5 | 0.55 | 64.2 |
| 5 | 91.5 | 68.9 | 0.28 | 80.7 |
| 6 | 83.9 | 63.7 | 0.27 | 74.6 |
| 7 | 85.1 | 59.7 | 0.34 | 73.1 |
| 8 | 79.9 | 69.1 | 0.14 | 74.8 |
| 9 | 92.8 | 75.0 | 0.21 | 84.3 |
| 10 | 90.7 | 67.2 | 0.29 | 79.7 |
| 11 | 91.3 | 64.0 | 0.34 | 78.7 |
| 12 | 92.6 | 68.6 | 0.29 | 81.1 |
| 13 | 77.2 | 48.9 | 0.44 | 63.8 |
| 14 | 77.7 | 37.2 | 0.48 | 63.5 |
| 15 | 94.2 | 73.3 | 0.24 | 84.5 |
| Total | 86.0 | 61.0 | 0.33 | 74.3 |

* Literacy is in percentage population below 7 is excluded.

*Source* : Computed from Town Director, Part IX-A, Series 8, Haryana, 1991.

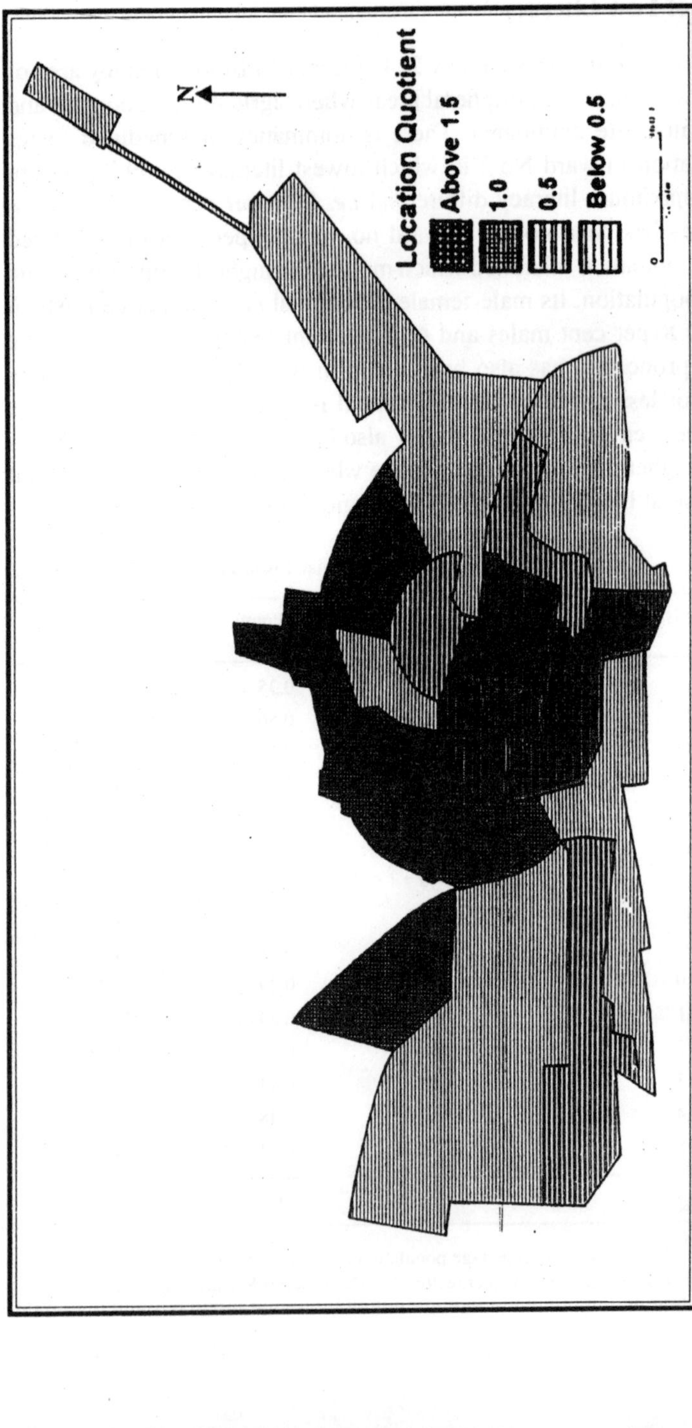


**Fig.22.7 :** Scheduled Castes Population of Jhajjar Town, 1991

## STRUCTURE OF SCHEDULED CASTE POPULATION

The term scheduled caste was first introduced by British Empire. There are numerous caste including in this caste in India but in Mariana 37 castes are included in it. They are considered as the lowest strata of the society and comprises about 16 per cent of the total population of the town which is higher than that of district's urban scheduled caste average population (14.96%) and of the state urban scheduled caste average population (14.20%). A slight increase in scheduled caste population is observed from A.D. 1981 (16.59%) to 1991 (16.89%). If we see the morphology of the town itself show the very process of setting down of different social groups in the urban space. The *mohalla, basti* and *tola* formation within the urban centre indicates the division of the urban space between the caste, community and occupation group as Ahmed (1999) also discussed in details in his book *Social Geography*. Each and every caste has separate *mohalla* for their respective caste and this pattern is valid for all regions in India.

## SPATIAL DISTRIBUTION AND PATTERN OF SCHEDULED CASTE

The concentration of scheduled castes is unevenly distributed over the town. It reflects the personalities of inhabitants and life style. Their main occupation is still pollute, unclean work, agricultural labours and some of them engaged in small scale industries. (Fig. 22.7) shows four categories of population distribution over the town *viz*., (i) Area of high proportion (>24%) of scheduled castes, (ii) Area of average high proportion (16% to 24%), (iii) Area of low proportion (8% to 16%), and (iv) Area of very low proportion (< 8%). The area of high concentration of scheduled castes found in Ward No. 1 where Khatik and Jatia are leading and engaged in leather works. Due to high dominance, this ward is known as Jatia mohalla. Another high concentration area is Beri gate which has mixture of many scheduled castes. Its southern part is also dominated by backward castes population like Gujar and Saini. The third highly concentration of scheduled population found in Mata gate area where Chamar, Dhanak, Doom and Balmiki are concentrated. Outer area of this agglomeration are generally performed clean services. In general it has been found that this category of highly concentrated of scheduled caste population has high percentage of agriculture labourer menial job, manufacturing processing other than household industry.

Area of average high proportion of scheduled caste population is recorded in Ward No. 10, 11, 12 and 13. All these wards lie in walled town but located at peripheral area. The southern part of Ward 12 is dominated while the west southern part of Ward 11 is concentrated by Chamar and Dhanak whose main occupation is unclean and polluted. Now it comes in the centre of old city.

The area of low population of scheduled caste has dispersed character lies in Wards 5, 9 and 14 where their proportion noted as 16.8 per cent below the average per cent of the Jhajjar town.

The area of very low proportion has been developed in the post partition expansion time. They spread over the entire Ward of 3, 6, 7, 13 and 15 in a form of isolated patches and do not form a compact contiguous area.

### Occupational Structure

Economic activity denotes man-land relationship including production and services. The status of the population depends on the degree of economic development of that area. Mehta (1967) observed that in most of the society of the world, the earning of bread was primarily a male responsibility. Hence the male participation rate is ubiquitously more than the female. Chandana (1986) also observed the same result that the female participation in work is low depending on the status which the female enjoy in the society. (Table 22.4) shows occupation and work force structure of town-Jhajjar–1991. It reveals three folds major division *i.e.* (i) Agricultural activities, (ii) Manufacturing and industries, and (iii) Services. The first category includes cultivators, agricultural labourers and livestock. Rearing share 28.53 per cent of the total workers followed by manufacturing and industries in which only 16.38 per cent population engaged and in the third category of working force *i.e.* services 55.05 per cent population engaged. It shows that the town is dominated by tertiary activities in which more than 55 per cent of workers are active while in agricultural activities only 28.63 per cent people are involved and less than 16 per cent population engaged in the industrial activities.

## SPATIAL DISTRIBUTION OF WORKERS

Fig. 22.8 shows active population by their occupation of Jhajjar towns. It reveals four categories of working forces *viz.* (i) area of very low

(<24%) proportion, (ii) area of low proportion (24% to 26%), (iii) area of moderate high proportion (26% to 28%) and (iv) area of high proportion (>28%).

AREA OF VERY LOW PROPORTION OF WORKERS (< 24%)

It has been noted that there are four wards *viz*., 5, 7, 8 and 13 of very low proportion of working force. The Ward No. 5 is centrally located in walled town while the Ward No. 7, 8, and 13 situated on south peripheral area. The central part of the town *i.e.* Ward No. 5 is mainly engaged in commercial activities as the percentage of workers in "trade and commerce" is high 43.27 per cent while its primary sector working force proportion is the lowest. But in Ward No. 7, 8, and 13 the proportion of working force is high in primary sector as noted 51.06 per cent engaged in agricultural activities as well as agricultural labourers.

**Table 22.5 :** Occupation and Work force Structure of Town : 1991

| Occupational Category | Number of Workers | | | Percentage of Workers | | |
|---|---|---|---|---|---|---|
| | Male | Female | Total | Male | Female | Total |
| Cultivators | 1129 | 153 | 1282 | 16.87 | 15.34 | 17.78 |
| Agricultural Labourers | 700 | 31 | 731 | 10.46 | 6.37 | 10.14 |
| Livestock Rearing | 42 | 1 | 43 | 0.62 | .20 | 59.81 |
| Mining & Quarrying | 1 | - | 1 | -.01 | - | 0.01 |
| Manufacturing including household industry | 142 | 6 | 148 | 2.12 | 1.23 | 2.05 |
| Industries | 759 | 5 | 764 | 11.34 | 1.02 | 10.59 |
| Construction | 253 | 2 | 255 | 3.78 | .41 | 3.53 |
| Trade and Commerce | 1666 | 6 | 1672 | 24.90 | 1.23 | 23.19 |
| Transport and Storage | 297 | - | 297 | 4.44 | - | 4.12 |
| Other Service | 1699 | 283 | 1982 | 25.39 | 58.23 | 27.49 |
| Total | 6689 | 486 | 7175 | 92.79 | 7.20 | 100 |

In total worker, male/female, marginal workers are also added.

*Source* : Computed from District Census Handbook. Part XA and XB. Jhajjar District. 1999.

Fig. 22.8 : Active Population by their Occupation, 1991

**Area of Low Proportion of Workers (24% to 26%)**

The area of low proportion of workers found in Ward 1, 4, 6 and 14 which are situated at peripheral part of the walled town. But Ward No.1 has dominance of workers who are dominated in manufacturing, trade and commerce which shares 26:38 per cent while in Ward 4, 14 there are 62.38 per cent of working force engaged in primary sector (including 30.23 per cent cultivators and 31.42 per cent) as agricultural labourers which reflects pure village economy.

**Area of High Proportion of Workers (26% to 28%)**

There are four Ward Nos. 2, 9, 10 and 12 lie in the high proportion of workers of the town. Most of the wards situated in the walled city except Ward No. 2 where high proportion of workers are engaged in territory activities. The highest proportion of workers (81.13 per cent) who are engaged in 'trade and commerce' belong to Ward No. 9 in which high commercial activities has already been found.

AREA OF VERY HIGH PROPORTION OF WORKERS (> 28%)

Table 22.5 clears that there are two wards 3 and 15 which belong to this category of very high proportion of worker as per 1991 census. As data shows that 51.22 per cent of working population are engaged in 'other services' in Ward No. 3 while 41.81per cent workers engaged in primary activities in Ward No. 15 in which 26.61 per cent people are engaged in cultivation, 15.86 per cent as agricultural labourers. Most of them are immigrants of the neighbouring villages. The statement of C. D. Deshpande (1980) is also proved that the proportion of workers is high in those areas where the proportion of immigrants is higher.

## CONCLUSION

The changing scene of population structure of Jhajjar town focuses on two facts : (i) Very slow growth of population (A.D. 1901-A.D.1941), (ii) Fast growth of population (post-freedom with a declined trained of population during A.D 1951-A.D. 2001). As facts and figures reveal that the trend of growth of population has been declined from 35.38 per cent (1951) to 14.21 per cent (1991) which is less than that of the natural growth rate of the state *i.e.* 22 per cent. Most of the population is concentrated in the central part of the town with their own castes, creeds while the peripheral areas inhabited by mixed population of various castes, creeds who come from nearby villages. Generally they use to stay/inhabit in the peripheral part of the town which is known as "colony". The area of high literacy is related to high income, availability of the educational institution and share of low percentage of scheduled castes population. The sex ratio is also related with literacy occupation of the people, such as businessmen did not bother about education. Hence low sex ratio *i.e.* 827 females per thousand males recorded in this community. All modern colony, sectors (private and government) along Jhajjar and Bahadurgarh road and some part of north-west and south-west occupied by district administrative employees have high literacy rate with low sex ratio *i.e.* 875 females per thousand males which is still lower than that of the average sex ratio of the town. It has been proved by going through the Ward No. 5, 7, 8, 9, 12, 13 and 15 of the area under study. These wards have low proportion of scheduled castes population, high income group of people with high literacy rate. In contrary the high proportion of scheduled *viz*, Khatik, Jatia, Chamar, Dhanak, Dom and Balmiki with very low percentage of the literacy rate have dominated in Ward No. 2, 3, 4, 6 of the town which may be characterized as high sex ratio *i.e.* more than 895 females per thousand males. The proportion of workers is also high in those areas where high percentage of immigration has been noted. For example, in Ward No. 3 more than 51.22 per cent of working population are engaged in "other services" and in Ward No. 15, 41.81 per cent workers engaged in primary activities in which 26.61 per cent population engaged in cultivation and 15.86 per cent engaged in agricultural labourer, which shows a dynamic characteristics of population dominated by younger in all walk of life in the area under study. It is an indicator of fast progressive nature of the town in the twenty-first century.

REFERENCES

Ahmad, Aijazuddin (1999), *Social Geography*, Jaipur: Rawat Publication.

Alam, Manzoor. S. & Fatima Ali Khan (1987), *Prespectives on Urbanization and Migration, India and U.S.S.R.*, New Delhi: Allied Publisher Pvt. Ltd.

Aziz, Abdul (July 1983), "Man-Land Ratio in Town of Uttar Pradesh", *The Geographer*, Vol. XXX No.2, p. 37.

Bali, Ram & Nisha Rani Gupta (June, 1997), "Size Distribution of Urban Centre in Bihar Uplands" *National Geographical Journal of India*, Vol. 43, p. 2.

Bawa, K. S. & Kainth. (1985), "Why this rush toward cities", *Yojana*, Vol.29, No.13, p.15.

Bhagwati, A K. & B. Sahariah (1984), "Urban Centre and Spatial pattern of their road accessibility in Assam", *The Geographer*, Vol.46, No.3, p. 14.

Bose, A. (1970), *Urbanization in India*; An Inventory Source Material, Bombay: Academic Books Ltd.

Brandnock, R.W. (1984), *Urbanization in India : Case Syudy of the Developing World*, London; John Murray Publisher Ltd.

Brunn & William (1983), *Cities of the World*, New York: Harper and Row Publishers.

Carter, H. (1981), *The Study of Urban Geography*; III Edition, New Delhi; Heinemann Chandna, R. C. (1986) Geography of Population, Kalyani Publisher, New Delhi.

David Ley (1983), A Social Geography of the City, New York: Harper and Row Publishing

Desai, Anjana (June 1981), "Differential Perception of Residents to Environmental Quality' of an Urban Area–An Ecological Approach: A Case Study of Pune City, Trans. Inst *Indian Geography*, Vol. 43, No. 2, p. 155.

Deshpande, C. D. (July 1986), Urban Models and Indian Realities, *Trans. Inst. India Geography*, Vol. 8, No. 1-2.

Diddee, Jaymala and Semi Octania (July 1983), " Medium Towns as Development Nodes Trans Inst. *Indian Geography*, Vol. 15, No. 2, p. 57.

Debe, K. K. and C. S. Kumar. (June 1997), "Environmental Problem in Varanasi City, / Geographical Perspective" *National Geographical Journal of India*, Vol. 43. p. 2.

Garg, H. S. & Amar Singh (July 1997), " City size and the Industrial Location in the N. C R." *The Geographer*, Vol. XXIV, No. 2; p. 37.

Ghosh, Bonani (March 1976), "Geographical Note: Trend and Pattern of Population Growt of Calcutta City," *Geographical Review of India*, Vol. 38, No. I, p 85.

Kulkarni, K. M. (1984), Geography of Crowding and Human Response, Concept Publishin Company, New Delhi.

Kulkarni, K. M. (1984), *Urban Structure and Interaction*, Concept Publishing Compan New Delhi.

Kumar, Ashwani ( March 1981), "Changes in the Occupational Structure of Urban Populatio of Rohtak and Gurgaon Districts, 1961-71" *Geographical Review of India*, Vol. 4: No.1, p. 89.

Malathi, S. (Dec. 1993), "Structural Characteristics of Small Towns" *The India Geographical Journal*, Vol. 68, No. 2, p. 18.

Mehta, S. (1967), "India's Rural Female Working Force and its Occupational Structure. / Geographical Analysis" *The Indian Geographical Journal*, Vol. 12, No. 1 & 2.

Milling, Joseph (1980), *Housing, Social Policy and the State*, Groom Helm, London.

Mishra, G. K. *et al.* (1997), *Sustainable Urban Development*, Uppal Publishing House, New Delhi.

Mishra, H. N. (July 1990), "Reflection of Indian Urban Geography," *Trans Inst. Indian Geographer*, Vol. 12, No.2, pp. l, 4, 5.

Mishra, H. N. (Jan. 1975), "The Size and Spacing of Town in Umland of Allahabad" *The Geographer*, Vol. XII, No.1, pp. 5 & 45.

Mukherjee, S. (1993), Functional Classification of Indian Towns by Factor Cluster Method (1981-91), Monograph, I.I.P.S. Bombay.

Murphy, R. E. (1960), *The American City: An Urban Geography*, McGraw Hill, New York.

Phogat, S.R. (1978), *Inscriptions of Haryana*, Vishal Publications, Kurukshetra.

Piggot, S. (1945), *Some Ancient Cities of India*. Oxford University Press, Bombay.

Prabha, K. (1976), *Towns: A Structure Analysis*, Inter India Publications, New Delhi.

Prasad, Lalta (1984), *A Growth of Small Town—A Study of Ballia (U.P.)*, Concept Publishing Company, New Delhi.

Rao, B. K. ( Dec.1977), "Urban Land Use Map for Towns and Urban Agglomeration in Census of India," *National Geographical Journal of India*, Vol. XXII, Part 3-4, p. 60.

Rao, M. P. (1990), *Planning for Metropolitan Cities—A Suggestive Approach*, Concept Publishing Company, New Delhi.

Rao, R. M. & Simhadri (1999), *Indian Cities: Toward Next Millennium*, Rawat Publications, New Delhi.

Schnell G. A. & Mark S. M. (1982), *The Study of Population : Element, Pattern, Process*, A Bell and Howell Company, London.

Shandil, S. (Dec. 1992) "Evolution of Simla", *Geographical Review of India*, Vol. 54, No.4, p. 26.

Sharma, R. C. (1984), *South Asian Urban Experience*, Criteria Publications, New Delhi.

Singh, R. L. & R. P. B. Singh (Dec. 1978), "Concept of Morphological Analysis : Some Theoretical Postulations" *The National Geographical Journal of India*, Vol. 24, Part 3-4, p.16.

Wrong, H. D. (1956), *Population and Society*, Random House, New York.

Yadav, K. S. (1986), *Residential and Social Structure*, Inter India Publications, New Delhi.

# SECTION-III

# Asian Case Studies

23

# Supply and Demand of Compost in Rural Japan

## A Case of Tokyo Metropolitan Region

**HIROMICHI NAGASHIMA**

Environmentally conscious agriculture has become to be noticed in Japan after the new agricultural policy called "The Basic Direction of New Policies for Food, Agriculture and Rural Areas" in 1992. Specific section to promote this policy was opened at the Ministry of Agriculture, Forestry and Fisheries in the same year. Same kind of section was opened also at the office of all prefectures. The policy for environmentally conscious agriculture seems to be influenced by the consumer movement. There are several ways to realize environmentally conscious agriculture, *e.g.*, conservation of soil fertility with suitable use of compost, management of idle lands, organic farming, farming with less use of chemical fertilizers and agricultural chemicals or introduction of crop rotation systems. Compost is related to some of these ways to promote environmentally conscious agriculture.

The purpose of this chapter is to make clear the current situation of supply systems and demand for compost and to discuss the factors to give incentive for farmers in relation to the use of compost. The study area is Tokyo Metropolitan Region. This region shares 15.2 per cent of total number of dairy cows, 11.5 per cent of beef cattle and 20.8 per cent of poultry.

Number of cows per one dairy farm is 36 heads, beef cattle is 34 heads and poultry is 2,894.

### COMPOST USE IN FARMING

Compost has been the most fundamental fertilizer to conserve soil fertility in Japan. Fish manure or oil cake became to be used in the nineteenth century. Ammonium sulfate was introduced in 1930s. In case of rice cultivation in paddy fields, compost use per 0.1 ha. was 649 kg in 1960, but decreased to 115kg in 1996. Diffusion of chemical fertilizers since 1960s, introduction of agricultural machines instead of domestic animals and increase of elderly farmers are pointed out as reasons of the reduction of compost. Recently, however, production of compost has increased since 1980s, namely 72 thousand tonnes in 1970, 650 tonnes in 1980 and 3000 tonnes in 1997.

**Production and Supply of Compost**

Almost all compost is made by use of animal waste, although garbage became to be used for compost. Livestock industry developed as one of the growth sector of Japanese agriculture since 1960s. As a result of development of livestock industry, water pollution and smell were complained as environmental problems. This situation was amplified through urbanization, especially in Tokyo Metropolitan Region. Complaints reached the peak in 1973. Equipment for animal waste handling facilities was an urgent issue for livestock industry. The projects to improve animal waste handling facilities were carried out by use of their own fund and subsidies of the government. Now almost all livestock industries have their own handling facilities. Compost is treated through several ways *e.g.* for domestic use, to be sold, exchanged with other materials such as straw, etc. Recently they are very positive to sell compost as a way to gain income. Compost as centre of agricultural cooperative is another equipment to deal with animal waste in the community.

**Table 23.1 :** Number of Farm Households and Livestock in Tokyo Metropolitan Region (1995)

| | Number of Farm Households | Number of Livestock (thousand) | Average Number of Livestock per Farm Household |
|---|---|---|---|
| Dairy cattle | 8363 | 297 | 35.5 |
| Beef cattle | 7934 | 271 | 34.2 |
| Swine | 3788 | 1691 | 446.4 |
| Poultry | 4881 | 14123 | 2893.5 |

*Source :* Agriculture and Forestry Census, 1995.

## Demand for Compost

### *Demand for Compost is as Follows*

— *Conserving soil fertility.* Compost is used to avoid damage caused by successive planting of same crop. Compost is indispensable for vegetable production. Compost use of this type is observed in traditional vegetable production areas such as Miura, Kanagawa or Tomisato, Chiba. Crop rotation system used to be introduced together.

— *Organic Farming.* Organic farming is introduced in the production of rice, vegetable, fruits and specific crop such as arum root.

— Farming with less use of chemical fertilizers and agricultural chemicals. This type of farming seems to be suitable for the condition of high humidity like in Japan.

### *Development of Organic Farming*

(i) According to the guideline established by the Ministry of Agriculture, Forestry and Fisheries, organic agricultural products

**Table 23.2 :** Market for Organic Agricultural Products

| | Social Background | Organization for Marketing | Market System |
|---|---|---|---|
| 1970s | Movement of City Dwellers to Take Safe Foods | Co-partnership between Farmers and Consumers (Teikei) JOAA* | Delivered Directly from Farm (Sanchoku) |
| 1980s | Increase of Demand for Organic Agricultural Products Increase of Female with Job | Special enterprise dealing with Organic Agricultural Products Consumer's Coop. | Delivered to each house (Takuhai) |
| Second Half of 1990s | Standard of Indication of Organic Agri. Products | Department Store, Supermarket, Family Restaurant Trading Company (Shosha) | Organic Section at Wholesale Market |

* JOAA : Japan Organic Agriculture Association.

are the products produced without chemical fertilizers and agricultrural chemicals in the field where chemical fertilizers and agricultural chemicals have not been used for three years. Special agricultural products are the products produced by less use of chemical fertilizers and agricultural chemicals. In this chapter both of these agricultural types are shown as organic farming and products are shown as organic agricultural products.

(ii) Development of organic farming is divided into three phases. *First phase (1970s)* : The problem of environmental pollution became a serious social problem as a result of rapid economic development since 1960s. Movement to take safe foods were proceeded by city dwellers. One of the association for these movements was Japan Organic Agriculture Association established in 1971. The basic policy of this association was co-partnership between farmers and consumers (*Teikei*). Commodity was supplied directly from farmers to consumers (*Sanchoku*). *Second phase (1980s)*: This phase characterized is by special enterprises dealing with organic agricultural products. These special enterprises composed of citizen and student, vegetable man *etc*., include a feature of movement body aiming agriculture without agricultural chemicals. These types of enterprises were expanded rapidly through introducing delivery service to each member's house (*Takuhai*). Organic agricultural products were spread also through the enlargement of consumer's co-operatives in 1980s. Now total number of members is 14 million. Organic farming was introduced in some municipalities as a way to proceed ecological agriculture producing value-added products. *Third phase* (*Second half of 1990s*): Organic agricultural products have been sold as a value-added commodity at department store or supermarket. Organic vegetables have become to be served as a healthy menu at family restaurant. Trading companies (*Shosha*) have been expecting to expand their business in the market of organic foods.

### *Farmer's Attitude to Organic Farming*

Motivation for farmers to introduce organic farming is to supply safe foods, anxiety for the influence of agricultural chemicals on their health or to produce value-added agricultural products. Compost is supplied by themselves, or others such as stockbreeding farms or compost centre managed by agricultural co-operative. There are some issues to be conquered in farming with use of compost. For example, use of compost needs more labour, development of new market for products, yield per acre is reduced etc. According to the survey in Tokyo Metropolitan Region, compost are sometimes delivered by stockbreeding farmer or farmer's group to farmers with labour shortage or elderly farmers. Market for organic agricultural products have been expanded gradually from personal relation such as relatives or friends to organization such as consumer's cooperative or special enterprises. Recently organic agricultural products are dealt with by some agricultural cooperatives. Now farmers have some routes to sell their products. Some groups sell their products at farmer's market in the morning.

## Share of Organic Farming

According to the survey of the Ministry of Agriculture, Forestry and Fisheries in 1997, percentage of organic farmers in Japan is as follows :

Rice planting : 1,07,300 farms (5% of total farms in 1995)

Vegetable : 14,900 farms (1% of total farms in 1995)

Fruits : 23,200 farms (5% of total farms in 1995)

Cultivated land for organic farming in 1993 was estimated between 1,29,000 ha. (2.5% of total farmland) and 2,94,000 ha. (5.7%). Sixty to seventy per cent of organic farmers in Japan will continue their farming with the same size. Twenty to twenty-five per cent of farmers expect to enlarge the size of organic farming. In Tokyo Metropolitan Region, organic farming not including farming with less use of agricultural chemicals is introduced in 123 municipalities (5.2% of total municipalities, 1995) Table 23.1.

## New Policies to Promote Compost Use by the Prefecture and Agricultural Cooperative

In Saitama, a project to promote organic farming has been carried out by the prefectural government since 1997. The goal of this project is

**Table 23.3 :** Some Special Enterprises dealing with Organic Agricultural Products

*Person, Yen*

| Management | Number of Members | Number of Farmers | Admission Fee Membership Fee/Year | Main Area of Delivery |
|---|---|---|---|---|
| Citizen's Association for Recycle Movement (Tokyo) | 55,000 | 2,000 | 5,000<br>5,000 | Tokyo Metro. Region<br>Hokkaido<br>Osaka etc. |
| Daichi Corporation (Tokyo) | 46,400 | 2,500 | 5,000<br>1,000 | Tokyo Metro. Region |
| Polan Organic Food Delivery Corporation (Tokyo) | 7,000 | 1,200 | 5,000<br>5,000 | Tokyo Metro. Region |
| Shizenha Network* (Ibaraki) | 1,000 | 23 | 3,000<br>0 | Ibaraki Pref. |

* Agricultural Producer's Co-operative Corporation.

to reduce the use of chemical fertilizers and agricultural chemicals by half until 2010 (1995 basis). Use of non-used local resources such as animal waste, straw or garbage are expected to be recycled. A group of farmers composed of eleven farmers with the age of 30-40 years was organized in Fukaya in 1998. In Chiba, a project called Network System to Promote Use of Compost was introduced by prefectural government in 1995. Information of compost such as compost producer's name, quality chart of compost, compost price, is shown on the board of personal computer. More than 300 farmers have joined this system. In Yamanashi, linkage of compost and value-added rice production has been proceeded by agricultural cooperative.

## CONCLUSION

(i) Production and supply system of compost have been prepared already. Demand for compost seems to have been increased with the diffusion of organic farming.

(ii) Organic farming is mainly carried out by farmers who have their own idea about farming. Conservation of soil fertility is recognized as the most fundamental factor for farming. Therefore, compost is treated as indispensable materials. Organic farming or farming with less use of chemical fertilizers and agricultural chemicals is sometimes conducted by agricultural cooperatives as their own way for survival. These cooperatives are very positive to research and to develop their own market.

(iii) Organic farming has been noticed as an alternative agriculture in Japan since 1970s. However share of farmer and farmland for organic farming is limited.

(iv) Market of organic agricultural products seems to have a tendency to be expanded with the increase of consumers who would like to take safe foods. But an amount of demand will be supplied by farmers who have already introduced organic farming. In case of special enterprise, demand brought by new member was fulfilled by increase in production of contracted farmers. Agricultural products with value-added price and development of marketing system for these products will be incentive factors for farmers to introduce organic farming. In Chiba, a farmer's group involves part-time farmers as quasi member who produce specific crop. Such a type of organization suggests a way to increase the use of compost to the farmers.

### REFERENCES

Japan Organic Agriculture Association: The First IFOAM Asian Conference 1993, JOAA, 1994.

Kokumin seikatsu centre:Tayouka suru yuki nousanbutsu no ryutsu (Diversified Marketing Systems of Organic Agricultural Products) Gakuyo Shobo, 1992.

The Ministry of Agriculture, Forestry and Fisheries: The Prompt Report of Environmentally Conscious Agriculture *Crop Farming*, 1997.

Tokyo Metropolitan Government : Report of the Commission on Providing Marketing Systems for Organic Agricultural Products, 1996.

# 24

# Vulnerability and Institutions

## The Role of Towns for Rural Livelihood Security in Nepal

**des. MARTIN RAITHELHUBER**

### URBANIZATION AND RURAL-URBAN INTERACTION IN NEPAL

Often, development planners as well as researchers treat urbanization as a process that affects towns and the urban population while neglecting the effects of urbanization on rural areas. The problems for urban development caused by massive rural in-migration, for example, are well documented whereas little is known about the problems of rural households with or through urbanization.

Nepal is often pictured as a country of villages with most people doing agriculture and living in rural areas. However, this is only part of the truth. During the last decades, Nepal has experienced a rapid urbanization process, which is characterized by the evolvement of small and medium sized towns in the country's southern Terai flatland. While in the early 1950s, just 3 per cent of the population was living in a small number of towns, today, about 15 per cent of the total population is living in 58 towns (unpublished census data, CBS 2001). Although the majority of the population is still living in rural areas, their connection to towns through roads and telecommunication is improving. This chapter presents the results of a household survey performed in 1998-99 in the rural hinterland of Butwal Municipality in Western Nepal (Raithelhuber, 2001). The study sets focus on those who stay back in the village, and investigates how and why they live there while migration to urban areas is a major process in rural areas.

Most rural households are somehow involved in a grain-based, mainly rain-fed subsistence agriculture, and depend strongly on natural resources such as land, grassland and forest. However, a constant population growth of about 2.4 per cent per year means that more and more people have to share the same natural resources, and that there is increasing pressure on these resources. The use of industrially produced inputs like chemical fertilizers and high yielding varieties is not widespread. Therefore, the productivity of the fields is stagnant or even declining. Consequently, the food self-sufficiency of rural households, *i.e.* the number of months a household can live on food from own agriculture, is decreasing. In the study area, around half of the households have a food self-sufficiency for six months or less.

The main hypothesis of the study is that the rural economy is changing rapidly due to population growth, limited natural resources, better accessibility of towns, and rapid urbanization. This change implies increasing rural-urban interaction because the possibilities to make a living based on subsistence agriculture are diminishing. Some rural households will profit from new opportunities like access to urban markets. Others will not benefit but face new risks or old risks in a different way.

A number of questions arise from this hypothesis. Where does the income come from to cover food demand for the rest of the year? How does improved accessibility of towns affect rural livelihoods? Which households can profit from new income opportunities that might come up, and which households cannot? Which risks do rural households face when pursuing these strategies?

## STUDY AREA IN WESTERN NEPAL

Butwal is a medium-sized foothill town of 80,000 inhabitants (2001), situated in Western Nepal just 20 km north of the Indian-Nepalese border. The opening up of vast areas in the adjoining Terai flatland for settlement after the eradication of malaria in 1950s and its location at a major highway junction, has led to a rapid growth of the urban population. At the present rate, Butwal is doubling its population every 10 years. The town is a business centre of regional importance, and the location of a large retail and wholesale market for vegetables. For the field study, three villages with different accessibilities from Butwal were selected, representing the different ecological settings in the hills and in the Terai flatland (see Fig. 24.1). The results from two of the studied villages, the hill village Kachal and the Terai village Semlar, are presented here.

Kachal is a typical hill village. The houses of the village are scattered on a south-facing slope between 700 and 1200 m.s.l. There is no electricity supply, no telephone line and no road access. The inhabitants of Kachal can reach the highway leading to Butwal with a five hours walk, during which they have to cross a river twelve times without bridges. After having reached the highway, it is just another

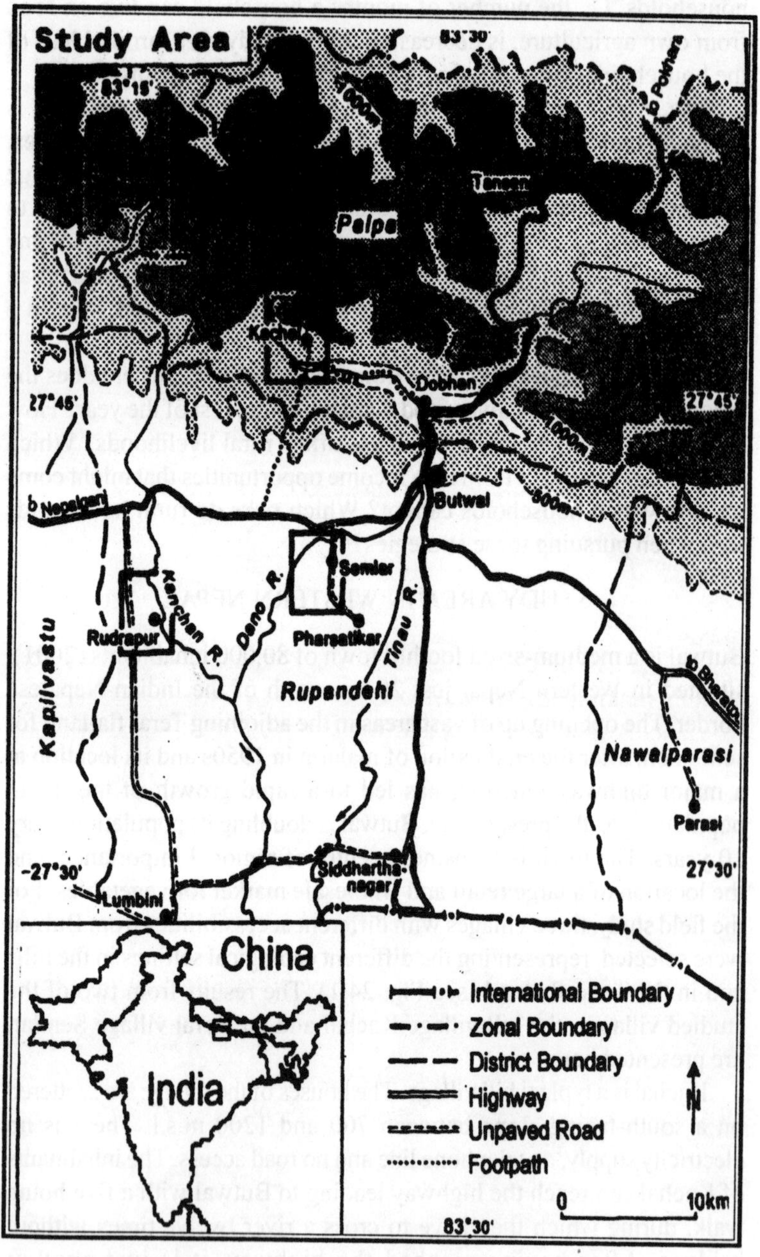


**Fig. 24.1 :** Study Area. Draft : M. Raithelhuber Cartography : H. Nischk.

5 km by bus to Butwal. The main features of Kachal are an extremely high percentage (60%) of temporary male labour migrants, most of them heading for Indian towns and a high percentage of households (75%) which are involved in cottage production (grass ropes, brooms, strings, bamboo baskets).

Semlar is a peri-urban village in the outskirts of Butwal. The village is well connected with the town, which can be reached either by one of the frequent busses and jeeps or by bicycle. In contrast to Kachal, where most households have at least some land, although not enough to produce enough food for their own consumption, 28 per cent of all households in Semlar have no land at all. At the same time, 47 per cent of the households produce grain surplus, which indicates a high unevenness in land distribution. Some households are engaged in commercial vegetable production, an income strategy, which could not be found in the other study villages.

The field survey in the study villages included a quantitative phase based on PRA methods (participatory rural appraisal) and a 30 per cent random sample questionnaire survey. The centrepiece of the PRA was a wealth ranking of all households in the study villages by key informants (I being the wealthiest and IV the poorest group). This wealth ranking served to stratify the sample, in order to include households of all socio-economic strata. In every village, 36 to 39 households were interviewed about their livelihood strategies over the last twelve months.

## VULNERABILITY AND INSTITUTIONS

In order to analyse rural-urban interaction and its role for rural livelihood security, new concepts from the field of institutional theory and the concept of vulnerability with its main elements "risk" and "coping strategies" were used.

The vulnerability concept originates from a critique of poverty research, which was mainly based on econometric parameters (*cf.* Swift, 1989). However, these approaches could not explain why people became poor and which groups had an especially high risk of becoming poor. The vulnerability concept aims to overcome these shortcomings with an analytical, multi-perspective approach (see Fig. 24.2). Vulnerability has two analytical sides (*cf.* Bohle, 2001; Watts & Bohle 1993):

- An external side (exposure to risks), which can be analysed using political economy, political ecology and entitlement approaches.
- An internal side (coping capacity), which is defined by political, social, ecological, and economic assets.

Households can be considered as actors (*cf.* Long & Ploeg, 1994) who try to make a living. Their action space expands between the exposure to risks and their capacity to cope with these risks. A high degree of exposure and a low coping capacity results in a limited space of action, and causes vulnerability. The more or less successful attempts of households to make a living are strategic actions of some regularity pursued over a certain time. These strategic actions over time are called

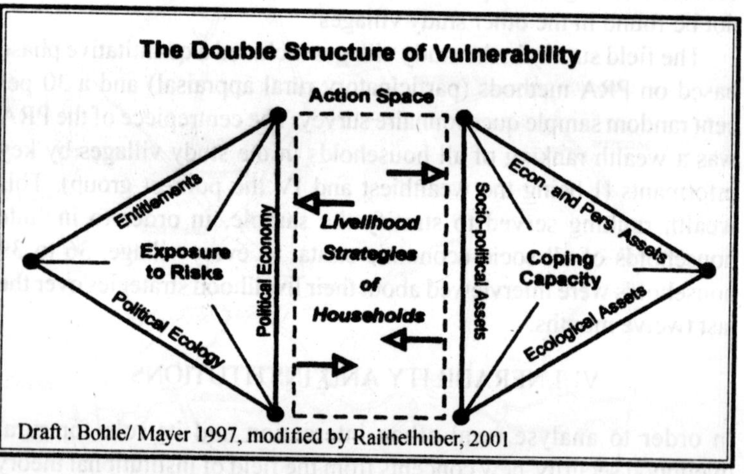

Draft : Bohle/ Mayer 1997, modified by Raithelhuber, 2001

**Fig. 24.2 :** The Two Sides of Vulnerability

livelihood strategies, here. Together, all livelihood strategies form a household's livelihood pattern. The study does not only cover the livelihood strategies of rural households, *i.e.* the activities to make a living, but also the conditions, which constitute the framework for these activities. These conditions can be analysed by sharpening the analytical categories of the vulnerability concept, risk of exposure and coping capacity, with an institution-theoretical perspective.

In recent years, there have been various contributions to institutional theory from scientist with different scientific backgrounds. Anthony Giddens' Theory of Structuration and Douglass C. North's work about the New Institutional Economics are among those with the greatest influence. Giddens developed the concept of "duality of structure and action" (Giddens, 1984). According to him, institutions are social structures, which are continuously produced and reproduced by the interaction of individual actors. In a simplified definition, his institutions are patterns of behaviour, which change slowly over time. The New Institutional Economics deals especially with those institutions, which structure the economic activities of actors. North's considers institutions as "the rules of the game in a society" (North, 1990, p. 3), which have a dual function. On the one hand, institutions reduce the number of possible ways of behaviour. Thus, they restrict the action spaces of actors and constrain human interaction. On the other hand, institutions enable interaction and make interaction easier, because they reduce the complexity of situations by limiting choice to a manageable range of options (*cf.* North, 1995). Although the New Institutional Economics acknowledges the reciprocal relationship between institutions and action, it still considers institutions as something external to human interaction. Institutions, in the context of the New Institutional Economics, are shaped and changed by actors, which means that they are rather institutionalised social rules than structural properties of human behaviour. North's "rules of the game" and Giddens' institutions are not directly compatible, as they argue on different levels of abstraction. However, irrespective of their grade of formalization, all social rules in a society have their base on underlying institutions, which, consciously or unconsciously, help human beings to interpret the actions of their interaction partners, to understand the meanings to their actions, and to choose a reaction they think appropriate. While Giddens' rather abstract institutions help to understand the reciprocal relationship between individual actions and long-lasting structures of human interactions on a theoretical level, North's 'institutions as rules' are helpful to analyse how and why social rules structure human interaction in the 'real world'.

Keeping in mind the different levels of abstractions, the term institution is used in this study for an institutional analysis of livelihood

people from Kachal is the unpredictability of prices. The prices offered by the wholesalers change frequently and sometimes within minutes, depending on the number of wholesalers present, the time of the day, and the amount of products offered by the villagers at a certain point of time. Prices can fall up to 50 per cent of their average. These changes do not depend on the season or customer demand. The cottage products are storable, and customer demand is more or less stable over the year. The villagers are forced to sell once they have reached Dobhan as there is no storage facility, and they need the money to buy grain. Going down to Butwal's weekly market, which takes place at the same two days of the week, would consume even more time and involve the cost for the bus ticket plus a luggage fee. In contrast to the informal weekly market in Dobhan, in Butwal there is an entry fee for the weekly market (rupees 10 per vendor irrespective of the amount of goods brought for sale). This is not attractive for the majority of the villagers who sell only small amounts of goods. Those who sell are mostly women, because a majority of the men (60%) are gone for temporary migration in the dry winter season, when cottage production is on a peak. Many women (42%) are illiterate and have been educated not to speak up against men. They feel that they are not in a position to bargain successfully with the male, literate and eloquent wholesalers. People from Kachal do not organize their marketing activities, nor do they have delivery contracts with the wholesalers. Interestingly, the wholesalers try to avoid the market situation at times when supply is low. Then, they move to places closer to the villages in order to intercept villagers on their way to the market.

The fact that the bargaining position of the villagers is low compared to the wholesalers' and marketing risks are almost entirely on the shoulders of the villagers explains partly why the production and marketing of cottage products contributes only to a small extent to the income of the study households. Labour input for cottage production is high while it is unpredictable how high the profit will be. The main rationale of their livelihood pattern is to spread and avoid risks by keeping a balance between long-term strategies cash income (like long-distance labour migration) or food security (like subsistence agriculture) and strategies providing cash income at shorter notice.

## Marketing of Vegetables in Semlar

Having analysed the marketing activities at Dobhan, the question arises what are the preconditions to more profit from rural-urban interaction? The livelihood patterns of households living in Semlar give some hints (see Fig. 24.4).

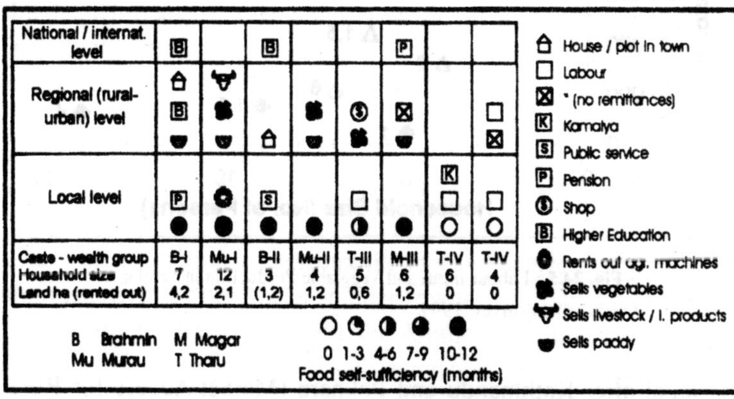


**Fig. 24.4 :** Exemplary Livelihood Patterns in Semlar

*Source:* Own survey, 1999.

In Semlar, several households, most of them belonging to the Murau caste, are highly engaged in commercial vegetable production. These households grow paddy in summer, and use pump-wells for vegetable irrigation in winter. They sell their vegetable produce at the weekly market in Butwal and at several smaller weekly markets in nearby rural market centres, and earn up to rupees 60,000 per year. Labour input is the main factor that determines vegetable production whereas the size of the land holding is of secondary importance (see Fig. 24.5).

In recent years, *dal bhat,* the staple food consisting of lentils and rice, has become *dal bhat* tarkarari, lentils and rice with vegetables, for more and more people. Now, vegetables are a part of the daily food of the growing urban population, at least for those who can afford it. Therefore, the demand for vegetables is high all the year round. The weekly market in Butwal is the third largest wholesale vegetable market

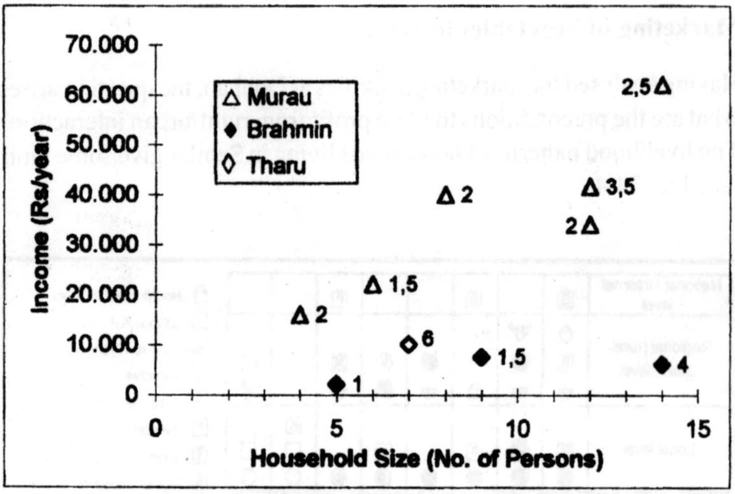


**Fig. 24.5 : Labour Input and Vegetable Production in Semlar**

*Source:* Own survey, 1999.

in Nepal after Kathmandu and Pokhara (Market Access for Rural Development, 1998). Given these promising circumstances, it is not plausible why only households, which can produce grain surplus, use this strategy. Why do not more households engage in vegetable production to earn the cash money, and prefer to look for wage labour?

Households, which engage in vegetable farming, have to cope with various risks. Although there is demand for vegetables all the year round, prices show high seasonal variations. The price for white cabbage sometimes falls from rupees 10 to just rupees 2 per kg in the high season. In addition to that, the vegetable farmers have to sell off their perishable produce in a short period after the harvest, as there are no cold stores available in the Butwal area. Vegetable prices in Nepal are highly influenced by the Indian vegetable market. About 75 per cent (weight) of the vegetables traded at the weekly market in Butwal are Indian imports. A harvest failure of a booster harvest in India can cause considerable price changes in Nepal. All the vegetable producing households do the production, transport and retailing of vegetables themselves without employing workers. Thus, they get a higher share of the price difference between farm gate prices and retail prices. However, all these activities are time-consuming and require workforce.

In contrast to a grain-based production pattern with its slack season in winter, vegetable farming requires the full workforce of all household members throughout the year. Labour migration, therefore, is no viable option for the vegetable farmers, and none of the vegetable-producing households has labour migrants.

Currently, the strategy of commercial vegetable farming is no attractive option for households with low food self-sufficiency, firstly because of the high risks of production losses either through pests and diseases or during transport and because of the perishability of certain vegetables. Secondly, vegetable farming is not compatible with livelihood patterns, which include wage labour, a permanent job or labour migration. Households with few assets and no regular income have to keep the balance between long-term and short-term income strategies. They have to rely on wage labour to meet their short-term cash needs, a strategy which does not harmonize with the labour-intensive vegetable farming. Households with a secure asset base consisting of a large land holding and enough work forces can profit most from vegetable farming. However, some households, which have the preconditions for vegetable farming, prefer other strategies such as higher education for the next generation, renting out the land, getting office and government jobs. These households are involved in a restructuring of their livelihood pattern, which eventually leads to giving up farming altogether, renting out the land, and transferring the residence to towns.

## RESULTS AND CONCLUSIONS

Almost all households in the study area rely partly on non-agricultural livelihood strategies on regional and or national/international levels. In contrast to a common assumption that households which are located in a greater distance to the nearest urban centre are less engaged in rural-urban income strategies than households living closer to town, the highest percentage of rural-urban livelihood strategies could be found in the remotest study village. Road access is no precondition and no trigger for rural-urban interaction. However, the scope for cottage production as a livelihood strategy is extremely limited given the present institutional set-up and livelihood patterns. Similarly, the commercial production of agricultural products and their marketing on regional urban markets is only possible for food secure households. Temporary labour migration, which plays a major role as a source of foreign exchange on the national level (*cf.* Seddon *et al.*, 1998), does often not provide livelihood security on the household level.

In the study area, there is no typical rural household or a typical rural income pattern. The situation can rather be described as a wide variety of livelihood strategies and livelihood patterns. Rural livelihood patterns tend to include more and more strategies, which are not based on local, risk-distributing institutions. This seems to be because livelihood patterns, which encompass a combination of complementary strategies on different spatial levels of interaction, are especially successful. The preconditions for the establishment of such a livelihood pattern are a medium asset base. In the study area that means a landholding of 1 ha, a pair of oxen, and a good balance of adult workforce and dependent persons in a household.

The institutional analysis of rural livelihood patterns gives insights into the rationales of households and the risks they face. The analysis gives hints how and where the institutional setting can be changed in such a way that rural households can strengthen their livelihood security, expand their coping capacity, and reduce risks. A first step for the improvement of regional development strategies in Nepal would be, if planners would take into account the complexity of rural livelihood patterns. There is no typical Nepalese farmer ready and able to produce cash crops for an open market providing free and equal access for all. Livelihood security of rural households and especially their ability to earn short-term cash money depends to a large extent on interaction with regional markets. Nevertheless, the conditions of marketing are unfavourable for many rural households. Changing the institutional setting and introducing more risk-sharing or risk-avoiding elements would help rural households to optimise their marketing strategies. Market access must become cheaper and the market fees should be more appropriate for small farmers. Small suppliers and farmers should get a seat in the managing boards of weekly markets, which are currently dominated by the municipality and wholesale businessmen. It is necessary to strengthen women's bargaining capacities and encourage women to join the wholesale business. Moreover, the existing local institutions with risk distributing elements like the cash free labour exchange system or communal work can be utilised for marketing strategies. It is especially necessary to improve the institutional setting along the marketing chain with the help of regional actors in order to reduce marketing risks through externally induce price fluctuations or the seasonality of prices, and improve the predictability of income. Wage labour is a strategy of major importance for rural households, and seasonality, periodicity, and local non-availability poses a major risk for many rural households. Therefore, regional development measures have to focus on regional labour markets.

Finally, switching livelihood strategies and restructuring a livelihood pattern is not an easy task for a household. Regional development programmes should, therefore, start to strengthen those strategies, which rural households already employ instead of trying to introduce new and different ones. That will help to widen the action space of rural households and enable them to find additional income strategies appropriate for them when the need arises.

## REFERENCES


Bohle, Hans-Georg (2001): Vulnerability and Criticality: Perspectives from Social Geography. In: *IHDP Update. Newsletter of the International Human Dimensions Programme on Global Environmental Change* (2/01): S. 1-5.

Giddens, Anthony (1984): The Constitution of Society. Outline of the Theory of Structuration. Berkeley.

Kunzmann, Klaus R. (1992): Rural-Urban Linkages. A Discussion Paper. Dortmund. (Arbeitspapier 109).

Long, Norman & Jan Douwe van der Ploeg (1994): Heterogeneity, Actor and Structure: Towards a Reconstitution of the Concept of Structure. In: Booth, D.: Rethinking Social Development: Theory, Research and Practice, S. 62-89.

Market Access for Rural Development (1998): An Action Plan for Development of the Butwal Horticulture Market. Unpublished project report, prepared by James Diller. Kathmandu. (MARD/Lumbini-Gandaki Technical Report No. 28).

North, Douglass C. (1990): Institutions, Institutional Change and Economic Performance. Cambridge; New York; Victoria. (Political Economy of Institutions and Decisions).

North, Douglass C. (1995): The New Institutional Economics and Third World Development. In: Harriss, John, Janet Hunter, *et al.*: The New Institutional Economics and Third World Development, S. 17-26.

Raithelhuber, Martin (2001): Der Einfluss expandierender Mittelstadte auf die Existenzsicherung ländlicher Haushalte in Nepal. Eine institutionenorientierte Analyse der Stadt-Land-Beziehungen in den Distrikten Palpa und Rupandehi. Heidelberg University, Faculty for Geosciences. Dissertation.

Seddon, David, Ganesh Gurung, *et al.* (1998): Foreign Labour Migration and the Remittance Economy of Nepal. In: *Himalayan Research Bulletin,* Vol. XVIII (2): S. 3-10.

Swift, Jeremy (1989): Why are Rural People Vulnerable to Famine? In: *IDS Bulletin,* Vol. 20 (2): S. 8-15.

Unwin, Tim (1990): Urban-rural Interactions in Developing Countries: A Theoretical Perspective. In: Potter, R. B. & Tim Unwin: The Geography of Urban-Rural Interaction in Developing Countries, S. 11-32.

Watts, Michael J. & Hans-Georg Bohle (1993): The Space of Vulnerability: The Causal Structure of Hunger and Famine. In : *Progress in Human Geography,* Vol. 1 (1): S. 43-67.

# Urban Development

## A Challenge for Frontier Regions—Sri Lanka Experience

**H. P. SUSIRIPALA**

### WHAT IS URBANISM?

Before we discuss about the challenges for urban development, it is worthwhile to know what is urbanism and why it is needed by the people.

Urbanism may be defined in two ways: as a "way of life" and as a settlement pattern[1]. As a way of life urbanism is characterized by *complex social organization,* as a settlement pattern, it is a exemplified by the city as a relatively *permanent habitation for a large heterogeneous population that is densely settled and not engaged in producing its own food.* These two aspects of urbanism are analytically separable. The most impressive fact of cities is that they appeared so recently in the history of mankind. By early centuries of Christian era, cities had been established on all of the world's continents except Australia. As per Kingsley Davis[2], urban development based on two revolutions took place in the Europe: Agriculture Revolution and thereafter the Industrial Revolution that ultimately paved the way for urban development in the world and enabled cities to grow to very large size and in many instances, the city population eventually became the majority population of entire nation. It may be said that the Agricultural Revolution made it possible for cities to exist and that the Industrial Revolution made it possible for cities to dominate the world. The date 1750 is usually assigned as the "beginnings" of the Industrial Revolution in England where it originated. Pre-industrial world was characterized by the small percentage of population living in cities. In countries where cities existed usually no more than 10 per cent and after less than 5 per cent of population were able to live in urban settlements. The best available figures indicate that in 1800 only 2-4 per cent of world population lived in cities. (defined as communities of at least 20,000 inhabitants.

As long as industry was in the handicraft state, there was no reason why concentration of population for the industrial purpose alone should take place on a very large scale. Labour supply was inadequate for workers were characterized more by their immobility than their mobility. Even the factories operated by water driven machinery, the geographical location of cities usually forbade any ground expansion of industries. Any way the steam driven engines came in to operation, workers tend to concentrate in large numbers in industrial centres. The modern industrial towns are, therefore, partly a product of steam and more recently electrical power. By its nature steam is economical when applied to large manufacturing units concentrated within a smaller area. Consequently, the power driven machines drew manufacturing out of the home and placed it in a centralized location. As factory system expanded to meet the needs and demands of a growing population more workers were required to tend the machines and dispose the factory products.

The factories in towns and cities thus flocked rural people and attracted not only by the novelty of city life but also by the possibilities of greater economic rewards. In 1750 great majority of labour force (85-90 per cent) was engaged in agriculture sector.

This percentage was steadily declined to 80 per cent in 1805, 70 per cent in 1830, 50.3 per cent in 1870 until it declined to 5 per cent in 1970 in the United States. In 1970 this small group produced not only enough foods to maintain US as one of the best fed nations but also great quantities of food and raw materials were shipped abroad and keeping surpluses piled up in storage bins. This is a result of not only mechanization but also the application of scientific knowledge to increase soil fertility improve plants and animals and reduced wastage in various ways. US cities are of such size that presently the urban segment of total population occupied only 1.53 per cent of nations' land area[3].

Most of developed and developing countries now have large scale movement of population into outer rings of metropolitan areas may be ushering in a phase of metropolitan development. In regions where there are many metropolitan areas as the outer ring of one metropolitan area expand it often overlaps with the outer ring of another metropolitan area. If this process continues the urbanization will cover the entire country in a shorter period. This phenomenon has been called city region, super metropolis or galaxy.

## TRENDS IN DEVELOPING COUNTRIES

There is same tendency to view urbanization in developing countries as a later-day version of what occurred earlier in countries that are now highly industrialized and urbanized. However countries under which urbanization and industrialization occurred in the industrialized societies are in many aspects quite different from conditions that prevailed in developing countries now. Functions performed by cities in developing countries are different in certain respects from the functions of cities in developed regions. Most contemporary developing countries were at one time or another subject to colonial domination and many have only recently emerged from the status of a colony which was exploited by the colonial powers. Indeed, cities like Bombay or Colombo were actually created by colonial powers to serve their own economic, political and military interests.

Raw materials produced in the colonies were usually transported to the occupying country to supply its urban factories and mills and therefore provide employment for city dwellers. Major cities have attracted much attention not only because of their size but also because of their economic, political and cultural influences. Yet there are thousands of small and medium sized cities. The properties of a country's total population living in urban centres under 100,000 persons vary considerably from one area to another.

Most of the cities in developing countries could be cited as *primate or principal* cities whose development are much more superior than any other cities in the country. In such a situation policies for the development of the less advanced regions are frequently justified on the grounds of economic justice although it is sometimes also argued that such policies serve to accelerate total national economic development. These urbanization and regional policies often converse and complement to each other. The former tries to steer development away from over urbanized regions and the latter tries of attract and promote development in backward regions. It must be noted that two major policy goals are involved in those policies; efficiency and equity. By efficiency is meant growth measured in terms of per capita national product. By equity is meant a more equal distribution of income.

## SRI LANKAN EXPERIENCE

Urban development is considered as a challenge for frontier regions in Sri Lanka as it is a common phenomenon in almost all third world countries. If we take Sri Lanka as an example, urbanization is basically found in the city of Colombo (Fig. 25.1). It is the capital of Sri Lanka. In addition, urbanization is prevalent in nearly fourteen medium towns which are governed by Municipal Councils (MCs). Besides that urbanization is also found in forty small townships. All these medium and small townships are scattered in the island (Fig. 25.2).

The rest are the frontier regions which show visible characteristics of urban and rural. They are neither considered as urban nor rural. These regions are partly shown as urban and partly shown as rural.

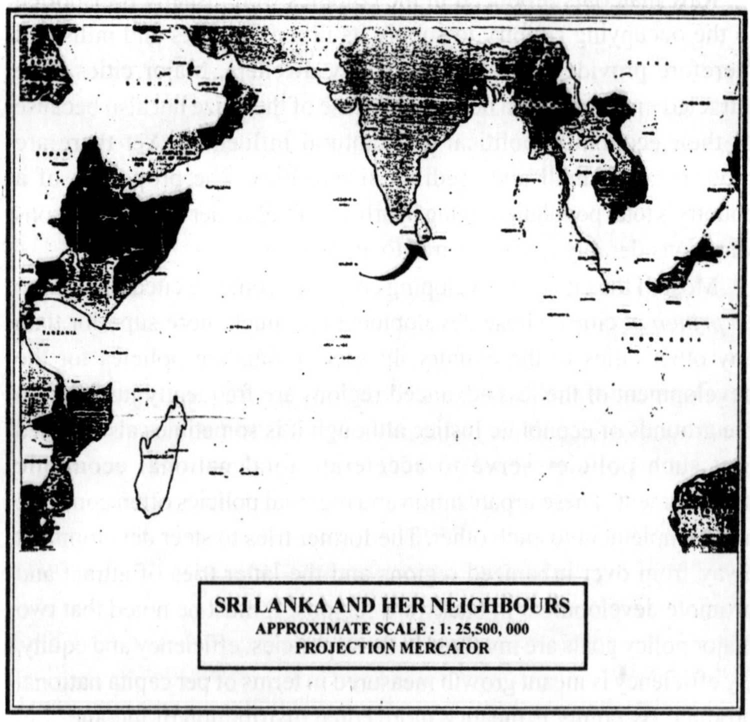


**Fig. 25.1 :** Sri Lanka and her Neighbours (Approximate Scale 1 : 25,500,000 : Projection Mercator)

Settlements of this nature are formed in bulks of villages scattered over the island. The people of these frontier regions have linkages with the urban centres and fascinated with the urban services which are not found in frontier regions. So the attraction towards urban centres

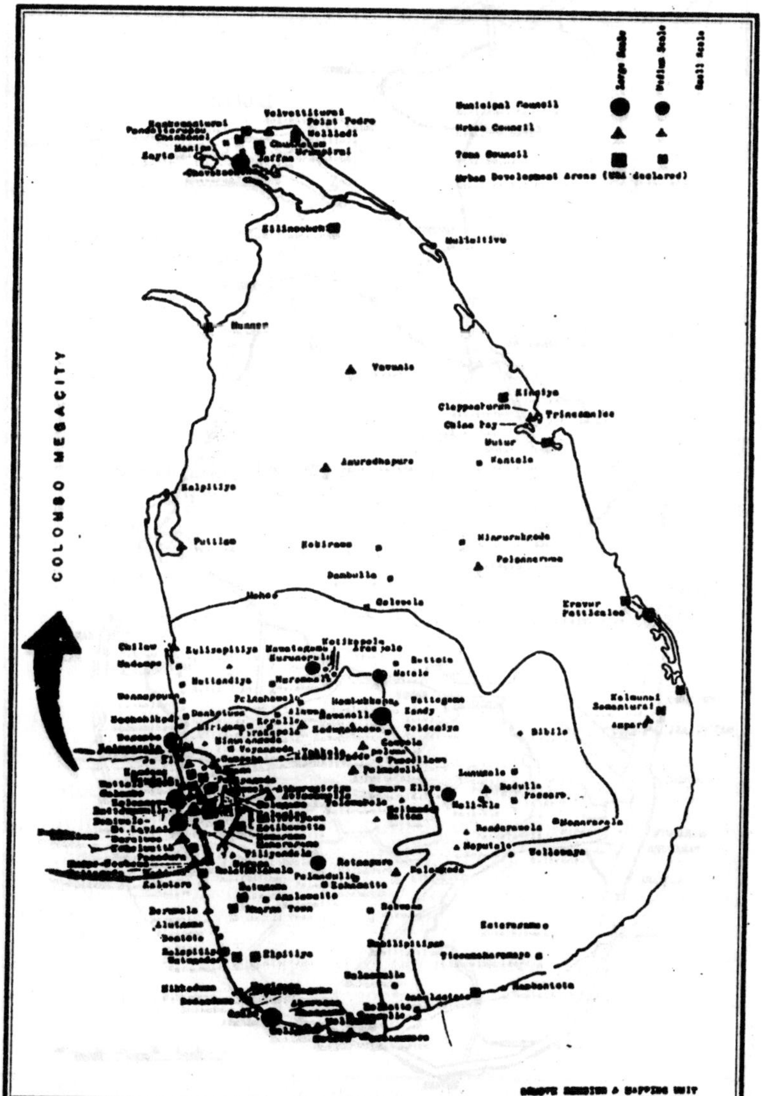


Fig. 25.2 : Urban Areas of Sri Lanka

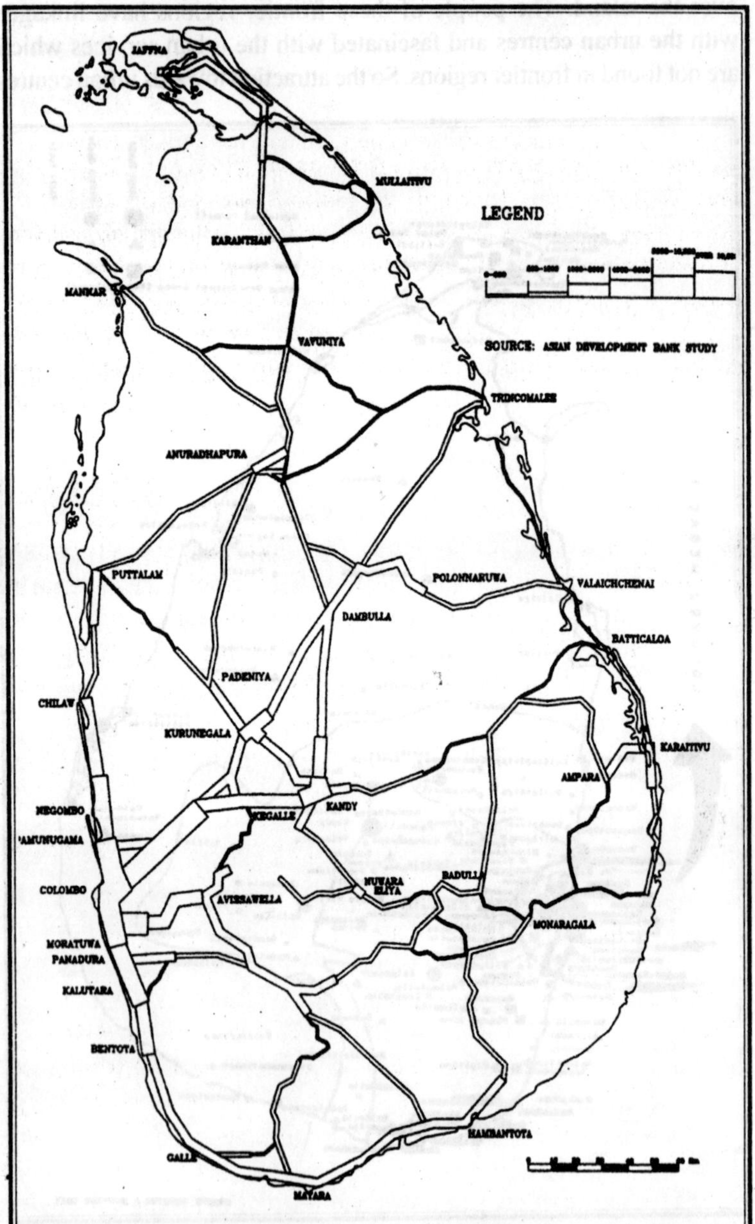


**Fig. 25.3 :** Average Daily Traffic on 'A' Road Network—1986

resulted agglomeration and thereby numerous problems cropped up which could not be solved easily by city administrators. The simple reason is that people in frontier regions seek urban services by shifting their residences or commuting daily to the towns which causes traffic congestion (Fig. 25.3).

The urban facilities are basically infrastructure, housing, and social services. Urban infrastructure includes potable water supply, solid waste management, electricity, transport and telecommunication. Further, acquiring education for children, health facilities, alleviation of poverty and enjoying social welfare, parks and play grounds, cultural facilities such as cinemas, theatres are some of physical and social infrastructures expected by people.

It is worthwhile to see how far provision of urban services could be accommodated in these regions. It is in fact a challenge. There are justifiable reasons why it is a challenge. Of course it is a challenge for developing countries. Perhaps it may be a challenge for developed nations as well in considering the viability of providing these facilities and maintenance. Basically it is a costly affair. Settlements are scattered in the region thereby provision of infrastructure like laying pipes for potable water, laying cables/wires for electricity or telecommunication involve lengthy and large areas which require large physical needs and vast amount of money which has to be recovered from the people who live in those regions. Probably viability to maintain the supply could not be justified with cost and benefits.

If people concentrate into an urban centre the cost-benefit of providing such supply will be viable since it limits to a particular area where density of population is higher (Fig. 25.4). In highly urbanized areas like Colombo, the residential density per hectare is 974 persons (gross density around 190) whereas it is 9 persons per hectare in a frontier region like Moneragala. This shows that large number of people scattered in a larger land area of the region whereas it is concentrated in a limited land area in the town. Under this situation, how far it is viable to provide infrastructure facilities needed by them. This matter is to be considered with the cost factor *i.e.* capital cost for the provision of potable water, telecommunication or electricity in rural areas is generally more than a supply of such facilities in a concentrated (urban) settlement. Similarly the maintenance cost also be very high compared

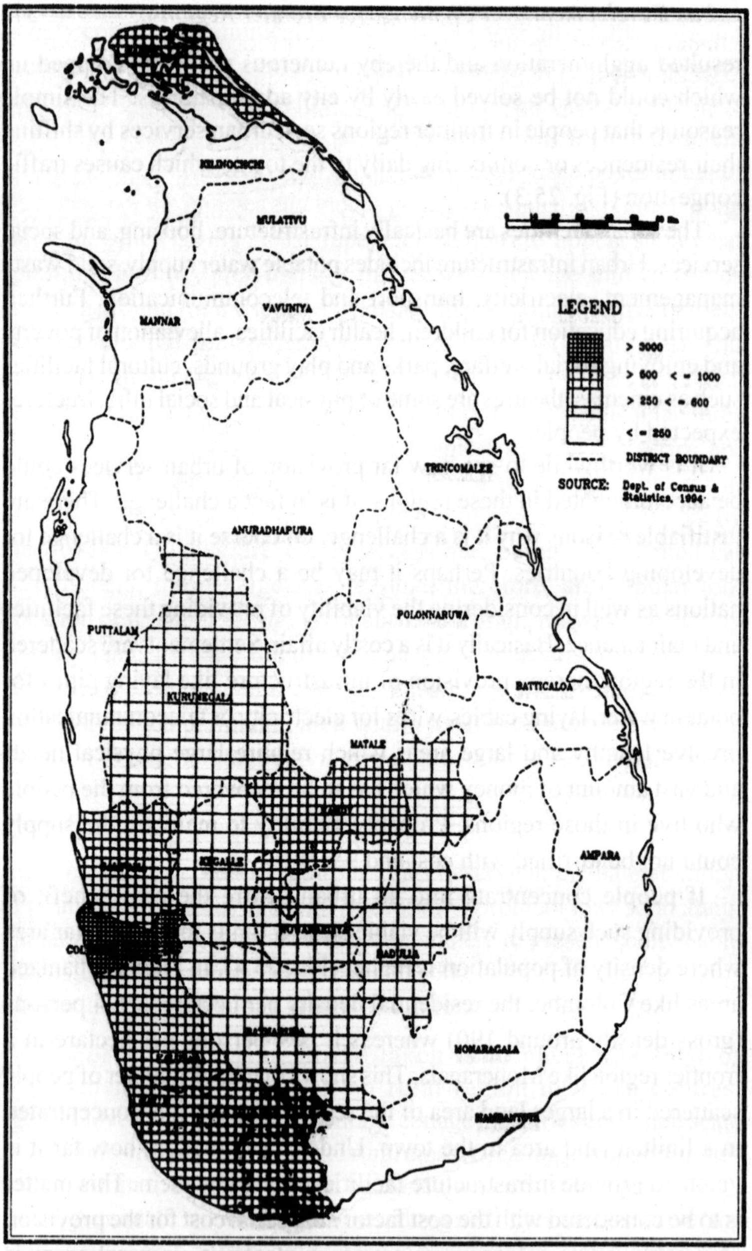


Fig. 25.4 : Population Density of Districts

to supply in urban areas. So it is a well known factor that it is a costly affair to provide urban facilities in frontier regions.

Viability to maintain such a supply would also depend on the threshold of a particular supply even if the capital cost for such services could be ignored for the simple reason that it is met by the government as an obligation to the people. So there is a dilemma in the operational aspect of the services. This is why the urban development is considered as a challenge for frontier regions that every nation face.

Will there be solution to this problem? One solution would be to leave aside frontier regions and concentrate on highly urbanized areas thereby discouragement ultimately leads to exodus of people from frontier regions to towns. Other solution would be by way of incentives or regulatory enforcement to settle down in urbanized area and allowing frontier regions to grow as agricultural areas or industrial areas where large investment could envisage. One can see that this would be a simple solution to meet the challenge. But it would not be an answer to the problem in real sense. We may have to study in detail by analyzing the current situation in the country and arrive at a solution that would be largely practical. This chapter is an exercise in analyzing the Sri Lankan experience based on current settlement system prevailed in the country (Fig. 25.5).

## Urban Hierarchies

Frontier Regions of Sri Lanka comprise of secondary townships excluding some larger towns in each provincial capitals.

Presently there are 100 urban areas including Municipal Councils, Urban Councils (MCs, UCs ) and those small rural centres which could also be considered as emerging towns. These are distributed throughout the country as per geographic, historic, economic and political factors (Fig. 25.6). Most salient feature of this distribution is the overwhelming dominance of Colombo as the Island's primate city. Colombo and its contiguous urban areas *i.e.* Dehiwala M., Laveniya, Kotte, Moratuwa, Kolonnawa and Panadura contain an estimated population of 1.64 million inhabitants and an additional number of urban inhabitants live on the semi-rural fringes. Thus Greater Colombo contains at least 56 per cent of the Island's total urban population excluding Northern province which not accessible at present due to terrorist activities.

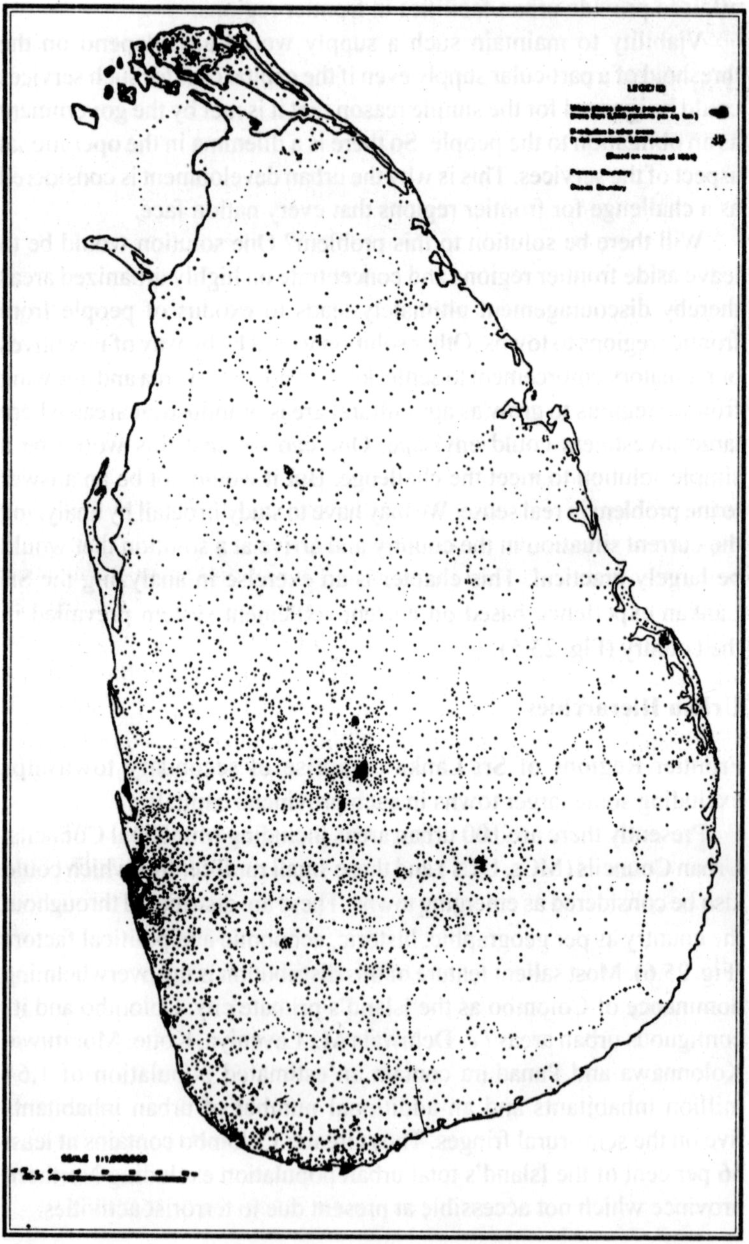

**Fig. 25.5 : Population Distribution**

There are no really "second order" urban centres in the sense of centres with a sufficient economic weight to even begin to compete with Colombo. However there are three towns Kandy, Negambo and Galle with around 100,000 inhabitants which can be considered third order cities with roughly one-fifteenth the population of Colombo. All of these towns in the south quadrant of the island relatively close to Colombo and in what is called the wet zone. Below these towns are six urban areas in the 30,000 to 50,000 population band (Ratanpura, Matale, Kurunegala, Gampola, Nuwara Eliya, Anuradhapura and Trincomalee) which function as regional administrative, trade, and service centres.

Below these towns are a number of what could be called "fifth order" provincial administrative and market centres, most of which contain between 15,000 to 30,000 inhabitants towns. Finally, there are numerous small and emerging centres in the 5,000 to 15,000 population band which function as agro-marketing and service centres or as administrative towns. These smaller towns with population below 30,000 are found throughout the Island, but again there is a concentration in the south-west and central quadrants. Such towns rely heavily on road transport corridors for their importance.

This shows that there is considerable bias in urban locations towards Sri Lanka's south-west quadrant. Not only Colombo and its satellites located there, but so too are most other important towns. The reasons are historical emphasis put upon Colombo by the colonial powers, the development of the central hill region for plantation agriculture, the higher agricultural productivity of the land due to the plentiful rains and consequently the higher rural population density; the radial arrangement of regional transport and infrastructure which reinforced Colombo's dominance and lent considerable locational advantages to urban activities placed along the radials, especially those near to Colombo (Fig. 25.3).

Fig. 25.4 and Fig. 25.7 present the location of the main urban centres in Sri Lanka and indicate their relative importance in population terms.

## Urban Morphology of Secondary Towns in Frontier Regions

It is difficult to generalize about the urban form of frontier regions in Sri Lanka since geographical differences are pronounced. For example,

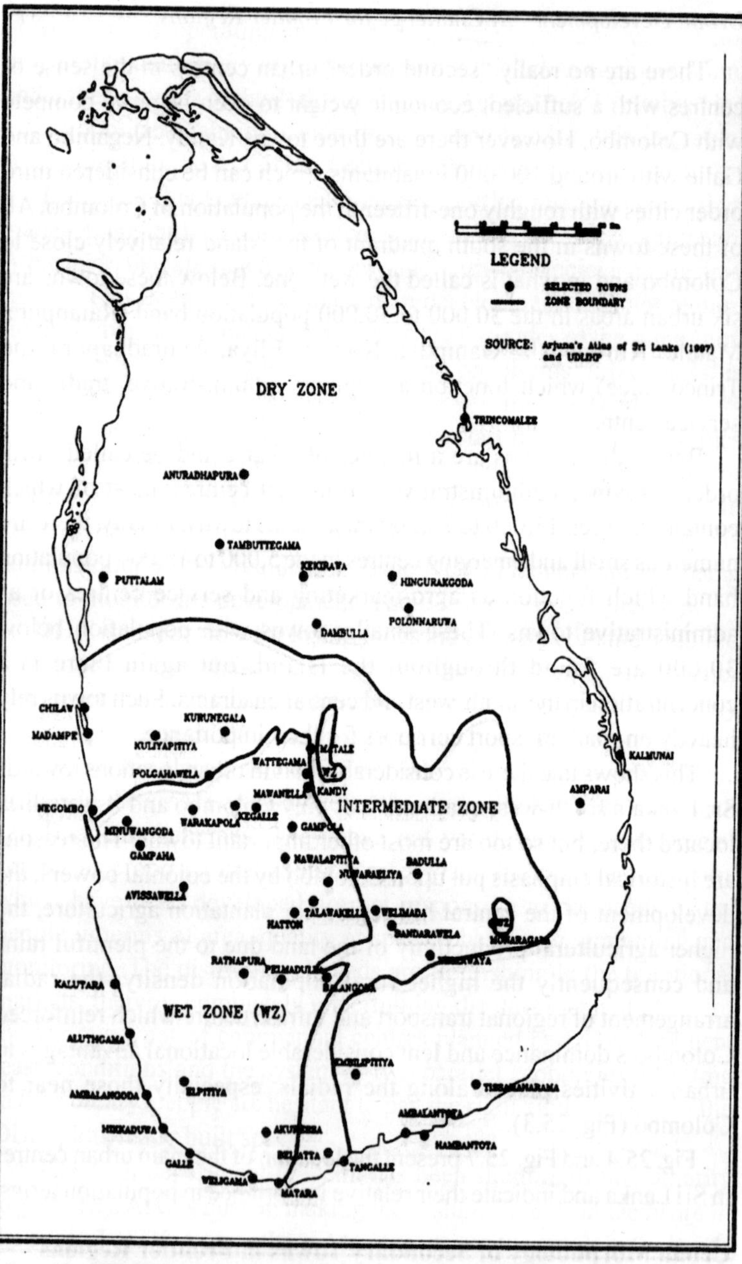


**Fig. 25.6 :** Locations of Selected Towns and Geographical Zones

hill towns in Sri Lanka topography and rivers, coastal towns by sea and lagoons, and dry zone towns by tanks (Wewa) and lakes. Even so, certain commonalties should be noted in larger towns especially those with considerable colonial history like Kandy.

Added to this form of secondary towns are the surrounding residential areas. With few exceptions, these are low density unplanned individual with lots of developments, with detached bungalows and huts. At initial development these neighbourhoods are indistinguishable from rural house-garden areas. They slowly densify through individual subdivisions, and the process extends to a general sprawl with access roads and services following development. Thus it is difficult to use the term "built up area" as a well defined envelop of an urban area. For the same reason, it is also difficult to talk about specific town extensions and directions of urban growth.

## Socio-economic Conditions and Urban Poor

### *Urban Demographic Trends*

Urbanization is taking place on the island but only at a moderate pace—at a rate less than 1 per cent above natural increase (given that there has been a considerable refugee movement from the north and east in the inter-census period, this growth is extremely moderate). Furthermore, it shows that while Colombo and its contiguous urban areas have captured the absolute majority of this increase in the urban population the growth rate of Greater Colombo's has only been 1.91 per cent per annum which is again moderate.

The rate of population growth in provincial towns such as Anuradhapura are growing at rate above 2.6 per cent annually. Implications of this data are, firstly, that Greater Colombo is not metropolitan area appears to be expanding out "into a vast functional urban region includes the city of Colombo an inner crescent of suburbs comprising 6 towns, an outer crescent of 11 new suburbs, 18 non-suburban towns and numerous urban settlements" (Somasekaran *et al.*, Atlas of Sri Lanka Colombo 1997, p.54). In general, rapid growing secondary towns tend to be those closer to Colombo. Increase of population is indeed somewhat a challenge for urban development.

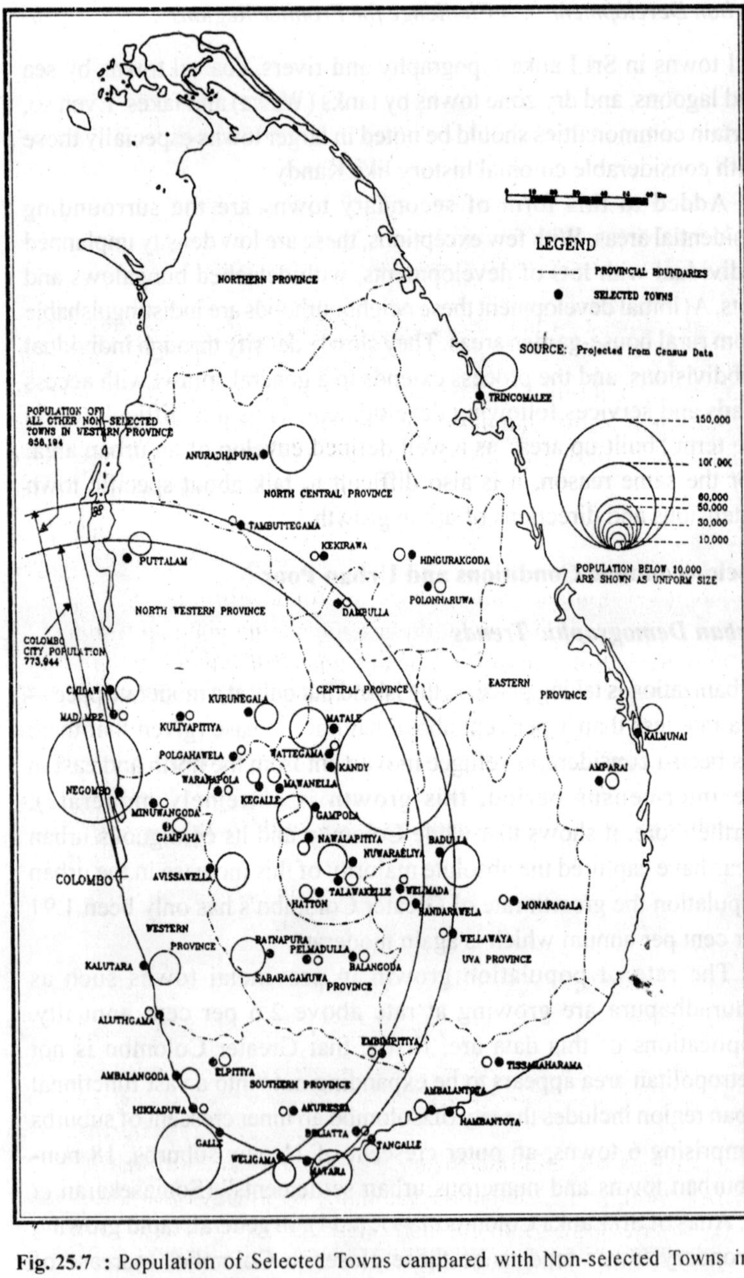


**Fig. 25.7 :** Population of Selected Towns campared with Non-selected Towns in WesternProvince

### *Urban Employment and Unemployment*

The 1995, Labour Force Survey estimates that the total potential labour force amounted to 6.12 million persons of which 5.34 million persons or 87.7 per cent were employed. The male/female split of this active population was roughly 70/30. The survey thus estimated the 1995 national unemployment rate at 12.7 per cent showing a slight decline from 1991 when unemployment stood at 13.8 per cent.

In 1995, 81.7 per cent of employed persons were employed in the rural sector while only 18.9 per cent were in the urban sector. Since over 20 per cent of the national population is urban, this implies that the employment rate in urban areas is somewhat higher than that in rural areas. This is evident that substantial portion of employed persons is residing out of cities and daily commuting to the towns which creates multifaceted problems. Overall the unemployed are younger and relatively more educated than total labour force (In 1990 the unemployment rate for the age group 15-19 was 30 per cent and for the age group 20-29 was 27 per cent while for the 30-39 age group was only 9 per cent). Urban development in the country is considered by providing employment opportunities for younger generation.

### *Urban Poverty*

The World Bank carried out a poverty assessment survey in 1994 (World Bank South Asia Region, Sri Lanka Poverty Assessment, January, 1995) which allows an overall view of the incidence of and trends in urban poverty. Two indices were constructed, the poverty incidence index, which is the proportion of the population below poverty line and the poverty depth index, which measures the gap between consumption of the poor and the non-poor. Using the results of the household income and expenditure survey of 1990/1991 and constructing a reference consumption poverty line of Rs. 471 per month per person in 1991, the World Bank study found that 22.4 per cent of the island's population were deemed to be poor and that the poverty depth index was 4.8. For the urban population the indices were 18.9 per cent and 4.14 respectively.

### *Welfare and Income Transfer Efforts*

The Government has set up in 1950s a number of welfare and income transfer programmes aimed at poor families. The *Food Stamp*

*Programme* (consuming on average 0.7 per cent of GDP) started in 1979. The *Janasaviya Programme* a two-year upliftment programme for the poor persons was started in 1989. Both these programmes suffered from considerable "leakage" and the new government elected in 1994 ended both programmes replacing them with the *"Samurdhi Programme"* which so far is more restricted to deserving poor families. The Samurdhi Programme is concentrated almost totally in rural areas, leaving poor urban families. It must be noted that the strongest "income transfer programme" in Sri Lanka today is made up of the remittances that hard working Sri Lankan send back from the Middle East. Continuing state welfare is immense burden if urban development is a priority of the nation.

**Urban Infrastructure and Services**

The economic development of the frontier regions is closely related to the effectiveness of infrastructure provision. For demand driven infrastructure, such as roads, transportation, water and power supply and telecommunications, there are resource generation thresholds which need to be identified and analyzed to discern if there may be a constraint to urban development. For environmental infrastructure, such as liquid or solid domestic and industrial waste, it is important to identify and ensure safe collection and disposal from both public health and resource protection aspects.

The infrastructure sector covers in this section thus comprise a mix demand driven requirements and environmental sanitation. The demand driven sectors are defined as infrastructure which is required to encourage inward investment and stimulate economic growth. Included for review were roads, power and water supply and surface transportation (mainly bus and taxi services). Telecommunication was not included as this sector has recently been partially privatized and the introduction of various cellular networks has relieved the pressure on terrestrial exchanges. The main telecommunication issue in secondary towns is upgrading of old analog exchanges and extending the cellular network coverage. Sufficient social infrastructure services, particularly education, health facilities are also prerequisites for achieving urban development and economic growth of frontier regions. (Fig. 25.8)

The main infrastructure deficiencies as perceived by the Urban Local Authorities (ULAs) themselves. As can be seen, water supply and stormwater drainage are the major infrastructure concerns, while stormwater drainage is also by far the major environmental issue and cause of natural disasters. Poor solid waste management and the attendant environmental issues arising from poor disposal is another major concern.

Infrastructure deficiencies stem from various sources. The ULAs often quote a lack of financial resources for capital investment and their major constraint to meeting basic infrastructure and service deficiencies. However this is frequently exacerbated by poor operation and maintenance and inefficient land-use arising from weak or non-existent planning and development controls. In addition, much infrastructure is provided by central or provincial government agencies. These agencies also often lack resources to meet the ULA infrastructure requirements while their planning and timing of interventions may not correspond with the ULAs' own plan. Most of infrastructure improvements are dependent on external, especially foreign, assistance as loans given to government which represents around 25 per cent of the total expenditure of the annual budget which is a major constraint.

### *Institutional Responsibilities*

Responsibility for infrastructure delivery lies with the ULAs or central or provincial government line agencies (Table 25.1). Private sector involvement is negligible, although a few initiatives are underway to contract out some services. An example is solid waste collection for Colombo.

In general the demand-driven infrastructure (*i.e.* that which can provide revenue and for which people are usually willing to pay) is supplied by line agencies, while environmental sanitation is the responsibility of the ULA. Same are responsible for the operation and maintenance and tariff collection for their water suppliers. Many ULAs were also previously responsible for their power supply distribution but this has in nearly all cases been transferred to Central Government organizations such as Lanka Electricity Company (LECO or the Ceylon Electricity Board (CEB) (Fig. 25.9). It would be seen that although decentralization and devolution of powers have been a government

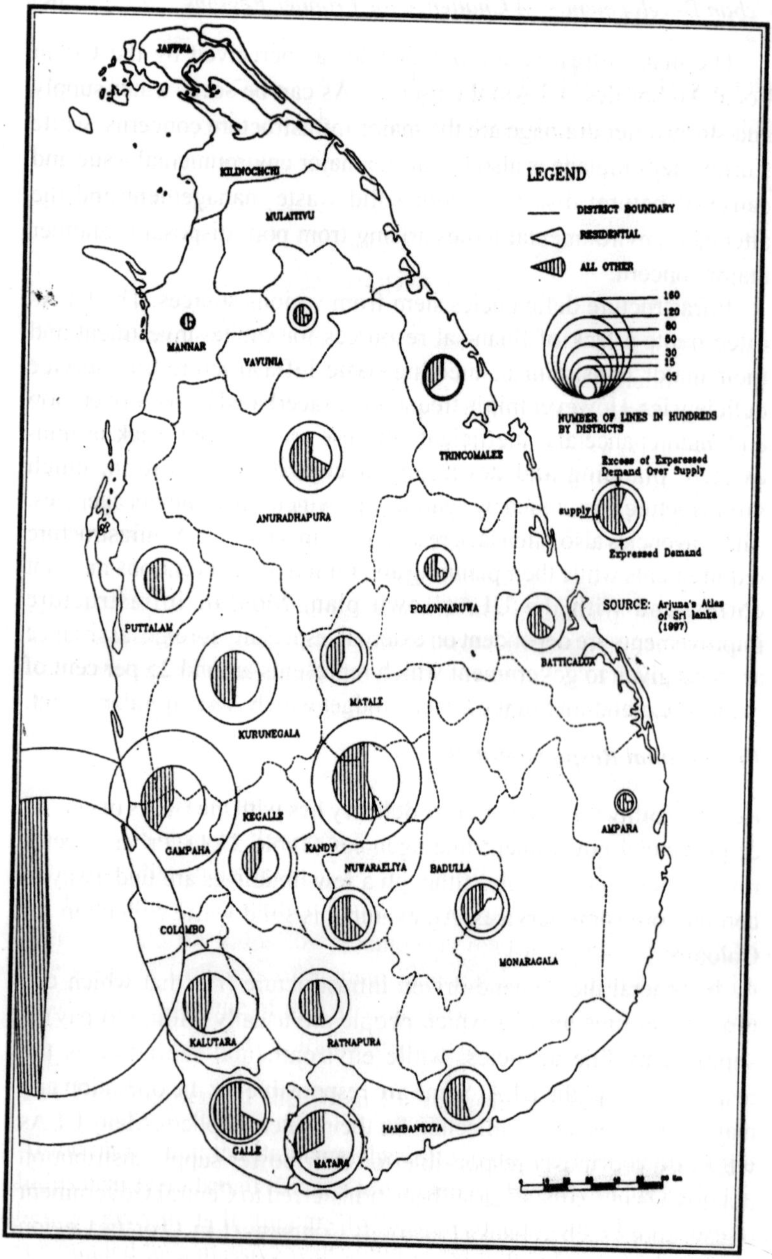


Fig. 25.8 : District-wise Provision of Telephone Lines

priority, the ULAs themselves prefer the national line agencies, with their skills and resources to provide technically complex infrastructure.

***Roads and Surface Transportation***

The Road Development Authority (RDA) seem to have the resources and technical ability to maintain the trunk roads in the country. They have also received substantial donor assistance (Table 25.2) for road rehabilitation and upgrading. It is at the provincial and ULA level where road conditions are poor. This is due to a combination of;

* inadequate drainage, caused either by inundation of solid waste or encroachments blocking drains;
* lack of resources for maintenance,
* road not designed for present day traffic loads, and
* poor construction.

Drainage is also an issue on RDA roads as the drain cleaning in the towns is the responsibility of the ULAs. If this is not carried out properly, then the RDA roads may also be damaged by rain water. A recent survey reveals that only an estimated 25 per cent of ULA roads are considered to be in good condition.

Within the town centres traffic congestion is becoming a problem. This is not due to inadequate roads, but also to poor traffic circulation, narrow right of way, inappropriate junction designs and priorities and lack of enforcement of driving and parking regulations, particularly for buses and taxis. Pedestrians and vehicular separation is not well demarcated and increases the potential for accidents. Many ULAs own land in the town centre which is not efficiently utilized. In some cases the ULAs have constructed a shopping centre but generally there is no overall plan to improve land-use efficiency or traffic circulation and safety in these areas.

In many towns the railway station is quite distant from the town centre and not really integrated with the commuting population, town centre circulation and economy.

***Storm Water Drainage***

Many towns declare this sector as being their greatest infrastructure constraint. Even ULAs in hill areas where topography should lend

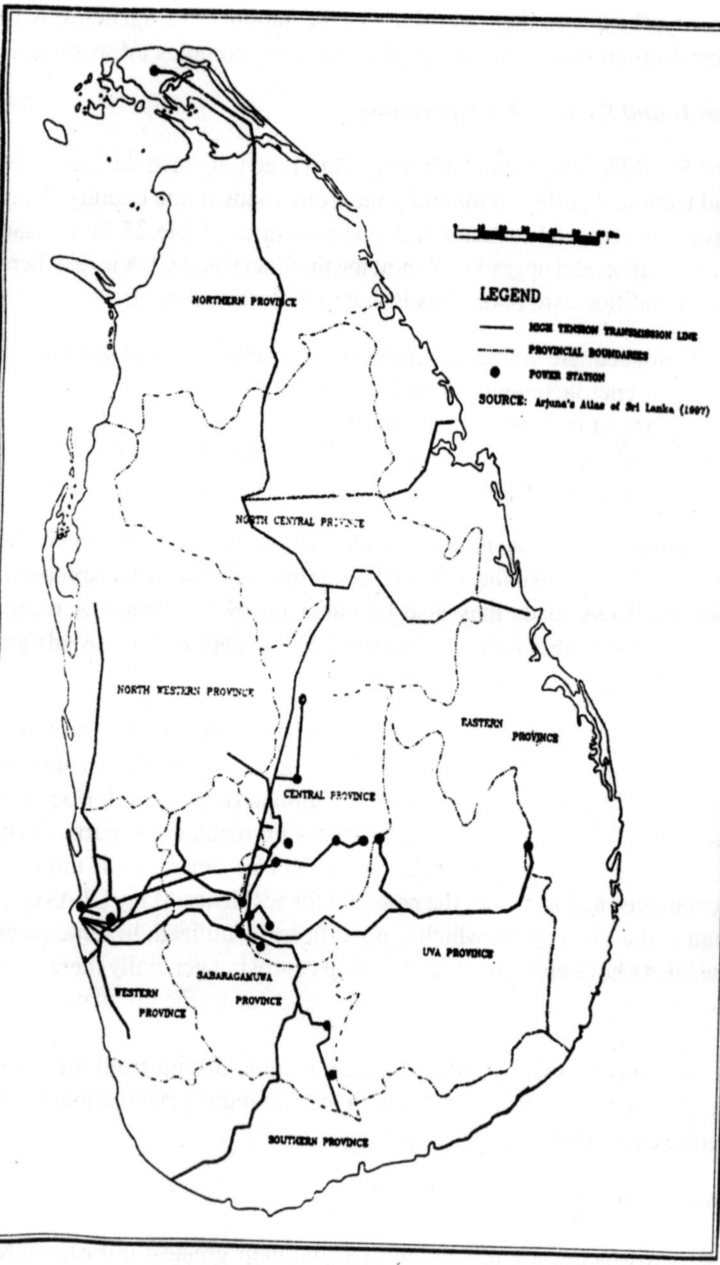


**Fig. 25.9 :** Generation and Distribution of Energy

**Table 25.1 :** Institutional Responsibilities for Infrastructure in Secondary Towns

| Sector | Agency |
|---|---|
| ***Roads and Surface Transportation*** | |
| Trunk Roads (A & B Class) | Roads Development Authority (RDA) of the Ministry of Transportation |
| Main Roads (C & D Class) | RDA of Provincial Ministry of Transport |
| Access and Side Roads (C, D and E Class) | ULA |
| Traffic Management | Police |
| Private Bus Parks | ULA or bus operators |
| Peoplized Bus Service | ULA |
| Railway Stations | Ceylon Railways |
| ***Water Resources, Supply and Standards*** | |
| Ground Water Resources | Water Resources Board |
| Surface Water Resources | Irrigation Department |
| Water Supply Headworks Mains | Usually NWSDB, some large and Trunk ULAs |
| Water Distribution and Tariff Collection | NWSDB, ULA |
| Drinking Water Standards | NWSDB |
| ***Liquid Waste Management*** | |
| Sanitation | ULA |
| Sewerage and Treatment | NWSDB |
| ***Solid Waste Management*** | ULA |
| ***Stormwater Drainage*** | ULA |
| ***Power Supply*** | |
| Generation & High Voltage Transmission | CEB |
| Low Voltage Transmission, Distribution & Tariff Collection | LECO |
| Street Lighting | ULA |
| ***Pollution Control*** | Central Environment Authority |

itself to effective drainage, quoted flooding and blocked drains as a problem. Landslides during rain storms are also a problem. Many coastal towns are also inundated during high tides. If the high tide happens to coincide with heavy rainfalls and run-off to rivers, then these towns can face severe flooding. However many stormwater drainage problems accrue from a combination of man-made factors which are given below:

* plans do not consider stormwater drainage implications and land-use conflicts with the drainage regime,
* poor enforcement of planning regulations encourages *ad hoc* development with encroachments and blocking of drains,
* drains are blocked by solid waste, and
* pressure on urban land increases development in areas prone to flooding.

This sector requires a vast amount of money which secondary towns find difficult to resolve and always seek foreign assistance which has to be channelled through provincial and national government.

***Water Supply***

Adequate water supply is vital for urban development of a town and in meeting public health requirements. This sector has and continues to receive much government and donor assistance. Unaccounted for or non-revenue water is estimated to average around 25 per cent. This is relatively low figure for small towns and possibly reflects the level of investment in this sector. The key issue with water supply is meeting ever increasing urban demands. Three compounding factors are the cause of this increase in demand:

* an increasing population;
* a rising proportion of urbanization with higher water needs, requiring; and
* improved level of service.

Resource allocation conflicts is becoming a major issue with agricultural and increasing urban demands. In many areas, where water is pumped from rivers to meet these demands, salinity is increasing as sea water moves up river. This occurrence has been checked in few cases by constructing bands across the rivers to prevent sea water intrusion.

Within the towns the number of unnerved households has been decreasing while the percentage of households with direct connections to the reticulation system has been increasing due to reduced number of standposts. The ULA has to pay for the water delivered through the remaining standpoints. Infixing and augmentation of water supplies is in many cases failing to keep pace with urban devilment and identification. This sector presently depends mainly on foreign assistance as shown in (Table 25.2).

## Waste Management

### *Liquid Waste Management*

Only towns in the Colombo and Dehiwala Mt. Laveniya Municipal Council areas are served by a piped sewerage system. In secondary towns most middle and high income households have water sealed latrines which discharge to septic tanks. Low income households are served by a combination of unsanitary pit latrines communal latrines or no service. As per information available at ULAs around 20 per cent of population are not served latrines.

In many towns, watercourses, road side and main drains receive seepage and sullage from households and industries. Water pollution is increasingly becoming a problem particularly for poor and disadvantaged groups living in marginal land. A particular constraint to effective sanitation in many towns have high watertables which some towns also have rock outcrops, easily transferred through saturated soils. In coastal towns much liquid waste is disposed of to sea which substantially reduces the tourism potential.

### *Solid Waste Management*

Solid waste disposal is a pressing problem to many towns since many ULAs have no suitable sites to dump wastes. In many occasions, ULAs have no equipment or vehicles to collect and transport solid waste. Collection efficiencies in town areas averages 66 per cent. Waste minimization and recycling could be improved to reduce the amount of landfill required. The ULAs themselves recognize that solid waste management is a problem and is a key issue today.

**Table 25.2 :** Summary of Ongoing Projects by Sector

| Project | Donor | Amount in Millions | Funding Type | Start Date | Finish Date |
|---|---|---|---|---|---|
| **Housing and Urban Development** | | | | | |
| Urban Development and Low-Income Housing T A | ADB | 1.10 US$ | Grant | 5/97 | 5/98 |
| Low-Income Housing Improvements | Japan | 670 Yen | Grant | 12/96 | 12/97 |
| Housing for Government Staff | Republic of Korea | 8,200 Won | Loan | 8/96 | 4/99 |
| Clean Settlements Programme | IDA | 0.45 US$ | Grant | 5/96 | 3/97 |
| Urban Development Sector | ADB | 19.2 SDR | Loan | 1/93 | 6/98 |
| Urban-Land Management T A | ADB | 0.29 US$ | Grant | 1/93 | 12/96 |
| Low–Income Housing | ADB | 14.9 SDR | Loan | 10/91 | 10/97 |
| Institutional Support to HDFC & SMIM, T A | ADB | 0.63 US$ | Grant | 10/91 | 12/94 |
| Municipal Management | IDA | 8.79 SDR | Loan | 7/86 | 1/96 |
| **Water Supply and Sanitation** | | | | | |
| Kalu Ganga WSP for Colombo | Japan | 11,280 Yen | Loan | 8/97 | 11/03 |
| Greater Colombo Sewerage | UK | 1.92 UKP | Grant | 7/97 | 7/99 |
| Vavuniya Rural Water Supply and Sanitation | Germany | 1.50 DM | Grant | 6/97 | 12/98 |

*(Contd.)*

**Table 25.2 :** *(Contd.)*

| Project | Donor | Amount in Millions | Funding Type | Start Date | Finish Date |
|---|---|---|---|---|---|
| Towns East of Colombo Water Supply | Japan | 2,000 Yen | Loan | 3/88 | 1/98 |
| Towns North of Colombo Water Supply | Japan | 5,310 Yen | Loan | 10/96 | 7/02 |
| Rural Water Supply and Sanitation | ADB | 0.60 USD | Grant | 9/96 | 3/97 |
| Water Supply in Am & Na | Germany | 20.00 DM | Loan | 10/95 | 12/97 |
| Water Sector Development | UNDP | 0.63 USD | Grant | 2/95 | 12/98 |
| Matara and Nimlambe Water | Lloyds Bank | 13.29 GBP | Loan | 8/94 | 6/97 |
| Kalmunei Water Supply | Australia | 3.51 USD | Loan | 1/94 | 1/06 |
| Comprehensive Water Resources Management | ADB | 0.19 USD | Grant | 9/93 | 12/95 |
| Greater Colombo Water Supply Extension | Japan | 3,730 Yen | Loan | 8/93 | 10/99 |
| Second Water Supply and Sanitation | ADB | 28.31 SDR | Loan | 7/93 | 9/98 |
| Community Water Supply and Sanitation | IDA | 16.90 SDR | Loan | 12/92 | 12/98 |
| North West Province Water Resources Development | ADB | 21.53 SDR | Loan | 7/92 | 12/99 |
| Kurunegala Water Supply | Germany | 12.55 DM | Grant | 5/84 | 12/95 |
| Second Water Supply and Sewerage | Saudi Arabia | 99.90 Riyals | Loan | 1/81 | 6/90 |
| Polunnarawa Water Supply and Sanitation | PRC | 50.00 CNY | Grant | 1/80 | 12/89 |

*(Contd.)*

**Table 25.2 :** *(Contd.)*

| Project | Donor | Amount in Millions | Funding Type | Start Date | Finish Date |
|---|---|---|---|---|---|
| ***Surface Transport*** | | | | | |
| Kalutara Galle Railway Signals | Netherlands | 27.33 NLG | Loan/ Grant | 12/96 | 5/99 |
| Ratnapura-Banderawela Road Reconstruction | Republic of Korea | 24,512 Won | Loan | 8/96 | 2/01 |
| Southern Provincial Roads | ADB | 0.60 USD | Grant | 11/95 | 12/96 |
| Bridges Reconstruction and Rehabilitation | Kuwait | 3.30 KWD | Loan | 3/95 | 12/99 |
| Third Road Improvement | ADB | 38.11 SDR | Loan | 2/95 | 12/99 |
| Quarry Industry Study | ADB | 0.43 USD | Grant | 2/95 | 12/98 |
| Road Network Improvement | ADB | 0.70 USD | Grant | 2/95 | 12/98 |
| Road Safety Study | ADB | 0.80 USD | Grant | 2/95 | 12/98 |
| Transport Planning | UNDP | 0.60 USD | Grant | 7/94 | 12/97 |
| Railway Bridges II | Germany | 21.50 DM | Loan | 12/93 | 12/96 |
| Colombo Urban Transport | IDA | 14.40 SDR | Loan | 6/93 | 6/99 |
| Third Roads | IDA | 30.60 SDR | Loan | 11/90 | 6/98 |
| Various Road Construction, Maintenance and Rehabilitation | Japan | 33,339 Yen | Loans | 7/88 | 11/00 |
| Various Rail Improvements | Germany | 8.08 DM | Grant | 4/88 | 12/98 |
| Ceylon/German Technical Training School | Germany | 10.60 DM | Grant | 4/81 | 12/96 |

***Country name implies that country's government unless otherwise stated.***

*Source:* External Resources Division, Ministry of Planning and Finance, CS-DRMS Report of 03/12/97.

Main issue with solid waste is its disposal. Nearly all dump sites are an environmental hazard which pollute water courses and many are poorly located and affect adjacent residential areas. Only very few towns are fortune enough to receive assistance from donor agencies to operate sanitary landfills. Under the urban Development Sector Project launched by the Urban Development Authority (UDA) in 1993 with assistance of Asian Development Bank (ADB) provided funds for only four ULAs out of seventeen ULAs selected for the project. Provision of suitable lands for landfillings is found most difficult task in order to qualify them for such assistance.

***Supply of Electricity***

Provision of electricity for the purpose of residential and non-residential use is vested with the Ceylon Electricity Board (CEB) under an Act of Parliament. The maintenance and operation of all major power stations in the hill country is managed by the Board and distributed over the island (Fig. 25.9). Distribution is being handled with the assistance of a private Electricity Company called Lanka Electricity Company (Pvt) Ltd (LECO) formed by the Government few years ago but its activities mostly limited to part of Colombo city and its suburbs. The CEB is purely dependent on foreign funds for its almost all capital expenditure. Current ADB project is expected to spend Rs. 2,600 million to extend supply lines to consumers of nineteen (19) districts. This Board finds it difficult in extending its services in towns in frontier regions specially in rural areas to comply with the requests of government Members of Parliament. However it tries to see the feasibility to arriving at a minimum EIRR of 10 per cent to commence a sub-project under this loan package which is not advisable in monitoring towns.

**Housing**

Housing is considered as one of the major sector in urban set-up. The present occupancy rate in urban areas is 8.37 $m^2$/person in low and middle income units, well above UN minimum standard of 5.0 $m^2$/person. Analysis data collected through the 1994 Demographic Survey done by Department of Census and Statistics shows that for Divisional Secretary Divisions containing 49 to 53 towns under study there were an average of 1.04 household units. These data indicate that overcrowding is not a problem in most of the towns. At the same time average unit sizes for lower and middle income households is 15 per cent of 53 towns were estimated to be less than 250 square feet (23.23 square metre). Household Survey done by PADCO 1997[4] reveals that average household size is 5.43 persons per household.

Housing supply in secondary towns is also largely dependent on the residential land sector. Most residential land is produced through an *ad hoc* semi-formal sub-division process at the periphery of the built-up area. Once agricultural or existing residential lands are subdivided, households generally inherit or purchase the remaining lots on the private market. Almost three-quarter of households surveyed organized the construction of their unit; 8 per cent purchased completed units on the open market, while 15 per cent inherited their houses. Less than 2.5 per cent of household received their units from a government agency. Although private sector developers are active in bulk sale housing market in the CMR with the exemption of Kandy and limited number of other regional centres little housing is produced by developers in secondary towns in frontier regions.

Housing tenure arrangements reflect the individual housing delivery process obtaining in secondary towns, ninety (90%) per cent of households surveyed own the houses they live in five (5%) per cent are renters and 5 per cent have other tenure arrangement including squatters.

## Government and Donor Experience in Low Income Housing

Substandard housing conditions in low income settlements particularly in the Colombo area have been a serious Government concern for some time. A wide range of intervention over the last 25 years have attempted to improve slum and shanty housing. These attempts have included:

- *modification of legal framework, application of island wide policies and programmes, establishment of community based organizations, use of foreign funding for pilot upgrading activities and development of social sector programmes to complement the physical upgrading of low income neighbourhoods.*

Despite these efforts the overall deterioration of substandard housing areas continue to out pace their improvement.

Neighbourhood upgrading efforts over last 25 years have evolved in line with the government major housing policies and programmes. They briefly can be summarized as follows:

- *Hundred Thousand Houses Programme*
- *Million Houses Programme*
- *1.5 Million Houses Programme*

### *Current Initiative and Direction*

With the change in government in 1994, the Million Houses Era came to an end. Ministry of Housing is still in the process of refocusing its efforts in the housing field as evidenced by lack of an official urban policy in Sri Lanka today. Emerging priorities include the production of higher density housing. Government today is willing to revert the earlier model of direct provision in order to achieve higher residential densities. One instrument for implementing this policy identified by housing officials is redevelopment of shanty and slum areas in central city locations.

This approach is evident in the Clean Settlement Project currently under preparation in the Ministry of Housing and Urban Development. It aims to improve the physical, social, economic, political and environmental situation of slum and shanty area in the Greater Colombo area and significant part of the Western Province through redevelopment scheme.

At the same time previous enabling approach is still being employed in the on-going Jana Udana Housing Programme. This Programme aims at to facilitate the construction of 100 new houses in each electorate.

## CONCLUSIONS AND RECOMMENDATIONS

The above analysis clearly indicates that Sri Lanka has limited resources to invest on infrastructure since its substantial proportion has to allocate for defence activities and state welfare and income transferring as a measure of rectifying unequal distribution of wealth. This paved the way to seek foreign assistance from various donor agencies around the world especially World Bank, ADB, ODA, JAICA etc. The assistance expected is not coming at the time when the country is ready for such development. This resulted to initiate construction by different agencies at defferent time frame without an overall development plan. So, one project constructs a road section under road improvement project and by another project would demolish the road section to lay pipes to provide water supply or telecommunication to the neighbourhood under a different project. This causes heavy losses to the country with the burden of debts repayment as spelt out by donor agencies.

On the other hand, government's emphasis on urban development throughout the country bring more and more problems. This resulted to attract more and more people to urban areas ultimately *few would live in rural areas*. For this, Government should have a clear urban policy and a clear rural policy. I suggest that the national government should give policy guidelines to all provincial and local level governments on policies that should be adapted in respect of urban and rural. This implies that in rural areas people should allow to enjoy rural facilities such as streams for bathing, wetland and highland for farming, forest for timber and hunting, open areas for recreation. The rural community should not be burdened with modern electronic environment. This may discourage more and more people to come to urban centres which may pave the way for concentrated settlements. It is a good strategy to minimize expenditure in the national budget.

## GENERAL RECOMMENDATIONS

There was a well known Economist called *Mark Jefferson* who had been constantly quoted in *"The Law of the Primate City"* said that "countries which have one dominant city are countries that are really not grown up." They are not grown up cities, not grown up countries. Historically he was referring to how London and Paris were primate cities in England and France respectively and how with the development of other urban centres in England such as Manchester, Glasgow, Birmingham *etc.* in the rest of the country and how London's dominance was gradually eroded and the rest of the country developed with rapid urbanization.[5]

Situation in Sri Lanka wherein if industrialization is taken to the regions outside Colombo, some provincial capitals will grow and challenge Colombo's dominance over the years and introduce spread effect growth in the rest of the country with urban industrial investment and urban industrial jobs. This is already happening through the dictates of political necessity with the establishment of some 200 garment factories throughout the country and agro industrial large scale investments such as Pelwatta Sugar Company in Moneragala and several other agro industrialization programmes planned and implemented in the rest of the country under Mahaweli Economic Agency and more recently through BOI initiatives.

Rapid industrialization and urban jobs close to provincial urban centres needs to be pursued very effectively if Sri Lanka is to avoid the terrible calamities underwent during 1988-1989 youth uprising. The cry of these youths was "why milk for Colombo Cucumber for us"! Economists/Planners both local and foreign state that without rapid urbanization in the frontier regions, Sri Lanka will not be able to move. So long with this attempt towards urbanizing—towards development of secondary towns—towards the development of infrastructure of those provincial towns.

Upliftment of frontier regions will no doubt continue to be important in the national development effort for the next few decades but with two important modifications. One concerns the likelihood of reaching the finite limits soon in the extension of peasant resettlement and subsistence farming in the dry zone.

As more and more of the rural population move away from subsistence farming, diversifying a segment of agriculture, and fostering of small scale agro-businesses to ply an increasingly important role in the development strategy.

There will also be the necessity to foster the development of the provincial centres and few more as medium-size towns. Social and economic infrastructure should be improved to provide higher order goods and services to their respective hinterlands. Some of the hitherto centralized public sector offices along with private and informal sector business and industries should be encouraged to locate in these towns. The new population of these urban places will also require much better facilities especially well equipped hospitals, secondary schools. These towns should be of sufficient enough standard to attract new migrants from small towns and rural areas.

On the other hand, frontier regions could be developed under urban set-up creating social environment for private and public investments on infrastructure which ultimately enhance urban development. Investment experience in some of the developing countries provides lessons for rest of the developing countries to adjust their policies towards urban development. Here are some general investment proposals:

## Investments as a Gear for Frontier Development

### *Joint Partnership—Private and Public*

Private and public investors now are forming new partnership to invest in urban development and in doing so are heralding a new approach for local governments around the world. The two sector hope that by holding hands they will be able to introduce a broader and more holistic approach to city investing. The private and public investors on the forefront of this innovative new thinking are developing comprehensive investment "Package"; for the long health of cities and their continued sustainable development. Instead of scattershot approach to invest a total road here, a subway there, a water system elsewhere their new approach built may ultimately stimulate additional economic return. The trends toward increasing private investment in infrastructure construction and services that have traditionally been provided by the public sector has had and will continue to have an impact in two significant ways: It frees up public resources to invest in the public realm and it leverage private investment so that it can be funnelled into the public realm. Urban assets such as land and building and even infrastructure have long time been privately owned by households, business, community organizations and religious groups. Those with sufficient wealth to invest usually benefited from city growth, as asset values appreciated and new investment opportunities emerged. People without adequate income and assets were locked out of their areas of wealth creations. However managing public and private investment in an integrated manner can often achieve a beneficial transfer of the value added by urban growth between categories of assets. This can lead to improved public as well as private assets and hence benefit those who do not hold assets as well as those who do. It can leverage the total volume of investment beyond what might be achieved without positive coordination and good public private partnership.

### *Investment Plan*

Investors and decision makers can work together to develop an investment plan for both public and private expenditure in key areas of city based infrastructure investment. The objective should be to maximize economic returns to the city not just commercial returns to investors but to improve city and public realms. If there is a strong need for private investment in a rail system both should consider where and when the benefits will flow to whom and what consequential investments might be encouraged or stimulated by the investment.

### *Certainty*

For the private sector the appeal of this approach is that it offers them a measure of certainty about the policy, reducing their risks when investment is diversified it allows investors to gain returns from more than one source. Package can be implemented faster and with more certainty reducing delays. By doing this the Government could expect:

(i) a living environment appealing to private investors by financing infrastructure to offer needed services.

(ii) generate adequate income, offered housing, or pay for health, education and other basic necessities.

(iii) public realm or spaces between the private investments.

NOTES

1. Louis Wirth. "Urbanism as a Way of Life" *American Journal of Sociology*, 64, July 1938.
2. "The Origin and Growth of Urbanization in the World". *American Journal of Sociology*, 60, March 1955.
3. *HUD Newsletter*, 3 July 1972, p. 3.

REFERENCES

1. *Urban Age*. Vol. 5. No. 2, 1998, p. 8.
2. *Small and Medium Towns for Regional Development in Sri Lanka*, p. 25, Institute of Town Planners, Sri Lanka, Colombo, 1993.

26

# Indus Towns and Huanghe Towns

## The Origin of the Grid Pattern Town Plan

JIRO YONEKURA

## INTRODUCTION

The excavation of Mohenjo-daro by Sir John Marshall (1931) and Earnst Mackay (1938) revealed the most ancient town planning in the world. The first geographer who devoted himself to study the origin and spread of the grid pattern town was Dan Stanislawski (1946). He demonstrated that Mohenjo-daro could have been the origin of the grid pattern town, but his explanation was very similar to Marshall and Mackay's. He, however, laid stress on the spread of the plan from the Indus to the Orient, Greece and so on.

Recently many archaeological town sites in and around the Indus Plains, which we call Indus towns, were excavated. The present writer will try to systematize the development of the town planning in these Indus towns and especially to ascertain the grid pattern of Mohenjo-daro itself.

In the Huanghe Plains, many of the ancient town sites (we will call them Huanghe towns) were discovered since World War II. This chapter will discuss these ancient Chinese towns and will compare them with the Indus towns.

This author has written some articles in Japanese over the last several years on Indus towns, and has read a paper at the XXXI International Congress of Human Sciences in Tokyo in 1983 and a short English resume of this Abstract has been published. This is the revised paper comparing Indus towns with Huanghe towns.

### The Development of the Town Planning in the Indus Towns

At the moment at the Rahman Dheri site in the western plains of the Indus near Dera Ismail Khan, a town plan of the early Indus period is being excavated. It appears to be a well laid out oblong town, surrounded by a massive wall and divided in two by a street running north-west to south-east. At right angles to this road, houses divided by regularly laid out straight narrow lanes are visible (Allchin and

Allchin, 1982). The settlement comprised an area of 22 hectares, and uggests a population of around 12,000. It is approximately 550 by 400 m, and by radiocarbon dating it belongs to the first half of the ourth millennium.

The Surkotada site (Joshi, 1971-1972) in Kutch was rather small n scale but it seems to have succeeded the plan of Rahman Dheri. This settlement was surrounded by stone rubble and a mud-brick ortification, and the area enclosed comprises two quadrates each of oughly 60 m square. The date of this site is said to cover the mature ndus civilizations, namely from *c.* 2550 B.C. to *c.* 2050 B.C. (Fig. 26.1).

The Kalibangan site (Thapar, 1973), about 200 km south-east of Harappa on the bank of the now dry Ghaggar river, was surrounded by a massive rampart of mud-brick. The site was composed of two mounds. The west and smaller one was "the citadel" and the east and larger one "the lower city". The former was a parallelogram, some 240 m from north to south and 120 m from east to west; the latter is also a parallelogram about 240 m from east to west and 360 m from

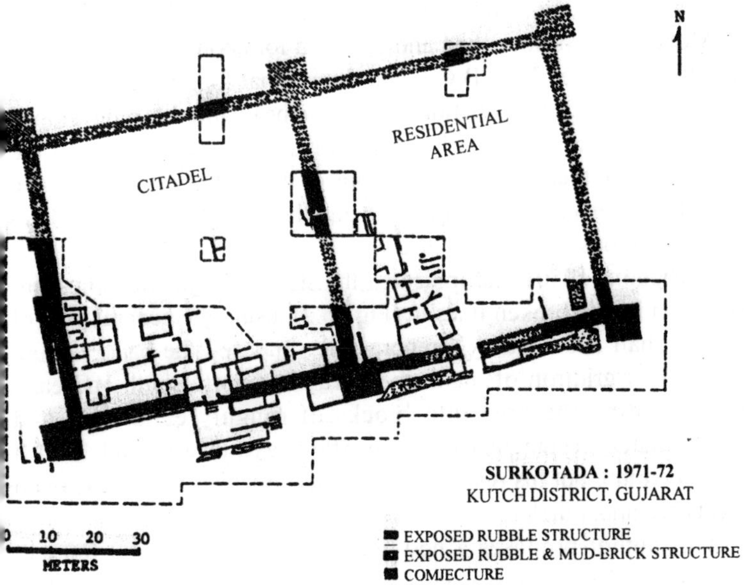


**Fig. 26.1** : Surkotada, Site Plan (after Joshi)

north to south, and lies about 40 m eastward from the citadel mound Within the lower city there is a gridiron plan of streets running north to south and east to west, dividing the area into blocks, of which the east-west side was usually 40 m in width. The width of lanes and streets ranged from 1.80 m to 7.20 m corresponding to multiples of 1.80 m.

The date of the site belongs to the "pre-Harappan" or early Indus period, 2920 B.C. Its lay-out could be called the direct antecedent of Harappan and Mohenjo-daro. Now we know that the town planning of the Indus towns developed at first from oblong walled towns with twin parts : at the west the citadel, and at the east the down town area. Afterwards, these two quarters were divided by an open space.

## On the Town Planning of Mohenjo-daro

The development of the town planning of the Indus towns reached its climax at Mohenjo-daro. It was situated on the flood plain of the lower basin of the Indus. This city area covered about 1 km square, six times bigger than that of Kalibangan, with the lay-out of the city being a mangification and elaboration of Kalibangan.

Mohenjo-daro flourished and survived for about 500 years (from *c*. 2500 B.C. to *c*. 2000 B.C.), and during that long time it suffered severe flooding and destructions and had to be repaired or redeveloped many time, changing its original plan here and there. Thus, in the excavated site there are accumulations of many deformations, so we must distinguish the original lay-out and the older plan from the later transformations.

S. Piggott (1950) first indicated the street plan of Mohenjo-daro as shown by the broken lines in (Fig 26.2), using the general plan of the Marshall and Mackay's reports. He supposed the basic lay-out would be a gridiron of main streets running north-south and east-west dividing the area into blocks of roughly equal size and approximately rectangular in shape, 800 ft east to west and 1200 ft north to south, but his restoration is rather rough, and even the main streets are unparallel.

This author proposes a new idea, shown by the solid lines in (Fig. 26.2). The main reasons for the differences between the two restorations are as follows: Firstly, the north-south street running in the Dk area B section was drawn in a N1-2° W direction in the

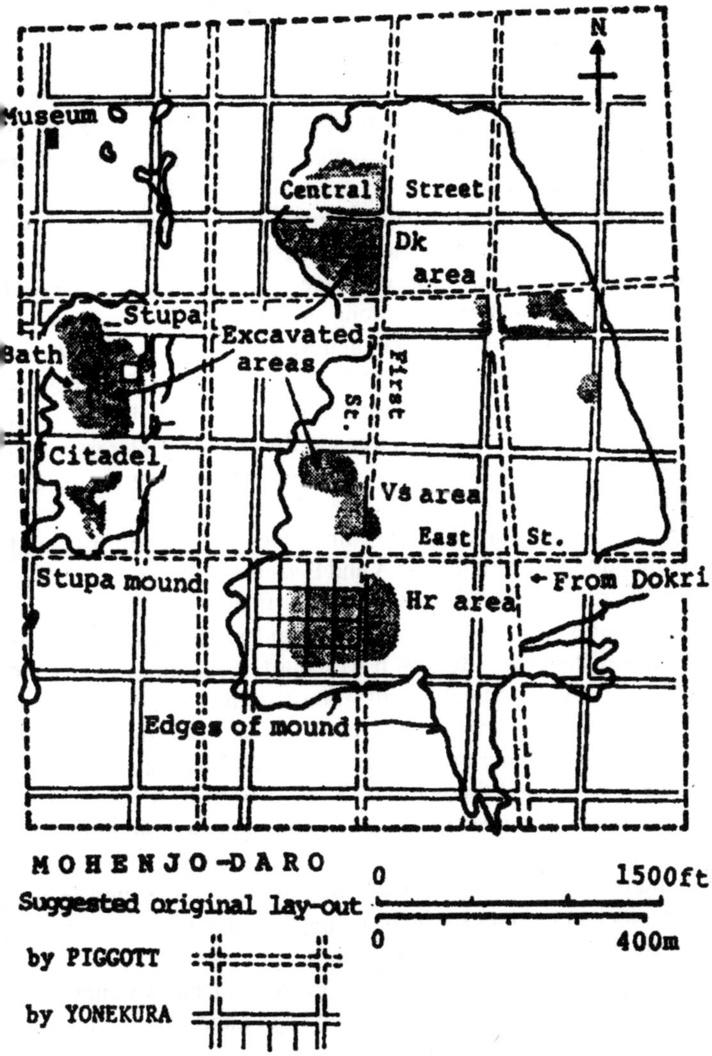


Fig. 26.2 : Suggested Original lay-out of Mohenjo-daro.

general plan, but according to the detailed map of the site (P1. LXII in Vol. 3 of Marshall's report) (Fig. 26.3), it is clear that the direction is almost N 6°E, parallel with First Street (the supposed principal meridian), and contrary to Piggott's restoration. Second, the space between these two streets is about 580 ft or nearly 600 ft, and it is supposed that Central Street in the Dk area was one of the main east-west streets which ran parallel to East Street (supposed the main parallel), the distance between the two streets being about 1750 ft, just three times 580 ft. Thus this author is convinced that the streets ran parallel to 1st and 5th streets, demarcating blocks of 580-600 ft (nearly 180 m) square as shown by the solid line in Fig. 26.2.

The measurement system of the Indus towns could have been adopted from ancient India. In the fourth century, in the Guptan Ages, 1 cubit was called *"hasta," 4 hasta* made 1 *"dhanu"* (or *danda*), and 1 *dhanu* was about 6 ft or 1.8 m long. A hundred *dhanu* was called *"nalwa"*. The lanes at Kalibangan and Mohenjo-daro were a *dhanu* wide or its multiples; for example, the width of First Street in Mohenjo-daro was about 30 ft or 9 m, corresponding to 5 *danda,* the blocks of Mohenjo-daro were 1 *nalwa* square, and the citadel of Harappa was composed of two parallelograms, the two sides of which were 1 *nalwa* each.

As to the subdivision of the dwelling blocks, this author has paid special attention to the Hr area in A and B sections. Street 1 (so called First Street) runs north to south with a 30 ft width and divides the area into A and B sections. At B section Street 2 runs almost parallel to Street 1 at a distance of 130-140 ft westward, the width of the street being 10-14 ft. Again Street 3 runs almost in the same direction as Street 2, this time the north-south direction deviates a little so that the east-west distance of the two streets is 150 ft at the north, but only 120 ft at the south, and the width of Street 3 is 10 ft. If we suppose that only Street 3 deviated from the original plan, we can conclude the spacing of Street 1, Street 2 and Street 3 is about 130-140 ft. Further more, we can imagine that Street 4 was constructed in the same way, so that the block which section A covers was divided into four, north-south parts by three streets.

In the east-west direction we find many lanes, namely Lanes 1, 2, 3, 4, 5, 6, 7, 8, 9, and 10 in B section, and High Lane, South Lane and Deadman's Lane in A section.

Lane 1 continues eastward to High Lane, and westward to Lane, 7 though interrupted by buildings from later ages.

Lane 2 is parallel to Lane 1, the distance between them being about 250 ft, and the width of the lanes is 5-10 ft.

Lane 7, Lane 5 and Lane 3, though they are interrupted partially, are spaced about 120 ft apart, and the width of the lanes is 10 ft, so we can conclude that the blocks which include B section were subdivided lengthwise equally spaced about 130 ft (40 m).

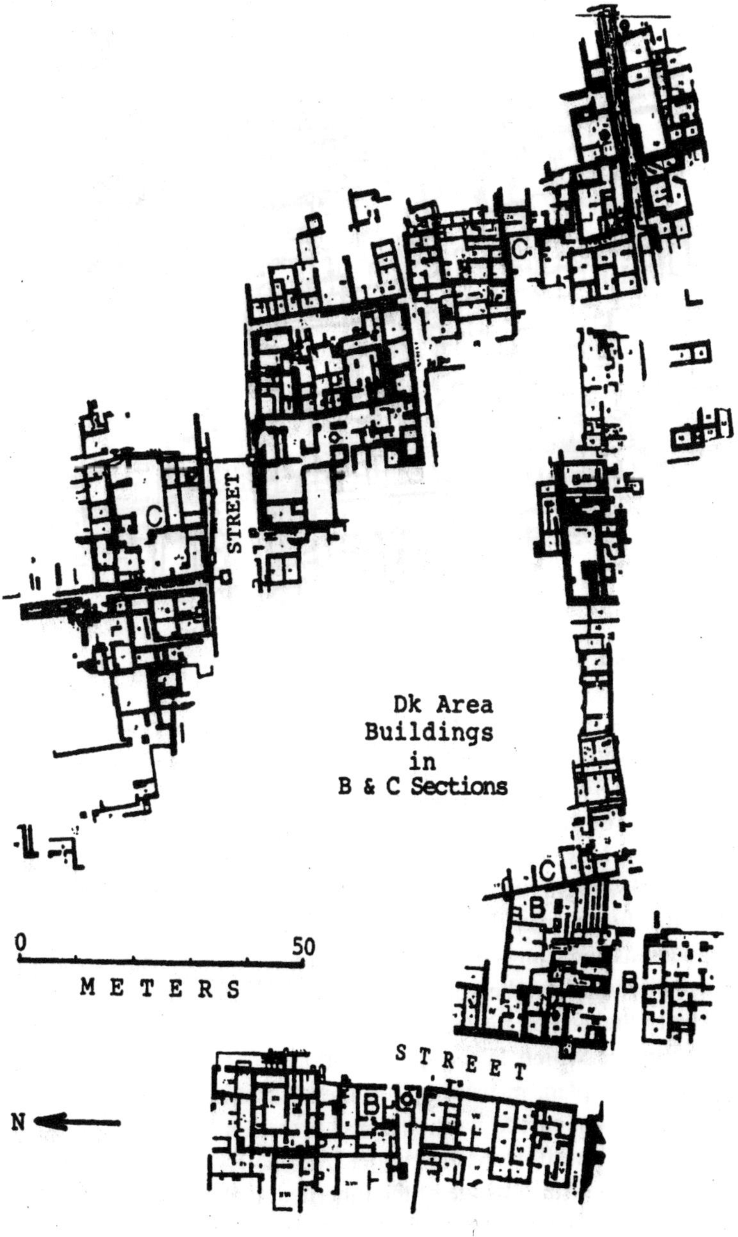


**Fig. 26.3** : The Street in the Dk Area in B Section (After Marshall)

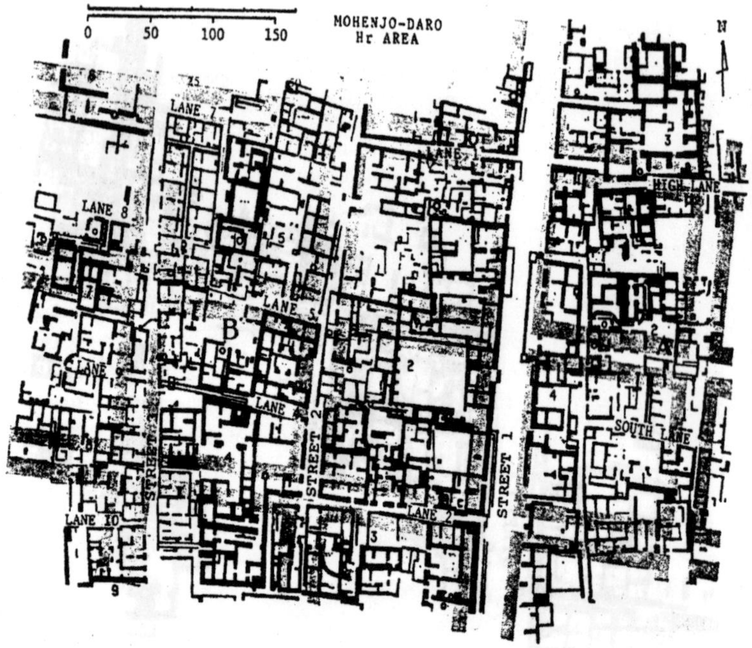


**Fig. 26.4 :** Supposed Original Lanes at the Hr. Area of Mojenjo-daro

The present writer supposes that the original lanes, as shown in Fig. 26.4, were such that a basic block (580 ft or 180 m square) was divided into 16 sections (Fig. 26.2), and by reserving 20 m for the total widths of the streets and lanes, the length of a section would be about 40 m. If we calculate it with Mohenjo-daro's foot, that is 13.2 inches or 33.53 cm, then it would be about 120 ft. A section of 120 ft was introduced into the town planning at Miletus, Olynthus by Hippodamus and many Greek and Roman cities followed this standard. This plan could have been introduced from the Near East.

The Lothal site on the Gulf of Cambay was a large port-city of the Indus Empire which lasted up to 1600 B.C. Initially Lothal was rectangular in plan, measuring 300 metres from north to south and 400 metres from east to west, and was protected against floods by a 13-metre thick wall. Here the citadel (Acropolis) was erected inside the lower town. This change of the inherited dual system is not clear, but it seems this tendency was adopted from the ancient Indian towns (Rao, 1973, pp. 52-63).

## Huanghe Towns in the Hsia and Shang Dynasties

The Huanghe Basin was another centre of ancient civilization in the East. Since the Second World War, Chinese archaeologists have been excavating many sites in the middle Huanghe Basin (Murata, 1981). Wangchenggang is situated about 100 km south-west of Zhengzhou, and at the foot of the noted Songshan. In 1977 a walled town was discovered. Its western wall was about 95 m, and the southern wall about 98 m. The northern and eastern walls were partially destroyed by the flooding of the neighbouring river. The southern wall was elongated eastwards at right angles to the eastern wall. These parts seem to be the remnants of another walled town. The eastern wall of the western town was also the western wall of the eastern town. This lay-out of twin towns with one wall in common resembles very much that of Surkodata of the Indus towns (Fig. 26.5). The radiocarbon dating of this town shows 4010 ± 85 y. B.P., which corresponds to the early ages of the Hsia Dynasty and the end of the mature Indus

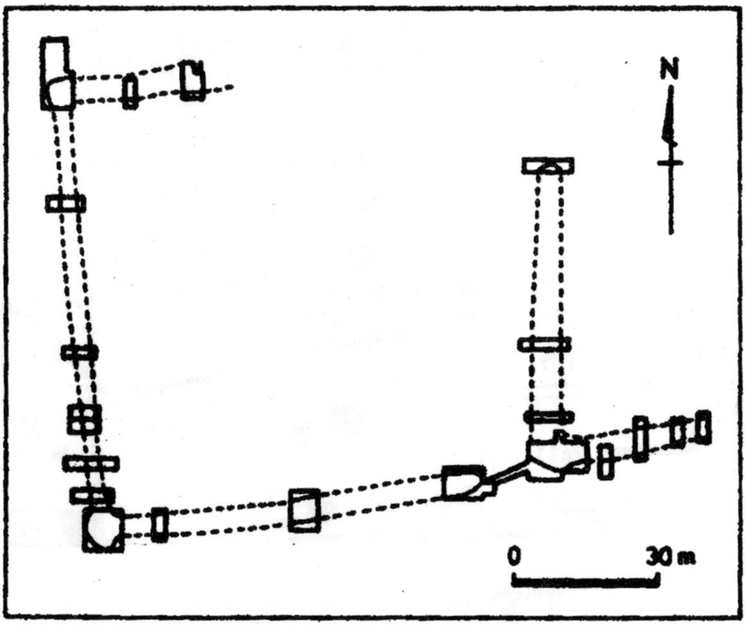


**Fig. 26.5 :** Plan of the Old Fort of Wangchenggang (after Henan Sheng Institute, 1983)

civilization. The Dongxiafeng site in Hsia Xian, Shanxi Province was also a walled town 140 m square, dated 3950±135 y. B.P.

Panlongcheng, north of Wuhan city was an oblong walled town, east-west about 260 m and north-south about 290 m. This was a provincial town in the Shang Dynasty. The so-called Shangcheng of the present Zhengzhou city was the capital of the Shang Dynasty, with its great wall 2 km north to south and 1.7 km east to west.

Thus Huanghe towns in the Hsia and Shang Dynasties had an oblong or square lay-out, surrounded by walls of hardened earth. They have many resemblances to the Indus towns.

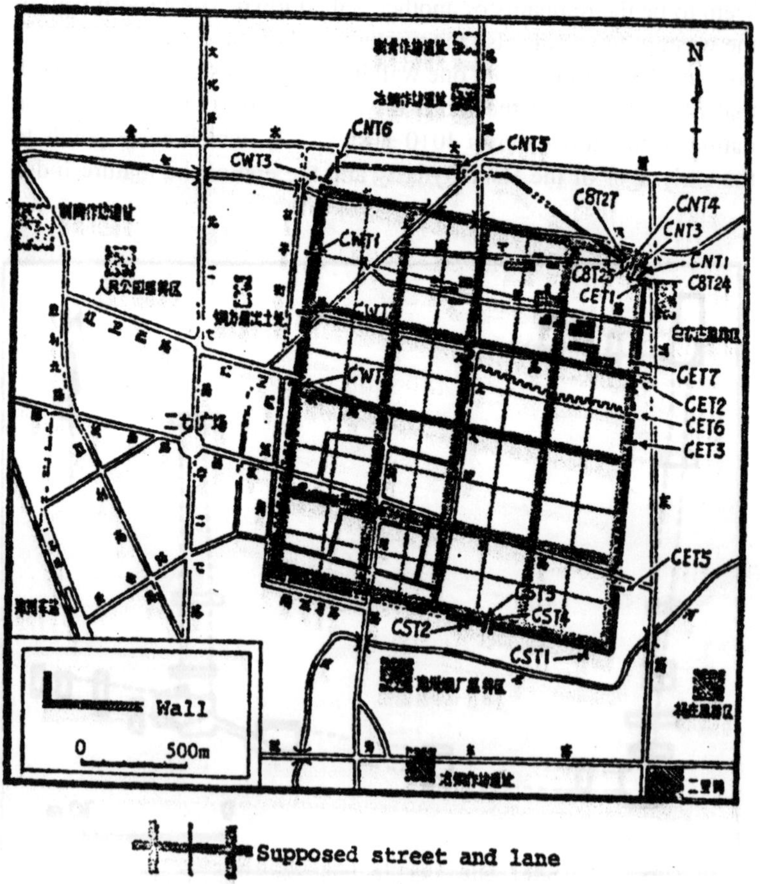


Fig. 26.6 : Supposed Lay-Out of the Shang Capital in Zhengzhou (after Wenwu, 1977)

For planning, a measuring system has to be developed in advance. The so-called *Shangchi* (scale) was about 17 cm long. It was just half of the shell scale of Mohenjo-daro, which was 1 foot, equal to 13.2 inches or 33.53 cm. In Harappa, the remnant of a copper scale was found, and it has a grading of 0.367 inch or 0.936 cm. This is half a digit, and 28 or 24 digits was 1 cubit. The former was 20.7 inches or 52.6 cm long, and the latter was 46 cm. The former was also used at the Indus towns as well as at the foot of Mohenjo-daro.

In China the so-called Qin and Han scale was about 23 cm. This is also just half of 1 cubit in the above mentioned latter case (Sono, 1968). It is probable that the foot and cubit scales were also used in China. In the Shang Dynasty the foot system was mostly used, but in the latter ages the cubit system was practised generally.

We can confirm that the Indus and Huanghe towns had almost the same measuring system, so the town planning of Huanghe towns could have close relations with those of the Indus towns.

**Shang Capital of Zhengzhou**

The lay-out of the Shang capital, at present Zhengzhou, seems to have been at first 1.7 km square (Fig. 26.6). The northern boundary was the Jinshuihe, which flows almost parallel to the southern wall, and later the northern wall was built further north beyond the river, so that the whole outline of the wall became a pentagon. This capital city continued its glory till the Han Dynasty and was revived again later as an important railway junction in North China. Tsou held the opinion that the capital was Bocheng, which was established by Tang, the first king of the Shang Dynasty (Tsou, 1984). But a very recent research has revealed that a big, relatively complete, walled town site was excavated at Yanshi (between Luoyang and Zhengzhou). It has an oblong plan, 1700 m north to south, and 1200 m east to west. It also has straight streets running at right angles to each other and seven castle gates have already been discovered. They believe this could be west Bocheng, which was first planned by Tang. In the Shang Dynasty the capital was changed so many times that site at Zhengzhou seems to be a later enlarged capital succeeding the first capital of Yanshi.

In ancient China the measuring system had 1 "*bu*" equal to 8 "*shi*" with 300 *bu* equalling 1 "*li.*" If the original lay-out of the Shang capitals were 1.7 km × 1.2 km, and 1.7 km square, then the former was 10,000 *shi* (1 *shi* was ca.17 cm), or 1250 *bu,* or 4 *li* and 50 *bu* × 3 *li*, and the latter was 4 *li* and 50 *bu* square. It is reasonable to suppose that the original lay-out of the cities might have been 4 *li* × 3 *li* and 4 *li* square; then the streets which were spaced 1 *li* each would have crossed each other north-south and east-west at right angles making 12 or 16 blocks of 1 square *li.* It is difficult to excavate the Shang capital at Zhengzhou because it is a filled up area, but some of the present streets follow along the original plan. For example, the central north-south street could have been the main avenue. Then, Huayuanlu and Peidalu would follow this ancient principal street, with Xiangyanglu running about 1 *li* westward. As for the east-west street, Hongweilu is situated in the middle, and Chengbeilu and Jiefanglu run almost parallel spaced 1 *li* apart north and south of Hongweilu.

Each block of 1 *li* square would have two lanes north-south and east-west, crossing each other at the centre of the block. Thus the original road system of the Shang Capital would be 9 roads (5 streets and 4 lanes) crossing each other a right angles, and there would be three gates on each side.

This lay-out was stated as the capital plan in the Zhou Dynasty in *Zhouli,* and this could have been modelled after the Chang capital of Zhengzhou.

Even in the Warring States Period (475-221 B.C.), the capital of Yen State Xiadon (the present Xixian, Hebei Province) and the capital of Chi State Linzi (the present Zibo, Shandong Province) were planned after the dual system. The former was composed of East and West castles; the latter had big and small castles side by side. They followed the plan of Wangchenggang in the Hsia Dynasty. The tradition of the Hsia Dynasty was preserved for a long time in the eastern part of ancient China.

The plan of the Shang capital was followed by the Zhou Dynasty. In the *Zhouli,* the handbook of the Zhou Dynasty, the capital plan stated that it had nine *li* square, and had nine streets running north to south, and east to west crossing each other at right angles with three gates on each side. This idealistic plan was not realized fully in the later ages, especially in east China, yet from 493 A.D., when Northern Wei changed the capital to Luoyang, this idealistic plan was at first practised on a larger scale and it was further improved at Chang'an in the Sui and Tang Dynasties (Mori, 1970).

## CONCLUSION

The grid pattern town planning could probably have started in the Indus towns. It seems to have been developed to the highest at Mohenjo-daro. As restored by this author, the basic grid was about 180 metres (100 *danda* of ancient India) square, and further was subdivided into 16 sections of about 40 metres (120 Mohenjo-daro feet) square. This pattern has influenced later town planning in the Orient, Greece and Rome and the whole of Europe and the New World, as Stanislawski has already written.

In India it is becoming clear that the Indus civilization had a strong influence on the making of Indian civilization, not only in the Indian measuring system but also in the town planning which owes some inheritance from the Indus towns. For example, the Sisupalgarh site in Bhubaneswar, which was established in the third century B.C. has a 600 *danda* square plan, and the Taxila site in East Bengal was divided into 120 ft long sections. The latter has followed the Greek plan that was originally started in the Indus towns and then reimported there.

The idea of grid pattern planning was crystallized in the *Silpa Shastras,* a technical book in the fifth and sixth centuries, but the villages and towns with grid patterns are now seen only in southern India, for the Islamic occupation destroyed this idea in northern India.

In the Huanghe Plains also, a very similar grid pattern town planning was started not so much later than that of the Indus towns, and the ancient Chinese scales belonged to the same cubic and foot system with those of the Indus towns, so it is suppossed that the grid pattern town planning in both civilizations developed from the same root.

The dual or twin town system changed afterward to one oblong town with inner and outer walls and a grid pattern street setting. The basic grid was 1 *li* (about 400 metres) square. Though the idealistic capital plan in *Zhouli* was not practised fully in the beginning, it inspired the idea of town planning not only in China but also in Korea, Vietnam and Japan.

For example, Heian Kyo (the present Kyoto) was planned after the Sui and Tang capitals in Chang'an and Luoyang; it covered 9.5 *ri* north-south and 8 *ri* east-west. (A Japanese *ri* was a little longer than the Chinese ancient *li:* it was about 545 metres.) The big streets traversed one *re* apart in a grid pattern, the basic grid was one *ri* square, and it was subdivided into 16 sections of one *cho* (120 metres) square.

In conclusion, the grid pattern town planning originated in the Indus and the Huanghe Plains. It was propagated from India to the west and from China to the east.

## REFERENCES


Allchin, Bridget and Allchin, Raymond (1982) : *The Rise of Civilizations in India and Pakistan*. Cambridge, 151-152.

Henan Sheng Institute of Cultural Relics (1977) : The excavation of Wangchenggang site, Dengfeng Xian. *Wenwu*. No. 3 (in Chinese).

Joshi, J.P. (1971-1972) : A review explorations and excavations. *Indian Archaeology*. Archaeological Survey of India, New Delhi.

Mackay, E.J.H. (1938) : *Further Excavations at Mohenjo-daro*. 2 vols., New Delhi, Vol. I, 718 p., Vol. II, Plates I—CXLVI.

Marshall, Sir J. (1931) : *Mohenjo-daro and the Indus Civilization*. 3. vols., London, Vol. I, 364 p. Vol. II, 367-716. Vol. III, Plates XV-CLXIV.

Mori, Shikazo (1970) : *Toyogaku Kenkyu. Rekishi Chiri Hen*. (*Asian Study, Volume Historical Geograhy*). Toyoshi Kenkyukai, Kyoto, 244–261.

Murata, Jiro (1981): *Chugoku no teito* (*Caitals in China*). Sogeisha, Kyoto, 378 p.

Nara Prefectural Museum (1983): *Chugoku no tojo iseki* (*Capital sites in Ancient China*). Nara, p. 84.

Piggott, S. (1950) : *Prehistoric India*. Harmondsworth, p. 293.

Rao, S.R. (1973) : *Lothal and the Indus Civilization*. Asia Publishing House, London, p. 215.

Sono, Toshihiko (1968) : Indus bunmei no shaku 2 rei ni tsuite (Two examples of scales in Indus Civilization). *Tokyo Daigaku Kyoyobu Kiyo Hikaku Bunka Kenkyu (College of General Education, University of Tokyo. Comparative Studies of Culture)*, No. 8, 34-45.

Stanislawski, Dan (1946) : The origin and spread of the grid pattern town. *Geograhical Review*, 36, 105-120.

Thapar, B.K. (1973): New traits of the Indus Civilization at Kalibangan. *South Asian Archaeology*. International Conference of South Asian Archaeologists in Western Europe, London.

Tsou, Heng (1984) : The theory of Zheng-Bo. *Proceedings of Papers. XXXI International Congress of Human Sciences in Asia and North Africa*. Vol. II, Toho Gakkai, Tokyo, 930-932.

Yonekura, Jiro (1973) : Jiwari no genryu-Mohenjo-daro toshi puran no saikento (The origin of land demarcation—A new interpretation of the town planning of Mohenjo-daro). *Chirikagaku* (*Geographical Sciences*), Hiroshima, No. 20, 1-6.

Yonekura, Jiro (1981) : Indus toshi to sono shankudo—Gobanwari toshi puran no kigen saiko—(A new interpretation of the town planning of Indus towns—The origin of grid pattern town planning). *Chirikagaku* (*Geographical Sciences*), Hiroshima, No. 36, 1-15.

Yonekura, Jiro (1983) : On the town planning of Mohenjo-daro. *Abstracts of Papers I, XXXI International Congress of Human Sciences in Asia and North Africa.* Toho Gakkai, Tokyo, p. 193.

Yonekura, Jiro (1984) : Comparison of Indus towns with Huanghe towns in Hsia and Shan Dynasties—Especially the town planning of Mohenjo-daro and Shang capital of Zengzhou. *Proceedings XXXI International Congress of Human Sciences in Asia and North Africa.* Vol. 1, Toho Gakkai, Tokyo, 68-69.

# Index